D1301096

CARRIER BATTLES

CARRIER BATTLES

Command Decision in Harm's Way

Douglas V. Smith

NAVAL INSTITUTE PRESS
Annapolis, Maryland

Naval Institute Press
291 Wood Road
Annapolis, Md. 21402

This book has been brought to publication with the generous assistance of Edward S. and Joyce I. Miller.

Library of Congress Cataloging-in-Publication Data

Smith, Douglas Vaughn, 1948–
Carrier battles : command decision in harm's way / Douglas V. Smith, PhD.
p. cm.
Includes bibliographical references and index.
ISBN 1-59114-794-8 (alk. paper)
1. United States. Navy—Aviation—History—20th century. 2. Naval strategy—Study and teaching—United States—History—20th century. 3. United States. Navy—Education—History—20th century. 4. Aircraft carriers—United States—History—20th century. 5. World War, 1939–1945—Campaigns—Pacific Area. 6. World War, 1939–1945—Aerial operations, American. 7. World War, 1939–1945—Naval operations, American. 8. Air warfare—History—20th century. I. Title.
VG93.S58 2006
940.54'5973—dc22

2006019836

Printed in the United States of America on acid-free paper ♾

13 12 11 10 09 08 07 06 9 8 7 6 5 4 3 2
First printing

This work is dedicated to

Professor Timothy H. Jackson,

sailor, scholar, mentor,

and friend,

and to Professor James Pickett Jones,

from whom I have learned so much,

and to my mom, Grace,

and my wife, Paulette.

Contents

Tables

Figures

Foreword

LEADERS AND THE DECISIONS THEY MAKE determine the outcome in war. In World War II it was Fleet Admiral Chester W. Nimitz more than any other single leader who determined the outcome of war in the Pacific. The critical year in the American struggle against Japan was 1942. Crushed by the six powerful carriers of Vice Admiral Chuichi Nagumo's *kido butai,* or fast mobile force, the United States Pacific Fleet lay crippled at Pearl Harbor. With eight mighty battleships now out of action and twenty-seven ships in all damaged or sunk, Admiral Nimitz surely realized the grave nature of his assignment when he arrived at Pearl precisely at 7:00 AM on Christmas morning 1941 to assume command of the remnants of the Pacific Fleet for the life-and-death struggle that was to follow.

Nimitz understood the implications of the Japanese attack. The Washington and London naval treaties had given the United States an elusive advantage over Japan in warships. In 1934 an act of Congress authorized naval construction up to treaty limits. In 1938 another act of Congress allocated a billion dollars for the construction of a two-ocean navy. In reality, the two-ocean requirement for American naval power had shifted the balance slightly in favor of the Japanese in the Pacific. The attack on the fleet at Pearl Harbor had shifted it tremendously in favor of the Imperial Japanese Navy. Moreover, all the navies of the world still adhered to the paradigm that naval strategy revolved around the battleship—all, perhaps, except Japan. Nimitz was faced with a huge strategic dilemma—defeating a vastly superior naval force that outnumbered his own in all important classes of ships but one.

Both Admiral Nimitz and the commander in Washington, D.C., under whom he served, Adm. Ernest J. King, believed that Japan's geographic position made it vulnerable to attack by submarine. In this category only did the units available to the United States roughly equal Japan's—both nations had around fifty. Unfortunately, the failure of many of America's submarine-launched torpedoes in the early phases of the war negated the advantages Nimitz and King saw. The tremendous size of the Pacific Ocean—the largest geographical wartime dominion in recorded history when Nimitz took command in 1941—and the vast number of Japanese warships also militated against Japan's defeat by submarine action alone. This barrier of superior numbers and distance would crumble as the war progressed.

As soon as it was understood that submarines were not going to execute U.S. strategy in the Pacific singlehandedly, however, it was obviously essential to conduct an offensive war of attrition, severing the crucial supply lines between Japan and its overseas sources of materials and deployed troops. In 1939 Japan had purchased 80 percent of its oil from the United States and most of the remaining 20 percent from the Netherlands East Indies. U.S. oil exports to Japan were, of course, ended in July of 1941. Like Germany, Japan was able to stockpile almost every critical material but oil before the attack on Pearl Harbor. The denial of oil to the Japanese economy and war machine would ultimately destroy the industrial foundation of Japan's war effort.

Things could have worked out much differently in the Pacific. Favored by President Franklin D. Roosevelt, Nimitz was offered the position of Commander in Chief, United States Fleet (CINCUS) in early 1941. As such he would have been second in the Navy hierarchy only to the Chief of Naval Operations—an assignment of extraordinary power and influence for so junior an admiral. To his credit, Nimitz declined. He rightly felt that he would not be able to garner the necessary support of the many admirals senior to him he passed over in taking the command. Nimitz's good friend, Rear Adm. Husband E. Kimmel, did accept the post and jumped over thirty-one admirals his senior in taking the temporary rank of full admiral and assuming his post in Hawaii on 1 February 1941. Nimitz would have had to make a jump over three times that many. Had Nimitz accepted the promotion it would have been him, and not Kimmel, in Pearl Harbor on 7 December.

Instead Nimitz was assigned as Chief of the Bureau of Navigation, responsible for manning and equipping the hugely expanded American Navy. In this capacity he worked relentlessly. Resisting pressure from above and below, Nimitz refused to follow the British lead in differentiating the insignia for reserve officers, preserving his preference for including them indistinguishably from regular officers in the fleet. This proved to be a very wise move, as Nimitz found it necessary to man and officer the Navy primarily with members of the reserve force. At the height of Navy officer personnel tallies in 1945, over 85 percent of all officers were reservists.

Nimitz was similarly responsible for forming the infrastructure necessary for the submarine campaign against Japan. Some twenty years before the Japanese attack on Pearl Harbor he had constructed the submarine base at Pearl with borrowed equipment from East Coast naval stations and shipyards. This base was critical to the war effort. The London Conference treaty of 1930—signed by Britain, the United States, and Japan—stipulated that a submarine "may not sink, or render incapable of navigation, a merchant vessel without having first placed passengers, crew and ship's papers in a place of safety. For this purpose the ship's boats are not regarded as a place of safety unless the safety of the passengers and crew is assured in the existing sea and weather conditions." When the Japanese attacked the Pacific Fleet the U.S. had to repudiate this treaty.

Some planning had in fact been done in anticipation of this eventuality. In the spring of 1941 members of the staff and students at the Naval War College recommended at their annual war game that "War Zones into which all merchant ships would enter at their own peril" be created as required in the Pacific. This recommendation was made with the knowledge that the Germans in the Atlantic and British and Italians in the Mediterranean were in effect already conducting unrestricted submarine warfare. The General Board of the Navy, adhering to the U.S. tradition of defending nations' rights to freedom of navigation under all circumstances, categorically rejected the War College's recommendation. Nonetheless, war plans Rainbow 3 and 5 authorized fleet commanders to establish strategic zones or areas from which commercial planes and merchant shipping would be excluded. On the afternoon of 7 December 1941 Admiral Stark, the Chief of Naval Operations (CNO), telephoned the White House to report on the Japanese attack on Pearl Harbor. President Roosevelt instructed him to put plans for war with Japan into effect. Stark read him the text of a telegram to Pacific commanders instructing them to commence unrestricted submarine warfare. The message was authorized and sent shortly after six that evening.

In the 1930s Japanese and American strategists had envisioned submarines mainly as scouts and ambushers serving the main fleet. They trained to conduct barrier operations, pick off enemy ships outside bases, and destroy units during fleet actions. Subs had to make seventeen knots to keep up with the fleet, and this limited their utility in directly supporting fast-moving task forces during most of the period. By 1941, however, the U.S. Navy had a powerful and reliable enough engine to meet nearly all fleet requirements. The *Tambor*-class sub displaced about fifteen hundred tons, had a top speed of close to twenty-one knots on surface, a range of about ten thousand miles, and could crash-dive in around thirty-five seconds. It also had good handling capabilities and habitability when submerged. In comparison, the Japanese I-class subs had heavier deck armament but took a long time to dive; they were crowded, and difficult to handle and very noisy when submerged. They also lacked radar until very late in the war.

On balance American submarines were somewhat superior. All U.S. skippers were Annapolis graduates at the war's outset. By war's end almost 50 percent of the initial enlisted crews had become officers. However, almost 30 percent of all U.S. submarine skippers were relieved for unfitness or lack of results during 1942. Around 14 percent were relieved during 1941 and 1944. Their Japanese counterparts were not much more successful. Many Japanese submarines arrived back in port after a patrol without expending a single torpedo. Failure to arrive at a "perfect" targeting solution, rather than lack of aggressiveness, probably best explains the Japanese dilemma.

The real difference between success rates for the Americans and Japanese was the torpedo with which they were equipped. The Japanese Long Lance torpedo has been venerated over time for its effectiveness and lethality. On the other hand, defective torpedoes seriously hampered U.S. success. The MK-14 torpedo ran two and a half times deeper than set. Its magnetic fuse often failed to work in the Pacific area where the magnetic signature was different from that in Newport, Rhode Island, where the MK-14 was made. The MK-14's contact detonation pin also tended to jam on contact. After twelve months of war the defects were finally identified, and they were corrected by September of 1943. Thus the U.S. submarine onslaught began in earnest in late 1943.

By July 1944 about one hundred submarines operated out of Pearl Harbor and another forty out of Australia. Additionally, the new MK-17 electrical torpedo, which left no wake, had been developed. Codebreakers (working on the JN-25 Japanese naval code) also helped the U.S. submarines locate Japanese merchant convoys and thus eliminate time-consuming searches. From that point in the war on the submariners of the U.S. Pacific Fleet did in spades to the Japanese what the Germans who had developed "wolf pack" tactics in late 1943 had hoped to do to the United States.

At war's beginning the Imperial Navy had no units assigned exclusively to antisubmarine warfare. In November 1943 a Grand Escort Command Headquarters was established to oversee protection of shipping, but the Combined Fleet continued to get the best escort vessels and Grand Escort Command received only older ships. By mid-1943 Japanese losses to U.S. submarines were becoming a problem. U.S. submarines operating from advanced bases in New Guinea, the Admiralties, and the Marianas sank more than six hundred Japanese ships during 1944 for a total of about 2.7 million tons—more than the 2.2 million tons sunk during 1941, 1942, and 1943 combined.

This was a phenomenal rate of attrition, considering that Japanese ship construction totaled just over 6 million tons during the entire war, or roughly equivalent to the tonnage Japan had at the war's outset. Competition with construction requirements for warships, which were also being sunk in significant numbers, further limited replacement merchant ship construction. About two-thirds of Japan's tanker fleet had been destroyed by the end of 1944. By late 1944 Japanese naval and aviation fuel stocks were critically low. By February 1945 oil imports were completely stopped, and in July 1945 total stocks—which had stood at 43 million barrels in December of 1942—were down to 3 million barrels. Fleet activity was restricted to the immediate vicinity of the home islands through most of 1945. Shortages of oil and steel were the most destructive, but by 1945 coal scarcities were also crippling the country. The entire Japanese economy was on the verge of collapse by the spring of 1945. Flow of oil from the East Indies was almost completely cut and general bulk imports fell by close to 40 percent. The U.S. submarine offensive against Japan was one of the decisive elements in ensuring the empire's defeat.

It is worth noting that the submarine force comprised less than 2 percent of U.S. Navy personnel and accounted for 55 percent of Japan's losses at sea. U.S. submarines sank over thirteen hundred Japanese ships, including a battleship, eight aircraft carriers, and eleven cruisers in the course of the war. The cost was high. About 22 percent of U.S. submariners who made war patrols in World War II failed to return—the highest casualty rate for any branch of the Service. For the Japanese the cost was even higher. Around sixteen thousand seamen were killed and another fifty-three thousand were wounded as a result of U.S. submarine attacks. Indeed, the U.S. submarine offensive was the "third prong" of the two-prong strategy.

The importance of the submarine campaign against Japan notwithstanding, America's Pacific war effort had to make it to September of 1943 before the campaign became effective. Admiral Nimitz deserves the lion's share of the credit for making that possible. Aside from constructing the infrastructure that enabled offensive submarine operations and expanding fleet manning through training reservists, his greatest impact on the war came as a result of the decisions he made at critical junctures.

Less than five months after taking command of the Pacific Fleet, Nimitz was faced with a Japanese move to take Port Moresby on New Guinea and the likelihood of rapid sequential moves to sever U.S. sea lines of communication (SLOCs) between Hawaii and Australia. Such moves would also make the Japanese Southern Resource Area in the former Dutch and British controlled areas of the southwestern Pacific nearly impenetrable. Believing the intelligence on these moves that was given to him, Nimitz responded firmly by sending two of his four remaining carriers—half his remaining strategic assets—to thwart the Japanese onslaught. Given the necessity of preserving his main defensive assets until newly constructed warships started arriving in the Pacific in mid-1943, this was a courageous and well-considered move. Failure to respond could have made the strategy of attrition or any future drive toward the Japanese home islands considerably more difficult to execute.

Only a month after defeating Japan's drive to sever American SLOCs to Australia Nimitz was confronted with another strategic decision of gigantic proportions. Intelligence once again indicated a Japanese move to take the Midway Islands. Nimitz's response was brilliant from both a strategic and operational standpoint. Of course much has been made of the intelligence coups—indicating that Midway was running low on potable water and inducing the Japanese into responding in the JN-25 naval codes that "AF" was low on water —by which it was firmly established that Midway was the Japanese operational objective. But what is not emphasized is that only about 10 percent of the JN-25 code had been deciphered at the time. In sending all three of his remaining operational strategic assets to Midway, Nimitz was rolling the dice based on what he knew to be incomplete intelligence. He was, in effect, accepting a risk that could have lost the war in a single day.

Nimitz not only accepted that risk, he devised an operational plan that enabled his carrier task force simultaneously to be in position to move against a primary Japanese offensive against the Aleutian Islands; to place Nagumo's *kido butai* in a position between his three carriers and the "fourth carrier" of Midway itself, thus compounding the Japanese battle problem; and to beat a hasty retreat to the east should the situation become untenable. Thus Nimitz simultaneously accepted and mitigated a significant risk, and in the process placed the U.S. Navy in a position to contemplate offensive operations against the Japanese navy for the first time in the war.

In the most critical stages of the war in 1942 the American carrier commanders were invariably outnumbered, deficient technologically, and saddled with unproven doctrine and tactics. Most of Nimitz's carrier battle group commanders had battleship or cruiser backgrounds with little or no carrier experience. Few aviators were senior enough to qualify for carrier battle group command. Yet they were arrayed against formidable and experienced foes in the Imperial Japanese Navy, and while Admiral Nimitz deserves the credit for putting his operational commanders in the best position to win battles, those battles still had to be fought. Only the operational acumen of the American carrier battle group commanders could make up for these huge disadvantages.

Rear Adm. Frank Jack Fletcher stepped into the breech at Coral Sea and again at Midway. By stopping the Japanese move to take Port Moresby on New Guinea he prevented the Japanese from gaining the land-based air supremacy that was critical for their advance to sever U.S. SLOCs to Australia and for protecting the Southern Resource Area so critical to both the Japanese navy and its army in Manchuria and China. The degree of damage that Fletcher and Rear Adm. Aubrey Fitch inflicted on Japan's two newest carriers and largest air wings created the environment that enabled Nimitz's strategy at the Battle of Midway a month later. By depleting the air wings of the *Shokaku* and *Zuikaku* at Coral Sea they not only stabilized the situation in the areas adjacent to Australia, but balanced the force levels at the tip of the spear at Midway. Through sound decisions arrived at quickly, decisive action was also the order of the day in the Battle of Midway. Fletcher and Rear Adm. Raymond Spruance sent the four remaining Japanese fleet carriers to the bottom and thus made limited offensive action possible for the United States Navy for the first time in the war. The "Incredible Victory" at Midway let Admiral Nimitz's audacity and shrewd strategic reasoning ability come fully into play. America no longer had to wait and respond to Japanese initiatives. A strategy aimed squarely at bringing American military power to the Japanese home islands was now possible. The next step was Guadalcanal.

Nimitz's actions in turning the tide of the war to the offensive in the Guadalcanal and Upper Solomons campaigns were no less courageous and spectacular. Realizing that the Japanese still had several viable strategic options after their resounding defeat at Midway, he correctly concluded that their main objectives would be to consolidate and defend their Southern Resource Area and to revitalize their initiative to sever SLOCS between Hawaii and Australia. The two carrier battles that ensued—the Battle of the Eastern Solomons and the Battle of Santa Cruz—were critical to gaining the initiative and transforming U.S. strategy from reactive to proactive. Convincing Admiral King to promote Frank Jack Fletcher to vice admiral to place command in the hands of the man most experienced in carrier battle was critical to success in the Battle of the Eastern Solomons.

Even more critical to success in the Battle of Santa Cruz, and to the ultimate American victory on Guadalcanal, was the last-minute decision to relieve the defeatist Vice Adm. Robert L. Ghormley with the warrior-spirited Vice Adm. "Bull" Halsey. Working as he had become accustomed to before and throughout the war on a "shoestring," Nimitz's extraordinary judgment of character at critical junctures turned likely defeat into overwhelming victory. Moreover, Nimitz was again willing to risk his last two strategic assets to achieve his military objective. When *Hornet* was lost, only *Enterprise* remained to oppose the Imperial Japanese Navy until *Saratoga* returned to action in the invasion of New Georgia in July of 1943.

Nimitz's leadership was constant throughout the remainder of the war, but perhaps less critical when new construction warships started arriving in the Pacific. With the Battle of the Philippine Sea/Marianas Turkey Shoot, the tide was irrevocably turned against the Japanese. Also, with torpedo problems corrected the submarine offensive became a decisive factor in victory. Yet the leadership of Fleet Admiral Chester W. Nimitz remained a constant without which the United States had several opportunities in 1942 to prolong or possibly lose the war. Foremost of Nimitz's accomplishments were the following:

1. Having the strength of character to accept substantial risk when he was convinced that the potential rewards warranted aggressive action.
2. Balancing the intelligence he was provided. As has been true throughout history, intelligence is never clear-cut and rarely definitive. Many senior commanders shy from decisions while waiting for something

approaching complete accuracy in the intelligence they are provided. Nimitz made the judgments he needed to make precisely at the most critical points in World War II—and in ways that maximized his prospects for success.

3. Knowing and trusting his subordinates, and making changes in command responsibilities when they were needed. In this area perhaps most of all Admiral Nimitz showed consummate good judgment and an impeccable decision process.

While we have begun this discussion with comments on the criticality of Nimitz's leadership and the submarine offensive against Japan, the pages you are about to read are about the five carrier battles of World War II. The key considerations throughout are about the decisions made by those in command at the highest levels in the Pacific, and the way their professional education may have contributed to correct decisions for the situation at hand. It is not likely that anyone will agree with all, or even most, of the assessments made by the primary commanders in each of the battles. But the purpose of critiquing the decisions of these commanders is to engender an appreciation for the decision process as it relates to national strategic goals and operational success in achieving them in war. Fleet Admiral Chester Nimitz was only one of dozens of operational commanders whose decisions contributed to truly complete victory in World War II. *Carrier Battles* will provide an insight into the leadership decision-making process and rationale that secured the seas and won the war—a thorough understanding of which will make each officer a better leader and a better commander.

Thomas B. Fargo
Admiral, U.S. Navy (Retired)

J.B. Nathman
Admiral, U.S. Navy

A Note on the End of an Era

PEARL HARBOR CHANGED EVERYTHING. It was as if all the predictions and tactical possibilities of Alfred Mahan, Billy Mitchell, Joseph Reeves, and Isoroku Yamamoto came together over the Pacific Fleet on that Sunday morning in December 1941.

Certainly, there had been a foreshadowing of the destructive potential of naval air power. An example that has been noted by many historians is the British naval air attack upon the Italian fleet anchored in the shallow-water harbor at Taranto. Some critics disclaimed that event because the ships were in harbor. But in May 1941, British carriers were successful in disabling the battleship *Bismarck* with torpedo attacks. The argument that an attack on a "sitting duck fleet" proved nothing was countered with an example of a victory over a battleship fully maneuvering at sea with screening antiaircraft fire.

A few officers and tacticians imagined the carriers' possibilities as an offensive weapon, but not until the dramatic events of 7 December had unfolded could that reality be fully realized. After the attack, photographers documented the devastation of Battleship Row in unflinching detail. Even today, these images reflect the power and the horror of a carrier strike force. But these images also serve as a metaphor for the end of an era. The supremacy of the battleship navy was stripped away.

The emergence of the carrier and the development of task force tactics became a reality in World War II. The tactical implications were clear. The Pacific war would become a carrier war. The Japanese and American navies soon realized that because of the distance and vastness of the Pacific, aircraft carriers could narrow the margins of battle. Controlling the air was controlling the sea. In the six months after Pearl Harbor, American and Japanese carrier forces played a cat-and-mouse game over critical and strategic areas of the Pacific. The U.S. Navy, realizing that its surface fleet was now limited by the damage and losses of its main battle line, relied on aircraft carriers and the support vessels that comprised the task force.

As the Japanese sought to secure their primary invasion targets, they also sought to eliminate American military bases at Wake Island, Guam, the Philippines, and Midway. These key areas became part of the Japanese chessboard. In an effort to counter Japanese moves, American carrier forces played out the tactic of "hit and run." The carrier actions primarily took place in the southern Pacific region, from December 1941 to July 1942. They set the stage for combat strategies and the development of American carrier operations.

During that difficult period, naval aviators sought to reconfigure the tactics, material, and equipment that had been developed during the prewar years for actual combat. This, of course, had its trials and tribulations, but above all, it had risk. The pesky American carrier forces became a dominant concern for Japanese planners—in particular, Admiral Isoroku Yamamoto.

In an effort to move the Japanese conquests forward in the area of the Coral Sea, a dramatic carrier action unfolded in 1942. It was the first serious carrier battle to take place in the Pacific. The result of that battle would play a larger role in the one that was about to come.

Sandwiched between the Coral Sea and Midway was the extraordinary foray of American forces with the daring plan to attack the mainland of Japan. In the wake of Pearl Harbor, American planners and politicians wrestled with the idea of striking back. The result was the Doolittle Raid, named after the officer who led the mission.

With unorthodox training and the innovative use of a U.S. Army bomber, the B-25, the idea of a raid on Japan became a reality. What the Army and the Navy proposed to do was launch medium bombers off of a pitching deck of an aircraft carrier. Once launched, the aircraft could not return to the carrier. It was a one-way mission to Japan. After the mission was accomplished, the aircraft were to land in prescribed airfields in China.

All of this planning was negated when the American forces were detected nearly five hundred miles from their target, forcing a premature launch. Sixteen bombers were launched against the Japanese mainland. Although damage was minimal, the psychological effect on the Japanese government and its navy was significant. The Doolittle Raid underscored the reality that not only Japanese carrier forces were capable of going long distances and striking wherever they chose, American forces could as well.

The drama of the Pacific war would unfold, not within the first six months, punctuated by the Battle of Midway, but rather in three years of intensive carrier operations that would decide the outcome of the war in the Pacific. Many factors shaped the command decisions regarding carrier battles, among them assumptions, personalities, planning, intelligence, tactical superiority, training, and seamanship. Professor Douglas Smith carefully reviews these concerns with a straightforward approach. How did the combat experiences of operational commanders of both sides shape their decision-making processes? This is the question that Professor Smith addresses with precision and insight.

Nearly sixty-five years have passed since the Pearl Harbor attack. Only now are we able to broaden our perspective of the Pacific War. We are no longer burdened with the prejudices and hatred that permeated the war with Japan. As the World War II generation passes, we honor them. These veterans were stakeholders and guardians of the historical narrative of World War II. We also understand that their experiences, in many ways, prevented the type of historical investigation needed to comprehend the dramatic conflict that was the Pacific War. In the aftermath of Pearl Harbor, those who had witnessed it sought to close the chapter on the U.S. Navy's greatest defeat. Adm. Chester Nimitz, who is considered one of the greatest military leaders of World War II, felt that it was a mistake to remember defeat by undertaking a memorial at Pearl Harbor. But he was wrong. He was simply too close to that painful memory. The lessons of history were lost.

Although Pearl Harbor was a defeat, it left us with new lessons and understanding. It was the end of an era; the passing of the battleship and the emergence of the aircraft carrier. Out of the ashes of Pearl Harbor arose a new U.S. Navy. It was a reflection of a nation. It showed resiliency and purpose. The greatest maritime salvage operation in history would be the raising of the Pacific Fleet. Pearl Harbor would become a springboard for the retaking of the Pacific from the Japanese. Today, the USS *Arizona* Memorial gives mute testimony to the sacrifice on December 7, 1941. It embodies America's ability to remember Pearl Harbor as a battle cry of the nation in 1941 and, today, as an eloquent statement to remember the sacrifices of Americans during World War II.

During those war years, the great aircraft carriers that sailed forth in harm's way silently passed the remains of the USS *Arizona*. Often, sailors would stand to the rail in silent salute in reverence of that day. But memory and perception come in many forms. Professor Smith's book gives us those perspectives to understand the failures and successes of carrier operations in the Pacific.

Daniel A. Martinez
Historian
USS *Arizona* Memorial
National Park Service

Acknowledgments

I WISH TO THANK Professor Timothy H. Jackson, director of the College of Distance Education, U.S. Naval War College, for his faith in me and his continuing support, without which this book would not have been possible. I also wish to thank Professor James Pickett Jones of the Florida State University Department of History, who has encouraged and mentored me for almost a decade. Professor of strategy and policy and my deputy at the Naval War College, Stanley D.M. Carpenter also deserves my most grateful acknowledgement for taking on the responsibilities of my job as well as his own for more than a year in order to allow me to complete this project. A fellow product of the Florida State University Department of History, Stan's constant encouragement provided a source of inspiration for reaching my goal. So too do I wish to thank Professor L.W. Wildemann, deputy director of the College of Distance Education at the War College, for his encouragement and for sacrificing progress toward his own doctorate to allow me the opportunity to complete requirements for mine. I would be remiss if I did not include Professor Charles C. Chadbourn III, director of Washington, D.C., Programs and the Non-resident Masters' Degree Program, for his friendship and advice along the way. I owe deep respect and gratitude to Professor Hal Blanton, associate chairman of the Naval War College Department of Joint Military Operations at the Naval Postgraduate School Detachment in Monterey, California, who, besides providing every sort of help to me along the way, taught me French, enabling me to fulfill that language requirement for doctoral candidacy. I also want to thank Professor John E. Jackson, director of Development and Long-range Planning at the War College, for hiring me and providing encouragement and support for almost a decade.

I also wish to thank those who provided the intellectual basis for this project. Mr. Gary A. LaValley, archivist of the Nimitz Library at the United States Naval Academy, was of great help in providing source material on the education of officers at the Academy in the interwar period. Mrs. Alice K. Juda, reference librarian at the Naval War College, found material I'm convinced no one else could find by doggedly pursuing any lead she could uncover. Moreover, Mrs. Juda provided daily encouragement for me to complete this project, without which my enthusiasm could have easily vanished. I owe her a great debt of thanks. Likewise, Mr. Dennis J. Zambrotta, library technician at the War College, spent countless hours locating and retrieving microfilm from the College's microfilm library. His attention to my every request was essential to this project.

Dr. Evelyn Cherpak, Naval War College archivist, was a font of knowledge on every document in her archival holdings. Dr. Cherpak not only helped me conceptualize this project, but uncovered a vast array of original source material for it. Ms. Gigi Davis, head of the Naval War College Graphic Arts Department, gave life to this project through her suggestions and personal attention to the graphics included here. Mr. Jason Peters, assigned by Ms. Davis exclusively to support this project, is a credit to his profession. Without them this project would lack the critical spatial orientation required in any consideration of military or naval history.

I also wish to thank Professors Donald D. Horward, Jonathan Grant, and James Sickinger, whose mentoring and encouragement have been so instrumental in focusing this project and guiding it toward completion. I will be forever in their debt.

I owe my lasting gratitude to Professor Emeritus Frank Snyder of the War College Joint Military Operations Department. I'm convinced that he knows more about the Battle of Midway than any man alive, and his careful consideration of Vice Adm. Frank Jack Fletcher and his contribution to the Navy's success in the Pacific theater has earned him the nickname of "Frank Jack Snyder." Editor Emeritus Frank Uhlig of the Naval War College Review has also provided insights invaluable to this project. Likewise, author John B. Lundstrom has added his considerable insight whenever requested for the first six parts of this work. Daniel Martinez, historian and archivist of the USS *Arizona* Memorial, has also provided information and insights critical to this study. Professor Ned Willmott has reviewed my work in progress and offered many critical comments that have improved every aspect of this work. Professors Charles S. Thomas II of Georgia Southern University and John H. Maurer, chairman of the Strategy and Policy Department at the Naval War College, both friends and respected colleagues, have provided both encouragement and valuable insights on all aspects of World War II. Professor Brad Lee of the War College, a respected expert on Japan and World War II, has also infused valuable insights in this project. To each of these powerful intellects I will be forever grateful.

I owe my heartfelt thanks to Ms. Debbie Perry, graduate assistant for the Florida State University Department of History. Like every graduate student in history before me, I could not have gotten this far without her.

To my wonderful bride, Paulette, I owe more than I can ever repay. She has put up with me for a decade and run every sort of errand necessary to my studies. Her help on and intellectual contribution to this book has been crucial to its completion. Her advice and counsel have enlivened this project and she shares in any success I may have achieved in it.

Special thanks go to Adm. Tom Fargo, Commander in Chief of the United States Pacific Fleet and thence United States Commander in Chief, Pacific, classmate in the Naval Academy Class of 1970 and friend, for graciously taking the time to evaluate, offer his intellectual contribution to, and provide the foreword for this work. Likewise I thank Adm. John B. "Black" Nathman, also a classmate in the Naval Academy Class of 1970, for his contribution to the foreword. As the former Commander, Naval Air Force, United States Pacific Fleet and Commander, United States Naval Air Forces, as well as former Vice Chief of Naval Operations, now Commander, Fleet Forces Command, Adm. Nathman has shared his insight and expertise generously.

Most of all I thank Edward S. Miller for more than a decade of support and insights on his own book, *War Plan Orange*, which has served as a guide and inspiration for my own work. Thanks also go to Edward S. and Joyce I. Miller, whose generosity and interest made publication of this book possible.

Others who have provided help along the way but who are not named here are gratefully acknowledged. I owe you all so very much.

The views expressed in this book are mine and are not to be construed as those of the Naval War College or the Department of the Navy. All errors in fact or analysis remain my own.

CARRIER BATTLES

Introduction

THERE WERE FIVE CARRIER BATTLES in World War II. There will be no more. Technology—the advent of precision-guided missiles, nuclear weapons, high-yield conventional weapons, and above all exceptionally accurate target locating and delivery systems—has been paired with a comprehensive operational concept for its use. In an increasingly integrated global economy, such technology makes future manpower-intensive conventional warfare in the open ocean unlikely.

Nonetheless, warfare today employs the same decision-making processes that determined the outcomes of past battles, including the carrier battles of World War II. Commanders make decisions in war, and although technology has tremendously increased the rapidity of the decision process during combat, the way in which that process is refined and optimized is the key to military success.

This book will examine how the United States Navy produced warriors capable of maintaining an offensive mind-set and making correct decisions in harm's way at sea in World War II. As the carrier battles were key to successfully matching strategy with political objectives in the naval arena in that war, we will evaluate the decisions made in those five battles: Coral Sea, Midway, the Eastern Solomons, Santa Cruz, and the Philippine Sea.

History generally equates to a story—describing what happened and who was involved, and often analyzing the significance of courses of action and events. Seldom do historians consider the anatomy of the decision-making process that led to those actions and events. Yet in the study of military history, decisions are the key to the interaction at arms between hostile nations and societies. Thus evaluation of the decision-making process in battle becomes all-important. Moreover, because combat is interactive, the relative capacity of the combatants to make correct decisions becomes a determining factor in the relations among nations.

This book examines the command decisions made by the U.S. Navy's top leadership in World War II to evaluate the utility of each leader's preparation, through military education and study before and during combat, for making such decisions. The victory of the United States over Japan in World War II seems to validate the adequacy of U.S. leaders' preparation. However, scholars have also ascribed the victory in the Pacific to luck, good intelligence, and the personal characteristics of the Navy's leaders. To determine the source of the battle's outcome as it relates to the decision processes of those in command during the five carrier battles of the war, this book will evaluate the following:

1. The commander's estimate of the situation and grasp of the strategic and operational significance of the decisions he would be required to make
2. The commander's demonstrated ability to formulate a course of action, his ability to convey his decision in mission orders to subordinate commanders concisely and unambiguously, and his flexibility in modifying those orders through strategic and/or operational reappraisal if required
3. The adequacy of command arrangements, the chain of command established, and the communications procedures put into effect to facilitate the exercise of command in battle
4. The commander's adherence to established operational and tactical doctrines where appropriate, his adherence to procedures established prior to the engagement of forces, and his ability to deviate from the same when warranted
5. The commander's communication of mission requirements to subordinate commanders and the suitability of complementary actions by those subordinates to engage the enemy more effectively
6. The commander's understanding of the engagement's importance within the wider context of achieving U.S. political objectives and his

concomitant appreciation for the appropriate risk and determination of the proper circumstances in which to end the battle

7. The commander's audacity and brilliance in conceptualizing, articulating, and executing a plan of action
8. The commander's ability to learn from the situation and rapidly pass lessons along to the advantage of those commanding in later engagements

Evaluation criteria one through three and six above particularly reflect the tenets advanced in *Sound Military Decision*—the key text for optimizing combat decisions used at the U.S. Naval War College in the interwar period—as key to arriving at the most advantageous understanding of the circumstances under which combat at sea will take place and arriving at a sound decision as to how to conduct the ensuing battle. To the extent possible, we will examine the factors responsible for either success or failure in the command decision process as a means of identifying the efficacy of institutional development of the Navy's top leadership in preparing the Navy's leaders to make good decisions in combat. In particular, we will scrutinize the educational and operational experience of the considered commanders as a basis for their command decisions. The relative lack of experience of virtually all of the U.S. Navy's operational commanders in World War II will be inspected in depth, as will the adequacy of the Navy's educational system to compensate for that lack of experience. The utility of officer education in the Navy will thus be evaluated, demonstrating the benefit and misdirection it provided as the war played out from 1942 through 1944. Through this process, we will highlight those of the eight evaluation criteria offered above most responsible for success or failure.

What Created Success?

Various scholars have credited the U.S. naval successes in the Pacific theater in World War II to luck or good intelligence. Certainly a strong case could be made for either of these, given the enemy advantage in relative force levels in several of the battles and the exceptional code-breaking efforts of members of the U.S. Naval Intelligence Service. More than anything else, however, the outcomes of the five Pacific carrier battles can be attributed to the relative merit of decisions made by the opposing commanders. But the success of U.S. commanders in making appropriate and timely decisions at sea in World War II is also a function of the correct or erroneous decisions and actions taken and executed by their Japanese counterparts.

The Japanese naval leadership had considerable combat experience even before the decision to attack the United States at Pearl Harbor. Japan's aircraft carrier commanders—particularly Adm. Chuichi Nagumo, who commanded all major carrier operations, including the six-carrier attack on Pearl Harbor, prior to U.S. Fleet opposition—had considerably more operational experience in a combat environment than any admiral the United States could muster to oppose them. For instance, the first carrier commander of the U.S. Pacific Fleet to see action and the senior commander in the first three of the five Pacific carrier battles, Rear Adm. Frank Jack Fletcher, was not even an aviator. He thus lacked conceptual insight into air battle out of sight of the carrier that launched the attack and in an additional dimension compared to battle on the ocean's surface. Nor had he seen any opposing surface naval action while in command of a Navy fighting vessel, though he had received the Medal of Honor for service as a lieutenant during the United States' occupation of Vera Cruz and the Navy Cross for service in European waters in 1918.

This imbalance in relative combat experience coupled with the Japanese advantages of superior numbers, an aviation complement with considerable combat experience, and aircraft newer and more technologically advanced than anything in the American arsenal should have given the Japanese a decided edge in combat situations. The American admirals had merely pondered in the classroom and on the gaming board situations that their Japanese adversaries had experienced in real life.

History, unfortunately, has not often been kind in battle to those who lack experience, who have inferior weaponry and outdated tactics, or who are numerically inferior. Thus the success of the U.S. Navy in the Pacific in World War II—particularly during the critical year of 1942—can be seen as an anomaly of some proportion. This book will examine that anomaly to determine what created success in situations ripe for disaster. While such historical enquiry may not help predict the future, it may uncover a method of educating officers to create an analytical and decisive mind-set that can compensate for inadequate experience in the most deadly of human endeavors.

Strategic Culture

Combat commanders often develop a style and a way of looking at war that is, in a sense, a product of their civic and military acculturation. The U.S.

military has had several defining moments in its history. Before World War II, these included the American War of Independence, the American Civil War, and World War I. In combination, these moments produced an attitude toward war peculiar to the American situation. Americans tend to look at war as a failure of diplomacy, rather than as a continuation of policy by other means (as it was regarded by the theorist of land warfare, Carl von Clausewitz). Americans abhor loss of life. Hence we attempt to compensate for men in battle with superior technology and logistics. Americans are driven by "moral" causes—hence "the war to end slavery" and "the war to end all wars." And, perhaps most of all, Americans' approach to war can be characterized as "wargasm," the desire to right a wrong swiftly and at as little human cost as possible, and then to get back to the normalcy of civilian life.

It is within this culture that the U.S. Navy's top leadership came to command in World War II. Such strategic culture bodes well for decisiveness and aggressiveness in waging war. What remains is the catalyst for decisive action to be inculcated in naval (and military) leadership. This study will examine how the U.S. Navy approached the development of such a catalyst and how it institutionalized it in its leadership cadre during the first four decades of the twentieth century.

Relevance of the Study

While the technologies of war have changed, its fundamental elements have not. Preparing warriors for war by methods that do not require them to actually engage in it will remain the norm rather than the exception. The study that follows intends to accomplish four things. First, it will employ critical analysis of the decision process during five key naval battles of World War II. Second, it will provide a single-source history of all five carrier battles of World War II. Third, through evaluation of the decision processes of the commanders concerned, it will identify the interwar educational system—particularly *Sound Military Decision*—as the cornerstone of success in those battles. Finally, it will discuss institutionalization of the educational processes that led to success in harm's way at sea in World War II as a model for the future education of naval officers in time of peace.

CHAPTER 1

Preparing for War: Naval Education Between the World Wars

FIGURE 1. USS *Arizona* This photo and the following caption appeared in an Army/Navy football program, on 29 November 1941, just nine days before the attack on Pearl Harbor: "A bow on view of the USS *Arizona* as she plows into a huge swell. It is significant that despite the claims of air enthusiasts no battleship has yet been sunk by bombs." This was a clear shot across the bow of naval aviation. —*Courtesy of U.S. Naval Academy Archives*

Introduction

NAVY 14, ARMY 6. This victory on 29 November 1941 was the Navy's last before a resounding and unexpected defeat only nine days later, the attack on the Navy's Pacific Fleet at Pearl Harbor on 7 December 1941. It demonstrated conclusively that bombs—and aerial-launched torpedoes—could indeed sink battleships, despite claims to the contrary by the "Gun Club" or "Battleship Navy," which declared that battleships could survive, and were thus superior to, the destructive power of aviation (as shown in the blatant advertisement above*). Mainstream thinking within the Navy's top leadership held that naval aviation was an adjunct to battle fleet operations rather than an

*Obviously the claim made in the football program ignored the lesson learned by the Italian Navy on 11 November 1940—almost a year to the day before the Japanese attack on Pearl Harbor—

integral part of its offensive lethality. The Japanese attack established beyond doubt that this philosophy was seriously in error.

Having made such a monumental error in judgment, it remained to be tested what strengths of insight and decision that same leadership group could throw against Japan in a war of unlimited political objective* and military commitment. Some among them felt hope borne of confidence in their preparation to fight and win a war contested in open ocean areas and inland seas.

Fleet Adm. Chester W. Nimitz, who took up the post of Commander of the Pacific Fleet and Pacific Ocean Areas as a three-star at the end of 1941, wrote in a letter dated 19 September 1965 to Vice Adm. Charles Melson, then president of the U.S. Naval War College in Newport, Rhode Island, that "The enemy of our games [at the War College] was always Japan and the courses were so thorough that after the start of WW II—nothing that happened in the Pacific was strange or unexpected."[1] This chapter examines the veracity of Nimitz's statement by evaluating the adequacy of the flagship U.S. Navy educational institutions—the United States Naval Academy and the United States Naval War College—in preparing the Navy for combat in World War II. Specifically, we will explore how naval "lessons" from World War I were treated and how the curricula were structured to consider their adequacy and impact in transforming a predominantly defensive navy into a well-honed organization with an offensive mind-set capable of conducting operations in both inshore and open-ocean areas.

Of equal importance to intellectual preparation for war was the attitude of the naval leadership in the interwar years toward the nature of "the next war." This attitude toward doctrine, which has recently been described as "technology, and an intent for its use," was sure to manifest itself in Navy doctrine. Education, the interpretation and application of lessons from recent past wars, the adaptation of new technologies to offensive lethality

---

when the battleship *Cavour* was sunk and two other battleships were disabled at anchor by British air attack in the harbor of Taranto. Ironically, of the twenty-one warships sunk by the Japanese at Pearl Harbor, only one battleship—*Arizona*—was sunk by a single bomb.

*Richard Storry, *The Double Patriots: A Study of Japanese Nationalism* (Westport, CT: Greenwood Press, Publishers, 1957), appendix II, pp. 317–319. The Japanese Land Disposal Plan laid out a detailed schedule for Japanese conquest of Asia and much of the Western Hemisphere over two wars, and allocated the most suitable form of government to each territory. Alaska, for example, was to be under a governor-general. Because this document establishes the grandiosity of Japanese political objectives at the war's outset and is central to the analysis found later in this book, it is reproduced in its entirety as an appendix.

and ship survivability, a doctrine establishing new warfare concepts, and war gaming to validate those concepts dominated the professional preparation of the Navy officer corps. Navy leaders' attitudes toward future war structured the debates intrinsic in all of these pursuits.

While Nimitz's statement above speaks strongly of the proper intellectual preparation for World War II at the Naval War College, it also implies that the Navy was being properly structured in the interwar period with respect to the kind of war it was likely to fight in the near future, the doctrine it would require to fight that war, and the implements of war it deemed necessary to succeed against a capable and motivated adversary. Inherent in all of that, since war is above all an interactive process, is the assumption of a likely enemy. All concerned got that right in selecting Japan.

Studying "The Right Stuff"

In the letter mentioned above, Nimitz continued, "Each student was required to plan logistic effort [*sic*] for an advance across the Pacific—and we were well prepared for the fantastic logistic efforts required to support the operations of the war. . . . One of my classmates [both in the Naval War College (NWC) Class of 1923 and United States Naval Academy (USNA) Class of 1905] Captain R.C. MacFall . . . devised the circular tactical formations used so successfully during WW II."[2] Nimitz went on to say, "I credit the Naval War College for such success I achieved in strategy and tactics both in peace and war."[3]

Admiral Nimitz's ringing endorsement of his prewar educational experience was most assuredly validated by his performance in the Pacific during World War II. Yet the realities of that war indicate that his assessment of the prewar naval educational effort—as it applied to the Navy in general—could not have been farther from the truth. Although the focus on Japan as a primary threat and the elements of course composition, which stressed analysis of the situation and sound decision processes, were sufficient to produce a professionally grounded officer cadre with a superbly analytical and adaptable group mind-set, the most forward-looking elements of technology and doctrine were conspicuously absent from naval education of the interwar period. What was evident in the Navy's officer leadership during World War II, however, was a universal offensive orientation borne of a distinct strategic culture ingrained in that leadership cadre from their first days in Annapolis. They had studied the "wrong stuff," but in precisely the right way.

Study, Gaming, and Wartime Reality

The U.S. Navy was indeed unprepared for the type of war it was to experience in World War II. It took the Allies some time after the fall of France to relearn the importance of building enough destroyers to serve as screens for convoying ships on the logistic train following the sea routes across the Atlantic. Expectations in the Navy were for a battleship war akin to World War I, as institutionalized in the major war game of the interwar period conducted at the Naval War College, the Battle of Sable Island.

The Sable Island game was essentially a replay of the Battle of Jutland, another important element of study and critique, with east and west inverted, off Nova Scotia, and the United States arrayed against Britain.[4] In that part of the War College curriculum, the utility of the aircraft carrier as anything other than a scouting platform was completely neglected. Other major elements of the curriculum centered on the Battle of Jutland as well. *Jutland Decisions* (eighty-eight pages), by Capt. William Glassford, received substantial classroom attention after 1930. *Jutland* (forty-one pages), based on the eyewitness account of Vice Adm. Sir Matthew R. Best, RN, a member of Admiral Jellicoe's staff during the battle, entered the curriculum in 1936. Thus offensive carrier interactions were relegated in importance to the study of gun platform battles bereft of radar (not available until 1936) or reconnaissance aircraft fixing of enemy units.

Other games were conducted at the Naval War College that explored the use of naval air assets and aircraft carriers, even before the latter were introduced into the fleet in late 1924 with the commissioning of USS *Langley*. Those early games were conducted under Rear Adm. William S. Sims while he was president of the college from April 1919 to October 1922. But the emphasis on the battleship as demonstrated in the Sable Island series of games was clear through the late 1930s. Only gradually, starting with Sims's presidency and experiencing ebbs and advances under succeeding presidents, did naval aviation in an offensive role gain gradual acceptance.

There were, of course, major advocates of air warfare in the Navy at the time. Adm. William A. Moffett was one, the first Chief of the Navy Bureau of Aeronautics created on 10 August 1921. Adm. John H. Towers, who became naval aviator number three in an attempt to refine the precision of battleship targeting and gunnery by aviation spotting of enemy targets, and Adm. William F. Halsey, who qualified as a naval aviator at an advanced age, were also supporters. Perhaps the most vocal early proponent of the aircraft carrier was Capt. Washington Irving Chambers, who served for a period under Acting Secretary Franklin D. Roosevelt while assigned as chief aviation adviser to the Secretary of the Navy. That Chambers never made flag rank speaks volumes about the battleship predilection of the Navy's top leaders.[5]

Even Halsey was less than totally enthusiastic regarding the offensive potential of the carrier. Commenting on his qualification as a pilot and taking command of the carrier *Saratoga* in 1935 at the age of fifty-two, Halsey declared, "I regarded the privilege of commanding the *Sara* merely as a pleasant bonus."[6] Battleship admirals, members of the Gun Club or Black Shoe Navy, held firmly that cruisers and destroyers could not be spared from "the main formation" to protect carriers in an offensive role—carriers should have a scouting-observation function, remaining the "eyes of the Fleet."[7] This bias in the senior Navy hierarchy was reflected in the War College course of study.

The Naval Air Debate

Pivotal to the way in which the Navy approached future war at sea was the debate that raged during the 1920s and 1930s within the Service's hierarchy over the role of naval aviation. Oddly, that debate is perhaps best summed up by Col. William "Billy" Mitchell—a distinguished officer and combat veteran of the Army Air Service who had risen to the rank of brigadier general during World War I and become one of the leading spokesmen for military aviation. In September 1925 he leveled serious accusations against the Navy Department and War Department in the press. Of the eight specifications brought against Mitchell in the court-martial proceedings against him as a consequence of his charges, the first was the most serious and set the terms of reference for the other seven:

> *Specification 1*: In that Colonel William Mitchell, Air Service, did, at Fort Sam Houston, Texas, on or about the fifth day of September, 1925, conduct himself to the prejudice of good order and military discipline and in a way to bring discredit upon the military service by making, uttering and publishing to Harry McCleary, A.H. Yeager, Kenneth McCalla and to the Associated Press, a news gathering and news promulgating agency, and in the *San Antonio Express*, a public journal, and in divers [*sic*] other public journals of the United States, a statement which in its entirety reads in substance as follows . . .[8]

Mitchell indicated that his statement was his opinion, and it was particularly critical of the Navy for its handling of aviation matters. He brought as evidence the deaths of two aviators at the annual Army and Navy Air Races as a result of the shifting of the races between the two Services each year for "propaganda purposes" rather than "service" and those competing having to fly "old crates," "dilapidated racing airplanes" built for the race two years prior and rendered unfit and unsafe for racing, rather than new aircraft for which ample funding was available. He also singled out the Navy for the loss over land of the airship *Shenandoah* and with it the Navy's most experienced airship captain, "going west on a propaganda mission . . . over mountains," which he maintained was totally inappropriate for a Navy air asset.[9]

Mitchell further decried the Navy's conception of a war in the Pacific, specifically its recent "great Pacific naval maneuvers—the main features of [which] were the assembling of a fleet of some 148 surface vessels in the Pacific, the parade up our Pacific coast and entrance into San Francisco Harbor and then the trip to Honolulu"* as the operational objective of the maneuvers.[10] Mitchell challenged the concept of a march across the Pacific to secure Hawaii from foreign occupation, sending the operational force's antiquated ships through mines off San Francisco and submarine operating areas en route to the objective area. (The mines were intended to protect the approaches to Hawaii from ships coming from known U.S. naval ports. Mitchell stresses that the ships were "antiquated" to reinforce his position that ships of whatever vintage were too antiquated to defend themselves against land-based aircraft, or mines, or anything else, for that matter.)

Mitchell also criticized the attempt to demonstrate, with three airplanes, the ability to fly nonstop from California to Hawaii, which resulted in the loss of the entire five-man crew of the only aircraft to make it a reasonable distance from takeoff.[11]

> These accidents are the direct result of the incompetency, criminal negligence and almost treasonable administration of the national defense by the navy and war departments [*sic*]. In their attempts to

---

*Here Mitchell is undoubtedly referring to the Fleet Problem V of March 1925. A complete listing and abbreviated description of these Fleet Problems is contained in *Records Relating to United States Navy Fleet Problems I to XXII 1923–1941*, National Archives Microfilm Publications, National Archives and Records Service General Services Administration, Washington: 1975. This series of Fleet Problems will be discussed in greater detail later in this chapter.

> keep down the development of aviation into an independent department, separate from the army and navy and handled by aeronautical experts, and to maintain the existing systems, they have gone to the utmost lengths to carry their point. All aviation policies, schemes and systems are dictated by the non-flying officers of the army or navy who know practically nothing about it. The lives of the airmen are being used merely as pawns in their hands.[12]

Mitchell went on to say that "officers and agents sent by the war and navy departments to Congress have almost always given incomplete, misleading or false information about aeronautics, which either they knew to be false when given or was the result of such gross ignorance of the question that they should not be allowed to appear before a legislative body."[13]

"The conduct of affairs by these two departments, as far as aviation is concerned, has been so disgusting in the last few years as to make any self-respecting person ashamed of the cloth he wears. Were it not for the great patriotism of our air officers and their absolute confidence in the institutions of the United States, knowing that sooner or later existing conditions would be changed, I doubt if one of them would remain with the Colors—certainly not, if he were a real man."[14]

Such a direct and flagrant attack on the highest levels of leadership of the Army and Navy by one considered perhaps the most experienced combat aviator of the nation—and the obvious consequences for its exponent for initiating such an attack—certainly gave credence to Mitchell's charges.

With respect to the utility of aircraft against surface combatants, Mitchell specifically attacked the Navy's decision to forestall congressionally authorized and funded tests of aircraft in the "aerial bombardment of battleships and shipping board vessels while under their own steam and moving, so as to set at rest any doubt of aircraft's ability to destroy and sink any seacraft which floats on the water."[15] Here he maintained that "steam was gotten up by the navy . . . to deprecate the value of air power and show the value of the surface vessels and battleships."[16] In discussing both the Navy's failure to allow bombing tests on underway combatant ships and its previously discussed Pacific campaign exercise against the Hawaiian islands in 1924, Mitchell opined that "if any ship of the fleet survived the [mines outside San Francisco Harbor and the] submarine attacks, crossed the sea and came within hundreds of miles of the hostile coast, they [*sic*] would be sent to the bottom forthwith, by aircraft. If the Pacific maneuvers showed anything conclusively, it was that aircraft acting from land bases can destroy any surface fleet coming within its radius of operations.[17]* This already had been amply proved by our bombardment tests in 1921."[18]

Mitchell referred to the bombing tests conducted between 21 June and 21 July 1921 as a result of the momentum he personally generated to "prove" that aircraft could sink ships at sea. In October of 1920 the Navy had started bombing tests of its own on obsolete ships anchored in the Chesapeake Bay, and though the tests were conducted in secrecy, photographs of the damage to the decommissioned battleship *Indiana* were smuggled to the *London Illustrated News* where they were published in December 1920.[19]

This gave Mitchell just the opportunity he wanted. He pressed openly and publicly, as well as when called to testify before Congress for Army participation in a series of similar bombing tests to be conducted against Navy ships.[20] Ultimately Secretary of the Navy Josephus Daniels agreed, and the tests were conducted, culminating with the sinking of the interned German dreadnought† *Ostfriesland*.[21]

Despite the outcome of the tests, the debate Mitchell had created surrounding naval aviation had several consequences he had not anticipated. On 12 July 1921 Congress created the Bureau of Aeronautics for the Navy, strengthening the institutional independence of naval aviation and in large part negating Mitchell's goal of a single aviation service supporting both the Army and Navy.[22] Ultimately the Joint Board of the Army and Navy, under the chairmanship of Gen. John J. Pershing, accepted the Navy's view of the implications of the bombing tests: carrier aviation and other uses of aviation assets at sea should enjoy greater support and funding. This finding directly opposed Mitchell's position that the success of the bombing tests demonstrated conclusively that surface fleets were obsolete.[23]

Mitchell remained undeterred in his effort to convince appropriate leaders of the vulnerability of Navy ships to aerial attack. By the time of his attack

---

*It is indeed ironic that Grand Joint Exercise No. 4 of February 1932 would evaluate a land-based attack on Rear Adm. Harry E. Yarnell's carrier force northeast of Hawaii as having destroyed a carrier fleet, with aircraft claimed by Yarnell as destroyed on the deck in a previous raid from his carriers during that exercise. Grand Joint Exercise No. 4 will be discussed at greater length later in this chapter.

†*Ostfriesland* was actually surrendered to the United States as reparation for war damage, commissioned into the U.S. Navy, and then decommissioned when she arrived on the East Coast to be used in the trials.

on the Navy's handling of aircraft and those who flew them in September 1925, his position had evolved into complaints over safety, administration, and reasonability of force structure.

Mitchell's specific objection to the Navy's handling of air power is best summed up below:

> The navy, to maintain its position, keeps asking for more aircraft, which it cannot use legally, because the legal defense of the land is entrusted to armies. In spite of the legal restrictions, however, but to keep control of aviation and not let it get away, the navy department continually gets more money from congress by its Washington lobby so as to keep the political support of the aircraft manufacturers and, possibly, some others interested in them. This year, the navy's estimate for the aircraft amounts to $37,360,248. They only have one aircraft carrier, the *Langley*, which can go about half as fast as a battleship, and which is an obsolete collier. It can hold 36 small airplanes. They are building two aircraft carriers [the *Lexington* and *Saratoga*] which can hold 60 to 70 planes. These are practically obsolete before they are completed.
>
> Where is the thirty-seven million for aircraft going? It is going into land aircraft which have nothing to do with the navy's operation on the seas and which will be used as a political lever for the maintenance of their existing systems.
>
> The War department, that now is entrusted by law with the serial defense over the land areas of the United States and its possessions, including the protection of navy yards, asks for $24,582,000. Consider how foolish it is. The navy, an organization charged with going to sea and which must operate from surface vessels, which as a matter of fact are practically obsolete now, and which will afford no real protection to the country in case of an air attack, asking for two-thirds more than the army does, which acts from land bases and is specifically charged with the defense of the land areas. The amount allotted to the navy for new aircraft is three times as much as the army.[24]

It should be noted that as early as April of 1917 the Navy had 54 aircraft, and by November of 1918 it had 2,107 aircraft—yet the Navy's first carrier, the experimental USS *Langley*, was not commissioned until late 1924.[25]

Edward S. Miller, author of the award-winning book *War Plan Orange*, maintains that congressional funding for Navy aircraft and building rates indicate the Navy's proactive position on incorporation of air assets into fleet operations during this period.[26] Mitchell's statement above contradicts that contention by reinforcing that, though the Navy was highly involved in the procurement of aircraft, it was fixated on land-based air operations and lacked a concrete plan for employing its air assets in operations with fleet units. Though the Navy was spending plenty on land-based aircraft, it had no real plan for constructing carrier air wings. The Navy's aircraft carrier building and commissioning plan, discussed later, seems to support Mitchell's analysis of the situation.

But was Mitchell's contention that the Navy Department was "incompetent, criminally negligent and almost treasonable in its administration" of the national defense credible, or merely the futile outcry of a disenfranchised aviation proponent? Perhaps the best answer comes from the testimony, elicited by Mitchell's military defense attorney, of Rear Adm. William Sowden Sims, USN (Ret.), the Navy's most highly placed operational leader in World War I and a highly respected and knowledgeable advocate of the Navy's role and mission in the United States' global involvement.

An 1880 graduate of the U.S. Naval Academy, Sims reached the rank of admiral in 1918 and reverted to two-star rank at the close of World War I.[27] He served in the Atlantic and Pacific and on the China Station, where he was for a time on the staff of the commander in chief, and he was a naval attaché in St. Petersburg, Russia and in Paris.[28] From 1907 to 1908 he was one of President Theodore Roosevelt's aides, and commanded the battleship *Minnesota* from 1911 to 1913.[29] After attending the U.S. Naval War College in Newport, he commanded the Atlantic Fleet Torpedo Flotilla from 1913 to 1915, the battleship *Nevada* from 1915 to 1916, and in 1917 received orders to become president of the Naval War College.[30] "A month or two before the war broke out, 1917, until the end of the war [he] was in command of the United States Naval forces operating in European waters."[31]

On his return from World War I and reversion to the peacetime rank of rear admiral, Sims became president of the Naval War College until his retirement in October of 1922.[32] He was highly decorated as an intellectual. He declined the Distinguished Service Medal from the United States government for his wartime service, but did accept the Grand Cross of the Order of St. Michael and St. George from Great Britain in 1918, the beginning of a long list of awards he would receive by 1922.[33] Admiral Sims had also served as a member of the nation's General Board while president of the Naval War College. All things considered, he was in an excellent position to critique the Navy's situation as a naval power, and of aviation's role in that equation.

Under questioning, Sims stated that as he understood the situation, "the Navy Department [had] not any defined policy [as regards how the Navy handles aircraft] . . . going along from day to day, more or less in a higgledy-piggledy way,"[34] indicated that if you got into contact with an enemy who has more airplanes than you at sea, he will "drive down your airplanes until he gets command over your fleet, and then it is a question as to whether the airplanes that command the water over the fleet can destroy the ships or not . . . in the Navy Department they tell you that they can."[35] He further testified, "It seems to me it is perfectly absurd to take any different attitude, in view of the experiments that have been carried out on modern battleships, how easily they are sunk with bombs that are dropped on board of them, or alongside, and it seems to me it is entirely inevitable that any ship at all is at the mercy of airplanes or bombing planes that command the air over it."[36] Sims stressed the importance of having more or at least approximately the same number of aircraft carriers (or other combatants) as any potential adversary, stating that as an objective over any conceptualization of a "balanced fleet," a meaningless term except in the context of a specific opponent with an identifiable force structure.[37]

Sims also stated that Britain, for instance, had constructed "two or three" aircraft carriers after the war, and had another near completion, which were of the shape and hull of a battle cruiser, longer and narrower than a battleship, and capable of a speed of thirty-odd knots.[38] Thus they would be able to keep up with battleships and battle cruisers and act as integral parts of the battle fleet, unlike *Langley*, which had a top speed of fourteen knots.

In all his testimony, Sims—a battleship commander without any personal military aviation experience—came across as a staunch supporter and advocate of naval aviation. When asked what he considered the "backbone of the fleet" he responded:

> The backbone of the fleet is of course the group of capital ships, but it depends on what those capital ships are. It seems to me that in view of the power of the plane used and the battleship, when he commands the air over it, it is a foregone conclusion that if the battleship should meet an airplane carrier at sea, the two of them alone, the battleship carrying no plane except a couple of spotting planes,

> the airplane carrier would command the air over the battleship, and we would have a reproduction of one of the bombings off the coast [the bombings conducted from 21 June to 21 July, 1921, mentioned above]. In other words, there would not be any hope at all for the battleship because the airplane carrier would stay out of range of the guns. So therefore it seems to me that the battleship of the future is the airplane carrier.[39]

When questioned about the vulnerability or likelihood of success of a surface fleet against well-organized air forces operating from a land base, Sims's answer was similar:

> I do not see why it could not. . . . A land force that has more planes than can be brought on the decks of the ships of the attacking force can get control of the air and it seems to me absurd that the attacking fleet can remain within the radius of action of those planes and, for that reason, if the United States has a certain amount of air force on its coast that can be concentrated at a point of attack, it need fear nothing about what has been called the simon-pure naval operation we read about in history, because they can not bring as many planes against you on the decks of ships as can be assembled on land.[40]

Sims was consistent throughout his testimony in establishing himself as a strong proponent of aircraft in an offensive military role—both from land bases and from carriers designed to accommodate them. His message was clear. Aircraft in larger numbers over fleet units—including battleships—could "force down" the aircraft of their opponent and destroy the ships below. His position sums up that of the officers of the Navy who advocated concentration on the aircraft carrier as the principal capital ship of the near-term and future navy: that aircraft would replace surface ship gunnery as the main offensive weapons in the fleet's arsenal.

Yet in every debate there is another side. Such was the case when Rear Adm. William V. Pratt, U.S. Navy, then serving as president of the Naval War College and later to become Chief of Naval Operations, was called to the stand. Pratt had risen to flag rank through perhaps less glamorous, but no less distinguished, assignments than Sims, his predecessor as War College president. Pratt stood out in a variety of assignments for the first part of his career, and was rewarded with a tour of duty as a member of the staff at the Naval

War College. After that he went to sea as chief of staff for Admiral Sims; as the captain of USS *Birmingham*, a light cruiser; and as commander of the destroyer force of the Atlantic Fleet.[41] Pratt next served in the Office of Naval Operations in Washington, D.C., in the Canal Zone orchestrating defense of the Panama Canal, and then at the Army War College during the early stages of World War I, where he ultimately rose to the position of aide for operations.[42] In August of 1917 Admiral Pratt was made Assistant Chief of Naval Operations, serving under Adm. William S. Benson, where he was assigned for the rest of the war.[43] In February of 1919 he assumed battleship command of USS *New York*, after which he was appointed commander of the destroyer force of the U.S. Pacific Fleet.[44]

In 1921 Admiral Pratt was ordered again to Washington, where he became a member of the General Board.[45] During that assignment he was tasked to provide data and analytical material and to serve as a technical advisor for the Conference on Limitation of Naval Armament, together with Assistant Secretary of the Navy Franklin D. Roosevelt and Adm. Robert E. Coontz.[46] In 1923 he again received command afloat, and then assumed his position as president of the Naval War College on 5 September 1925. During his time with the General Board, Pratt was party to the development of most of the important directives for structuring and administering the Navy, and it was this period that was of most interest to the counsel for the prosecution.

When asked specifically if U.S. Navy policy regarding air forces afloat showed that the Navy Department fully realized its responsibility with respect to national defense, Pratt answered "I think the general policy is perfectly sound."[47] Like Sims's in earlier testimony, Pratt's position regarding the relative merits of the battleship and aircraft carrier was quite clear. When asked, "What do you consider the main part of the fleet?" Pratt answered, "Well, I consider the battleship is the backbone of the fleet."[48] When asked, "Is there any other element in the Navy at the present time that tends to take the place of the battleship, in your opinion?" he responded, "No; I do not think there is anything [that] can take its place."[49] Finally, asked if he would tell the court what he thought the relationship between battleship and airplane should be in the fleet, he opined, "I consider the airplane one of the most valuable adjuncts to the fleet . . . and an extremely useful weapon."[50]

Thus the testimony offered by Sims and Pratt—both knowledgeable and responsible men with considerable experience in both conducting and observing operations and in the classroom at the Naval War College—chose diametrically opposed positions on the relative merits of the battleship and the aircraft carrier with respect to the composition of the United States Fleet. So too were their contemporaries divided as regards the merits of carrier aviation. Sims's and Pratt's well-considered positions, which they translated into the areas of curriculum emphasis as presidents of the Naval War College, reflect the mood of the times that prevailed in both the Navy and the Aviation Service of the Army. Not surprisingly, their positions also reflect a similar controversy taking place within the nation's political and diplomatic services.

The Carrier Debate

The Treaty of Naval Limitations—emanating from the Washington Naval Conference of 1921–1922—was ratified by the U.S. Senate on 20 March 1922.[51] It concerned the five major technological advancements that had dominated war at sea in World War I: radio communications, the submarine, steam turbines, the dreadnought battleship, and the airplane.[52] Conference attendees determined that it was necessary to curtail the combination and scope of these technological advancements to mitigate their lethal power. In accomplishing that, the U.S. Navy's way of looking at its future force structure—including the numbers of and role of naval aviation assets, including aircraft carriers—was fundamentally altered.

The treaty imposed both quantitative and qualitative limits on Navy carriers, setting an overall carrier tonnage of 135,000 gross tons, from which USS *Langley* (CV-1) was excluded owing to her agreed-upon status as an experimental ship unable to sustain movement with the fleet.[53] No new-construction carrier could exceed 27,000 tons, and not more than 3,000 tons could be added to that during modernization.[54] The building program that followed as authorized by Congress included the conversion of cruiser hulls for construction of two "33,000-ton carriers," the *Lexington* and *Saratoga*. When built, these ships' gross displacement was actually closer to 36,000 gross tons, and the British took exception to the American assertion that these ships displaced about 33,000 tons, but to no avail. However, the construction of these two aircraft carriers created yet another debate centered on building options within the constraint on tonnage imposed by the Washington Conference.

Of a total of 135,000 allowable tons for construction of aircraft carriers under the Treaty of Naval Limitations, the United States had committed to 66,000 tons for *Lexington* and *Saratoga*. That left a total of 69,000 tons with which to complete the remainder of carriers to be employed with the fleet. Under treaty limitations that allowed no carrier of new hull-up construction above 27,000 gross tons, construction of two such carriers would eat up 54,000 tons of the remaining construction permissible under the treaty, leaving only 15,000 for a possible fifth fleet carrier.

Amid evidence from war gaming conducted by the Navy at the Naval War College (primarily under the presidency of Sims) many within the Navy strongly believed that smaller carriers, which would enable the launching of more aircraft in shorter periods of time, an advantage critical in battle, were what the Navy needed. Thus, even before *Saratoga* and *Lexington* were launched, on 7 April and 3 October 1925,[55] respectively, there was a constituency in favor of scrapping them for more small carriers.

The Japanese carrier-building program that paralleled U.S. construction took a somewhat more balanced approach. The Imperial Japanese Navy (IJN) ship *Kaga*, built on a battleship hull of 39,000 designed tons under the 1917 "Eight Four" Fleet Law, was launched on 17 November 1925 as a carrier of 26,900 gross tons, capable of carrying sixty aircraft, though her normal observed load of aircraft was around half that. (At Midway *Kaga* carried sixty-four aircraft, plus another nine earmarked for Midway once it was captured.[56]) *Akagi*, built on a battle cruiser hull of 42,000 designed tons (also laid down under the 1917 "Eight Four" Fleet Law), was launched on 22 April 1925 as another carrier of 26,900 gross tons, with a smaller maximum load of fifty aircraft.[57] A smaller carrier of just under 7,500 tons and capable of carrying between twenty and twenty-six aircraft, *Hosho* was launched in November of 1921. *Ryujo* followed this trend, laid down in 1929, launched in April 1931, and entering service in 1933, just over 8,000 tons and carrying around twenty-four aircraft.[58] When she was found to be too small, *Ryujo* was rebuilt, tipping the scales at 12,732 tons and carrying an Air Group of thirty-eight aircraft in her second state.

The Japanese construction program built a combination of carriers that very nearly approached the tonnage allowed by the Washington Naval Conference, but supplemented by smaller carriers that could enable the time-critical launching of requisite offensive aviation assets as deemed necessary by their American counterparts in war games conducted under Sims in the early 1920s. This combination of platforms could produce air superiority in battle without broaching the upper limit of overall carrier tonnage allowed under the terms of the Washington Conference. Independent of what the U.S. Navy was doing in Newport, it would appear that the Japanese had come to the same conclusion—that the side able to get the most aircraft in the air quickly would likely be the victor in a carrier battle.

The United States Navy, on the other hand, remained undecided on what size of carrier best suited the needs of the fleet. Inhibiting design considerations was a conservative estimate of the likely near-term enhancements to aircraft performance, such as speed, climb, power, and maneuverability. In December of 1926 the navy generated a report synthesizing the opinions of the bureaus of Aeronautics and Construction and Repair recommending construction of carriers of 23,000 tons with speeds of 23 knots but delayed construction of an initial purpose-built carrier pending fleet exercises with *Saratoga* and *Lexington*.[59]

Unfortunately, those carriers were not ready to join in fleet exercises until Fleet Problem IX was conducted off Panama in late January of 1929.[60] Thus the first American aircraft carrier to be designed from the hull up—*Ranger* (CV-4)—was not scheduled for completion until May 1934.[61] Commissioned in June of 1934, *Ranger* was the only carrier other than the *Saratoga* and *Lexington* to operate with the fleet until the *Yorktown* and *Enterprise* were commissioned on 30 September 1937 and 12 May 1938, respectively.[62] Designed for only 13,800 tons and launched at 14,500 tons as a compromise, *Ranger* proved to be too small to be involved in the type and scale of operations that were under consideration at the time.

Thus throughout most of the 1920s and 1930s the Navy was faced with determining the best use for carriers and their capabilities in various roles with three carriers ill-suited for the job from a design perspective. Nonetheless, most senior officers in command of fleet units gradually accepted the offensive potential of the carrier and its air wing. This did not, however, dispel the notion that the battleship remained the cornerstone of the fleet's offensive might. Even as World War II approached, the Battle of Jutland remained a fundamental consideration in the education of officers preparing for war at the Naval War College.

The Debate over Doctrine

Between February of 1923 and April of 1940 the U.S. Navy conducted twenty-one Fleet Problem exercises.[63] (A twenty-second Fleet Problem scheduled for January 1941 was canceled because of the outbreak of war in Europe.) These exercises were the Navy's vehicle for refining operational skills and for testing new technologies and ideas to enhance the fleet's combat effectiveness.

The Fleet Problems produced doctrine—they determined the way in which the Navy would use new technologies in its operations and tactics to meet the requirements of warfare.

At the forefront of consideration during these Fleet Problems was the way in which naval aviation would be incorporated in fleet doctrine. Endemic to many in leadership positions in the U.S. Navy, however, was a firmly held view that the battleship remained the "cornerstone of the Navy," and that the proper roles for carrier aviation were scouting for the fleet, gunfire spotting for battleship main batteries, and employment against submarines. This predilection may well have unfairly inhibited carrier air potential in the exercises.

In addition to the Fleet Problems, and usually immediately following one, the Navy also took part in "Grand Joint Exercises" with the Army and, on occasion, the Marine Corps. Grand Joint Exercise No. 4 was conducted in February of 1932, in the aftermath of Japanese occupation of Manchuria in autumn of 1931. In this exercise, which commenced on 1 February, Rear Adm. Harry E. Yarnell, who had been the first commanding officer of USS *Saratoga* when she was commissioned in 1927, returned as the commanding officer of *Saratoga*'s task force. Yarnell launched a surprise attack on the Hawaiian island of Oahu from a position to the northeast. His operational objective was as follows: "The BLUE Commander [Yarnell] is ordered to recapture and hold OAHU and occupy such other islands as may be necessary to reestablish our control of the HAWAIIAN AREA. To accomplish this task he has available the BLUE Battle Force plus an Expeditionary Force, approximately two divisions, one of Army and one of Marine Corps Troops."[64]

The situation surrounding the objective was summarized as follows:

> A powerful BLACK Atlantic Fleet, concentrated to cover the movement of large BLACK Army forces overseas for invasion of the BLUE Atlantic Coast, has been decisively defeated. BLACK naval power in the Atlantic has been reduced to a definite inferiority. The remnants of the BLACK Fleet and the BLACK overseas expedition have retired to Eastern Atlantic Bases.
>
> The BLACK naval forces which participated in the capture of OAHU withdrew from that vicinity, leaving a garrison of approximately eighteen thousand troops of all arms, coast defenses in good condition, some fifteen submarines, a small mine squadron and a military air force component.

> No information exists as to the location or strength of any remaining BLACK naval forces in the Pacific. BLUE's naval superiority is such as to make reasonably certain no naval interference outside of local units, with the operations against OAHU.[65]

Yarnell, drawing on his experience as commanding officer of *Saratoga* and taking advantage of the prevailing weather in the vicinity of the Hawaiian Islands, launched his raid on Oahu under conditions of almost complete surprise. He ordered an attack on Sunday morning, 7 February 1932. "In summary, Raid Plan No. One, initiated at 0540, 7 February, from a point forty miles off KAHUKU, was executed with 150 airplanes [from a total embarked aircraft inventory of 171 airplanes]. All aircraft returned to carriers, the operations being carried out in the face of overcast and squally weather, rough seas and high wind. The constructive opposition was slight. Carriers were notably vulnerable to submarine attack during launching and recovery phases due to high surface wind requiring slow speed (six to ten knots) on part of carriers."[66]

Yarnell's report of Grand Joint Exercise No. 4 indicates that bombs were expended on prescribed targets on the island of Oahu as described in table 1. No aircraft were sighted at Waipo or Puena Point fields.[67]

Several hours after the launch, at 0720, a submarine was sighted on the port quarter of *Saratoga* at twenty-eight hundred yards, with umpires assessing 19 percent damage to that carrier.[68] Similarly, as the last planes from her "attack" on military targets in the vicinity of Pearl Harbor were returning onboard, submarine S-42 launched four torpedoes against *Lexington* at a range of about eighteen hundred yards on her starboard beam, with "no damage" assessed by umpires.[69] Thus both *Saratoga* and *Lexington* had successfully launched and recovered their aircraft and executed a nearly unopposed raid on a plan devised by then-captain John Towers.

According to historian Brian M. Linn's award-winning book, *Guardians of Empire: The U.S. Army and the Pacific, 1902–1940*, "Hawaii's vulnerability to carrier raids had been graphically illustrated in 1932, when, during Grand Joint Exercise No. 4 the invading side's two aircraft carriers delivered a strong attack at dawn on Sunday, 7 February. The aggressors were credited with destroying several defending airplanes on the ground and with seizing temporary control of the air over Oahu."[70] Linn explains, however, that the purpose of the exercise was for the Blue Force, commanded by Yarnell, to take and hold territory on Oahu, and that their mission thus

TABLE 1 Bombs expended by *Saratoga* and *Lexington* aircraft

Saratoga		
VF One-B	36 bombs	Eighteen on hangars; eighteen on antiaircraft batteries at Wheeler Field
VF Two-B	28 bombs	Hangars at Luke Field
VF Five-B	44 bombs	Hangar at Wheeler Field
VF Six-B	30 bombs	Twenty-four on hangars at Luke Field, six on one plane near hangars
VS Two-B	18 bombs	On eight bombardment plans
	6 bombs	At Rodgers Airport
Lexington		
VT One-B	45 bombs	Ammunition depot at Schofield Barracks
VT Two-B	45 bombs	Chemical depot at Schofield Barracks
VS Three-B	24 bombs	Four designated targets at Schofield Barracks

Source: Information in table from H.E. Yarnell, Rear Admiral, USN, Commander Aircraft, Battle Force. *Operations of the Blue Air Force in Grand Joint Excercise No. 4*, 1–12 February 1932, 27 February 1932, 7. USNWCA: RG-8, Box 61, Folder 3.

negated significant destruction of airfields and infrastructure on the island that they were subsequently going to try to take for their own use.[71] While this is indeed a plausible and reasonable explanation for the umpires' failure to credit the raid with the extensive damage that was claimed by the admiral, it contradicts the mainstream interpretation of the events. According to historian Clark G. Reynolds,

> The Army minimized the extent of the damage in the sneak attack, claimed its planes had critically damaged the carriers, and protested the legality of attacking on Sunday (!). When the umpires and admirals agreed with the minimal damage estimate to Pearl Harbor, [Capt. John] Towers protested violently, so much so that he was reprimanded. Still, the message was clear enough for those who cared to read it. . . . The fact that Japan nearly duplicated this attack on Pearl on Sunday morning, 7 December 1941, was no accident. Early in the 1950s Towers dined in Tokyo with a Japanese vice admiral who had

participated in the planning. "He told me they simply took a page out of our own book!"[72]

Yarnell, though less adamant, protested the umpires' decision to allow "destruction" of *Saratoga* in the exercise by a Black Force bombing squadron attacked in detail by four Blue fighter squadrons:

> On Wednesday, 10 February, 1932, after learning the BLUE Force Commander's intention to conduct his demonstration, Raid Plan No. 4 was executed, with some slight change in objectives. Heavy losses resulted both to the enemy and to *this force* [emphasis mine], largely through the application of damage rules in a manner not foreseen by us. An enemy bombing squadron, though it was attacked first by three BLUE fighting Squadrons, simultaneously, and then by a single fighting squadron, was allowed, under the rules as applied by the Chief Umpires, sufficient strength to carry out a bombing attack on *Saratoga* and *Lexington*, and awarded a hit with a 1000 lb. bomb on the *Saratoga* placing the flight deck permanently out of commission. . . . *Saratoga* was ordered to the base at Lahaina for repairs.[73]

This rebuttal to the findings of the exercise umpires refers to the attack and constructive (i.e., evaluated by umpires, drawing on their expertise rather than based on actual observation) damage to *Saratoga* by Black aircraft that were attacked both on the ground and, three days later, in the air by Blue carrier aircraft. The result indicated the Navy's perception of carrier survivability while attempting to attack a set of targets ashore—and its overall attitude toward the utility of carriers in the attack role.

Thomas Fleming points this out with respect to the carrier raid of 7 February: "The BLACK commanders put up a vigorous defense—after the fact. They persuaded the umpires to rule that 45 of Yarnell's planes had been hit by antiaircraft fire. They also pointed out that their battleships were at sea when Yarnell attacked and insisted that in a real war they would have soon caught up with his carriers and massacred them with their long-range guns."[74] He also notes that, between 1936 and 1940, the U.S. Navy laid the keels for ten battleships, but only a single aircraft carrier (America had, of course, laid down six carriers and no battleships between 1919 and 1936).

While the lessons of Grand Joint Exercise No. 4 were unheeded by many leaders in the U.S. Navy, the Japanese saw fit to draw conclusions from their adversary's fleet exercise that proved most costly to the U.S. cause. Fleming reports that the Japanese Navy War College circulated a paper entitled "Study of Strategy and Tactics in Operations Against the United States in 1936" that stated "In case the enemy's main fleet is berthed at Pearl Harbor, the idea should be to open hostilities by surprise attack from the air."[75] The Japanese also sent Lt. Cdr. Minoru Genda,* their primary planner of naval air operations, to view the aftermath of the British air attack that sunk the Italian battleship *Littorio* and damaged two other new battleships and one cruiser at Taranto on 1 November 1940.[76] Clearly, the Japanese appreciated the offensive potential of a carrier air strike under the proper circumstances.[77]

It deserves mention that, despite a dedicated search at nine major archives and an electronic search of national libraries and archives, it was impossible to locate or access copies of the umpires' reports for Grand Joint Exercise No. 4 to include analysis of them in this book.[78] The "disappearance" of the reports hinders any potential public scrutiny and disagreement with the official position, that is, the limited viability of an attack on land targets by carrier-launched aircraft and the susceptibility of carriers to attack by land-based aircraft, submarines, and battleships while entering their launch envelopes. Dr. Albert A. Nofi, who is completing a book on the Fleet Exercises from 1923 through 1940 and the associated Grand Joint Exercises, is similarly skeptical of the motives of the umpires in denying reasonable damage from the Blue Force raid, as well as the subsequent allowed success of Black Force air and submarine attacks against *Saratoga* and *Lexington*. He too has been unable to locate the official umpires' reports on the exercise, but ascribes their absence to the lack of attention to record keeping in general during that period rather than any more sinister motive.[79]

Nonetheless, Grand Joint Exercise No. 4 represents a failure of considerable proportion, whether through an honest misinterpretation of the likely success of carrier-based aircraft attacks on military land targets or through a Navy attempt to structure the official outcomes of the exercise to conform to the predispositions of the Service's senior leaders. Beyond the scope of the exercise, the same misguided thinking introduced an ambiguity in the way in which the carrier and its air wing were handled in the curriculum and war gaming effort at the Naval War College.

---

*The Japanese traditionally use surnames first, followed by given names. To conform to the conventions used in most Western nations, Japanese given names will appear first, followed by surnames, throughout this text.

War Plans

Planning for a war with Japan through the period from 1897 to 1941 was institutionalized in War Plan Orange. While the nuances of that plan from its inception through the Japanese attack on Pearl Harbor on 7 December 1941 go far beyond the limitations of these pages, an outstanding detailing of the plan is provided by Edward S. Miller in *War Plan Orange: The U.S. Strategy to Defeat Japan, 1897–1945*. In that volume Miller postulates two schools of strategic thought within the Navy—the "thrusters," who advocated a dash across the Pacific Ocean to "save" the Philippines as a base of forward operations, and the "cautionaries," who understood the difficulties such a huge undertaking presented and supported a more gradual drive, fully realizing that the Philippine garrisons probably would not be able to hold out until the fleet could reach and support them.[80] Once again the relative importance of carrier air power was a critical component of the debate.

"In the 1920s aircraft carrier strikes on Japan were . . . pondered, but the planners considered them blows unsuitable for economic warfare and better concentrated against naval bases such as Yokosuka and Kure, preferably as surprise raids early in the war."[81] In 1928 the Joint Board "reckoned [that] . . . Blue would have to rely on outnumbered carrier planes since its seaplanes would be outclassed . . . Rear Admiral William A. Moffett of the Bureau of Aeronautics considered the air complement too weak unless augmented by 'temporary' carriers. Some army planners wondered if Blue had enough aviation 'to go over at all.'"[82] But the capabilities of carriers became more apparent over time, and "studies in the 1930s indicated that a lesser fleet, perhaps of two-thirds the opponent's strength, could win a sea-air battle. Victory in the future engagements would depend on striking first and thus on intelligence from long-range scouting aircraft."[83]

Amidst differing institutional prejudices concerning the relative merits of battleships and aircraft carriers as the fundamental offensive weapon of the Navy, the course of study, war gaming, and operational and tactical consideration of doctrine for the officers assigned at the Naval War College continued in support of the planning effort. With only *Saratoga, Lexington,* and *Ranger* available in the fleet inventory before *Yorktown* and *Enterprise* were commissioned in 1937 and 1938,[84] the flexibility of that group in considering new and audacious uses for air assets was limited.

Implications for the War against Japan

Thus the United States prepared for war in the Pacific, institutionalizing in the Navy strategic culture a reliance on capital ship engagement akin to that theorized by Alfred Thayer Mahan (1840–1914): a large battle between capital ships would decide which side gained "command of the sea." The U.S. Navy did not fully appreciate the importance of the carrier as a primary element of offensive warfare. Moreover, it expected and prepared for daylight gunnery action; the main type of encounter fought in the war's early stages was night torpedo action. How, then, could the man best placed to evaluate the utility of naval preparation for World War II—Nimitz—be so convinced that "nothing that happened in the Pacific was strange or unexpected"? The answer lies not in *what* was studied, but *how* it was studied.

Preparing for War

Experience is essential in the conduct of war. From the chronicles of Thucydides in the Peloponnesian War to the present, history is replete with examples that demonstrate the importance of experience in combat. Yet few societies since 431 B.C. have been immersed in conflict to the extent of the classical Greeks.[85] In fact, many nations face the prospect of war without any significant recent opportunity for experience in how to conduct it. Such to large extent was the case with the United States Navy in the period leading up to World War II.

Prior to World War II the United States Navy, though extremely important to the nation's emancipation from British rule and to the protection of homeland security and national interests during the century that followed, was fundamentally defensive in character. During most of the nineteenth century, with the exception of the U.S. Civil War, the Navy was predominantly employed in coastal defense and commerce protection roles. Even during World War I, which resulted in significant naval expansion, the Navy's role could not accurately be characterized as an offensive one. Practically none of the major U.S. Navy commanders in World War II saw significant action during that war, and virtually all entered service after the Spanish-American War.[86]

How, then, could such a navy hope to engage against and prevail over foes with much more recent and extensive offensive experience—particularly against the Japanese, who could boast a warrior tradition, albeit almost exclusively on land, without significant blemish for the previous seven hundred years, and an offensive-minded Mahanian naval doctrine of their own? In the case of the Unites States Navy during the interwar period, the answer, of necessity, was education and training. Yet meaningful training could only emanate from an educated assessment of the probable circumstances of a future war. Education—particularly of the senior leadership and officer corps—was the essential ingredient in any hope of preparing the Navy adequately for the type of conflict that was becoming increasingly likely in the period after the Japanese military established dominion over Manchuria in 1931.

The United States Naval Academy and Strategic Culture

Academic emphasis at the Naval Academy changed very little from the time Nimitz entered as a plebe in 1901 until the eve of the World War II. In 1939, the "evolved" curriculum centered on marine engineering; seamanship and navigation; English, history, and government; electrical engineering; ordnance and gunnery; languages; and hygiene.[87] Several aspects of the Naval Academy curriculum stand out in contrast to other elements.

First, according to Capt. W.W. Smith, who was charged to examine the adequacy of the Naval Academy curriculum in early 1939, "The curriculum [was] designed to accomplish our objective . . . basic Service requirements. . . . The course content and the method of instruction [were] so planned that midshipmen [would] retain as much as possible of the material offered in the four-year Naval Academy course and graduate with a clear perspective, equipped with a 'set of useful tools.' To accomplish this the course must have depth. Emphasis must be placed upon clear thinking, not on memorization."[88] Smith was sure that best results could be achieved by "*covering less ground and by covering that ground more thoroughly, concentrating upon fundamentals rather than upon details*" [emphasis in the original].[89] The Naval Academy stressed thorough immersion in professional fundamentals and the development of a clear, analytical mental acuity.

Smith postulated that "The Naval Academy [faculty was] fortunate in having a high turnover in officer personnel. The annual replacement of approximately forty percent of the officer instructors by officers direct from the Fleet [enabled] the professional departments to keep in close touch with Service requirements and make frequent changes in curriculum to conform with modern practice and new developments in naval science."[90] It is interesting that Captain Smith considered a high turnover of officer instructors a good thing. His conclusion indicates that conformation with new developments in the fleet was more important, in the view of the academy leadership, than academic proficiency. Thus, by extension, the curriculum was designed to be practical and highly reactive to "developments in naval science" rather than purely academic as late as 1939.

Civilian instructors at Annapolis were essentially equal in number relative to their officer counterparts. Their qualifications, however, were impeccable. Of the pool of available civilian educators, a highly select and credentialed group of around seventy usually applied for vacant academy positions. Approximately eight of these would be competitively tested through written examination as well as appropriate standards of personality and fitness before an examining committee in Annapolis, with one or two emerging as certified for employment.[91] Thus highly qualified civilian professors or instructors constituted between 50 and 65 percent of the teaching faculty, depending on department.[92]

Yet the Naval Academy curriculum centered on professional fundamentals rather than strategic concepts and the creation of an offensive mind-set. What resulted was, aside from graduates with a "clear perspective, equipped with a set of useful tools," a group of quality officers imbued with a deep sense of national destiny and convinced of the leading, offensively capable role the Navy would play in realizing that destiny.[93] Throughout their careers, both operationally and in intellectual pursuits, this cadre would interact to create and refine a sense of mission supporting their collective ethos and producing a strategic culture focused on offensive naval operations in distant waters.[94]

What, then, produced this refined sense of mission and the operational orientation to support it? Several formative events occurred during the Naval Academy days of the top Navy leaders in World War II.

"Everybody Works but John Paul Jones"

Thus starts a turn-of-the-century ditty celebrating the temporary resting place of the icon of United States offensive naval action beneath the steps of Bancroft Hall, home of the Brigade of Midshipmen at the United States Naval Academy. "Ceremonies [were] held on April 24 [1906], marking the removal of the body of Admiral John Paul Jones [a Russian two-star, but never an Admiral in the U.S. Navy] from the temporary tomb in which it was placed on July 24, 1905, to the niche in the memorial room of Bancroft Hall. . . . According to the program issued [that day], President [Theodore] Roosevelt, Secretary of the Navy [Charles J.] Bonaparte and a party of diplomats [arrived] in Annapolis from Washington shortly after noon. . . . The President and his party . . . the brigade of midshipmen, the battalion of marines . . . [took] part in the ceremonies."[95] President Theodore "Teddy" Roosevelt exuded the qualities of masculine virtue admired by the young men in attendance. The "Rough Rider," the "Hero of San Juan Hill," hunter, marksman, and adventurer, outgoing and perceived as fearless in all his endeavors, this magnificent overachiever could not have helped but invigorate the men of Annapolis. John Paul Jones likewise reenergized the brigade. "I have not yet begun to fight" captured the spirit of this master of fighting sail. In combination these two great symbols of America's warrior spirit surely energized the members of the Brigade of Midshipmen and gave them pause to contemplate their own role in the destiny of their nation.

Not too long thereafter, in 1907, President Roosevelt lent another hand in molding the outlook of the men of Annapolis. A "paralyzing" disagreement had arisen between the Army and the Navy over whether to fortify Subic Bay in the Philippines as Admiral Dewey, chairman of the Joint Army-Navy Board wanted, or Manila, as the Army wished.[96] While the mood in the Navy in general opposed Subic, this impasse prevented effective action of any kind, resulting in no fortified naval base west of Pearl Harbor. Deliberations in mid-1907 regarding the Philippines and U.S. posture in the western Pacific led to the recommendation that the American battlefleet might cruise there as a means of impressing Japan with American naval might.[97] On 16 December 1907 the sixteen battleships of the "Great White Fleet," commanded by Roosevelt's handpicked leader, Rear Adm. "Fighting Bob" Evans, steamed out of Hampton Roads. The fleet rounded Cape Horn, passed through San Francisco, and made port visits in New Zealand, Australia, the Philippines, and Japan before passing through the Indian Ocean, the Suez Canal, and the Mediterranean on its successful forty-six thousand–mile journey.[98] According to historian Kenneth J. Hagan, "Eighty years later the cruise remained synonymous with Teddy Roosevelt's naval policy."[99]

This monumental demonstration of naval power certainly influenced the aspiring officers of the Brigade of Midshipmen like no other event in U.S. naval history. The United States had laid down its marker as a nation with global reach and had established beyond doubt that its interests would henceforth not be confined to the North American hemisphere. Moreover, they—

those naval cadets by the Severn—were going to be part of it. The nation's destiny and their own were, for better or for worse, intrinsically linked. And by his act of defiance of Congress in sending a fleet on a global circumnavigation without funding authorization for the trip, President Roosevelt empowered the American people in support of that destiny. So also had then Captain Alfred Thayer Mahan, who articulated the advantages of a powerful fleet that could secure "command of the sea" as demonstrated in historical precedent. Mahan was not just a naval theorist and author, but a publicist and a powerful advocate of a great navy for the United States.

For three hundred years the British had presided over the "Pax Britannia," and for almost another hundred years the Dutch had kept a similar peace. They had created empires of wealth based on trade, and had placed themselves in a position to influence and shape events in Europe and beyond. The British Navy was indeed Britain's sword Excalibur, and Mahan articulated how it had made possible Britain's status among nations. But the sword had passed. An "American Excalibur" was soon to be in the hands of the brightest and most capable among those men attending the U.S. Naval Academy at the start of the twentieth century—men imbued with "a clear perspective, equipped with a set of useful tools."

Sound Military Decision

If the Naval Academy created a cadre of young men dedicated to naval service with a common vision of national greatness underpinning their view of the mission of the U.S. Navy, the Naval War College transformed them into elite intellectual leaders capable of unitary concepts of action and acceptance of calculated risk.* The key to this transformation was the honing of an analytical mind-set capable of reacting to rapidly changing circumstances and formulating sound military decisions. Indeed, the ability to enhance students' capacities to arrive at sound military decisions was the fundamental strength of the War College experience.

A good idea of the trends in educational philosophy at the Naval War College can be gained from the commencement and graduation speeches of some of the presidents of that institution.[100] As early as 1919, Sims stated in his graduation address that the primary mission of the War College was "the

*It is interesting to note that during the entire period between the world wars the Naval War College faculty was composed entirely of serving military officers, save for a single academician in the Department of Intelligence from 1933–1945.

development of principles, and training in the application of these principles to practical situations. . . . It has been the object of the college not only to develop and define the principles of naval warfare, but to indicate the methods by which these principles may be applied with maximum success."[101] He related in his commencement address to the class of 1920 that students "will gradually acquire confidence in [their] ability to estimate a situation correctly, reach a logical decision, and write orders that will insure the mission being carried out successfully."[102] Sims also indicated that "the service would be greatly benefited if all of our officers could take the course. As this is manifestly impracticable, it follows that if the whole commissioned personnel of the Navy is ever to acquire a working knowledge of the principles and practice of naval warfare, it must be through the efforts and influence of the college graduates exerted upon the personnel under their command."[103]

Thus Sims reemphasized the importance of a document that had been used at the War College since 1910—*Sound Military Decision*, or the "Green Hornet," so called because of the color of its cover. Starting in 1910 as *Estimate of the Situation*, this key guide to analysis of military operations evolved over time. War College president Rear Adm. Austin M. Knight summed up the importance of this document quite well in 1913: "The [*Estimate*] is not for the purpose of justifying a decision previously arrived at, . . . [it] is a reasoned solution of a problem where each step in the process approaches a decision, [which] without those steps could be arrived at by accident only."[104]

In his opening remarks to the Class of 1922, Rear Adm. C. P. Plunkett, Admiral Sims's chief of staff, stressed the importance of early familiarization with three pamphlets critical to the War College curriculum: *Training for Higher Command*, *Estimate of the Situation*, and *The Formulation of Orders*.[105] Admiral Plunkett continued, "The *Estimate of the Situation* must be kept at hand, and constantly referred to, to inculcate an orderly process of reasoning."[106] He reiterated that "Policy, Strategy and Tactics" remained supremely important to the curriculum, but added "Logistics and Command" to the list.[107] Plunkett also discussed "chart maneuvers" and "the tactical game" as methods of refining students' analytical abilities, reasoning, "The playing of a bad solution may be more illuminating than the playing of a good one. One learns much by exposition of mistakes."[108]

In 1927 Pratt extolled as a requirement for exercise of "supreme command" the "knowledge of . . . fundamental principles, based upon a background of sound practical experience."[109] He emphasized the importance of the War College course of instruction in refining the "traditions and foundations" imparted at the Naval Academy and the "broad perspective" gained through experience in the fleet.[110]

Rear Adm. Harris Laning, the president of the Naval War College in 1930, reflected the increasing concern of the times in emphasizing that the college was "in a better position than any other part of the Navy to reach sound decisions . . . as to how to organize, employ, and operate . . . ships in war."[111] This president also stressed, "It is through . . . war games, conducted in miniature where he can see the whole picture, that the student learns how to apply to actual war situations the principles he has learned through his study. . . . This institution is also a research laboratory of a very high type. Here we can try out, test, and weigh almost any idea that has to do with naval war operations."[112]

In 1933 the War College acting chief of staff, Capt. S. C. Rowan, again stressed the importance of war gaming and the "Green Hornet."

> In casting about for a practical means of avoiding the errors of the Civil War, attention was drawn to the methods of the Prussian Army so successful in the War of 1866 and 1870, methods having their roots in the teachings of Scharnhorst and the writings of von Clausewitz after the Prussian defeats in the Napoleonic Wars, but deriving more directly from the older von Moltke's school for staff officers. The success of those methods made an impression on a small group of American officers and specifically the German forms of orders appealed to them as filling a long felt need in the American Navy. Suffice to say from these origins evolved, among the many pamphlets of the War College, the *Estimate of the Situation* and the *Order Form*, which are merely means of arriving at a logical plan for a naval operation and embodying the plan in a clearly written order.[113]

When coupled with offensive Mahanian theory centered on decisive battle between opposing battle fleets and the prevailing military search for restoration of maneuver and offensive action on the field of battle after World War I, this fascination with the cult of the offensive associated with the wars of German unification underpins the mind-set that permeated the Naval War College course of study.

Even on the eve of World War II, Adm. Edward C. Kalbfus, after reluctantly accepting a shortening of the course to five months, noted to the graduating class of 1941 that "the number of officers who pass through the

College during the coming year will be more than four times the number of those who received their diplomas today."[114] He noted that the graduates were "schooled in the fundamentals of the warfare of today [and] they are prepared to apply them in terms of modern techniques. They go to join those other graduates of this College who, in this hour of need, are to be found in all the highest command positions, afloat and ashore, which it is the providence of the Navy to fill."[115]

Throughout the period between the world wars the importance of gaming, flexibility, and sound military decision properly conveyed to subordinates were emphasized and reemphasized as the essential ingredients for excellence in war. *Sound Military Decision* stressed several factors as "Universal Determinants in War"[116]

a. The nature of the appropriate *Effect Desired*,

b. The *Means Available and Opposed*,

c. The *Characteristics of the Theater of Operations*, and

d. The *Consequences as to Costs* [emphasis in original].[117]

Also stressed were the physical objectives involved, the relative positions utilized, the apportionment of fighting strength, and the provision for freedom of action with regard for suitability with respect to the desired effect, feasibility by reason of means available and opposed and acceptability as a factor of consequences and costs.[118]

The method stressed a pattern of logical analytical thought, developed by the contemplation of possible courses of action within the context of a likely future war and scrutinized, debated, and refined through war games. The War College in the interwar period focused on decision making in battle. The results among those who would shortly become the leaders of the Navy were an aggressive group mentality and an understanding of the types of actions that it would be advisable to take given the circumstances prevailing in a future battle. *Sound Military Decision* imbued a precise mental process in graduates regardless of the shortcomings of the Naval War College curriculum.

Strategic Culture in the Wartime Navy

A highly select group of the Navy's future leaders entered the Naval Academy at approximately the same time, at the outset of their careers. At the academy, this group developed a cultural bias centered on the expectation of national greatness borne of extra-hemispheric involvement and a group sense of the Navy's role in securing national policy. Long-term mutual interaction and professional education reinforced their proclivity for offensive naval action. When they emerged from the Naval War College, the same group of men possessed a warrior mentality and a firm expectation of the professional competence, sound decision process, and analytical mind-set of their wartime counterparts, irrespective of the War College's intellectual focus. This mind-set was so deeply imbued in them that it would dominate their actions throughout their careers in the Navy or Marine Corps.

Proof of this "cradle to grave" strategic culture can be found in the roles of prominent Naval Academy and Naval War College graduates in World War II. Little needs to be said of the role Nimitz played in that conflict. As mentioned above, Nimitz credited his classmate R.C. MacFall (USNA class of '05, USNWC class of '23)[119] with devising the circular tactics that proved so successful during the war. Adm. Harold R. Stark (USNA '03), later Chief of Naval Operations from 1939 to 1942, was also a member of the USNWC class of 1923. Adm. Charles M. "Savvy" Cooke (USNA '10, USNWC '34) went on to become, in the eyes of many of his contemporaries, the most brilliant naval planner of World War II. Fleet Adm. Ernest J. King (USNA '01, USNWC '33) was hugely instrumental in all aspects of strategic prioritization and planning during the war, and was the primary advocate of modifying the "Europe First" strategy taken up at the war's outset in favor of simultaneous offensives against both Germany and Japan. Fleet Adm. William F. "Bull" Halsey (USNA '04) was another member of King's War College class of 1933, and Adm. Raymond A. Spruance (USNA '07, USNWC '27) went on to become head of the correspondence course section of the War College during that same year. Halsey and Spruance rotated as planners and executors of the Navy's drive across the Pacific to Japan.

Vice Adm. Frank Jack Fletcher (USNA '06, USNWC '30) commanded the Carrier Task Forces, which forestalled and decimated the Japanese *kido butai*, or Fast Carrier Group, in the battles of the Coral Sea, Midway, and the Eastern Solomons—three of the five carrier battles of the Pacific War. Adm. Thomas C. Kinkaid (USNA '08, USNWC '30) and Spruance commanded during the other two, the Battles of Santa Cruz and the Philippine Sea. Adm. Richmond K. Turner (USNA '08, USNWC '36) was equally important in orchestrating the vital amphibious operations across the Pacific.

Other prominent World War II commanders also attended both schools: Adm. John S. McCain (USNA '06, USNWC '34); Adm. John H. Towers (USNA

'06, USNWC '34); and a host of others. In all, the U.S. Naval Academy produced 215 admirals in the decade between 1901 and 1910. Another 37 admirals came out of the Naval Academy Class of 1911, as well as 36 admirals and one Marine Corps general from the class of 1912. Yet the largest class in this entire period was 208 in 1907, with classes averaging just over 100. Even an academy dropout, Henry Latrobe Roosevelt (class of 1901), son of President Theodore Roosevelt, later became assistant secretary of the Navy.

Conclusion

To what extent, and why, was this cadre of offensively minded officers adequate as a core of naval leadership? In 1945, reserve naval officers numbered 270,893 out of 317,316 officers in the United States Navy—or 85.4 percent of the officer corps.[120] None of these were Naval Academy graduates, and the first reserve officers who saw service in the war entered the Naval War College with the class of 1942.[121] It is thus no coincidence that the overwhelming majority of senior officers in critical wartime billets during World War II were graduates of both Annapolis and Newport. While the specifics of their education—particularly at the Naval War College—may not have precisely mirrored the type of war they were about to fight, they demonstrated an ability to hone and reinforce their warrior mentality and create an offensive strategic and operational spirit in a Navy hitherto mainly concerned with coastal defense. This ability clearly emanated from their shared operational and intellectual experiences. Lifelong association and career interaction, an ethos centered on national greatness and the Navy's role in achieving it, and the analytical and offensive-minded decision process learned from *Sound Military Decision* prepared the senior officers of the United States Navy well for combat in World War II—in spite of their careful study of "the wrong stuff."

CHAPTER 2

The Battle of the Coral Sea

FIGURE 2. USS *Lexington* off Diamond Head in Hawaii. —*Courtesy of Naval Historical Center (80-G-416531)*

SOUTH OF THE LOUISIADES AND EAST OF AUSTRALIA there lies an expanse of water known as the Coral Sea. For ten days in the summer of 1942 it became one of the most important places on earth.

The world was at war and in the last four months things had only gotten worse for the Allies. Japan, already entrenched in Manchuria and China, had steamrolled across Southeast Asia and was threatening Australia. Without Australia, the United States, crippled at Pearl Harbor, had little hope of containing Japanese imperialism. Yet the American armed forces were in no position to go on the offensive. They could only wait for the next Japanese move and react as best they could.

That move came in early May. Intoxicated by Japan's recent successes, many in the Japanese leadership hierarchy sought further conquest. That conquest had to be stopped. The question was where, and the answer began to develop in late March and early April. United States Navy code breakers had been hard at work deciphering the complex Japanese naval code JN-25 since

1938. At this point, only about 10 percent of the code was actually broken.[1] However, as early as 25 March, intercepted orders began to indicate a Japanese move against Port Moresby, instructing air commanders to strike "RZP" with geographic designators "RQZ" and the codename "MO."[2] Subsequent intercepted transmissions equated MO more firmly with Port Moresby.

What follows is an analysis of the battle that was soon to take place in the Coral Sea, the reasons for its outcome, and an evaluation of the operational commanders' adherence to the eight tenets of a "sound military decision" described on pages 2–3.

Japanese Opening Moves and Plans

On 28 November 1941, the day before the Army–Navy football game, then Vice Adm. William F. "Bull" Halsey sailed from Pearl Harbor in his flagship *Enterprise* to deliver twelve Marine F4F-3 Wildcat fighter aircraft of VMF-211 to Wake Island in anticipation of a possible Japanese move against the United States.[3] USS *Lexington*, under the command of Rear Adm. John H. Newton, was to leave seven days later on 5 December from Pearl on a similar mission to reinforce Midway* with eighteen Vought SB2U-3 Vindicator scout bombers from VMSB-231.[4] On his departure from Pearl Harbor Vice Adm. Bull Halsey set Battle Order Number One—and thus became the first commander to assume a war condition on a U.S. Navy ship in the Pacific theater in World War II.[5] Oddly enough, he did this with full knowledge that the advisory from Harold R. Stark, the Chief of Naval Operations (CNO), did not specify any danger to Hawaii in the warning that war was imminent in the Pacific. Rather, it indicated that the western Pacific, including the Philippines and possibly as far east as Wake Island, were threatened.

Stark's warning influenced Adm. Husband E. Kimmel, commander in chief of the U.S. Pacific Fleet, to concentrate on his own plan for victory over the Japanese in the event of war. He planned in great detail for a force under the operational command of Halsey to lure the Imperial Combined Fleet out into an area west of Midway. After refueling at Truk Island, this force would engage the Imperial Navy under conditions of surprise and "decisively" defeat it on or about sixteen days after the commencement of hostilities (see fig-

*The Midway Islands are a chain of three closely located islands: Sand, the largest; Eastern, on which most of the action took place in the Battle of Midway; and Spit, a tiny island between them.

ure 3). In order to minimize wear on the engines of his eighty-four seaplanes, Kimmel elected to conserve their flight time: he refrained from using them to scout in the vicinity of Hawaii in early December 1941. Stark's warning of imminent hostilities was not enough to convince Kimmel that defense of Pearl Harbor and U.S. Army assets on Hawaii was of higher strategic priority than conserving assets, including seaplanes for adequate aerial search, for his planned offensive. Admiral Stark had inadvertently aided in convincing Kimmel that his estimate of the situation was correct.

In another strange twist, as war with Japan began to seem increasingly likely, President Roosevelt asked Stark whether it would be best to send Adm. Ernest J. King to the Pacific and move Kimmel to the Atlantic. Stark replied that there was no reason to switch their commands. Had Stark acted on Roosevelt's suggestion, one can only imagine what may have gone differently.

There was a reason that Stark had left Hawaii off his list of likely targets of Japanese aggression. Indications were that Japan would attempt to secure its sea lines of communication (SLOCs) and gain access to the oil resources of the Dutch and/or British to the south as a necessary prelude to any move to the east against the United States. The Philippine Islands, laying astride Japan's SLOCs in the South China Sea and hosting U.S. B-17 and B-18 bomber aircraft capable of reaching Tokyo, seemed the most likely target for initial Japanese aggression.

Moreover, Japanese naval capabilities were interpreted in the United States as inadequate to attack both south and east simultaneously. U.S. naval analysts concluded that, with only six large carriers available, the Japanese would have to use all of them in any move against Pearl Harbor.* With more pressing need for two or more carriers nearer to home, such an attack was viewed as too risky for the Japanese to conduct. Also, the shallow waters of Pearl Harbor would make aerial torpedo attack impossible in the estimation of U.S. intelligence experts. Even Vice Admiral Halsey considered an attack so far east extremely unlikely. His main concern was that the Japanese might be inclined to operate as far east as Wake Island, which also seemed improbable.

However, adaptations to two weapons systems enabled the Imperial Japanese Navy to overcome its limitations and strike as suddenly and unex-

*It should be noted that, at this time, U.S. Navy operational commanders and analysts believed that the Imperial Japanese Navy would operate carriers in groups not exceeding two, as was the custom in the U.S. Navy. The Japanese grouping of as many as six carriers in a single group, as was the case in their attack on Pearl Harbor, came as something of a surprise.

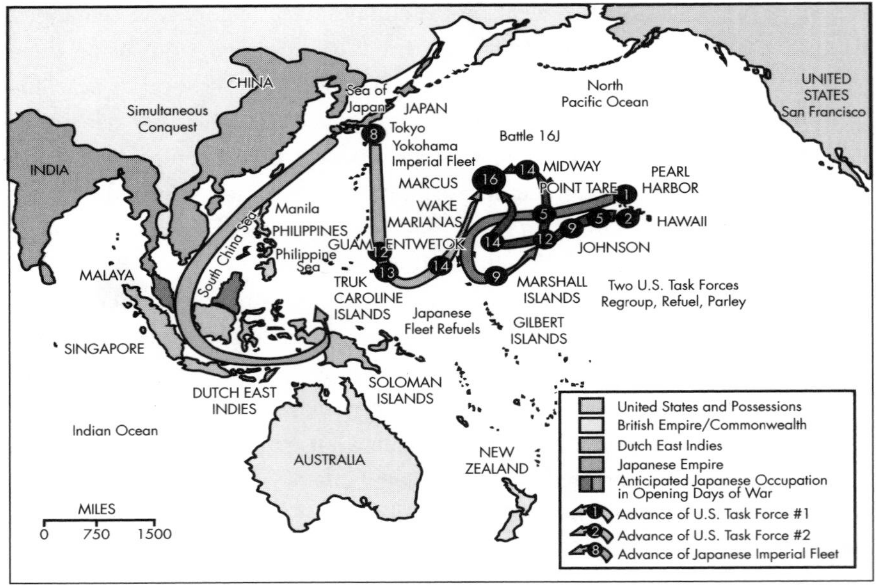

FIGURE 3. Kimmel's plan for Great Pacific offensive. —*Image provided by Edward S. Miller from his lecture "War Pan Orange," U.S. Naval War College*

pectedly as it had against the Russians at Port Arthur in 1904. In the month and a half before 7 December 1941 the Japanese made two technological breakthroughs. First, they added drop tanks to their Zero aircraft, enabling the Zeroes to accompany and protect the Japanese bombers against the Dutch and British oil holdings in Southeast Asia. Second, and only just in time for the operation, they fitted their 18-inch diameter aerial torpedoes with wooden stabilizer planes, which limited the depth to which the torpedoes dove enough that they could be used in Pearl Harbor.

Halsey was due back to Pearl Harbor in the late evening hours of 6 December 1941. Fortunately, the *Enterprise* group was slowed by a winter storm. Near dusk on 7 December, hearing of the Japanese attack on Pearl, he "bingoed" seven aircraft that had been airborne from his carrier at the time to land at Ford Island, the nearest suitable field. In the frenzy that followed the two-wave Japanese attack, only one of those aircraft—piloted by Lt. (jg) James Granson Daniels—arrived without being shot down by friendly fire.[6]

What was left of the U.S. Pacific Fleet at Pearl Harbor were two old battleships, *Maryland* and *Tennessee*, which could make way under steam in the not-too-distant future, and a third, *Pennsylvania*, which could be repaired. The other five of the eight battleships struck by the Japanese that day had been destroyed or were beyond immediate repair. The Navy could not count on another battleship to operate offensively in the Central Pacific until the arrival of *North Carolina* in June of 1942. On 11 January 1942 *Saratoga* was torpedoed in waters north of Hawaii and severely damaged. (The Japanese thought they had sunk *Lexington*.) *Saratoga* returned to San Diego for repairs that would take her out of the war for four months and eleven days.

So the United States began the war in the Pacific without the battleships that were the backbone of naval planning for War Plan Orange—the U.S. advance across the Pacific toward the Japanese homeland and the ultimate defeat of Japan. Kimmel's plan for a decisive victory over the Japanese, with a battleship task force under the command of "Bull" Halsey lying in wait for the advance of Adm. Isoroku Yamamoto's Combined Fleet, was no longer a possibility.[7]

Those members of the Gun Club or "battleship Navy" who had advanced the battleship as the cornerstone of naval might were further devastated by the sinking of the capital ships HMS *Repulse* and *Prince of Wales* in route to Singapore on 10 December 1941 by Japanese Nell and Betty bombers with torpedoes, the former while maneuvering at battle speed. The Gun Club proponents were forced to change their thinking drastically and embrace the carrier as the sole surviving centerpiece of offensive naval lethality with which to contest the Imperial Japanese Navy.

But what moves could be expected from the Japanese next? There were, as it turned out, three phases in Japan's plans. In the first phase the Japanese naval planners sought to destroy the carriers and battleships, and as many other large combatants as possible, at Pearl Harbor. They also determined to take Wake Island, Guam, and the Gilberts, cutting the U.S. line of communications to the Philippines. Hong Kong and Thailand would be overrun as a prelude for moves against Burma and Malaya. Then they would take Malaya and Sarawak, and British Borneo for its oil. In the second phase of operations the Japanese would take the rest of Malaya and Singapore, southern Burma, the northern islands of the Netherlands East Indies, and the Bismarck Islands. Finally, in the third phase, they would take the rest of the Netherlands East Indies to consolidate the oil resources there, as well as the rest of Burma.

Japan's timetable for conquest was astonishingly aggressive. Its rate of progress was for the most part even more astonishing. Japan planned to take the Philippines in 50 days. Though Gen. Douglas MacArthur and his air component commander, Maj. Gen. Lewis H. Brereton, were initially taken by surprise, they managed to defend Bataan until 9 April 1942. Corregidor fell on 7 May 1942 during the Battle of the Coral Sea, and the rest of the Philippines capitulated only three days later. Thus the Japanese actually took 155 days to wrest control of the Philippines—or roughly three times as long as they had anticipated.

But the Japanese advance was much more rapid elsewhere. They had envisioned taking Malaya and Singapore in 100 days. Singapore actually fell on 15 February, a full month earlier than expected. Similarly, the Japanese allowed 150 days for the conquest of the Netherlands East Indies. The Dutch holdings fell on 9 March 1942, only two months after the first landings. Thus, even though their success in destroying the U.S. Fleet at anchor in Pearl Harbor had been evaluated as marginal due to the absence of the U.S. carriers at the time of the attack, the overall military success gave rise to euphoria in both the ranks and the top leadership.

Japan's Forces in the Pacific Area

At the outset of its conquests, Japan had a total of fifty-one Infantry Divisions at its disposal. None of the armored divisions were ready yet for use. Japan had allocated only ten divisions for its new Southern Army, which moved forward with unanticipated success. It had thirteen divisions in China, and twenty-three divisions in Manchuria. The rest of Japan's Army Divisions were in Japan and Korea and on Formosa.

Japan's Combined Fleet was composed of four main task forces. The Main Body consisted of six battleships, two light cruisers (cruisers with six-inch or lesser diameter guns) and eight destroyers. This Main Body was stationed in home waters under the personal command of Yamamoto, commander in chief of the Combined Fleet.

The Mobile Force, or *kido butai*, boasted six large carriers, the *Akagi*, *Kaga*, *Soryu*, *Hiryu*, *Shokaku*, and *Zuikaku*—of which the latter two had newly formed air wings, which they would not embark until November of 1941. It also had two battleships, two heavy cruisers, one light cruiser, nine destroyers, and as many as thirty submarines. It was commanded by Vice Adm. Chuichi Nagumo and was used initially in attacking Pearl Harbor, and thereafter against Rabaul, Darwin, and Ceylon.

The South Sea Force consisted of four heavy cruisers, three light cruisers, twelve destroyers, and nine submarines. Commanded by Vice Adm. Shigeyoshi Inoue, this force was used initially against Wake Island, Guam, and the Gilberts.

Finally, the Southern Force, under the command of Vice Adm. Nobutake Kondo, consisted of two battleships, twelve heavy cruisers, four light cruisers, two light carriers (*Zuiho* and *Taiyo*), fifty-two destroyers, and eighteen submarines. It provided escort and cover for the landings in Thailand, Malaya, the Philippines, and the Netherlands East Indies.

Japan's naval aviation was divided into the 1st and 11th Air Fleets. First Air Fleet was carrier based. Eleventh Air Fleet was land-based and consisted of approximately three hundred aircraft on Formosa, arrayed against the Philippines, and approximately two hundred aircraft in Indochina, arrayed against Thailand, Malaya, and Burma.

Though Japan made tremendous initial advances, the army units allocated in support of naval operations were not its best. The best troops Japan could muster were employed in Manchuria and China. Moreover, only eleven divisions (ten at the outset) were allocated against Japan's southern and eastern enemies. This brings Japan's strategic thinking into question, especially in light of its grandiose expansionist plans to capture areas in North America and as far east as the Caribbean (enumerated in the appendix).

The Situation in the Pacific in the Summer of 1942

During the winter and spring of 1942 the Japanese conquered the Philippines, the Netherlands East Indies (now Indonesia), Malaya (now Malaysia), and most of Burma (now Myanmar), Wake, Guam, Rabaul, Hong Kong, and Singapore. They did so in roughly half the time they had planned and much more easily than expected. With the sinking of the *Repulse* and *Prince of Wales,* there were no Allied capital ships in the western Pacific to oppose the Imperial Japanese Navy.

The nonaggression pact signed by the Japanese and Soviets in April of 1941 had ensured that Japan could focus its navy in the Southern Resource Area and against America. While the Japanese had planned to establish a defensive perimeter to protect their gains to the east in the Pacific, the success of their operations both on land and at sea encouraged some among them to consider additional options. Three main naval options emerged:

1. Moving west to India in order to knock it out of the war, link up with German forces, and threaten essential British petroleum resources in Persia
2. Moving south to or toward Australia to sever Allied sea lines of communication, prevent American reinforcement of the Southwest Pacific, and protect against any major offensive against the Japanese mainland or resource area
3. Moving east, to the Hawaiian Islands. Though much has been made of this last option, and Japanese plans have been uncovered for it, it was not realistic. With only thirty-eight amphibious ships available, of which only thirty-four were operational at the time, the Japanese could not have hoped to invade the "armed camp" that Hawaii now represented—especially over an expanse of 3,650 nautical miles from Hashirashima (the Japanese Inland Sea).*

Each of the strategic approaches had its own constituency within the Japanese Navy, as well as within the more politically powerful Japanese Army, which had a land orientation toward Manchuria and China. The Naval General Staff initially advocated a move to the west. This concept proved untenable, however, when the headquarters received a copy of the new Tripartite Axis Military Agreement on 19 January 1942. Though it made passing reference to Germany's advance eastward and Japan's advance westward, the agreement said nothing at all about a future joint offensive effort.[8]

It was also abundantly clear that the Army did not want to commit forces for a move southward, and would have no part of an attempt to invade Australia. Thus the thrust eastward toward Midway, advocated by Yamamoto and the Combined Fleet, gained more support. Still wanting to move southward to cut off Allied SLOCs and fearful that an advance eastward to take Midway could not be sustained logistically, the Naval General Staff continued planning for the occupation of New Guinea and the Solomon Islands,

---

*Insights here were provided by Vice Adm. (then Capt.) Yoji Koda of the Japanese Maritime Self-Defense Force. Koda points out that all Japanese naval conquests and garrison activities were accomplished with only eleven divisions. Given the Japanese Army's requirement for thirty-six divisions in Manchuria and China and the rest of its fifty to fifty-one divisions in Korea, on Formosa, in the Philippines and southern resource area, or in Japan, and traditional fears of the Soviets after the debacle at Nomanhan in August of 1938 where the Soviets and Japanese clashed at the Corps level along the Mongolian front, invasion of Hawaii was merely an exercise in planning. See endnote 19 for more on Koda.

and contemplated the future occupation of Samoa and Fiji. The advocacy for future strategic moves sorted out as follows:[9]

1. Invade Australia. Supported by Capt. Morisada Tomioka, director of the Naval General Staff.
   a. Rejected by the army section of the General Staff.
   b. Cited reason was "lack of logistics."
2. Invade Ceylon. Supported by Vice Adm. Matome Ugaki, Chief of Staff, Combined Fleet.
   a. Rejected by the army section of the General Staff.
   b. First Air Fleet subsequently conducted air raids on Ceylon against Colombo and Trincomalee, the two British naval bases on the island. Of the five battleships and three carriers stationed there by the British, but at sea in anticipation of the Japanese attack, the heavy cruisers *Cornwall* and *Dorsetshire* and the light carrier *Hermes* and a destroyer escort accompanying her were sunk by Japanese carrier aircraft. Oddly, unlike other Japanese carrier operations before and to follow, the five carriers of the *kido butai* that conducted this raid were protected by four accompanying battleships, two heavy cruisers and one light cruiser, and eight destroyers. This precaution was not taken in subsequent major carrier operations, much to the chagrin of the naval hierarchy.
3. Coral Sea/Port Moresby Operation. Captain Tomioka's second choice after invasion of Australia.
   a. Conducted.
   b. Led to the loss of the two largest carriers of the 1st Air Fleet, *Zuikaku* for four to five weeks and *Shokaku* for eight weeks. The 1st Air Fleet lost approximately 35 percent of its aircraft capability for the Midway operation.
4. Invade Midway. Supported by Yamamoto, Commander in Chief of the Combined Fleet. This move would extend Japan's defensive perimeter to the east, but Yamamoto's ulterior motive was to lure the U.S. Navy's operational carriers out and engage them in a decisive Mahanian battle, completing the unfinished business started at Pearl Harbor.
   a. Conducted.

   b. Led to the loss of four of Japan's six large carriers from 1st Air Fleet.

5. Defensive Barrier. Supported by Rear Adm. Ryunosuke Kusaka, Chief of Staff of the 1st Air Fleet.
   a. Rejected by naval section of the General Staff.
   b. The rationale for rejecting this plan was that it did not address the pressures emanating from the League of Nations declaration of 1 January 1942, which called for nations to forcibly eject Japan from its recent conquests. The Japanese leadership had believed that Japan could set the terms of reference for the war and fight the Americans to exhaustion and a negotiated settlement. The League of Nations declaration negated that option, so the Japanese concluded they had to undertake offensive operations rather than settle for a defensive campaign.
   c. Also rejected because the 1st Air Fleet was held in disrepute by the Combined Fleet Staff.

Ultimately the decision clarified. Many historians attribute this directly to the "Doolittle Raid," which was launched by the United States over Tokyo on 18 April 1942. However, the decision was actually taken almost two weeks earlier.

> It was on April 2 that [Yasuji] Watanabe went to Tokyo bearing the Combined Fleet's more or less completed plan for the MI (Midway) and AL (Aleutians) operations. Once more, the Naval General Staff showed extremely strong opposition to the plan. . . . On April 5, in the operations room at the Naval General Staff, the results of [a] study [on the feasibility of the Midway and Aleutians plans] gave rise to another heated argument in the presence of Vice-Chief [of the Naval General Staff, Vice Adm. Seiichi] Ito. Vice Admiral [Shigeru] Fukudome [Chief of the First Division of the Naval General Staff] turned to Ito. "If the C. in C.'s so set on it, shall we leave it to him?" . . . Chief of the Naval General Staff [Adm. Osami] Nagano had no objections.[10]

Acceptance of Yamamoto's plan for increasing Japan's defensive perimeter to the east and using Midway as a forward base for reconnaissance and early air attack is confirmed by Ugaki's personal diary entry of Sunday, 5 April 1942: "Staff Officer Watanabe has been in Tokyo to consult with the high command on the second stage operations plan. And he telephoned back that the Naval General Staff seemed to have reluctantly agreed to it."[11] This was the Midway plan. As in the case of Pearl Harbor, the Naval General Staff caved in when Yamamoto exercised a bit of genteel blackmail, hinting he might resign if he did not get his way.[12]

The Doolittle raid certainly hardened Yamamoto in his resolve to attack to the east and take Midway. Convinced that he had failed in his duty to protect the emperor under all circumstances, Yamamoto increased his advocacy for a move toward Midway to expand the Japanese defensive perimeter and prevent a recurrence. Embedded in his motive was the expectation that the U.S. Pacific Fleet would have to defend Midway, thus enabling the Imperial Japanese Navy to engage a numerically inferior force in a great Mahanian battle akin to that of the Straits of Tsushima in the Russo-Japanese War. Yamamoto was the only serving officer in the Japanese navy who had participated in the Russo-Japanese War, though he had not shared in any of the engagements that had brought glory to the navy in World War II. Perhaps his personal motives for the move against Midway clouded his judgment. Nonetheless, his power and personality prevailed. The decision was made to press forward with both the Coral Sea/Port Moresby operations and those aimed at Midway, the latter on a compressed timetable.

For the Allies, the situation in the Pacific could not have been much worse. With MacArthur's expulsion from the Philippines the thrusters' hopes went dormant.[13] Maintaining SLOCs with Australia was second in strategic importance only to defense of the American mainland and Hawaii.

Relative naval strength after Pearl Harbor certainly favored the Japanese. In late December of 1941 the Japanese had ten carriers, six large and four small (including one escort carrier), and eleven battleships.[14] An additional light fleet carrier, *Shoho*, which was later to appear at Coral Sea, was launched in January 1942. In comparison, the United States had only three of eight existing carriers (*Lexington*, *Saratoga*, and *Enterprise*) operational in the Pacific. Of the twelve battleships remaining in the U.S. arsenal after the loss of or damage to eight battleships at Pearl Harbor,[15] most were required in the Atlantic theater. In fact, when the Battle of the Coral Sea took place, only seven heavy cruisers, one light cruiser, and thirteen destroyers were available to support the two American carriers operating there.[16]

Saratoga was torpedoed on 11 January 1942 by a Japanese submarine and underwent repair in Puget Sound, keeping her out of action between 11 January and 22 May.[17] She only reached Hawaii on 6 June—far too late to help at Coral Sea. *Yorktown*, which had been transferred to the Atlantic Fleet in April of 1941 when war appeared imminent, and desperately needed a yard period after extensive service in the North Atlantic, was transferred back from the Atlantic when the Japanese attacked Pearl Harbor. She became Flagship of Task Force 17 on New Year's Eve and the de facto replacement for *Saratoga*. The newly constructed *Hornet* was still in the Atlantic embarking her air wing and would not be operational, let alone available, for several months. The Navy could expect only defensive operations at best until newly constructed units entered fleet service in late 1943. This made U.S. planning, of necessity, reactive rather than proactive.

Japanese Plans and Preparations

The Japanese had two main purposes in extending their defensive perimeter to the south. First, they wanted to provide added protection for their new forward base, which they had just established at Rabaul. Second, they knew the importance of severing the Allied SLOCs between Hawaii and Australia. If the initial drive through New Guinea (taking Port Moresby) and the Solomons was successful, the Japanese planned to advance into New Caledonia, Samoa, and the Fiji Islands. To do this they attempted to adapt their naval doctrine to a concept of land warfare that would become characteristic of their operations in later battles, such as Midway and Leyte Gulf.

Japanese naval doctrine was Mahanian in nature.[18] It sought a decisive battle waged on advantageous terms, which were created by attrition of the enemy en route to the area of operations. This would be accomplished by placing submarine barriers in the enemy's path and attacking enemy ships using land-based aircraft, with the objective of destroying roughly 50 percent of the enemy's forces prior to battle. There was at the time a universally accepted principle that naval forces were reduced in combat efficiency 10 percent for every thousand miles' distance from their nearest base with support infrastructure. Thus the Japanese expected that the U.S. Pacific Fleet would be reduced in efficiency by at least another 30 percent as it moved into the western Pacific from its base at Pearl Harbor. Most important, the primary engagement would take place with forces massed under an umbrella of land-based air support.[19]

Significantly, the Japanese navy relied on applying tactical lessons of prior *land* battles, particularly the Battle of Cannae in the Second Punic War, rather than sea battles to their operational concepts. At Cannae, Hannibal presented a weak center. When his center collapsed, he enveloped the Romans on both flanks and won a resounding victory with a force of approximately thirty-seven thousand against a vastly superior Roman force of around seventy thousand. At sea, such a scheme would require concerted operations by several separate forces constrained to a rigid timetable. Such a timetable assumed success and even opposition in all areas and was thus as unlikely to succeed in concept as it proved in actual application. The Japanese naval hierarchy simply "scripted" outcomes without realistic consideration of the complexities of maneuver at sea.

Thus the Japanese set out to occupy the island of Tulagi in the eastern Solomons as a diversionary measure and for use as an advance base for staging air patrols, with the main objective—seizure of Port Moresby in New Guinea—to take place six days later. The two fast carriers assigned to the operation—*Shokaku* and *Zuikaku*—had the additional responsibility of striking any U.S. or Australian naval forces that might seek to prevent successful completion of the operation. Japanese intelligence, prejudiced by stereotypes of previous U.S. Navy operations in the area, underestimated opposing force levels. It also expected the U.S. Task Force(s) to enter the Coral Sea from the east and structured its air search plan accordingly. Rear Adm. Frank Jack Fletcher, the American commander, confounded his Japanese opponents by entering the area of operations from the southeast.

The Japanese combatants were organized into five groups.[20] The Tulagi Invasion Force was to take its objective on 3 May. The Port Moresby Invasion Force was to remain at anchor in Rabaul until six days after Tulagi was occupied. The Covering Force for both those operations (four heavy cruisers, a destroyer, and the small carrier *Shoho*) was to proceed to a position 150 nautical miles west of Tulagi and south of New Georgia Island. A Support Force (two light cruisers, some gunboats, minesweepers, and auxiliaries) was to take station in the same area about sixty nautical miles west of the Covering Force.

The two fast carriers *Shokaku* and *Zuikaku*, commanded by Rear Adm. Tadaichi Hara and on loan from the *kido butai*,[21] with a screen of two heavy cruisers and six destroyers, was initially about 630 nautical miles northwest of Tulagi proceeding on a southeasterly course. It was to enter the Coral Sea and attack any carriers or other Allied combatants or shipping it might encounter.

It was to do this, however, via a track east of the Solomon Islands, and was additionally tasked to conduct an air strike against the northern extremities of the Australian continent to eliminate or reduce land-based air opposition to the landings at Port Moresby.[22] Six submarines were also deployed to provide reconnaissance and sink any Allied ships in the area. All the units in the Japanese force were to be covered by land-based aircraft, which would also scout to a range of up to 650 miles.

As was their habit, the Japanese "scripted" the encounter to follow. Except for one instance of an air strike on Lae, American carriers had always operated alone in the Coral Sea. Thus the Japanese predicated their operational planning on the assumption that they would be up against a single U.S. carrier. That assumption was to prove costly.

Moreover, in accordance with their doctrine of conservation of air assets for rapid launch of superior numbers in the strike role, the Japanese relied exclusively on cruiser- or battleship-launched and land-based aircraft for search missions. This reliance on assets external to the carriers for search and location of enemy units introduced a divergence of intent and interest in the search process, as well as a barrier to accurate transmission and authentication of the locating information passed to the carriers. Because none of the Japanese ships or aircraft had radar and, except for Tulagi, the forward bases could not mount adequate reconnaissance missions over the southern and eastern areas of the Coral Sea, the Striking Force was needlessly vulnerable.

The Japanese plan called for a concerted strike or "double envelopment" of what turned out to be two U.S. carriers by widely separated forces that had no established time frame to mass for the attack. Scripting the expected U.S. operational patterns in the Coral Sea area produced an air-search plan that was not optimized to locate the carriers early and strike before they were close enough to attack. Moreover, the radio silence the planners required to maintain the security of the force compounded the difficulty of executing the Japanese plan.

The American Plan

The U.S. plan, in contrast, was quite simple. The strategic objective was to turn back the Japanese onslaught and maintain the necessary SLOCs to Australia to enable a buildup of U.S. forces there, give the nation's industrial base time to build ships and other equipment, and give the Armed Services time to train the men necessary to go on the offensive against Japan. The two American carriers, *Lexington* and *Yorktown*, and their supporting ships, were to conduct a raiding action to stop the Port Moresby landing. Their mission was to stop the Port Moresby invasion. Secondary to that mission, they were to sink as many Japanese carriers and combatant ships as possible without undue risk. Since *Lexington* and *Yorktown* represented half the operational carriers in the Pacific, their preservation was of utmost strategic importance. They would be hazarded only to accomplish the primary mission.

Operational Imperatives

As stressed in the interwar curriculum at the Naval War College, there were five general imperatives advanced as key to carrier task force success:

1. Defend the task force, and particularly the carriers.
2. Keep the task force or group together for mutual protection and support. The doctrine at the time of the Coral Sea battle called for separation of the carriers to enable optimum use of cloud cover to reduce the possibility of detection by aircraft. Therefore, the few destroyers available at the time had to be divided to support two carrier groups. The destroyers had to be rapidly repositioned to new stations when either carrier maneuvered or came into the wind to launch aircraft. This in turn halved the firepower of the antiair naval gun defense and exposed the carriers to attack by submarine, particularly while the destroyers maneuvered to reposition. As the learning curve advanced and the war went along, groups of carriers would be established in a single task force.
3. Locate the enemy's carriers.
4. Launch the strike first against the enemy.
5. Maintain radio silence to avoid detection.

In battle, several of these imperatives became mutually exclusive. This made the commander's decision process much more difficult. The Battle of the Coral Sea hinged on the respective commanders' ability to establish proper priorities and adhere to these imperatives.

The Tulagi Invasion

On 3 May 1942 the Japanese seized Tulagi. The Australians, yielding to a superior force, had departed the day before. The Japanese did not appear to have realized the importance of Tulagi to the Allied commander, Fletcher, who had been alerted to its seizure late that evening by the commander of the Southwest Pacific Forces.[23] Air searches from the island would seriously impede the Allied freedom of action in the Coral Sea, and thus Tulagi became a target for the American carriers—even at the expense of giving away their presence and approximate location in the area.[24] Figure 4 shows the area of the operations.

Fletcher was told that *Lexington*, en route to join his task force, would not complete refueling operations until noon on 4 May, preventing the carriers from rendezvousing as planned. Fletcher decided to attack the Japanese force, which had landed on Tulagi at 1100 on 3 May, as soon as he could close within striking range of the island—about a hundred miles.[25] He appears to have felt that his strength was adequate in relation to the Japanese force on Tulagi even without the *Lexington* task force commanded by Rear Adm. Aubrey W. Fitch. Fletcher also knew that he had been reported by a submarine, spotted by a *Yorktown* scout only thirty-two miles to the north.[26] His freedom of action and the security of his force would be jeopardized unless he struck immediately.[27] Therefore, he chose to take the first action.

Yorktown commenced its air search of the area at 0631, just after first light. By 0701 on 4 May the heavy cruisers in Task Force 17's screen, *Astoria, Chester,* and *Portland,* had launched an inner air patrol against submarines. At the same time the *Yorktown* launched her first attack group of twelve torpedo planes, thirteen scout planes, and twenty-eight dive-bombers, protected by only four fighters. The Americans hoped to catch the Japanese by surprise and practically no air opposition was expected.[28] Fletcher maintained a combat air patrol of six planes launched in three cycles to maintain air cover of the task force through the day.[29] The remaining fighters, only twelve of which were carried aboard *Yorktown*, were retained for the defense of the task force.[30]

Unwisely, no Strike Group commander was appointed because the Air Group commander was retained aboard *Yorktown* as fighter director officer.[31] Each squadron attacked at Tulagi with little or no coordination, internally or with the attacks of other squadrons. The air operation lacked a commander to reconnoiter and prioritize the objectives of the attack in the target area,

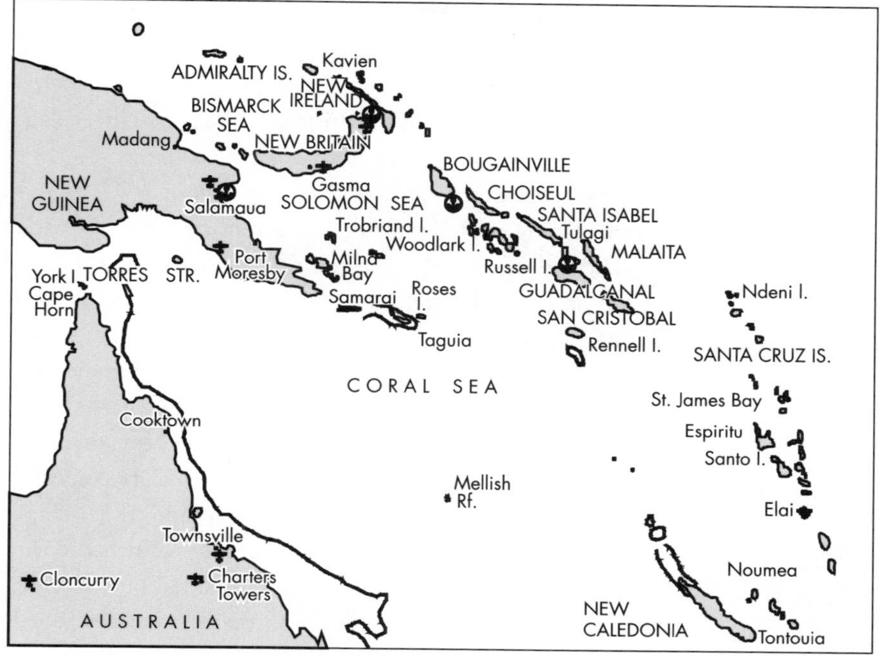

FIGURE 4. Chart of the Coral Sea and vicinity. —*Courtesy of U.S. Naval War College*

to assign targets to the squadrons and stipulate the order of attacks, and to observe and report the results of the overall attack.

Historian and author John B. Lunsdtrom notes that the inability of the U.S. carrier squadrons to coordinate their attacks was a marked contrast to the well-considered and organized attacks of the Japanese and continued through much of the war—and was particularly evident at Coral Sea and the Battle of Midway.[32] Midway, moreover, the fragmentation of the American attacks was the reason for their success.

Yorktown's second attack group was launched against Tulagi between 1036 and 1120 and was made up of eleven torpedo planes and twenty-seven dive-bombers.[33] The attacks by this group were not coordinated either. The *Yorktown* launched her third attack group at 1400. This consisted of twenty-one dive-bombers.[34] At 1632 this attack group returned, completing air operations against Tulagi.

The overall results were disappointing. Torpedoes were dropped at ranges of up to three thousand yards. To the green pilots of the *Yorktown* Air Group the antiaircraft fire appeared worse than it really was. The second attack group expended thirteen 1000-pound bombs and eleven torpedoes on a minelayer, but she was still operable after the attack. Thirteen 1000-pound general purpose bombs were expended by Bombing Squadron Five on three gunboats.[35] In fact, there were better targets for this type of bomb in the Tulagi area, but without a Strike Group Commander proper reconnaissance was not conducted and the better targets were not attacked.

The evaluation of the damage inflicted from pilots' reports after the battle indicated to the commanding officer of *Yorktown* that one light cruiser had been beached and sunk, that two destroyers, one cargo ship, and four gunboats were sunk, and that one heavy cruiser or aircraft tender (conflicting statements made it impossible to identify) was severely damaged, with one cargo ship and various small craft destroyed and five single-float seaplanes shot down.[36] In reality, as confirmed by Japanese sources available after the war, the ships that were actually lost were one old destroyer, *Kikizuki*, two special duty minesweepers, and one converted minesweeper. Three additional ships were reported damaged by the pilots of the *Yorktown,* and these included the old destroyer *Yuzuki*, the minelayer *Okinoshima*, and one small patrol craft. The five single-boat enemy float planes *Yorktown*'s pilots reported destroyed coincided with the Japanese records.[37]

The Tulagi operation was also disappointing in terms of the ratio of ordnance expended to results obtained.[38] Nimitz, the commander of the Coral Sea operations at the strategic level as Commander in Chief, U.S. Pacific Fleet (CINCPACFLT), stated on reconstruction of these events that the performance of the *Yorktown* Air Group demonstrated laudable willingness and effort to keep after the enemy, but there was a real need for target practice at every opportunity.[39] He thus instituted procedures to improve the targeting and accuracy of attacks of the Pacific Fleet carriers whenever possible, making good use of the available feedback from the Coral Sea experience with little time lag in disseminating lessons learned to the Fleet.

The attack on Tulagi was successful in eliminating a staging base for Japanese reconnaissance, but Fletcher nearly fell into a trap because of his relatively weak force. He gave away the approximate location of his force to achieve an objective secondary to the priority of maintaining Allied control of Port Moresby. However, the Japanese did not realize or exploit the favorable military situation they were creating for themselves. This may well have been because of the weather in the area. A moderate cold front had created a hundred-mile line of bad weather south and southwest of Guadalcanal. Tulagi itself, however, had clear weather. The cloud bank that had developed was a barrier to Japanese scout planes, but it was not too low for American planes returning to their carrier base. It was practically ideal for launching a strike, and Task Force 17 profited fully in terms of both achieving initial surprise and masking its returning strike aircraft.

The choice of launching position for the first strike was optimal. During the day it would be necessary to work north and then back south to maintain a hundred miles between the task force and Tulagi, and the southeast winds would be helpful since the carriers had to turn into the wind to recover aircraft and would thus be heading away from the unlocated Japanese carriers.[40] Also, if the Japanese were not caught by surprise and launched a strong counterstrike, the southeast wind would facilitate successful retirement. The Rennel Islands might have offered some interference to early withdrawal, but bad weather significantly reduced the possibility of early discovery by enemy search planes and thus decreased the risk involved in the operation.[41]

While the attack proved successful even though huge amounts of ordnance were needlessly expended on minor targets, Fletcher's inability to mass his force, which thus became more vulnerable, resulted from erroneous information from Fitch aboard *Lexington*. Task Force 11's refueling was completed by 1310 on 3 May, nearly a full day earlier than projected. Fitch apparently made no attempt to signal Fletcher, by detached destroyer signal lights or by air drop, of this change, and was thus almost 250 nautical miles to the south of Task Force 17 during the action.[42] Consequently, Fletcher pressed the Tulagi attack without his full resources.

Thus the Japanese were repelled from Tulagi by air attacks from *Yorktown*, which commenced with the first launch at 0631 on 4 May and ended when the last planes landed at 1632. Hara's Striking Force was still too far away (roughly six hundred nautical miles) to give battle. Figures 5 and 6 compare the abilities of Japanese and American aircraft.

The relative speeds of Japanese and U.S. aircraft were roughly equal. However, as figure 6 demonstrates, the ranges for important classes of aircraft were significantly longer for the Japanese. Striking range is normally limited by the least distance any aircraft in the strike can cover. Moreover, carrier strikes generally mustered at a point near their carrier(s) so that fighter cover could be provided for the entire group en route. Therefore, since the Devastator torpedo bomber, an integral part of any strike, had a range of only about 420 nautical miles, a U.S. strike could realistically only be flown out to about 150 miles, since time would be needed first to effect the rendezvous of the strike aircraft and then to locate the enemy force precisely. The Japanese,

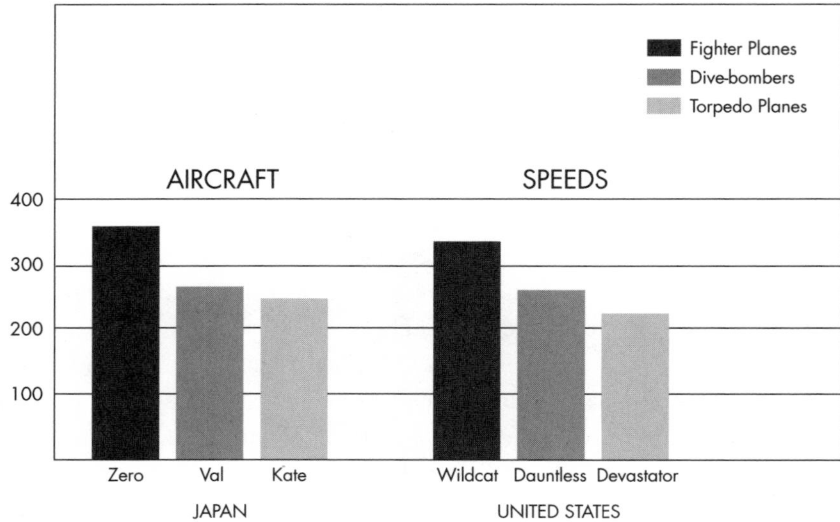

FIGURE 5. Aircraft speed (Japan and the United States). —*Courtesy of U.S. Naval War College*

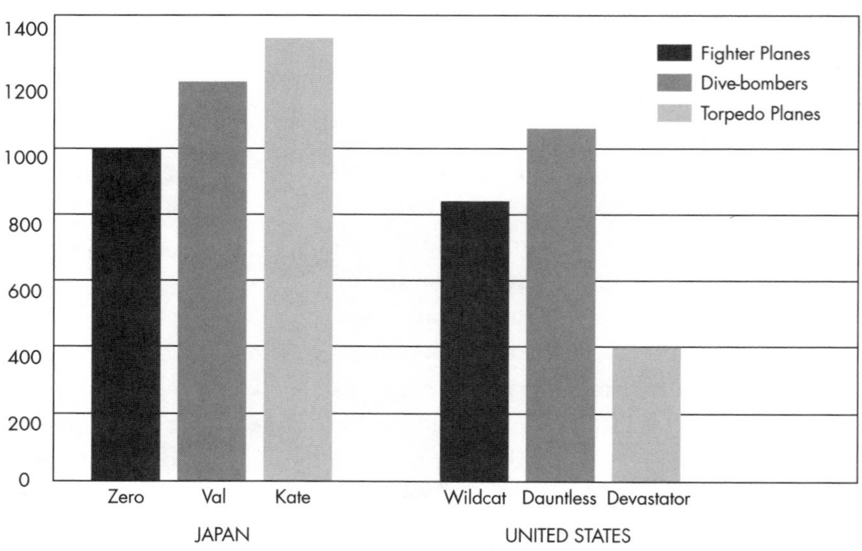

FIGURE 6. Aircraft ranges (Japan and the United States). —*Courtesy of U.S. Naval War College*

on the other hand, could fly strikes out to a distance of about 260 miles, giving a 100-mile advantage over their U.S. adversaries.[43] However, this advantage could only be exploited if Japanese area search plans were optimally devised, which, characteristically, they were not. Thus the Japanese squandered a decisive operational edge, primarily, it appears, because of their failure to grasp the significance of the better operational characteristics in terms of speed and range of their aircraft. Their failure to search the Coral Sea area adequately with carrier aircraft denied the Japanese a significant tactical advantage.

Notably, Fletcher launched the three attacks on Tulagi without fighter protection, save four fighters for the first of three attack waves. With only twelve fighters aboard *Yorktown*, he elected to retain them all to defend his carrier. Noting the lack of U.S. carriers in the Pacific, this defensive measure was a wise decision. After the battle Fletcher urgently recommended that all carrier air wings be upgraded to at least twenty-seven fighters in order to better provide for the conflicting demands of combat air patrol and escort for strikes.

Prelude to the Main Action

Considering the setback at Tulagi a minor inconvenience, the Japanese pressed on toward their major objective at Port Moresby. The Invasion Force had left Rabaul on 4 May. Japanese intelligence indicated the presence of a single U.S. carrier, as anticipated, in opposition. Moreover, the Task Force 17 attacks on Tulagi had given some indication of the likely location of that carrier. A Japanese four-engine flying boat had been shot down on 5 May by a *Yorktown* plane, and a Japanese submarine was sighted heading toward the now combined Task Force 17 (composed of Task Forces 17, 11, and 44, a command of cruisers and supporting destroyers under Rear Adm. John G. Crace, RN) after they had rendezvoused that morning.[44] For the Japanese, the situation was developing more or less as expected. That was about to change.

Figure 7 shows the movements of both forces, with the broken line indicating operations in company of *Yorktown* and *Lexington*, and Japanese forces and force movements indicated by the solid line. Note the proximity of the opposing forces. After the American attack on Tulagi, the Japanese and U.S. forces in the area tried to locate each other for two days. Hara's Striking Force proceeded east of the Solomon Islands on a southeasterly course to enter the Coral Sea from the east, rather than from the north through the Jomard Passage as Fletcher expected. False and misleading contact reports

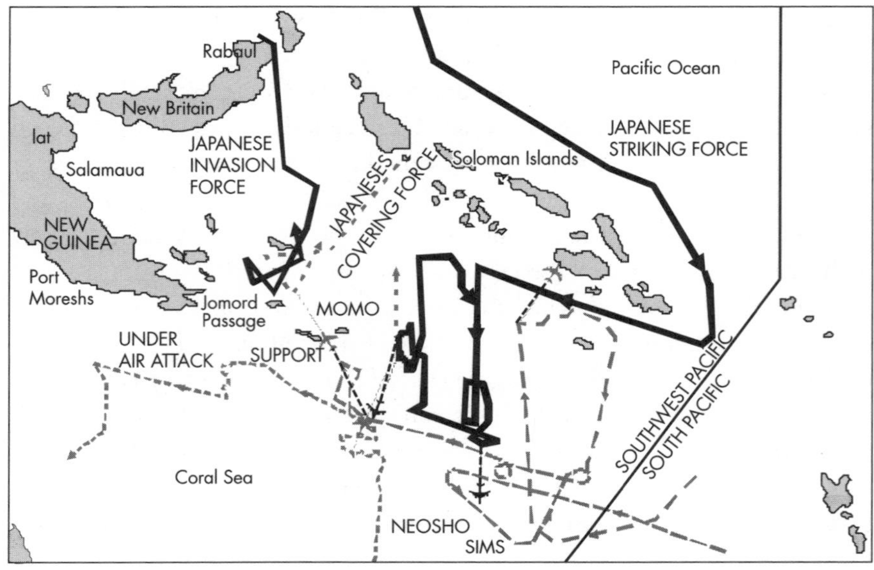

FIGURE 7. Chart of Coral Sea opposing force movements. The broken line indicates the movements of the U.S. task forces, and the solid line indicates Japanese force movements. —*Courtesy of U.S. Naval War College*

were generated during this period, which confounded both Fletcher's and Hara's decision-making processes. Fletcher's Task Force 17 rendezvoused as scheduled with Fitch's Task Force 11 at 0816 on 5 May, appreciably increasing the security of both forces. That morning a *Yorktown* scout plane had shot down a Japanese seaplane in the vicinity of Task Force 17, and a Japanese submarine had been spotted at about the same time inbound to the force about 150 nautical miles distant, but was later lost, giving Fletcher every reason to believe (albeit erroneously, as records would reveal after the war) that his carriers had been located.[45]

The carriers were located by the Japanese on the morning of 6 May, however, as two opposing aircraft sighted each other. The Japanese aircraft reported only a single carrier and a battleship, causing the composition of Task Force 17 to be underestimated.[46] Early the same morning, after heading northward during the night to close the invasion force in preparation for his attack, Fletcher issued his Operation Order 2-42, which combined Task Force 17, Task Force 11, and Task Force 44 into a single operational unit—an expanded Task Force 17.[47] Operation Order 2-42 directed destruction of "enemy ships, shipping, and aircraft at favorable opportunities in order to assist in checking further advances by the enemy in the New Guinea-Solomon area,"[48] not destruction of the Japanese carriers as a primary objective, in clear keeping with the strategic necessity Nimitz established for his force. A confluence of Antarctic polar and tropical air provided cloud cover and concealment for the American carriers as they readied for action. Unfortunately, Fletcher's directed air search plan supporting his operation order was inadequate in its northeasternmost extremes to locate the main opposing Japanese forces.[49] Observing radio silence, he did not coordinate a required search with the Commander of the Southwest Pacific Area, MacArthur, to rectify this problem.[50]

With expectations based on intelligence and land-based air searches that the Japanese would attempt to take Port Moresby on 6 or 7 May, Fletcher moved Task Force 17 toward the Jomard Passage to lie in wait.[51] He detached his only oiler, *Neosho*, and the destroyer *Sims* to a rendezvous area a safe distance from the expected action. The morning of 7 May, Fletcher sent out search planes to a distance of 250 nautical miles. The most critical east-northeast sector was terminated at 165 miles because of weather,[52] and the search generated no contacts.

Fletcher then detached Crace's cruisers and supporting destroyers (Task Group 17.3) to intercept the Port Moresby Invasion Force, which had been reported by land-based Army Air Corps planes as passing through the Jomard Passage en route to their objective at Port Moresby.[53] Fletcher was astute in aggressively pursuing his main mission of stopping the Port Moresby invasion, but sending Crace out without air cover, particularly during daylight, was extremely risky. Crace's force was attacked repeatedly—by U.S. Army Air Corps aircraft, which misidentified the Allied ships, as well as by the Japanese—but escaped with barely a scratch.[54]

These attacks highlight the problem created by Task Force 17 operating in the Southwest Pacific Area, Gen. Douglas MacArthur's area of responsibility. Mission priorities sometimes conflicted for MacArthur and Fletcher, and the use of different grids for reporting enemy contacts gave rise to the potential for misunderstanding enemy contact locations. Though Crace's force never engaged the enemy, it did distract Japanese land-based air reconnaissance, which might otherwise have located Task Force 17.

The fleet oiler *Neosho* and the accompanying destroyer *Sims*, both detached to the southwest of the American carriers away from expected enemy action, were harassed by Japanese planes, but without success. Fletcher never received confirmation of a Japanese carrier strike on these units, leaving him in a quandary over whether to counterattack. Had the position of

Neosho and *Sims* been plotted, it would have been obvious that they were beyond the range of the Japanese land-based aircraft staging from Rabaul. Thus their attackers were, by elimination, carrier-based.[55] Such information would have aided Fletcher greatly in narrowing down the possible locations of the Japanese carriers, but the types of aircraft making the raid were never passed to him.

The Main Action

At 0815 on 7 May *Yorktown*'s scouts reported two carriers and four cruisers over two hundred nautical miles away at 10° 03' S, 152° 27' E, heading 140 degrees true at eighteen-twenty knots.[56] This was the report Fletcher had been waiting for, and it seemed to give him the opportunity to carry out his strategic mission, since Japanese carriers would be essential to maintaining air defense against Allied planes from Australia until the Japanese could make a lodgment and base aircraft at Port Moresby. Without such air cover, it would be futile for the Japanese to attain and sustain their objective.

Ultimately, however, the contact was to prove about thirty-five miles south-southeast of the reported position—a good thing since the initial contact was well outside attack parameters for the American carrier aircraft—with only one carrier (*Shoho*) instead of two. Fletcher waited to close the contacts and launched strikes. The first, made up of twenty-eight bombers,* twelve torpedo planes, and ten fighters, along with the Air Group commander to direct the attack and three additional scout bombers, was launched from *Lexington* at 0926, only eleven minutes after the launch order was given.[57] The second, twenty-five bombers, ten torpedo planes, and eight fighters, was launched from *Yorktown* at 0944, in accordance with accepted practice at that time.[58] In the interval between sighting and launch the contacts closed to within 160 miles—just at the edge of strike range, another good decision by Fletcher.[59]

When the reporting pilot landed, however, not only was his positioning data incorrect, but he had also improperly encoded the type of contacts.[60]

*These were all SBD-2 or -3 aircraft, which composed the Bombing and Scouting Squadrons aboard U.S. carriers. Though there was a differentiation between squadrons, all pilots flew essentially the same planes and were equally trained for the dive-bombing mission. In practice, the Scouting Squadron was tasked with the bulk of the scouting missions, and was sometimes used at lower levels as defense against incoming torpedo planes.

He had really seen two heavy cruisers and two destroyers. Thus Fletcher's attack groups—the first U.S. carrier attack ever launched against an opposing naval force, with ninety-three aircraft in all but only eighteen fighters (not enough) in company—had been sent out on a false mission. Fletcher had adhered to the doctrine established in war games at the Naval War College and launched the first strike, but his operational intelligence had betrayed him.

Fletcher now had to decide whether to recall his strike or let it continue toward targets of lesser strategic and tactical importance when three unlocated Japanese carriers were known to be in the area. To his credit, he pressed forward the attack. To attempt to land fully armed aircraft on his carriers would have been foolhardy, and to have them dump their weapons loads before landing would render them useless until they could be rearmed. They would become an obstruction to defensive actions by cluttering the flight deck. With sufficient fighter aircraft onboard his carriers and in airborne defensive areas (fourteen fighters and two scout bombers to defend against incoming torpedo planes), Fletcher was putting his force at risk only for the duration of the attack. Moreover, if the Japanese carriers were located before his strike had reached its intended victims, he retained the option of vectoring the strike to the more important targets—an option he would lose if he directed the strike aircraft to return to their carriers. (See figure 8.)

At 1022 Fletcher received a message from MacArthur's command that an Army B-17 had sighted a carrier, sixteen assorted warships, and ten transports heading toward Port Moresby around thirty-five miles south-southeast of his pilot's reported sighting.[61] In the action that followed, the small Japanese carrier *Shoho* (believed at the time to be either *Ryukaku* or *Koryu,* but admittedly "not corresponding to any of the Japanese carriers for which we have silhouettes") was sunk, hit by multiple bombs and torpedoes, but no other Japanese ships were even damaged.[62] Pilots of Scouting Squadron 2 (VS-2) reported one hit on *Shoho*'s stern about fifty feet from the ramp and one about two-thirds aft on the center of the flight deck, and those of Bombing Squadron 2 (VB-2) one about two-thirds aft on the starboard side of the flight deck, another on the flight deck amidships, one aft on the port side of the flight deck, and two more amidships about halfway aft and on the near starboard side aft, all with either 500- or 1,000–pound bombs.[63] Japanese records show that all six fighters that *Shoho* was able to get airborne landed at Deboyne Island and their pilots were recovered, though their planes were lost.[64]

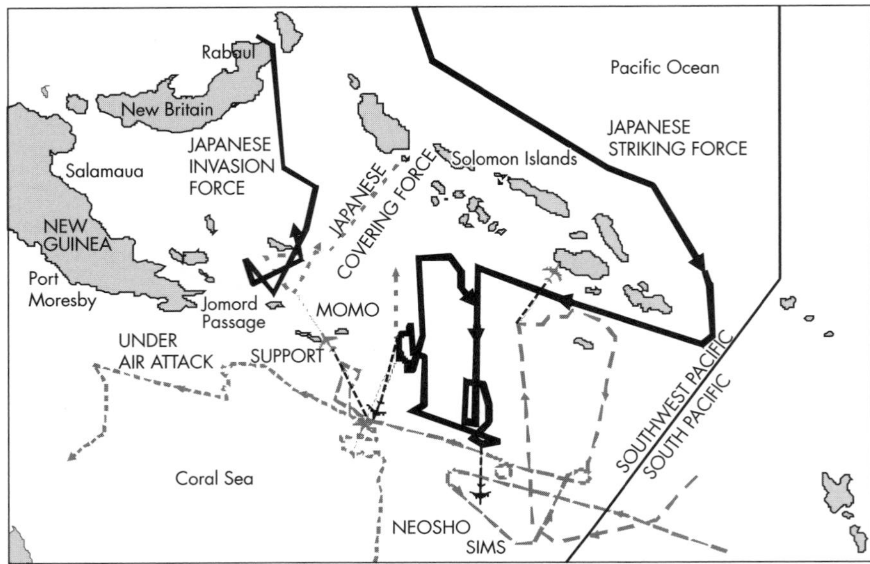

FIGURE 8. Another look at the developing action. —*Courtesy of U.S. Naval War College*

Given the amount of ordnance expended on the *Shoho*, and that only one light cruiser in company with her was hit, this encounter highlights the tendency of carrier aviators to focus on the opposing carrier force, even when sinking other ships might do more to ensure that the mission is completed.[65] The outcome of this attack was significant. Only 204 of *Shoho*'s crew of around 800 were rescued. More important to the American war effort, *Shoho*'s entire Air Group of eighteen aircraft—four Claude and eight Zero fighter aircraft and six Kate bombers—were lost in the action.[66]

So too were as many as six carrier-trained pilots, who were even harder to replace than their planes.[67] As Vice Adm. (then Capt.) Yoji Koda of the Japanese Maritime Self-Defense Force (JMSDF) points out, Japan was hit particularly hard by the Great Depression of 1929.[68] Its answer, in part, was to "de-mechanize" in order to keep more citizens productively employed in the workforce. Consequently, Japan had a far greater problem in training her pilots. Where virtually every young man in the United States had driven a car or tractor, most of their Japanese counterparts had never driven, and many had never even seen such a machine.[69] Training young pilots had to start in many cases with telling them, "This is a machine, and this is how you turn it on." Though the Japanese, to their credit, ultimately produced the very best pilots in the world at the time, it took them as long as three years and four months—three years being the norm—to complete the training cycle for each pilot.[70] With no acceleration of their training program at the outbreak of war, the inability to replace lost pilots quickly became a major obstacle to continued operational readiness in the Imperial Japanese Navy.

Koda offers another important insight on the limitation of a sufficient aviation leadership cadre in the officer corps of the Imperial Japanese Navy. In the years leading up to the attack on Pearl Harbor, the Japanese Naval Academy graduated and commissioned around one hundred officers per year. Of these, slightly over thirty were destined for aviation service. So, unlike the U.S. Navy, leadership positions in Japanese aviation squadrons aboard aircraft carriers were filled in part by enlisted personnel. However, when attrition set in over time, the most pronounced impact was on experienced leadership. This problem was exacerbated by the fact that, again unlike the U.S. Navy, where the most successful pilots in combat were often sent stateside for periods to recruit more pilots or serve as instructors to pass along insights on Japanese aircraft characteristics and pilot tactics, the best Japanese pilots remained in the front lines. Though this did make for a highly capable and aeronautically superior carrier squadron environment, it exposed Japan's best pilots to tremendous stress and great risk of being killed in action. It also removed the possibility of conveying combat experience to pilots in training, thus decreasing Japanese pilot skill in both embarked units and replacement pilots as the war went on. The Japanese loss of pilots and aircraft, even before and counting those aboard *Shoho*, placed Japanese carrier aviation on a slippery slide toward the ultimate defeat of Japan's navy.[71]

Because of the lateness of the hour and the presence of Carrier Division Five (*Shokaku* and *Zuikaku*), Fletcher did not fly additional strikes against the remaining Japanese targets.[72] Late that evening, *Lexington* obtained radar contact on what was believed to be a returning Japanese carrier strike. That information was not relayed to Fletcher until two and a half hours later, and since the planes could have covered a lot of ground returning to their carriers from the time they were sighted, Fletcher chose not to react.

Inexplicably, the Japanese Striking Force had received no useful locating information on the American carriers despite numerous opportunities since *Yorktown* struck Tulagi on 4 May. Estimating the carriers to be to the south, Hara altered course to position himself between the objective and the threat and deal with them before supporting the invasion of Port Moresby. Because the American carriers had not been located by land aircraft, Hara had to use his own carrier planes to extend the search to the south. At 0736 on 7 May he received word of contact with "the Allied Task Force."[73]

At 0859 on 7 May, just minutes after Fletcher had launched his strike against what he thought to be the carriers *Shokaku* and *Zuikaku,* the *Neosho* and *Sims* came under attack by a single reconnaissance plane, which made no hits. An hour later, the initial group of Japanese torpedo planes, coming upon the oiler and escort and realizing that no carriers were present, refrained from expending their torpedoes on lesser-value targets and departed.

Just after 1000 the first attack occurred, and at 1131 a second wave struck with more success. Also reacting to erroneous scout plane information indicating the presence of U.S. carriers, Hara had launched a strike of seventy-eight aircraft* almost simultaneously with that launched from the American carriers.[74] In this second attack *Sims* was torn apart and sank within minutes, while *Neosho* took seven bomb hits and eight near misses, and a plane she shot down crashed on her deck. In all, the Japanese lost six planes in this attack.[75] Figure 9 shows the relative strength of American and Japanese carrier-based aircraft, not including losses in battle, during the main action from 4 through 11 May, 1942.[76]

Severely damaged, *Neosho* was partially abandoned but resolutely refused to sink. Found on 11 May by a patrolling Catalina, she was intercepted by the destroyer *Henley*, specifically sent from New Caledonia for the purpose, and after rescuing 109 of her crew and fourteen crewmen from *Sims* who had taken refuge on the tanker, the destroyer scuttled the *Neosho* with two torpedoes.

At 2300 on 7 May, Inoue, commander of the 4th Fleet and the overall commander, canceled contemplated night action after the sinking of *Shoho*. He also delayed the invasion of Port Moresby for two days until the American carriers could be dealt with.[77] The Invasion Force retired to the north.[78] The result was a general clearing of the area other than both sides' main formations, and when battle was ultimately joined these were evenly matched. The Allies had one more heavy cruiser and destroyer than the Japanese, who outnumbered the Americans in remaining planes 122 to 121.[79]

The best information now available to Hara, however, credited the American force with two carriers, one battleship, two heavy cruisers and five

---

*Nine Zero fighters, thirteen Kate torpedo planes, and nineteen Val dive-bombers from *Shokaku* and nine Zeros, eleven Kates, and seventeen Vals from *Zuikaku*

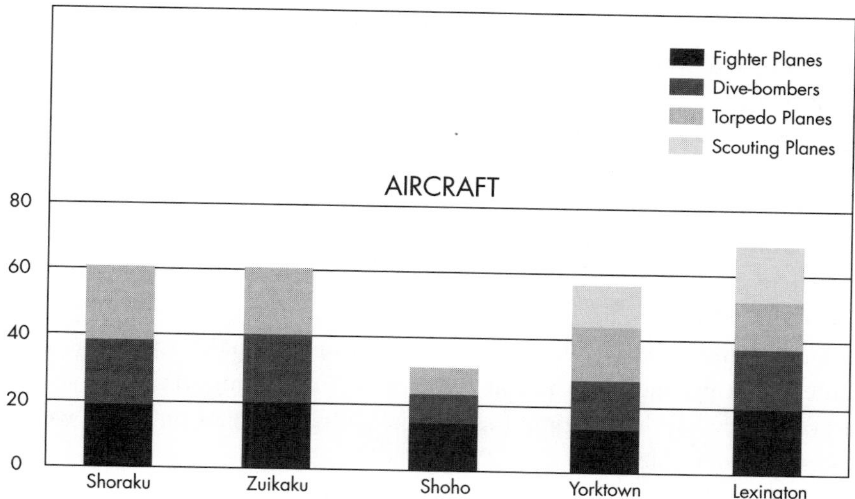

FIGURE 9. Aircraft (by type) aboard U.S. and Japanese carriers. —*Graphic provided by Jason Peters*

destroyers. The force actually had no battleships, four heavy cruisers instead of two, and seven destroyers instead of five. Fletcher's estimate was more accurate, underestimating only by three destroyers. Relative strength was important to the commanders in evaluating the feasibility and acceptability of potential courses of action.

As dawn broke on 8 May the opposing forces were within striking distance of each other. They reported sightings at virtually the same time. The edge now lay with the Japanese, however, since they were operating under the cloud cover enjoyed by the U.S. carriers the previous day, while Task Force 17 was operating in clear weather. At 0805 *Lexington* gained radar contact on an unidentified plane to the north-northwest inside 20 nautical miles. While unable to intercept it, a Japanese radio transmission was monitored only six minutes after the plane departed the vicinity. Three minutes prior to interception of that transmission, a *Lexington* scout plane radioed contact on "two carriers; four heavy cruisers; and three destroyers" at 028 degrees true bearing and 170 nautical miles from Task Force 17.[80] Both commanders had to assume that their locations had been compromised.

Shortly after the initial contact report, the commander of Scouting Squadron Two from *Lexington*, who had been searching an adjacent track, corrected that position on re-verification. His position, provided over an hour after the air strike had been launched, was roughly forty nautical miles north and just west of that initially given. This both complicated the ability of the strike aircraft to locate the Japanese force and limited their time over target.

Interestingly, in anticipation of the first carrier battle in history, where an entire engagement would be fought without forces ever coming within sight of one another, Fletcher, a cruiser commander by background, intended to transfer tactical command of his carriers to Fitch, an aviator.[81] Fitch was not informed of this decision, however, until just hours before the action of 8 May, and no mention of this change in operational responsibilities is made in the pertinent Operation Order.[82] Given the importance of such a responsibility, more lead time for Fitch to prepare a plan of action would have been advisable.

At 0838, fifty-two minutes before receiving the revised Japanese position, Commander Air (Fitch) directed both *Lexington* and *Yorktown* to launch their Air Groups. Eighty-two planes took off between 0900 and 0925.[83] In the interval, at 0907, Fletcher gave Fitch, Commander Air, tactical command of both American carriers in order to reduce signaling between carriers and to allow him complete freedom of action for his carriers and air groups.[84] This was a particularly generous decision, as it meant sharing his place in history in the first carrier versus carrier battle. The *Yorktown*'s aircraft were the first to reach the Japanese carriers. They attacked *Shokaku* as the *Zuikaku* was going under low-lying clouds in a rain squall. A total of three torpedo hits, six direct bomb hits, and several near misses were claimed.[85] Fires forward to port and amidships to starboard were reported.

Forty minutes after the initial attack, *Lexington*'s Air Group, which had trouble locating the Japanese, commenced its strike. As was the U.S. custom, the dive and scout bombers struck first, followed almost simultaneously by the torpedo planes. This was intended to force the opposing fighter protection high to counter the incoming bombers so that the low-level torpedo planes would encounter less resistance. Five torpedo and two bomb hits were claimed, including hits on *Zuikaku*. Information from Japanese sources shows conclusively, however, that *Shokaku* was the only Japanese carrier damaged, receiving three bomb hits.[86] While U.S. claims cannot be substantiated, in all likelihood the first two bombs on *Shokaku*, which caused her fires, were delivered by aircraft from *Yorktown*, while the last was dropped from a *Lexington* plane. Competent observers indicate that the bulk of the *Lexington* attack may have been directed against *Zuikaku* during a short emergence from cloud cover.[87] After this damage, *Shokaku* was able to recover, but not launch aircraft.

Task Force 17 then braced for the inevitable counterattack, having been alerted at 0832 by an intercepted enemy radio transmission giving the position, course, and speed of the U.S. force.[88] The enemy struck at 1118. U.S. fighter control was poor, and the Japanese neared weapon release point without much resistance. This is a bit surprising, in that the Japanese aircraft were detected by radar (of all the combatants, only the American carriers had radar) at seventy nautical miles and proceeded inbound for the attack on a constant bearing. In close, the Japanese split into three groups, with the dive-bombers in the center surrounded by two groups of torpedo planes. The attack group consisted of twenty fighters, seventy attack planes, and ten scout planes.[89]

Yorktown was attacked slightly before the *Lexington*, first by torpedo planes and then by dive-bombers. Skillful ship handling allowed *Yorktown* to evade all but one dive-bomber. The Japanese failed to bracket her bow, thus enabling *Yorktown* to turn away from the torpedo attacks. Now alerted, her fighters were successful in splashing a large number of the bombers before they launched their weapons. At 1127, however, *Yorktown* received her only bomb hit.[90] A 500-pound semi–armor-piercing bomb penetrated to her third deck before exploding in an aviation stores room.[91] The twelve-inch diameter hole left by the bomb in the flight deck was soon repaired without disruption to flight operations.

Lexington was not as lucky. She sustained two torpedo hits and two bomb hits.[92] Despite a six- to seven-degree list caused by the torpedoes, she was still able to make way with no reduction of her combat efficiency. The slight damage to the two carriers is quite remarkable, considering they were attacked by seventy Japanese planes, all with experienced combat pilots. Both the fighters and the scout planes that were thrown to the carriers' defense by necessity (because of lack of sufficient fighters and as a counter to the Japanese torpedo planes) acquitted themselves well.

Though attacked, the cruisers and destroyers supporting the U.S. carrier were unscratched. The Japanese nonetheless believed that they had sunk both *Yorktown* and *Lexington* (which their intelligence had led them to believe was *Saratoga*), as well as a battleship and cruiser.[93] Similarly, the U.S. Task Force 17 commanders reported that their antiaircraft fire and fighter/scout-bomber Combat Air Patrol had splashed many more Japanese planes than they actually had. In all they claimed twenty-seven Japanese fighters, fifteen dive-bombers, and thirty-one torpedo planes (including fifteen fighters and six dive-bombers claimed in the *Shoho* strike)—seventy-three in total were destroyed.[94] In reality, 92 Japanese planes from *Shokaku* and *Zuikaku* were recovered or accounted for after the action out of an initial complement of 122.[95] The excessive margin of error, forty-five—or one and a half times again the actual loss by the Japanese—attests to the unreliability of pilot reports, including contact locations and numbers and types of ships sighted, inherent in battle. The reliability of pilot-generated intelligence was questionable throughout the war, a factor of incalculable significance in compounding the difficulty of the decision process for all commanders at sea.

During the attack the American carriers became separated by six miles, while the Japanese carriers were separated by twelve miles. Some, such as Squadron Leader John S. "Jimmy" Thach, blamed the lack of mutual support between the carriers for the ultimate loss of *Lexington*. Thach later accused Fletcher of a similar "blunder" at Midway, resulting in the loss of *Yorktown*.[96] In retrospect, the separation of carriers under attack—given the commanders' awareness prior to actually experiencing combat of the tactical importance of keeping carriers together so they could support each other—was beyond the control of the respective commanders.

While the damage to *Lexington* was initially considered relatively minor, and she continued to launch and recover aircraft, her fate was yet to be realized. At 1247, an hour and fifteen minutes after *Lexington* sustained her last bomb hit, there was a severe internal explosion. Later theories suggest that the explosion was caused by aviation fuel seeping into a space secured for watertight integrity, with machinery still running, and igniting.[97] *Lexington* gradually regained headway and the crew had controlled the fires when a second explosion took place an hour later. The fires spread quickly, and by 1707 the commanding officer directed the crew to abandon ship.[98] Eighteen operational planes were transferred to *Yorktown* before *Lexington* lost way, but thirty-five went down with her.[99]

Of a crew of 2,952 all were saved except for 26 officers and 190 men.[100] The destroyer *Phelps* was detailed to sink *Lexington* with torpedoes. *Lexington*'s captain, Frederick C. Sherman, claimed one carrier (*Shoho*), another (*Shokaku*) probably sunk by *Lexington* and *Yorktown* aircraft in combination, four Zero fighter aircraft shot down and another two "probables," one type ninety-seven fighter destroyed by ship antiaircraft (AA) fire and another two splashed by *Lexington*'s fighters while attacking the *Shokaku*, and one three-place seaplane probably shot down during the action.[101]

At this point, the United States still had forty-nine aircraft aboard *Yorktown* available for a second strike against the Japanese, but only seven torpedoes remaining.[102] *Shokaku* was unable to launch aircraft, and, though the Americans did not know it, *Zuikaku* had only thirteen planes[103] ready for launch by 9 May. The rest were either severely battle damaged or pushed over the side during the recovery of *Shokaku*'s returning strike aircraft.[104] However, based on his information, Fletcher decided not to launch a second attack.

At 1422 Fitch relayed his strong indications, based on reports by one of his pilots, that an additional carrier had joined the Japanese force. This report was in error; the pilot had really detected *Zuikaku*. Fletcher, thinking he was opposed by two undamaged Japanese carriers, made the decision to withdraw his force to the south in preparation for renewed attacks the next day.[105]

COMSOWESPAC land-based aircraft were requested for follow-on attacks, but they were unable to locate the Japanese and on the afternoon of 8 May Fletcher received a dispatch from Nimitz ordering him to withdraw Task Force 17 from the Coral Sea.[106] With confirming reports by 80 percent of their returning pilots, the Japanese assumed they had sunk both American carriers. When this was reported to the commander of the 4th Fleet, Vice Adm. Narimi Inoue, the Port Moresby invasion was initially postponed for two days and then canceled. Hara had already ordered *Shokaku* to proceed north to Truk for repairs. *Zuikaku* lingered in the area on a southeasterly course, trying to locate the remaining American forces, until the early hours of 11 May, but was then directed to retire to the home islands via Rabaul to reconstitute her air group. There she was to make ready for impending operations against Midway.[107]

Inoue's rationale for this decision remains open to conjecture. Noting the lack of operational aircraft aboard *Zuikaku*, and accepting the report that both U.S. carriers were destroyed, he probably realized that not enough carrier aircraft were left to support the Invasion Force. Canceling the invasion was thus the only available option given the dominance of Allied land-based air power in the vicinity. The detection of two additional U.S. carriers in the area (Task Force 16 commanded by Halsey) bearing 098 degrees at 445 nautical miles from Tulagi certainly contributed to his decision.[108]

Coral Sea in Retrospect: Conclusions

If victory at sea was based only on ships sunk and damaged and temporary control of the action in areas of vital national or military concern, then Coral Sea would have to be classed a Japanese victory. Certainly, given the dearth of

U.S. carriers in the Pacific at the time, the loss of *Lexington* and bomb damage to *Yorktown* was a more severe blow to the United States than the loss of *Shoho* and major damage to *Shokaku* were to Japan. Yet more important things were at stake. The mission of the U.S. carriers was to maintain the SLOCs between Hawaii and Australia by stopping the Port Moresby invasion. That mission was accomplished. But the consequence of accomplishing that mission was far greater than merely maintaining U.S. SLOCs and preserving strategic options for an offensive directed at the Japanese home islands.

By early April of 1942 Yamamoto had prepared a plan to lure out and destroy the remaining three or four American carriers in the vicinity of Midway. In the process Midway would be captured and the defensive barrier around the Japanese home islands expanded by over a thousand miles. But Yamamoto undoubtedly had an offensive strategic objective in mind as well. Frank Uhlig, editor emeritus of the *Naval War College Review*, postulates that Yamamoto felt that, if necessary, Japan could invade and conquer Hawaii, despite the fact that since by mid-1942 Hawaii had become an armed camp and Japan lacked the requisite amphibious ships to stage an invasion.[109] In Professor Uhlig's opinion, Yamamoto reasoned that when the Americans were shoved back another thousand miles to Hawaii, and if necessary another two thousand miles to the West Coast, through naval dominance of that sea frontier, with lines of communication with the East Coast via the Panama Canal severed and commerce subject to attack by Hawaii-based Japanese submarines and surface naval forces, the United States would have to negotiate a settlement with Japan.[110] If indeed such a scenario was plausible, or even if Yamamoto was successful only in destroying the majority of the remaining U.S. carriers in the Pacific and extending Japan's defense perimeter, the Japanese strategic objectives in the Southwest Pacific would have been achieved en passant. Thus, in Uhlig's words, "In his decision, fortunately for the Americans, Yamamoto [made] success in a more important campaign [Midway] hostage to success in a less important one [Port Moresby]."[111]

Considering the stakes, the Battle of the Coral Sea must be qualified as a Japanese tactical victory and American strategic victory. With the loss of the carrier *Shoho* and the demonstration that the U.S. was a clear menace to their installations, naval units, and activities in the Coral Sea area, the Japanese temporarily gave up their expedition against Port Moresby. Though they tried again twice that summer to take the coastal village, MacArthur's Australian forces were able to foil both attempts.[112] The Japanese never again threatened expansion to the southeast of Guadalcanal, particularly not after their loss at

Midway. The effect of the Coral Sea operations thus had an important bearing on ultimate victory in the Pacific. The decisions of both the strategic level commander, Nimitz, and the operational level commander, Fletcher, at this critical stage in the Pacific Campaign were key to the achievement of U.S. national political objectives.

In joining a battle such as that in the Coral Sea, several aspects of the operational commander's decision process are key. The first is that the commander at sea must balance three separate and generally conflicting objectives:

1. To carry out the mission successfully.
2. To destroy as much of the enemy fleet as possible, and
3. To avoid being sunk, so as to be able to fight another day.

The commander must also be aware, as Halsey should have seen later at Leyte Gulf, that destroying the enemy fleet may well take second priority to carrying out the mission successfully.

Second, there are three universal tactical decisions that commanders must make about how to apportion the efforts of their forces: for offense, for defense, and for finding out what is going on. To the extent that certain ships and aircraft can be used for only one of the above (offense, defense, or scouting), the apportionment is simple. But naval forces are notoriously multipurposed, so allocating forces is necessarily difficult. These concepts will be examined below.

Certainly many operational and tactical lessons were learned at Coral Sea. Prime among them were the importance of optimizing a tactical advantage by using land-based support to maximum benefit and the haziness of intelligence—in terms of positions and composition of forces—supplied by pilots. Perhaps all the commanders involved in the battle, particularly the Japanese, should have paid more attention to massing forces. Also, both sides could have inflicted more damage to the operational objectives of the other if targets other than carriers had been dealt with more effectively. Pilots operated exclusively on the premise that if they got the carriers all else would follow.

Yet the most important lesson of this battle is perhaps the way to deal with operational success. Despite sinking *Lexington*, the Japanese had to forfeit their goal of securing a base at Port Moresby and severing Allied SLOCs. In tactical defeat, the Americans achieved their strategic objectives. Perhaps Carl von Clausewitz said it best: "War is merely a continuation of policy by other means."[113] The strategic, and thus the political, objectives must remain the prize in battle—on land or at sea.

Of perhaps greater overall significance to the outcome of the war against Japan was the attrition of Japanese pilots and aircraft. The length of time required to train a Japanese pilot and the paucity of officers with aviation experience in the ranks of Japanese carrier aviation put the Japanese at a serious disadvantage, and of the 105 aircraft confirmed lost by the Japanese at Coral Sea, ninety were carrier planes.[114] The toll on pilots, and especially those in leadership positions, during the Battle of the Coral Sea was significant, given the relatively few pilots who were carrier qualified. The Japanese estimated that they needed at least 3,500 pilots for the 3,029 aircraft in their first-line Striking Forces (1st and 11th Air Fleets) and second-line Striking Forces (Naval Stations).[115] Drawing from the methodology of Masatake Okumiya, who was air staff officer of the 11th Combined Air Flotilla and in charge of pilot training when the Japanese attacked Pearl Harbor, the Japanese had the number of aircraft assigned to its ten active carriers shown in table 2.[116]

Considering that Japan calculated that it needed a minimum of 3,500 qualified pilots to fly its 3,029 naval aircraft at the war's outset,[117] or 115.55 percent as many pilots as aircraft, it could by extension be expected that Japan had only slightly more than 563 fully trained pilots to man the 488 aircraft assigned aboard carriers of the First Air Fleet. Including the twenty-nine carrier planes lost during the two-wave attack on Pearl Harbor, seventeen more in the attacks of the British holdings at and around Colombo and Trincomalee on Ceylon, and another ten to twelve in attacks and operations in the Southern Resource Area, the Japanese had lost a total of at least fifty-six planes.

Fifty-six planes was not bad, considering the Japanese had sunk or disabled nine battleships, including those at Pearl Harbor, where a total of twenty-seven ships had been damaged; *Prince of Wales*, which had been sunk by land-based aircraft; the battle cruiser *Repulse*, again by land-based aircraft; the heavy cruisers *Cornwall* and *Dorsetshire*; and the British aircraft carrier *Hermes*, as well as over 300 aircraft in the air and on the ground. But the Japanese lost an additional 90 carrier aircraft at Coral Sea (by way of contrast, the U.S. lost 81 carrier aircraft at Coral Sea, including the 35 that went down with *Lexington*),[118] bringing the total number of carrier aircraft lost to more than 140 of the 488 initially assigned aboard Japan's ten active aircraft carriers—an astounding 30 percent of its total carrier complement.

TABLE 2 Number of aircraft assigned to Japan's ten active carriers

Akagi	63:18 Type Zero VF, 18 Type 99 VB, 27 Type 97 VCB
Kaga	63:18 Type Zero VF, 18 Type 99 VB, 27 Type 97 VCB
Soryu	54:18 Type Zero VF, 18 Type 99 VB, 18 Type 97 VCB
Hiryu	54:18 Type Zero VF, 18 Type 99 VB, 18 Type 97 VCB
Zuikaku	72:18 Type Zero VF, 27 Type 99 VB, 27 Type 97 VCB
Shokaku	72:18 Type Zero VF, 27 Type 99 VB, 27 Type 97 VCB
Ryujo	31:22 Type 96 VF, 18 Type 97 VCB*
Hosho	21†
Zuiho	30‡
Shoho	28§
Total	488

Note: Sources vary widely on the exact number of aircraft aboard carriers of the Japanese *kido butai*. An attempt has been made to determine the most reliable numbers possible, but these numbers are representative and there may be inaccuracies.

While many of the pilots Japan needed so badly had survived, it could be safely estimated that it had already experienced losses of slightly over 10 percent of her carrier-qualified pilot cadre. Moreover, this loss had been experienced primarily in a single action against an allegedly numerically inferior force. The worst was yet to come.

Fletcher's command performance will now be considered with respect to the methodology established on pages 2–3 to evaluate his adherence to the precepts of *Sound Military Decision* imparted during his educational tour of

*Hansgeorg Jentschura, Dieter Jung, and Peter Mickel. *Warships of the Imperial Japanese Navy, 1869–1945*. Annapolis, Md.: Naval Institute Press, 1977, p. 49.

†Anthony J. Watts and Brian G. Gordon. *The Imperial Japanese Navy*. New York: Doubleday & Company, Inc, 1971, p. 169. According to other sources the number of aircraft aboard *Hosho* could have been as high as forty.

‡Ibid., p. 293. *Jane's Fighting Ships 1941* lists *Zuiho* as carrying between thirty and forty aircraft. However, *Zuiho* was of the same class, displacement, and length as the two other carriers of the *Soryu* class, *Soryu* and *Hiryu*, and both are credited by Okumiya, Masatake, and Jiro Horikoshi in *Zero!* as having fifty-four aircraft embarked.

§Bates, *The Battle of the Coral Sea*, appendix II, p. vi.

duty at the United States Naval War College. Specifically, his decisions will be evaluated as they relate to the following.

1. The commander's estimate of the situation and grasp of the strategic and operational significance of the decisions he would be required to make. In this area Fletcher deserves high marks—perhaps a strong A-. His mission, as conveyed by his senior in the chain of command, Nimitz, was to forestall the Japanese from creating a barrier to American SLOCs between Hawaii and Australia by foreclosing Japan's attempt to take Port Moresby. Ancillary to that objective, Fletcher was tasked to destroy as many Japanese ships and aircraft as he could without unduly risking his carriers. Fletcher accomplished both aspects of his mission, but maintained his primary emphasis on stopping the Port Moresby invasion throughout. He should, however, have placed more emphasis on destroying ships other than carriers, as this would over time cause more damage to the Japanese war effort, especially as the Japanese also lost trained pilots. Fletcher deserves high marks for the performance of his assigned strategic role and also for the decision that preserved *Yorktown*, one of only three remaining strategic assets in the Pacific arsenal once *Lexington* had been sunk.

2. The commander's demonstrated ability to formulate a course of action, his ability to convey his decision in mission orders to subordinate commanders concisely and unambiguously, and his flexibility in modifying those orders through strategic and/or operational reappraisal if required. Fletcher undoubtedly formulated an aggressive and purposeful course of action, but his communication of the plan of action—particularly of his intent to have Fitch control aviation actions—was conveyed too late for Fitch to formulate a detailed plan of his own for this critical aspect of the mission. Fitch was thus forced to react to Japanese moves to a far greater extent than was necessary, which could have been costly and certainly increased the risk to the force. Also, Fletcher's coordination with COMSOWESPAC was less than optimal in both conveying requirements for areas to be searched to locate Japanese units and in providing locating information and ship types in order to direct land-based aircraft attacks on maritime units. Of course, the need to maintain radio silence to remain undetected by the enemy mitigates this lack of communication of necessary directives,

especially before the Allies' presence in the Coral Sea became known with Fletcher's attack on Japanese units at Tulagi. Fletcher's overall grade in this area would be a weak B.

3. The adequacy of command arrangements, the chain of command established, and the communications procedures put into effect to facilitate the exercise of command in battle. This was an especially strong point for Task Force 17, particularly in comparison with Japan's bifurcated command arrangements, under which five separate major fleet units and land-based air assets were controlled by a commander ashore. Except for the lack of coordination with COMSOWESPAC, in whose area of responsibility (AOR) Fletcher was operating, the U.S. Navy chain of command was direct, appropriate, and used to best advantage. Admiral Nimitz should share in the credit here, since he directed and established those command arrangements to which Admiral Fletcher reacted decisively and flexibly. Both deserve an A.
4. The commander's adherence to established operational and tactical doctrines where appropriate, his adherence to procedures established prior to the engagement of forces, and his ability to deviate from the same when warranted. Fletcher not only adhered to established operational and tactical doctrines, but also showed the moral courage to formulate doctrine where none was in place. He doggedly adhered to the principle of launching his strike first once the enemy had been located. Moreover, when confronted by a situation where he found out that the information he had been passed was incorrect and that the large Japanese carriers that were his main targets were not present, he resisted the temptation to recall the strike and pressed forward the attack—establishing doctrine in the process. There were, however, numerous occasions during the Battle of the Coral Sea when Fletcher adhered to doctrine that proved unwise, particularly regarding the doctrine of separating carriers to increase the likelihood that they would survive. Fletcher was a very strong proponent of operating his carriers in groups to provide mutual air support, simplify his strike planning profile of aircraft, and multiply the antiair and antisubmarine effectiveness of his screening cruisers and destroyers, which were in short supply and had to be spread thin to support independent carrier operations. Though he and Nimitz invariably instituted modifications to doctrine to correct shortcomings and practices shown not to work

during the battle, Fletcher obeyed Nimitz's order to operate separately in the Battle of Midway against his better judgment. For this Fletcher should not be criticized. Considering he was not an aviator himself, he deserves a strong A in this important area.

5. The commander's communication of mission requirements to subordinate commanders and the suitability of complementary actions by those subordinates to engage the enemy more effectively. This was another strong suit for Fletcher. He passed the responsibility for orchestrating the air defense and offensive to his junior, Fitch, since Fitch was as an aviator and thus more qualified—a very difficult decision for any senior. He also tasked Crace to detach cruisers and destroyers to attack the Port Moresby Invasion Force, thus increasing the risk from opposing air or submarine attack in order to increase the potential to succeed in his mission. The fact that this was overly risky during daylight and that Crace never contacted his target notwithstanding, Fletcher accepted decreasing the security of his force as a permissable tradeoff in optimizing his chance to accomplish his mission. Good leadership, but perhaps bad judgment—another A-.

6. The commander's understanding of the engagement's importance within the wider context of achieving U.S. political objectives and his concomitant appreciation for the appropriate risk and determination of the proper circumstances in which to end the battle. From start to attack to withdrawal, the foregoing discussion of Fletcher's decision process and performance should establish his grasp of this point unequivocally—A+.

7. The commander's audacity and brilliance in conceptualizing, articulating, and executing a plan of action. Fletcher entered the Coral Sea from the south and thus remained undetected in any useful sense by the Japanese until he had launched his attack against *Shokaku* and *Zuikaku*. He attacked the Japanese at Tulagi, giving away his *general* location to negate extended-range Japanese air searches that would give away his *specific* location. He launched first whenever the opportunity arose, doggedly adhering to the doctrine emanating from Naval War College war games that established that this enhanced the probability of success in attacks. He also had the good judgment and intestinal fortitude to press through the attack when, as was often the case, his pilot-

generated intelligence proved incorrect while the strike was en route to its intended target. He also increased the probability of achieving his main strategic objective by detaching a surface action group to attack the Port Moresby Invasion Force. While perhaps falling short of brilliant, Fletcher's ability to consider many things in exquisite detail and balance his responsibilities to seek out his foe, protect his own force, and press home his attack against the Japanese until his main objective was achieved, with all elements of his force informed of his intent and with no ambiguities in his directives, deserves a strong A.

8. The commander's ability to learn from the situation and rapidly pass lessons along to the advantage of those commanding in later engagements. One need only look at the way Fletcher and his subordinates captured, in clear, concise, and simple-to-understand terms, the many important lessons generated from the first naval battle in history where no ship in either force either saw or fired on an enemy ship to appreciate his mastery of informing those later to be "in harm's way." Nimitz similarly forwarded Task Force 17 action reports to those in his command immediately, enhancing their battle posture. Especially since this was the first ever carrier-to-carrier naval battle, and since lessons were transmitted to and acted on by other fleet units and commanders within days, Adm. Frank Jack Fletcher gets another A+ here.

From the analysis presented above, it is beginning to appear that at least one senior Navy leader had indeed learned something of importance in the interwar period.

In a recent article in the *Naval War College Review* by Thomas Wildenberg entitled "Midway: Sheer Luck or Better Doctrine?" the author defines doctrine as "the fundamental principles by which military forces guide their actions."[119] He postulates that elements of U.S. Navy doctrine, including those following, gave the United States a decided advantage over the Japanese in the Battle of Midway, and by extension, other battles of the Pacific war as well.[120]

1. The need for quick location of enemy carriers so that strikes aimed at their flight decks could be launched first, and the concomitant importance of carrier-based scouting assets

2. The predisposition toward bombers instead of torpedo planes on carriers to prevent an opponent from launching aircraft. Bombing the flight deck so no aircraft could take off or land was found to be more debilitating than torpedoing the waterline, which did not immediately impede flight operations.
3. The advantage of the flight "deck park," which enabled U.S. carriers to carry more aircraft than Japanese carriers of approximately equal displacement
4. The great advantage of conducting searches with indigenous carrier aircraft instead of relying primarily on battleship and cruiser aircraft, as the Japanese did
5. The relative strike advantage of the Japanese "box" tactical carrier formation and its defensive weaknesses. During wargaming at the Naval War College, it was found that the side that could get the most aircraft in the air soonest was likely to win the battle. Obviously the Japanese discovered this as well. Thus the use of the box tactic to mass aircraft was a major advantage; however, it placed all the Japanese eggs in one basket. An incoming American attack could strike at all Japanese carriers, whereas dispersed groups of about two carriers would have been less susceptible to destruction in a single American attack.

While Wildenberg makes a good case for the importance of doctrine, events at Coral Sea fail to support his findings. Both Japan and the United States adhered to doctrine based on getting the most aircraft airborne in the shortest time, and attacking first. Inherent to this plan was the need to locate the enemy before he located you. However, while almost all of Wildenberg's important elements of doctrine are derived directly from those universally held objectives, achieving them did not necessarily equate to success against the enemy. Even with a quarter of both embarked air wings composed of search aircraft, the U.S. was not guaranteed to locate the Japanese carriers first. Pilot errors on both sides introduced ambiguities where "first strikes" were launched against other than the desired targets. Though U.S. torpedo planes severely limited the range of a strike and required far too much time to muster over the carrier(s) and near the target to produce a coordinated high- and low-altitude attack, the Devastators were a hindrance not because of doctrine, but because of their antiquated speed and range characteristics. Moreover, while Wildenberg advocates the 50 percent bomber carrier load, the lack of adequate numbers of fighter aircraft was probably the greatest single lesson learned from the Coral Sea engagements, especially in the context of the need to balance fighter requirements for attack, defense, and scouting discussed above.

The absolute need for more fighters on U.S. carriers resulted in a 69 percent increase from the twelve on *Yorktown* and twenty on *Lexington* to twenty-seven on all U.S. carriers by the time of the Battle of Midway only a month later.[121] This increase highlights the importance of hedging against the ambiguities and fallacies of prewar doctrine concerning that balance. With more fighter aircraft on board the American carriers, a commander could hedge against the possibility of being attacked while his fighters were en route to attack the enemy by both sending fighters to protect the strike aircraft he launched against his opponent and keeping enough remaining aircraft to protect against a simultaneous attack by his opponent. Simultaneous strikes by both opposing carrier groups had not been adequately considered before the war. However, they were found to be the case much more frequently than expected. Indeed, after the Battle of the Coral Sea, Fletcher was at the forefront of those advocating multiple carrier formations for greater synergistic force protection, though he complied with Nimitz's direct order to operate his carrier groups independently at Midway.[122]

In his letter of 27 May 1942 to King via Nimitz, Fletcher twice justified his critical decisions on how to fight his carriers by relating his decision process to his "estimate of the situation."[123] In the first instance, Fletcher decided not to launch a second attack once *Shoho* and a light cruiser had been sunk, since other suitable targets were lacking and his mission priority was to move west to position for attack on the expected route of the Port Moresby Invasion Force and possibly a supporting carrier through the Jomard Passage.[124] In the second case, he explained rejecting the idea of making another air attack on *Shokaku* and *Zuikaku* since *Yorktown* had only eight fighters, twelve bombers, and eight torpedo planes (with only seven remaining torpedoes) still serviceable.[125] He also rejected a surface attack option because it would likely be located and subjected to a strong Japanese carrier air attack before dark.[126]

As discussed in chapter 1, "The Commander's Estimate of the Situation" was an integral part of *Sound Military Decision*, which was constantly used in conjunction with all aspects of the education of naval officers at the Naval War College. It was, in fact, an intrinsic and required part of the wargaming effort that went on in Newport and formed the basis of the doctrine that Wildenberg credits for American success in the Battle of Midway. Though that doctrine proved somewhat ill-advised and ineffectual at Coral Sea, the sound military decisions Fletcher made there reinforce the importance of *Sound Military Decision*.

CHAPTER 3

The Battle of Midway

FIGURE 10. Aerial view of Midway Islands with the runway on Eastern Island in the foreground, circa 1941. —*Courtesy of U.S. Naval Institute Photo Archive*

Shacked up in Shanghai when the war broke out—stop me if you've heard this story before.
—ANONYMOUS

Opening Phases

IN ALL OF HISTORY THE GODS OF WAR have sought a clash of Titans—a cataclysmic battle to decide the fate of nations and determine the course of history. In June of 1942 they got their wish.

As the four carriers of the *kido butai** bore down on Midway there was no doubt in the Japanese ranks of the victory that would follow. The battle had been gamed repeatedly with the same outcome—at worst one carrier lost. The Imperial Fleet was ready with what they thought was a sound plan of attack. Yet battles are won through clash of arms, not war games. As the Japanese were soon to learn, the outcome was anything but assured. The *kido*

*The *kido butai*, or "mobile force," was the striking group of large carriers in Vice Adm. Chuichi Nagumo's Third Fleet. (Note: All Japanese names herein have been westernized, with surname last and given name first.)

butai was defeated on such a scale that many have referred to it as the most decisive* rout in recorded naval history. What follows is an analysis of that defeat, the reasons behind it, and the decisions that contributed to it.

The Japanese Navy, born circa 1874, was modernized and expanded because of the inability to consolidate gains from the Sino-Japanese War of 1894–1895 due to lack of requisite naval strength. It developed a tradition that reflected Mahanian concepts of warfare at sea. The big or "decisive" battle was to be waged with the victor assured of command of the sea. The naval doctrine emanating from this tradition centered on attrition, aiming to decrease the enemy's forces by roughly 50 percent prior to actual engagement. During World War II, this attrition was achieved by placing submarine barriers in the enemy's path and attacking units with land-based aircraft. Most important, the primary engagement took place with forces massed under an umbrella of land-based air support.[1] The Mahanian Imperial Navy believed that such a plan enacted against an equal or inferior force would result in resounding success.

Yet at Midway the Japanese violated the very fundamentals of their doctrine. Their forces were not massed and the battle took place out of range of land-based air support. Though they could still have achieved victory, the combination of several other factors rendered the Japanese situation hopeless. But before those factors are considered it is necessary to examine the circumstances under which the battle took place.

The Situation in the Pacific in the Late Spring of 1942

During the winter and spring of 1942 the Japanese consolidated their gains in East Asia. While they had planned to establish a defensive perimeter to protect their gains, they had been stifled to the south by Fletcher in the Battle of the Coral Sea. Unable to provide what in their view was sufficient air power to protect their landing force while it attempted to take Port Moresby, the Japanese had called off that operation. At least for the time being, the Allied SLOCs between Hawaii and Australia were safe. The best way for Japan to sever those SLOCs, and to have a free reign to do as it might in the maritime regions of its Pacific domain, was to eliminate the U.S. carriers—

*The term "decisive" is illusory at best. Herein it is meant to indicate the creation of a situation after which the possibility of ultimate victory, save by the intervention of some type of radical technology such as atomic weapons, is unachievable.

the last strategic assets the United States had in the Pacific that could thwart Japanese intentions.

In late April of 1942 the Japanese had ten carriers and eleven battleships.[2] They had lost the light carrier *Shoho* in the Coral Sea battle, but were able to add an additional escort carrier, *Taiyo*, which was launched in September 1941.[3] However, Fletcher's victory at the Coral Sea in a strategic sense also included a major component almost as important in the long run as keeping the SLOCs open to Australia. The attack against the Japanese carriers *Shokaku* and *Zuikaku* had depleted their air wings to the point where neither was available for the Midway operation. This lack of additional carrier air assets to launch an attack against the American carriers at the critical moment may well have been decisive in determining the outcome of the battle.

In comparison, after the loss of *Lexington* and the damage to *Yorktown* at Coral Sea, the United States had only three of its six remaining carriers in operational status in the Pacific: *Yorktown*, *Enterprise*, and *Hornet*.[4] The odds could have been even worse at Midway if Adm. Ernest J. King, Chief of Naval Operations in Washington, D.C., had imposed his will on Nimitz. King wanted *Yorktown* to go directly to Puget Sound for repairs.[5] Nimitz, citing the lack of sufficient fuel aboard the *Yorktown* for a voyage of that length, convinced King that the best course of action was to send *Yorktown* to Pearl Harbor initially until the extent of her damage could be evaluated.[6] Once in Pearl Harbor, it was determined that *Yorktown* would need a minimum of a month and a half to repair. Through unbelievable determination and effort, she was given temporary repairs in only seventy-two hours, and was able to follow *Enterprise* and *Hornet*, under the command of Rear Adm. Raymond Spruance, to the northeast of Midway. As a result of the Japanese attack on Pearl Harbor, moreover, when the battle actually took place, only fourteen destroyers, seven heavy cruisers, and one light cruiser were available to support the American carrier groups.[7]

Saratoga, torpedoed in late December by a Japanese submarine, underwent repair in Puget Sound between 11 January and 22 May 1942.[8] Once *Saratoga*'s repairs had been completed she began training on the West Coast and was further delayed while waiting for escort units. She finally left Bremerton and Puget Sound on 22 May via San Diego. There she picked up aircraft and supplies. Leaving San Diego on 1 June 1942, *Saratoga* did not reach Pearl Harbor until 6 June—too late to take part in the battle of Midway.[9] *Yorktown* was transferred from the Atlantic as planned before the Japanese submarine's attack on *Saratoga*, and became flagship of Task Force

17 on New Year's Eve. This was fortuitous: *Yorktown* was much more flexible than *Saratoga* with respect to the number and types of aircraft that could be taken onboard, and this played out to significant advantage in the Battle of Midway. The U.S. Navy could only realistically expect to succeed with defensive operations, however, until new construction units entered fleet service in late 1943. Until then, U.S. planning had to be reactive rather than proactive in nature by necessity.

The Commander and His Opponent

The officer in operational command, or "tactical command" as it was termed at the time, for the Battle of Midway on the U.S. side was Rear Adm. Frank Jack Fletcher. Fletcher, nicknamed "Fletch" or "Flap Jack," was "a strenuous son of the Middle West. . . . Proud of Iowa's corn and hogs."[10] Born in Marshalltown, Iowa, on 29 April 1885, Fletcher was appointed to the U.S. Naval Academy from his native state in 1902, and graduated on 13 February 1906, after which he served for two years at sea as was then required by law.[11] After that, he was commissioned an ensign on 26 June 1908 while aboard USS *Eagle*.[12] Fletcher was promoted to lieutenant junior grade on 31 July 1911[13] and received his commission in the Regular Navy on 5 March 1912, only six years after leaving Annapolis.[14] Two years later Lieutenant Fletcher distinguished himself in action during the United States' occupation of Vera Cruz, Mexico, when President Woodrow Wilson backed Venustiano Carranza after Gen. Victoriano Huerta, who had overthrown the regime of President Francisco Madero by assassination, refused to step down.[15]

Fletcher received a commendation for operations conducted while under the command of his uncle, Rear Adm. Frank Friday Fletcher:

> Lieutenant Fletcher was in charge of the "Esperanza" [a merchant ship commandeered for the operation] and succeeded in getting on board over three hundred fifty refugees[,] many of them after the conflict had commenced. This ship was under fire being struck more than thirty times, but he succeeded in getting all the refugees placed in safety. Later he was placed in charge of the train conveying refugees under a flag of truce. This was hazardous as it was believed the track [was] mined, and a small error in dealing with the Mexican guard of soldiers might readily have caused a conflict, such a conflict

> at one time being narrowly averted. It was greatly due to his efforts in establishing friendly relations with the Mexican officers that so many refugees succeeded in reaching Vera Cruz from the interior.[16]

Lieutenant Fletcher's contribution to the important operations in the occupation of Vera Cruz ultimately were rewarded with the top American military honor, the Medal of Honor, "as a recognition of the distinguished service rendered by [Fletcher] in the line of [his] profession, upon the occasion of the seizure of Vera Cruz, Mexico, April 21st and 22nd, 1914, as recited in detail in Navy Department General Order No. 177."[17]

After serving as aide and flag lieutenant on the staff of the Commander in Chief of the U.S. Atlantic Fleet aboard the flagships USS *New York* and USS *Wyoming* from July 1914, Fletcher petitioned Adm. Cameron McRae Winslow, who was "to command a brigade of the division which Colonel Roosevelt hopes to take to France" in April of 1917, "to serve in [his] command."[18] Ultimately Fletcher was transferred from USS *Allen*, the first ship to which he was assigned in European waters, to take command of USS *Benham* "as relief of Commander William F. Halsey U.S.N."[19] Only two months later Fletcher was given a temporary appointment to the rank of commander, effective 1 July 1918.[20] Though there is no record of distinguished action in battle, Fletcher's papers having for the most part been lost when USS *Yorktown* was sunk during the Battle of Midway, then Commander Fletcher was awarded the Navy Cross,[21] one of the highest medals awarded by the U.S. Navy, as per the citation: "For distinguished service in the line of [his] profession as Commanding Officer of the USS *Benham* engaged in the important, exacting and hazardous duty of patrolling the waters infested with enemy submarines and mines, in escorting and protecting vitally important convoys, and in offensive and defensive action, vigorously and unremittingly prosecuted, against all forms of enemy naval activity."[22]

As it did with so many promising officers of this period, this award was intended in all likelihood to mark Fletcher as a man of great potential destined for successive assignments of greater importance rather than for any specific distinguishing act or acts.

Reporting for duty after his return from European waters in 1919 Commander Fletcher soon after commenced the intellectual part of his professional military education. In July of 1924 he was certified as completing the Naval War College Correspondence Course by Rear Adm. C.S. Williams, the institution's president.[23] Fletcher was subsequently stationed at the Navy Yard in Washington, D.C., from March 1925 to August 1927.

Assigned as executive officer of the battleship USS *Colorado*, Commander Fletcher requested aviation training, which was denied because he was found to be physically unqualified.[24] Fletcher had complained as a midshipman of problems with his eyesight, but Naval Academy doctors had found no detectible problem with his vision. He had petitioned for a second opinion from outside physicians, but his request had been denied. Thus the commander of the carrier task forces in three of the five carrier battles in history was to come to that leadership position without the benefit of firsthand experience as an aviator.

Thereafter Fletcher petitioned for[25] and was granted[26] assignment to the U.S. Naval War College, to commence on 1 July of 1929. On successful completion of his tour at the War College in early 1930, (where one of his classmates was Cdr. Thomas C. Kinkaid, another future key player in carrier warfare),[27] Fletcher was assigned for duty under instruction to the U.S. Army War College—a normal progression for those earmarked for continued demanding duty and positions of greater authority and responsibility.[28]

Fletcher's next assignment was as chief of staff for the Commander in Chief of the U.S. Asiatic Fleet aboard the flagship USS *Houston* from August 1931 through the summer of 1933, followed by duty from November 1933 through May 1936 as aide to the secretary of the Navy, Claude A. Swanson.[29] While in this position, Fletcher was given a temporary assignment starting in April of 1935 as an observer and advisor for Fleet Problem XVI with the commander of Battleships, Scouting Force.[30]

Fletcher assumed command of the battleship USS *New Mexico*, flagship of Battleship Division Three, Battle Force, in June 1936, where he served through December of 1937. He was then assigned as a member of the Naval Examining Board at the Navy Department in Washington, D.C., from June 1938 through September of 1939. His follow-on assignment was again in Washington as assistant chief of the Bureau of Navigation, where he was still serving when the Japanese attacked Pearl Harbor. Fletcher's shore assignments worked to his disadvantage with later Chief of Naval Operations Ernest J. King, who viewed those who he considered prone to accepting comfortable positions in Washington as "fixers," who went to easy jobs on shore to "fix" problems in the Navy while the real men went to sea.

Fletcher quickly returned to sea when war broke out, however, assigned as commander of the Scouting Force, with additional duty as commander of Cruiser Division Four, which he assumed on 31 December 1941. Already promoted to captain in August of 1930,[31] he was now, since his selection in December of 1938, a rear admiral. On 29 April 1941 Fletcher was designated commander of Cruisers, Pacific Fleet, with the continuing responsibility of commanding Cruiser Division Four. It was in this command position that he saw action in the Battle of the Coral Sea in May and the Battle of Midway in June 1942.[32]

While Fletcher was the only flag or general officer on active duty who had been awarded both the Medal of Honor and the Navy Cross when World War II started,[33] he did not have extensive combat experience by any means. His only real test under fire had been at Vera Cruz in 1914. Moreover, though he was an experienced cruiser and battleship man, he was not an aviator. Certainly his experience in carrier battle at Coral Sea had made him the only American equipped for the next encounter with the Japanese, but his knowledge was less than a month old when he was ordered to engage near Midway. He had little time to absorb its impact. Fletcher sailed into harm's way a relative novice in the art of carrier warfare.

By contrast, his adversary, Vice Adm. Chuichi Nagumo, had led the *kido butai* on every Japanese carrier strike except Coral Sea. Though not nearly as much is known about this hardened war veteran, it is safe to say that he was an extremely competent officer who had risen through the ranks through determination and demonstrated sound judgment. Not noted for his flamboyance or aggressive nature, Nagumo had reached the pinnacle of Japanese offensive command more by promotion of the most senior, as was the custom in the Japanese navy, than by any acts that set him apart from other officers.

Nagumo had been severely criticized in naval circles for not launching a third attack wave against Pearl Harbor, retiring instead for fear of being located and attacked by the as yet undetected U.S. carriers known to be in the vicinity. His actions had resulted in his being labeled as too conservative—something far removed from the samurai spirit imbued in all Japanese warriors. In all probability, Nagumo's actions in the Battle of Midway were influenced by his perception of the expectations of both those above him and those he led. His judgment was subject to considerations of criticism he might receive if he failed to uphold the traditions of the Japanese navy established in the Battle of Tsushima in the Russo-Japanese War.

Nagumo's junior and the commander of Carrier Division II under his direct command, Rear Adm. Tamon Yamaguchi, on the other hand, was generally considered the rising star of the Japanese navy. He had in many respects paralleled the career of the commander of the Combined Fleet, Adm. Isoroku Yamamoto, including his stint as a naval attaché in Washington, and was expected to achieve similar success through the rest of his career. Above all, Yamaguchi was considered a consummate warrior, aggressive in both outlook and action. Having such a shadow at Midway to offer recommendations and stand ready to critique any lack of aggressiveness on Nagumo's part placed Nagumo in a particularly delicate position with respect to the decisions he had to make.

Japanese Preparations

Japan's preparations for the Midway engagement were flawed. The plan drawn up by the Combined Fleet Staff had two central objectives. The first and more limited objective was to seize Midway as an advance air base for early detection of American warships operating west of the Hawaiian Islands. The second and much more important objective was to draw out the remaining carriers of the U.S. Pacific Fleet and to engage and destroy them in the "decisive battle" that had become the cornerstone of Japanese naval doctrine.[34]

Altogether, the Combined Fleet intended to employ over two hundred ships, including transports and auxiliaries, and approximately seven hundred planes in the Midway operation.[35] The ship count included eleven battleships, eight carriers, twenty-two cruisers, sixty-five destroyers, and twenty-one submarines.[36] These were to be divided into a Main Force, composed mostly of battleships and commanded by Yamamoto; a Carrier Striking Force, commanded by Nagumo; a Midway Island Invasion Force, commanded by Vice Adm. Nobutake Kondo; a Northern Force assigned to occupy islands in the U.S. Aleutian chain, commanded by Vice Adm. Moshiro Hosogaya; and an Advance Submarine Force, commanded by Vice Adm. Teruhisa Komatsu. Shore-based aircraft were to be commanded by Vice Adm. Nishizo Tsukahara. The Japanese primarily relied on Yamamoto's Main Force, Vice Adm. Shiro Takasu's Aleutian Guard (Screening) Force, Nagumo's First Carrier Striking Force, Rear Adm. Kakuji Kakuta's Second Carrier Striking Force (Aleutians) under Nagumo, and Komatsu's forces to crush the American fleet.[37] They would be arrayed as shown in table 3.

By any standard, this Japanese plan was complex, and its complexity was compounded by the compression of the schedule to prepare it for execution. On 1 May 1942 Combined Fleet Headquarters initiated a four-day series of

TABLE 3 Japanese force locations approaching Midway

Yamamoto Force	600 miles northwest of Midway
Takasu Force	500 miles north of Yamamoto Force
Nagumo Force	300 miles east of Yamamoto Force
Kakuta Force	300 miles east of Takasu Force
Submarine Forces To establish three cordon lines by D minus 5 [2 June 1942], disposed as follows, in order to detect the approach of enemy forces:	
Cordon A	(four units, the I-169, I-171, I-174, and I-175 from Submarine Squadron 3) between 19° 30' N and 23° 30' N, on longitude 167° W.
Cordon B	(Submarine Squadron 5, consisting of I-156, I-157, and I-159 of the 19th Submarine Division and I-162, I-165, and I-166 of the 13th Submarine Division, as well as I-168 from the 13th, which was also tasked with conducting a close reconnaissance of Midway itself) between 29° 30' N, 164° 30' W, and 26° 10' N, 167° W.
Cordon C	(I-9, I-15, and I-17 of Submarine Squadron 1) between 49° N, 166° W, and 51° N, 166° W.

Note: Projected force relationships are presented here to provide a picture of the difficulty in coordinating an operation of this magnitude from such dispersed locations. This theme will be considered later in the text as a contributing factor in the Japanese defeat.

Source: Information in table from Mitsuo Fuchida and Masatake Okumiua, *Midway: The Battle That Doomed Japan, The Japanese Navy's Story*, eds. Clarke H. Kawakami and Roger Pineau (Annapolis, Md.: Naval Institute Press, 1955 and 1992), 114.

war games designed to test the operational plan. Conducted under the direction of Combined Fleet Chief of Staff Rear Adm. Matome Ugaki, the games were attended by most of the commanders who would take part in the operation. All details of the plan were carried out without the slightest difficulty, owing in considerable measure to Ugaki's frequent intervention to set aside the rulings of the umpires.[38]

On the 6 May—only thirty-four days before the date that the Japanese expected to fight the battle, and with only four days of gaming and two days of briefing conferences and discussions—commanders were dispersed to their units. The constant operations that had preceded the games and the ensuing Battle of the Coral Sea (7–8 May) had provided the Navy some experience, but should have garnered a longer planning stage before the next step. The amount of preparation time both ashore and afloat was insufficient for an undertaking of this magnitude and complexity. Also, the outcome of the Coral Sea engagement modified the plan for Midway significantly; *Shokaku* and *Zuikaku*—both assumed available in the wargames and included in Japanese plans for the battle—were unavailable for the operation.* Still, Japan's scripting of the likely situation and actions of the U.S. Fleet and pride in its recent past successes gave rise to unbridled optimism.

Decisions vs. Intelligence

Samuel Eliot Morison and others, including John Prados, have characterized the United States victory at Midway as "a victory of intelligence," and undoubtedly intelligence did give the U.S. a crucially important edge in preparing for the battle. The celebrated test by which U.S. Navy code breakers induced the Japanese to indicate that "AF" was low on water after ensuring that they had intercepted U.S. transmissions that disclosed the same problem on Midway certainly gave valuable insight into specific Japanese plans intercepted in subsequent transmissions. This was particularly important in that the volume of Japanese message traffic and an incomplete deciphering of the Japanese JN-25 naval code† resulted in decoding only 10 percent of all JN-25 message traffic by May of 1942.[39] Fortunately, the high volume of Japanese message traffic after the Battle of the Coral Sea (and the indications of a planned strike against Port Moresby that emerged as early as 25 March[40]) had given the code breakers the opportunity to break down additional JN-25 number groups.[41]

Perhaps more fortuitously, the Japanese, probably because of the contemplated actions against Port Moresby, chose not to exacerbate circumstances at such a critical time by changing their naval codes as scheduled on 1 May. Instead, the change did not take place until midnight on 25 May.[42] The extra time to decipher more of the unchanged code helped make the "AF" intelligence coup possible.

---

*Aside from three bomb hits sustained by *Shokaku*, the air wings of both *Shokaku* and *Zuikaku* were diminished to the point that both carriers required eight weeks in the Inland Sea to make required repairs and reconstitute their air wings.

†JN-25 required the use of two books: a code book (with fewer than 33,333 entries) used to convert words or letters to five-number code groups, and a related cipher book (of 100,000 five-number cipher groups arranged in a random sequence). For encryption, each code group was then added to the next cipher group in sequence. No machine was involved. See endnote 1 of chapter 2.

Yet intelligence alone tells only part of the story. American historians tend to categorize victory in military encounters as a product of some major single factor. However, it is the decisions men make—in battle as in life—that shape their destinies. Surely intelligence alone can not explain the victory of the twenty-five U.S. ships, 227 carrier aircraft, and 110 Midway-based aircraft involved in the Battle of Midway against a Japanese armada of over 200 ships with 433 aircraft and sea planes embarked (not including the 33 earmarked to be flown off to Midway) and many more land-based aircraft. What follows is an analysis of the key decisions in that battle.

How the Plans Played Out

The pattern for the Battle of Midway, in many respects, was strikingly similar to that of the Battle of the Coral Sea a month earlier. In both battles the Japanese approached the area of operations in widely separated groups and sought to draw the U.S. carrier forces into a disadvantageous position where they could destroy them. In both actions secondary operations took place—at Tulagi in the Coral Sea and in the Aleutians at Midway. Weather was also an important factor in both operations.

The Japanese undoubtedly expected their operations in the Coral Sea to be successful. On 5 May Imperial Headquarters issued the orders for the Midway and Aleutian operations despite the fact that Tulagi, in the Solomon Islands chain and almost due north of Guadalcanal Island, had been attacked by carrier aircraft and the capture of Port Moresby had been seriously jeopardized by the presence of a U.S. carrier force.[43] On 12 May, after the Battle of the Coral Sea, Yamamoto issued the order for the operations at Midway. On 18 May Imperial Headquarters issued orders for the occupation of New Caledonia, Fiji, and Samoa.[44] The Aleutian Force carrier air groups were to make the initial blow on Dutch Harbor in the Aleutians on 3 June as a supplementary measure, not as a diversion as has often been thought in American circles. The *kido butai* would strike the main blow on Midway on 4 June.

Believing that they had sunk both the *Saratoga*, for which they had mistaken *Lexington* at Coral Sea, and *Yorktown*, the Japanese evidently considered their enterprise in the Coral Sea advantageous even though it became necessary to abandon the attack on Port Moresby when two carriers (TF 16, commanded by Halsey) were spotted bearing 098 degrees at 445 nautical miles from Tulagi.[45] Halsey was returning from launching the Doolittle Raid on Tokyo and was dispatched to assist Fletcher at Coral Sea. Fortunately, timely U.S. intelligence on Japanese movements had allowed the recall of all American carriers to the Hawaiian area, which made them available for the Midway action.

As the Japanese approached Midway, Nimitz instituted seven-hundred-mile patrol plane searches in the semicircle west of Midway and recalled his three carriers to Hawaii. While he remained in Hawaii, his opposite, Yamamoto, was aboard his flagship *Yamato* with the Main Force. This would limit Yamamoto's ability to communicate with his carrier forces and provide direction during the battle.

On arrival at Pearl Harbor, it was estimated that a month and a half's worth of work was needed to repair the damage Fletcher's carrier *Yorktown* sustained at Coral Sea. Nimitz ordered the work completed in seventy-two hours and, amazingly, she was returned to service in that short time. The U.S. plan called for countering the Japanese carrier forces northwest of Midway, and Halsey's Task Force 16 was to be dispatched immediately, with Fletcher to catch up when repairs to *Yorktown* were complete. Both task forces were to rendezvous at a predesignated point—appropriately named by Nimitz as "Point Luck." Unfortunately, Halsey was overcome by an attack of dermatitis and missed the greatest carrier battle in history because of a severe itch. His command went to the cruiser commander in his Task Force, Spruance. Spruance was placed in the position of having to coordinate with a new staff, though reputedly the best carrier air staff in the Pacific, within a brief period immediately before engaging the Japanese force.

Prelude to Action in the Aleutians and at Midway

The Battle of Midway took place from 3 June to 6 June 1942. Its consequences make it arguably one of the most important naval battles in history. This clash among two great navies was decided entirely by air power. No surface gunnery action took place at any time during the battle, and in fact no opposing surface ships came within sight of each other. In the Battle of Midway the Japanese repeated the pattern of the previous month in the Battle of the Coral Sea. Once again applying land tactics to battle at sea, they approached in widely separated and nonsupporting groups, seeking to draw out the U.S. forces in the area, and included an operation of less strategic importance akin to that aimed at Tulagi during Coral Sea. This time, the secondary target was the Aleutian Islands.

The Doolittle Raid on Tokyo of 18 April 1942, discussed in chapter 2, page 48, strongly influenced the Japanese to condense their timetable for execution of the MORYALMI (Port *Mo*resby, Ocean-Nauru (*RY*) [islands of Ocean and Nauru],[46] *Al*eutians, *Mi*dway) plans. The Japanese High Command responded by accelerating their advance into the Solomons and New Guinea. Further advances were planned to take New Caledonia, the Fiji Islands, and Samoa, and then capture the geographically strategic islands of Midway and occupy certain of the Aleutian Islands. Many of these objectives had been set forth in previous plans, but the Battle of the Coral Sea had checked the Japanese advance southward by sea. Imperial Headquarters ordered the advance to the east. They would cut the lines of American communications, mine the areas west of Pearl Harbor, and the balance of naval power in the Pacific would be for the time being more favorable to the Japanese.

Yamamoto believed that as a result of Pearl Harbor and Coral Sea the American Fleet was temporarily inferior, but that American industrial potential made a Japanese fleet action imperative. The approaches to Japan must be strengthened. By departing from the established naval policy of holding the fleet in Japanese-controlled waters and threatening something Americans prized, he reasoned that the Americans might feel compelled to commit their weaker forces and thus be brought to a vulnerable position. By offering irresistible bait, Yamamoto hoped to precipitate a decisive fleet action near Midway. Preceding the Midway attack by one day there was to be reconnaissance in force against Dutch Harbor, striking a paralyzing blow to cover the seizure of Adak, Kiska, and Attu Islands. This move would act as a complement to the main objective of taking Midway, rather than merely a diversion from it. Kiska and Midway could then be used as bases for barrier patrols to detect any surprise American penetration toward the Japanese home islands. They could also be used as staging points for air reconnaissance to the east and attack by air on U.S. and Allied shipping, as well as for surface ship and submarine action clear to the west coast of the continental United States.

Information Available to the Japanese Commander

Nagumo, commander of the Striking Force, believed, based on the intelligence available when he sailed from Hiroshima Bay toward Midway under conditions of radio silence, that there would not be any powerful American units, including carriers, in the vicinity of Midway. Though Yamamoto had better

FIGURE 11. Carriers of the Japanese kido butai. —*Courtesy of U.S. Naval War College*

KIDO BUTAI

*Akagi—Red Castle
Kaga—Increased Joy
*Hiryu—Flying Dragon
Soryu—Green Dragon
Shokaku—Flying Crane
Zuikaku—Lucky Crane

Note: Carriers in lighter shading were present at the Battle of Midway. Asterisks indicate those carriers with islands on their port sides.

intelligence, he failed to share it with Nagumo, believing that radio silence was imperative to prevent granting the U.S. force the advantage through detection of his Main Body or Nagumo's Striking Force. This highlights a major flaw in the Japanese organization for the Midway operation. Unlike Nimitz, his American counterpoint, who was stationed ashore and could communicate readily with his operational commander, Fletcher, Yamamoto saw fit to embark aboard his flagship in the Main Body of the attacking force. As a consequence, Yamamoto, the strategic commander, was of necessity unable adequately to communicate with his main offensive units—the four carriers of Nagumo's *kido butai*.

Thus Nagumo believed that the Americans patrolled west and south of Midway at a radius of five hundred miles but were not as likely to be in the area to the northwest of Midway from which he intended to approach. Frequent bad weather in this area might also serve to conceal his approach. He correctly estimated that the defenses of Midway would be strong and that submarines operated in the area. He believed that Midway had two squadrons of flying reconnaissance boats, one squadron of Army bombers, and one squadron of fighters, and that this air strength could be doubled in an emergency. This was an excellent estimate of the situation, except, of course, for the likely area in which the American carriers would be operating. (See table 4.)

Nagumo expected that there would be two to three U.S. carriers—a good estimate, as there were actually three. He also estimated that the Americans

TABLE 4 Japanese estimate of U.S. Navy ships possibly around Midway

JAPANESE ESTIMATE	Estimate	Actual
Strong Defenses	Yes	Yes
Reconnaissance Flying Boat Squadrons	2	2
Army Bomber Squadrons	1	1
Fighter Squadrons	1	1

The Japanese commanders' estimate of the American surface units in the Hawaiian area also included some accurate estimates. (See table 5.)

Source: Chuichi Nagumo, Admiral, Imperial Japanese Navy, Commander in Chief, First Air Fleet, *The Japanese Story of the Battle of Midway (A Translation)*, OPNAV P32-1002, Office of Naval Intelligence, United States Navy, June 1947, pp. 6–7. Department of the Navy, Naval Historical Center, 805 Kidder Breese SE, Washington Navy Yard, Washington, D.C. 20374-5060. This document can be accessed over the WEB at: http://www.history.navy.mil/library/special/midway/midway.htm.

TABLE 5 American surface units in the general area of Midway

AMERICAN SURFACE UNITS		
SHIP TYPE	Japanese Estimate	Actual
Heavy Carriers	2 to 3	3
Special (Light) Carriers	2 to 3	0
Battleships	2	0
Heavy Cruisers	4 to 5	7
Light Cruisers	3 to 4	1
Very Light Cruisers	4	0
Destroyers	30	14
Submarines	25	25

Source: Chuichi Nagumo, *The Japanese Story of the Battle of Midway*, pp.6–7.

would have two to three light carriers and two battleships, but there were none included in either task force arrayed against the Japanese. He estimated four to five heavy cruisers, when actually there were seven; three to four light cruisers when there was only one; and four very light cruisers, of which none were present. His estimate of thirty destroyers was correct, but at the time of the battle only fourteen were in the Midway area. His estimate of twenty-five submarines was also correct. Thus Nagumo's estimates—on which the very favorable outcomes of the four-day Japanese war games were predicated—were essentially correct.[47] The question remains how the outcome of the actual battle could be so far removed from the expectations those war games engendered.[48]

The Japanese commander of the Aleutian forces, Vice Adm. Moshiro Hosegawa, believed that there were considerable military installations and patrol craft at Dutch Harbor, but that the port and its bases could be captured easily. He also assumed that Kiska and Attu had military installations and patrol craft. He estimated that normally there were twenty patrol planes and ten fighters at Dutch Harbor, two squadrons of patrol planes at Kodiak, and one squadron stationed at Sitka. This was indeed a reasonable estimate. However, his failure to obtain intelligence on the construction of the new Army Air Field at Ft. Glenn on Umnak Island had an adverse affect on the conduct of his operations.

Japanese Force Deployments

All the Japanese fleet, including the naval air fleet but excepting the China Seas Fleet, was under the command of Yamamoto. For the Midway operation the Combined Fleet was organized into five coordinated task forces: the Striking Force of fast carriers (*kido butai*), the Main Force, the Midway Invasion and Occupation Force, a Northern Force, and a Submarine Force. Additionally, all of these were to be supported by land-based air forces. The strength of these task forces was as follows:

1. The First Carrier Striking Force consisted of four first-line carriers, the *Kaga* and *Akagi* of Carrier Division I, and the *Soryu* and *Hiryu* of Carrier Division II, commanded by the aggressive and fast-rising Rear Adm. Tamon Yamaguchi embarked in his flagship *Hiryu*.[49] The *kido butai* carried a total of 229 aircraft, plus 21 destined for Midway.[50]* The entire force was screened by two fast but lightly armored battleships, *Haruna* and *Kirishima*, the heavy cruisers *Tone* and *Chikuma*,

*It should be noted that such credible sources as Bates, op. cit., p. 82, and Fuchida, op. cit., p. 108, list the number of Japanese aircraft aboard the four carriers of the mobile force as 231 and 261 respectively. Other sources use these numbers as well. Willmott is used here, however, as his study had access to all sources in Japanese and American records.

the light cruiser *Nagara*, and eleven destroyers.[51] The *kido butai* was self-supporting and accompanied by its own supply ships. This powerful offensive force was designed to meet any U.S. threat—but in spite of the lesson they should have learned at the Battle of the Coral Sea, the Japanese did not include more ships for antiaircraft fire. Nor did they mass naval surface ships in a single group as they had, successfully, in their raid on Colombo. The compelling lesson of the Coral Sea had been lost on the Japanese.

2. The Main Force was composed of one aircraft carrier, *Hosho* (with nine A5M4 Claudes and six B4N1 Jeans); the sixty-five-thousand-ton battleship *Yamato* (Yamamoto's flagship); the battleships *Nagato*, *Mutsu*, *Ise*, *Hyuga*, *Fuso*, and *Yamashiro*; two light cruisers, *Kitakami* and *Oi*; twelve destroyers; and four supply ships.[52] This powerful surface force, combined with the *kido butai*, should have been able to defeat the U.S. task forces in the Midway area if Yamamoto had arrayed it against them, particularly if the engagement was made under conditions of darkness to negate American airpower. In combination with the four operable carriers of the *kido butai*, the Main Force would have been nearly invincible if properly deployed.
3. The Midway Invasion and Occupation Force consisted of five groups: the Second Fleet Group of two battleships, *Kongo* and *Hiei*; four heavy cruisers, *Atago*, *Chokai*, *Haguro*, and *Myoko*; one light cruiser, *Yura*; eight destroyers; and three supply ships.[53] The Transport Group totaled twelve transports and supply ships and a close screen with the light cruiser *Jintsu*, ten destroyers, and three patrol boats.[54] The Close Support Group included four heavy cruisers, *Kumano*, *Suzuya*, *Mogami*, and *Mikuma*, screened by two destroyers, as well as the Seaplane Tender Group and the Minesweeper Group.[55]
4. The Advanced Submarine Force
5. The Northern Force, organized to capture certain Aleutian Islands, was composed of three groups:
   a. The Second Carrier Striking Force, commanded by Rear Adm. Kakuji Kakuta, which included the light carrier *Ryujo* (twelve fighters and eighteen torpedo planes embarked), the carrier *Junyo* (six fighters and fifteen dive-bombers embarked), the heavy cruisers *Takao* and *Maya*, three destroyers, and a single oiler.[56]

b. The Kiska Occupation Group, which was composed of the light cruisers *Kiso* and *Tama*,[57] five destroyers, two auxiliary cruisers, two transports carrying a total of 1,250 troops for the landing, three gun boats, and eight submarine chasers.

c. The Adak-Attu Occupation Group, which included the light cruiser *Abukuma*, four destroyers, a transport with 1,250 troops,[58] a mine-layer, and one auxiliary seaplane carrier.

The Japanese forces proceeded toward their destinations more or less independently. The First Carrier Striking Force (*kido butai*) left Hiroshima Bay 26 May.[59] At a point 450 nautical miles southeast of Tokyo it rendezvoused with its supply units. On 3 June it was 600 nautical miles northwest of Midway.[60]

The Main Force also departed Hiroshima Bay 26 May.[61] On 3 June the Main Force divided into two groups—the Main Group and the Aleutian Support Group, which headed toward the Aleutians.[62] The Midway Occupation Force left Japanese waters in widely separated groups. The Minesweeper Group departed Saipan on 25 May for Midway via Wake Island. The Transport Group, the Seaplane Tender Group, and the Coast Support Group left the Saipan-Guam area on 27 and 28 May.[63] The Second Fleet Group left Japan at 0700 on 28 May as well.[64] This group took position on the left flank of the Transport Group, seldom closer than fifty miles.

The Northern Force left Japanese waters in three separate groups. The Second Carrier Striking Force left Honshu Bay on 25 May and headed for a point four hundred nautical miles from Dutch Harbor. The Kiska Occupation Group left Ominato on 27 May for Paramushiro To and from there departed for Kiska Island on 1 June. The Adak-Attu Occupation Group left Ominato on 28 May for Aleutian waters.[65]

Thus the Japanese had set in motion a plan of attack on two widely separated outposts, with the ultimate objective of luring out, locating, and engaging a group of U.S. carriers somewhere west of the Hawaiian Islands. With over two hundred ships at sea simultaneously, the Imperial Japanese Navy's was the largest single naval operation to this point in history. The complexity of that operation, requiring the various commanders' simultaneous estimates of the situation and decisions, was contingent solely on a series of war games taking place from 1–4 May. Some of the commanders had not even been able to attend because of the action in the Coral Sea, and the carriers *Shokaku* and *Zuikaku*, whose air wings were depleted at Coral

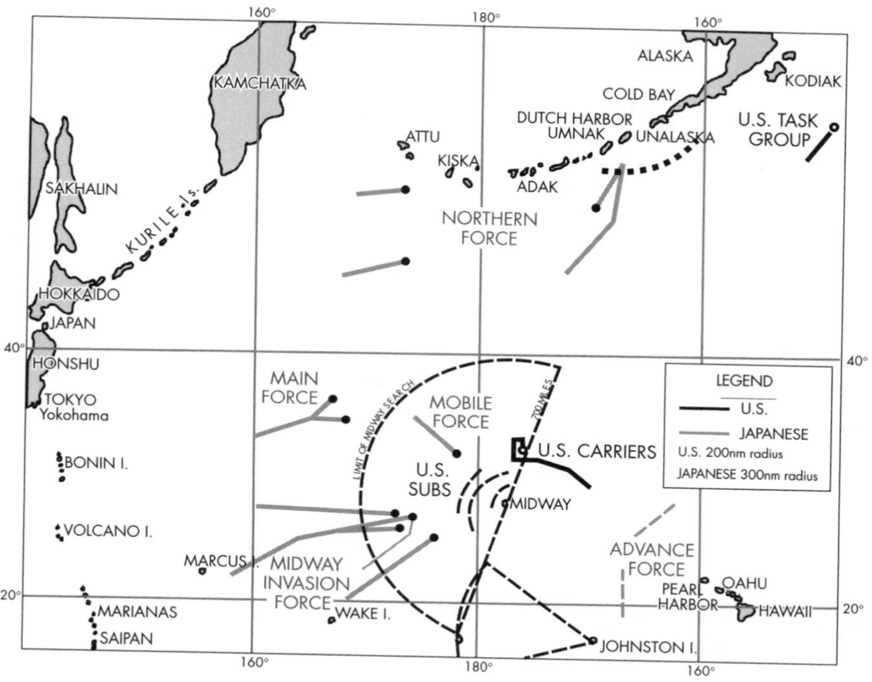

FIGURE 12. U.S. and Japanese force movements converging on Midway. —*Courtesy of U.S. Naval War College*

Sea rendering them unavailable for the Midway operation, had been integral to the contemplated action.

The wide dispersion of the Japanese task forces and their approaches to their objective areas, as well as the U.S. Strike Force and its route to the battle area, can be seen in figure 12. To allow his carriers the ability either to move to the north should the main thrust of the Japanese attack be against the Aleutians or to retreat to the east if their situation became untenable, Nimitz placed them where the Japanese carrier force would of necessity be between them and Midway Island. This created problems for the Japanese in the search plan they would need to establish and in prioritizing between Midway and the American carriers for their strikes.

As long as events unfolded exactly as anticipated, the Japanese plan for the Midway operation appears to have been reasonably sound, other than the wide separation of the principal forces that worked against the provision of mutual support and dissipated what should have been a potentially crucial advantage, namely superiority of numbers. The Main Force could not support the Striking Force or the Occupation Force unless they retired to the area of the Main Force, which was six hundred nautical miles west of the Striking Force and an equal distance to the northwest of the Occupation Force. The deployment of the Northern Force was well planned, nevertheless. The raid on Dutch Harbor did succeed in furnishing a diversion for the Midway operation in addition to its primary objective of taking a staging base for air surveillance and air, ship, and submarine attacks on U.S. shipping in the area.

Information Available to the American Commander

Nimitz was directed on 3 April 1942 to assume command of all the armed forces in the Pacific Ocean Area. Early in May Nimitz received intelligence that caused him to believe the Japanese planned an invasion thrust at Midway and the Aleutians early in June. This information was remarkably complete. In an intelligence coup of great significance, the garrison on Midway had been directed to broadcast in the clear (uncoded) that it was running low on fresh water. Consequently, decryption of Japanese JN-25 naval codes related that "AF" was running low on water—and subsequent intercepted transmissions provided details of impending Japanese moves against it.[66] Nimitz not only considered that he knew of the projected operations, but also he had quite comprehensive information on the strength of Japanese forces involved, their general direction of approach, and the approximate date on which each phase of the operation was to be launched. From this information Nimitz was able to make an estimate of the Japanese combatant ships to be used in the Midway action. (See table 6.)

The estimate of carriers, heavy cruisers, and submarines was reasonably correct. But his estimate of the number of Japanese battleships, light cruisers, and destroyers was seriously in error.

The commanding officer of the Naval Air Station at Midway, Capt. Cyril T. Simard, expected that the Japanese carriers would not launch their planes at a distance greater than two hundred miles, displaying an excellent knowledge of and appreciation for Japanese carrier aircraft capabilities. Simard therefore placed in operation a twenty-two plane search with flying boats (PBYs) to a distance of seven hundred miles.[67] These searches were augmented by an eight-hundred-mile search from Oahu and a seven-hundred-mile search from Johnston Island to cover probable approaches to Pearl

TABLE 6 Nimitz's 27 May estimate and actual number of Japanese ships present in Midway Islands operation

JAPANESE SHIPS	AMERICAN ESTIMATE	ACTUAL
Battleships	2 to 4	7
Carriers	4 or 5	4
Light Carriers	0	2
Heavy Cruisers	8 or 9	10
Light Cruisers	0	6
Destroyers	16 to 24	49
Submarines	8 to 12	16

Data from Bates, *The Battle of Midway*, p. 41. Bates lists eleven battleships present but there were actually only ten, seven of which were involved in operations near Midway. There were also two, not one, light carriers present—*Zuiho* with the Midway Invasion Force and *Hosho* with the Main Force.

Harbor. Captain Simard also knew that ordinarily an area of reduced visibility could be expected about three hundred to four hundred miles to the northwest of Midway. He reasoned that the Japanese commander, after leaving predicted bad weather, would wait for dawn to fix his position before launching planes. Since dawn was about 0415, the Japanese might be expected to strike Midway at around 0600. The Japanese actually struck at 0635 on 4 June.[68] Thus Simard's estimate of the situation optimized Midway's readiness to meet the expected attack.

Nimitz's commander in Aleutian waters, Rear Adm. Robert H. Theobald (commander of Task Force 8 and the North Pacific Force), had received intelligence on 28 May that the Japanese had one Task Group detailed for the capture of Kiska and another for Attu. He feared, however, that this information was a deception to draw U.S. naval forces westward so the Japanese could move in behind them. He estimated that the most likely area for a Japanese landing would be the Umnak Island-Dutch Harbor-Cold Bay area, and decided to defend there. His freedom of action was seriously affected, as he was forced to rely on land-based aircraft for reconnaissance and the essential protection of his ships. His airplanes in the bases in the Aleutians were limited in number, and there were no airfields west of Ft. Glenn (Otter Point) on Umnak Island.

The distances between Theobald's naval surface forces and the bases from which his supporting aircraft operated and the almost total lack of darkness to help his forces move without detection complicated his problem. Theobald's overall plan for the defense of Alaska appears to have been sound, but the means available to him to resist the Japanese were not adequate.

Considering the loss of ships incurred at Pearl Harbor and Coral Sea, the advisability of sending surface forces to the Aleutians presented Nimitz with a difficult decision. Nimitz believed that Midway was the primary objective and that he should maintain strength there. But the Aleutians were the gateway to Alaska and American soil. If the Japanese seized them, American morale would suffer and the country might perceive a developing threat to the west coast. Corregidor in the Philippines had fallen only three weeks before, so any further blow to American morale would come at the worst possible time. To his credit, this was a chance that Nimitz was willing to take.

American Command Relations

On 12 May 1942 King and his Army opposite, U.S. Army Chief of Staff Gen. George C. Marshall, informed all subordinates that command and theater boundaries should in no way restrict operations aiding the common cause against Japan. This was intended to avoid the Area of Responsibility (AOR) boundary restraints that resulted in an uncoordinated effort in the Coral Sea action.[69] On 14 May a state of "Fleet Opposed Invasion" in the Hawaiian coastal and sea frontiers was declared. This conveyed to the commanders in the Pacific that the primary responsibility to oppose the invasion was given to the Navy, with unity of command vested in Nimitz.[70] Land forces, including those the Navy assigned to repel invasion, would remain under the operational command of the Army.

On 21 May, King declared a prospective state of Fleet Opposed Invasion in the Aleutians.[71] At the same time Nimitz formed Task Force 8 under Theobald's command to oppose any advance of the enemy in the Aleutians. Theobald designated the Naval Air Detachment, Alaskan-Aleutian area as Task Group 8.1 under command of Capt. L. E. Gehres, USN, and the 11th Air Force as the Air Striking Group (Task Group 8.3) under the command of Brig. Gen. S.B. Butler, USA.[72] This was not in accordance with the Joint Chiefs of Staff directive that in order to obtain unified air operations, the commander of Alaskan Army Air was to command all Army and Navy air groups in Alaska. By this division, the unity of command of all air forces in Alaska ceased to exist.

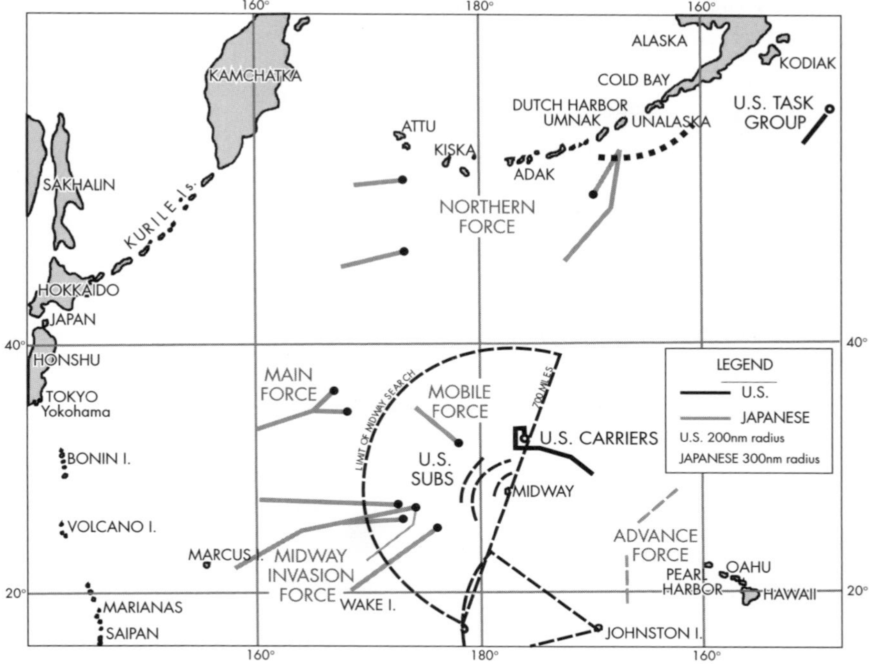

FIGURE 13. U.S. and Japanese force movements converging on Midway. —*Courtesy of U.S. Naval War College*

Task Force One, composed of the old battleships, was located at San Francisco. It took no active part in the battle, primarily because of lack of screening units for antiair and antisubmarine protection and lack of speed to keep up with the carriers should withdrawal from the Midway area become necessary.[73] The commander of Task Force 11, Rear Adm. Aubrey Fitch in the cruiser *Chester*, was anchored at San Diego on 3 June having arrived from Tongatabu two days earlier. Unfortunately, Fitch and his task force, built around the repaired carrier *Saratoga*, did not arrive in theater in time for the battle.[74] Task Group 11.1, which included *Saratoga*, the cruiser *San Diego*, and four destroyers, was en route to Pearl Harbor on 1 June under the command of Capt. D.C. Ramsey, USN, in *Saratoga*.[75]

Task Force 7, the submarine force, was divided into Task Group 7.1, the Midway patrol of twelve submarines; Task Group 7.2, the support patrol of three submarines; and Task Group 7.3, the Oahu patrol of four submarines.

Six submarines were detached to support Task Force 8 in the Aleutians.[76] The commander of Task Force 7 was Rear Adm. Robert H. English, USN. He stationed his twelve submarines on three arcs, one each at 200, 150, and 50 miles from Midway in sectors from 240 to 360 degrees true, as well as three submarines on a line from 045 to 225 degrees true with its closest point to Midway at 425 miles. English did this because CINCPAC's intelligence pointed to a Japanese attack through the northwest quadrant, and the second group of subs would be needed to support carrier operations, which might result in a forced retirement through their area.[77]

Task Force 16, under the command of Spruance, had been recently recalled to Pearl Harbor from the South Pacific area. It consisted of two first-line carriers, the *Enterprise* and *Hornet*; five heavy cruisers for screen, including *Vincennes*, *New Orleans*, *Minneapolis*, *Pensacola*, and *Northampton*; one light cruiser, *Atlanta*; and nine destroyers, *Phelps*, *Balch*, *Ellet*, *Maury*, *Monaghan*, *Worden*, *Aylwyn*, *Benham*, and *Conyngham*. Spruance assumed command of Task Force 16 as the handpicked replacement for the ailing Halsey.

Task Force 17, under the command of Fletcher in *Yorktown*, arrived in Pearl Harbor on 27 May. It consisted of *Yorktown*; the two heavy cruisers *Astoria* and *Portland*; and the destroyers *Russell*, *Hughes*, *Morris*, *Anderson*, and *Hammann*.[78] The rapidity of the emergency repairs allowed it to sortie three days later. Task Force 17 sailed on 30 May and rendezvoused with Task Force 16 at Point Luck near dusk on 2 June.[79]

On 3 June the two task forces, now under the operational command of Fletcher, were 320 nautical miles from Midway. On Nimitz's orders, which Fletcher reluctantly executed, the two task forces were to operate independently.[80] Based on war gaming conducted at the Naval War College, it was then believed that a one-carrier task group could maneuver better under air attack and avoid collision. Fletcher knew from Coral Sea, however, that the combined screening units—now insufficient in numbers to support multiple independent carriers—could provide a much safer antiaircraft screen when combined than with the carriers operating independently.

Probably because of *Yorktown*'s bomb damage and the resulting reduced efficiency in air operations, Fletcher chose not to challenge Nimitz's instructions. However, in the lessons learned he submitted to Nimitz after the Battle of the Coral Sea he probably provided the best rationale for purposefully operating Task Force 16 and Task Force 17 independently. Responding to a letter from Samuel Eliot Morison questioning Fletcher on who set "Point Option" for aircrews on launching the first U.S. strike against the Japanese carriers at Midway, Fletcher provided his rationale for the command arrangement he adopted. Spruance had told Morison in a previous letter that "he [Spruance] did not set Point 'Option' except for his own carriers . . . and was not O.T.C. [Officer in Tactical Command] until after *Yorktown* had been abandoned and [Fletcher had] sent him the signal at about 1820 'Will conform to your movements.'"[81] Fletcher explained, "Spruance is right. When the *Yorktown* Task Force arrived on the eve of the battle I Automatically [*sic*] assumed command of all the task forces. However, due to the lack of time for drill, conferences, preparation of plans, organization, et cetera, the clumsy and illogical method [of exercising command] was adopted of leaving Spruance in command of his two task forces while I retained immediate command of the *Yorktown* task force and the whole tactical command."[82]

Naval War College Prof. Emeritus Capt. Frank Snyder, USN (Ret.), holds that the single most critical decision taken before or during the Battle of Midway was for Fletcher to go against his instincts and operate Task Force 17 independently of Task Force 16. Though as aviator Jimmy Thach asserts in his oral history,[83] this may have contributed to the loss of *Yorktown*, it provided the flexibility to strike the Japanese carriers while maintaining a reserve strike capacity aboard *Yorktown*, thus hedging against possible ambiguity in the initial locating information on the Japanese carriers. It also facilitated a combat air patrol posture that optimized the overall protection of the American combatants, and ultimately compounded the Japanese problem in determining exactly how many carriers opposed them. This in turn contributed to the survival of *Enterprise* and *Hornet*.

Other than the aircraft and Marines on Sand and Eastern Islands, this Striking Force, Task Force 16 and Task Force 17, was the only real opposition to the Japanese seizure of Midway. Its air groups were well trained, although the *Hornet* crew lacked combat experience in the Pacific. Nimitz placed these formations where they could either outflank and strike the Japanese forces or move into Aleutians waters in response to a concerted Japanese offensive. King directed Nimitz to oppose the Japanese forces by attrition tactics only and not to unduly risk carriers and cruisers. In compliance Nimitz directed his Striking Force commanders to be governed by the principle of calculated risk, avoiding exposure to attack by superior forces without a good prospect of inflicting greater damage to the enemy.

Aleutian Phase of the Operation

The first strike by the Japanese came on 3 June against Dutch Harbor and consisted of two sorties of aircraft. The first launched from 165 miles south and resulted in minimal damage to the military outpost there. One of the three fighters and nine bombers involved in the raid was lost, along with its pilot, who suffered a broken neck while crash-landing.[84] A second attack was conducted the same day against American destroyers sighted on the return from the first strike in Makushin Bay, on Unalaska Island near Dutch Harbor, but weather obscured the targets. Two Army P-40 Warhawk aircraft shot two more Japanese planes down on their way back and damaged another two beyond repair.[85]

The first attacks set the stage for an all-out offensive the next day.[86] Early on 4 June the Japanese unleashed nearly simultaneous air attacks against both Midway and Dutch Harbor. Theobald, the commander of Task Force 8, charged with the defense of Alaska from attack from the sea, estimated the relative weaknesses of his situation quite well preceding the Japanese attacks. A USNA graduate of the class of '07 and twice a graduate of the Naval War College, first as a commander in the senior class of 1930 and again as a captain with the advanced class of 1935,[87] he was well equipped to do this; he had also served in the War Plans directorate in Washington in the early 1930s.[88] Theobald was convinced that the Japanese would most likely attempt a landing in the Umnak-Dutch Harbor-Cold Bay area, with an ultimate objective of Kodiak or Kenai.[89] He therefore structured his plan of action around the former area. He stationed a group of nine destroyers that could be used as an attack force in Makushin Bay near Unalaska Island, and directed a group of four cruisers with a four-destroyer screen to take station in the southern approaches to Kodiak Island.[90] He had fighter aircraft at Fort Glenn for the immediate defense of Dutch Harbor, but his main line of defense was two groups of land-based bombers, at Fort Glenn on Umnak Island and at Fort Randall on Cold Bay.[91]

Here lay the problem with Theobald's plan, and he knew it. The near-constant daylight in the northern latitudes made stealthy movement and concealment of his resources almost impossible. Far more important, Theobald's surface units had to rely exclusively on land-based air support that was located at significant distances from the ships they would have to defend. Fighter aircraft were few, and the radius of the ships' action would be limited significantly in an attack role if they were to be supported by fighters. Moreover, at Coral Sea, the utility of Army Air Corps bombing against ships at sea had been demonstrated as minimal at best. The lack of sufficient and capable aircraft was further complicated by the existing aircraft's distance from the ships they would have to support.

To give some idea of Theobald's problem, while the westernmost island in the Alaskan chain, Attu, was only 650 miles from the Japanese air and naval base at Paramushiro in the Kuriles, it was 725 miles from Attu to Dutch Harbor and from there another 1,158 miles to Juneau, the Alaskan capital.[92] On 24 May Theobald asked King for more and better-suited naval aircraft, but the best King could do was to promise him additional search aircraft from the west coast of the continental United States—and these were released for Theobald's employment on 7 June, too late to be of any use.[93]

Theobald's plans, unfortunately, were rendered totally inadequate. The Japanese chose to employ two light carriers, *Ryujo* and *Junyo*, first to do as much damage as possible to Dutch Harbor, and second to land on Attu and Kiska and support an advance party at Adak. The Japanese attacked on 4 June at 1600, after Rear Adm. Kakuta, commander of the Second Carrier Striking Force, had canceled a strike ordered by Yamamoto against Adak due to fog. *Ryujo* and *Junyo* launched a strike of seventeen bombers and fifteen fighters against Dutch Harbor. The attack was successful, destroying four new, full 6,666-barrel fuel tanks and significantly damaging the hospital and a beached barracks ship. This time visibility allowed one of *Junyo*'s returning planes to spot the newly constructed U.S. airfield at Otter Point on Umnak Island, from which they had been attacked by P-40s the previous morning. Until this point the Japanese had been unaware of the existence of this base.

Around the time of the launch at 1600, Kakuta's force was ordered south by Admiral Yamamoto to rendezvous with Nagumo's force, and further operations for 4 June were curtailed. At 1930, however, Yamamoto changed his mind and "temporarily postponed" that order, indicating to Kakuta that the occupation of the Western Aleutians must go on as planned.[94]

After rejoining Hosogaya's Northern Force Main Body, Kakuta's carrier force supported the landings on American soil. Rear Adm. Sentaro Omori, commander of the Adak-Attu Occupation Force, landed some twelve thousand troops at Holtz Bay on Attu and marched overland to their objective, Chichagof, losing their way in the process. Their occupation was complete in three days, having overcome the thirty-nine Aleutes—fifteen of them children—and two American missionaries at Chichagof and taking them prisoner.[95] The Kiska occupation force also landed on 7 June, opposed only by ten men from the U.S. weather station there. They met no meaningful resistance.[96] The planned occupation of Adak was canceled, probably since it was only 350 miles from the newly discovered U.S. air base on Umnak Island.[97]

Thus the Japanese had gained a foothold on U.S. soil, and the Americans believed (incorrectly) that they would soon develop an air base on Kiska Island. In reality, they never built one, and only operated seaplanes out of Kiska. Yet this face-saving conquest fell far short of extending the Japanese defensive barrier a thousand miles to the east. At best Attu and Kiska would provide an outpost to detect any U.S. surface ship movement from the northeast toward Japan. But the islands would prove difficult to supply, and would be no use whatsoever in staging any meaningful attacks against the United States.

In the month following the Battle of Midway, Nimitz contemplated forming a new task force comprised of *Enterprise*, *Hornet*, and *Saratoga*, the latter having returned to Hawaii from the mainland, but decided against this move when the limited extent of the Japanese operations became clear. That was definitely a good decision, as Yamamoto in the meantime had augmented Hosogaya's force with the fleet carrier *Zuikaku* and the light carrier *Zuiho*. *Zuikaku*'s orders were canceled on 12 June; she never sailed, but if the Japanese had located a U.S. carrier force with its land-based search aircraft, she could have been sent to join a task force sent to intercept and destroy it. The United States did fly periodic bomber attacks against the Japanese outposts, but did little to deter the Japanese from maintaining their hold on them. In the week following the Japanese landings, both PBYs and Army Air Force bombers attempted to locate and sink ships of Hosogaya's force, but without avail. As Morison noted, "During the entire course of the war no Japanese carrier (so far as I can discover) was hit by a PBY, a B-26 or a B-17."[98] There was little reason to hope that they would do better in the cold and bad weather of the Aleutian chain.

Midway Preliminary Action

The first contact with the Japanese was made at 0904 on 3 June when a Midway search plane reported two Japanese cargo vessels bearing 247 degrees true at 470 miles.[99] At 0925 Simard, the air commander at Midway, received a report from another search plane: "Main body, distance 700 miles, bearing 262 degrees true, six large ships in column."[100] At 1100 this report was amplified to indicate the presence of eleven ships, course 090 degrees true, speed 19 knots. This contact was on the Transport Group of the Occupation Force.[101]

At 1200 six B17s took off from Midway to attack the Transport Group.[102] At 1640 they reported, "Attacking target."[103] Twenty-four 600-pound bombs were dropped.[104] Though the flight leader claimed hits on one battleship and a near-miss on another, no hits were actually made in this high-level bombing on maneuvering targets.[105] However, the attack on the Transport Group caused the two commanders of the Japanese carrier groups, Nagumo and Yamaguchi, to make critical decisions regarding the number of fighter aircraft employed for defense and for escort and protection of their attacking air groups. At 2115 a second attack consisting of four radar-equipped Catalina PBY 5A airplanes each armed with one torpedo was launched from Midway.[106]

During this time Task Force 16 maintained its station about ten miles south of Task Force 17, approximately three hundred miles from Midway. Fletcher, in *Yorktown*, also received the two contact reports on the Japanese formations. Given his strategic and operational priorities, he decided these contacts were not important enough to expose his own position.[107] Fletcher was waiting for the Japanese carriers to be located. He launched an afternoon search without result. At 0001 on 4 June the U.S. Striking Force was approximately 270 miles northeast of Midway. All submarines excepting *Cuttlefish*, which was closing on Midway, were ready for contact with the enemy. But the Japanese Striking Force with its four carriers was not sighted at any time on 3 June.

Naval Air Station Midway 4 June Operations

At 0207 on 4 June the four Catalina PBYs that had departed Midway to attack the Transport Group of the Japanese Occupation Force sighted at 0925 on the previous day made contact with that force at a range of five hundred nautical miles on a bearing 260 degrees from Midway.[108] This group of ships had covered two hundred nautical miles since first sighted and was on the same approximate course, 080 degrees true at thirteen knots. Three of the four Catalinas attacked, but made only one torpedo hit, on the tanker *Akebono Maru*, and returned to Midway without damage.[109] This attack demonstrated for the first time the practicability of using long-range shore-based aircraft equipped with radar to deliver unsupported night torpedo attacks or low-altitude bombing attacks against ships.

At 0520 a Midway PBY reported, "Aircraft sighted."[110] At 0545 the same plane reported the most important contact of the battle, a carrier, 180 miles from Midway.[111] Then in plain English from PBY 3V58 came the feared message, "Many planes heading Midway, IMI Midway [repeat Midway], bearing 320, distant 150."[112] The air raid sirens sounded and all operable planes began to take off. All planes were directed to attack the Japanese carriers except the twenty-three fighter planes, which were ordered to defend Midway and were airborne by 0600.[113]

The fighter director broke the fighters into two groups. They discovered the Japanese bombers in three rigid V formations escorted by thirty-six fighters.[114] The Americans were outnumbered and outmaneuvered by the superior Japanese Zero fighters. All the Marine pilots were awed by the performance of this Japanese fighter, claiming it had 20 percent more speed, climb, and maneuverability than their own F4F-3 Wildcats.[115] The Marine fighters reported that they destroyed twenty-three bombers and eight fighters—a huge claim against a foe with such an admitted advantage.[116]

Nagumo's Attack on Midway

At 0430, the break of dawn on 4 June, at 240 miles from Midway the Mobile Force attack group of 36 fighters, 36 bombers, and 36 torpedo planes—a total of 108 planes—departed for Midway.[117] Nagumo allotted about 50 percent of his carrier-based planes to this attack (229 aircraft were embarked), keeping a second striking group in standby conditions for use against surface ships. Figures 14 and 15 show the number of each type of aircraft embarked on the Japanese carriers and the way in which Admiral Nagumo elected to use them in his first and contemplated second strike against Midway. Nagumo assigned roughly half the fighter aircraft from each of his carriers for each strike, but all of *Akagi* and *Kaga*'s bombers and all of *Hiryu* and *Soryu*'s torpedo planes to the first strike, and the reverse for the second strike. This was indeed an odd combination, and it reduced Nagumo's flexibility considerably during the battle.

Although Nagumo's intelligence indicated that there was no American carrier force in the area, he did not trust this information fully. Immediately after his attack groups had departed he sent out seven search planes from his accompanying cruisers. The search was not dense enough to cover all the entire area beyond 150 miles from the Mobile Force, however, and therefore inadequate to ensure the detection of enemy forces. Using carrier aircraft

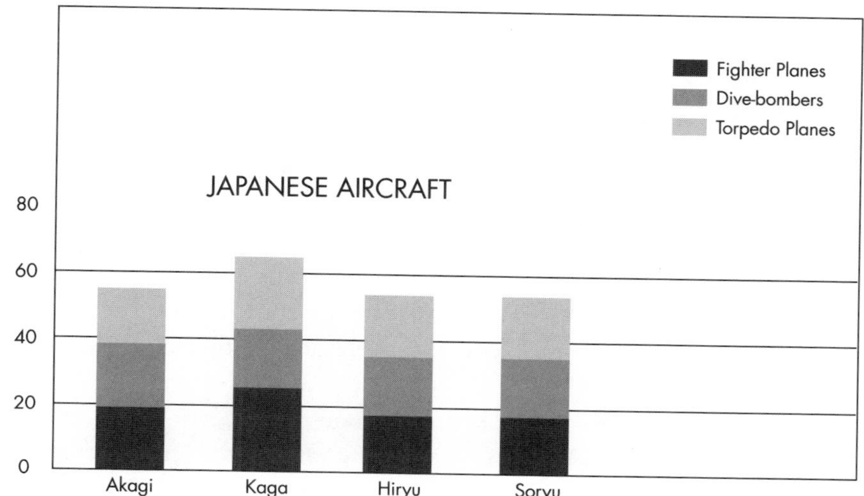

FIGURE 14. Aircraft, by type, available aboard Japanese carriers at Midway. —*Courtesy of U.S. Naval War College*

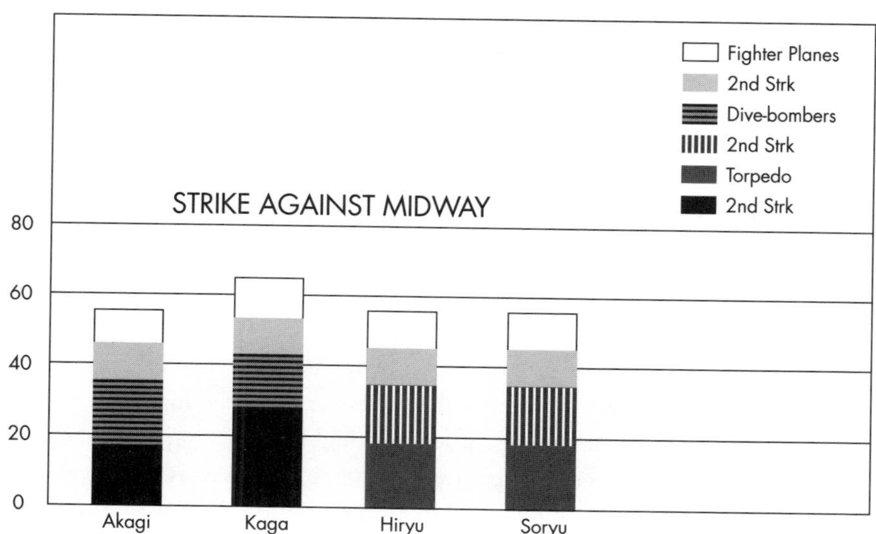

FIGURE 15. Aircraft assigned to attack Midway by Vice Adm. Nagumo. —*Courtesy of U.S. Naval War College*

to augment the search (Nagumo used the only two available—one from *Akagi* and one from *Kaga* specifically designated for this purpose) would have further reduced the number of bombers available to attack should an American carrier force be located. It was the Japanese practice to use only battleship and cruiser aircraft in the search role. Since all Japanese bombers were either in the air—most having already expended their ordnance—or were embarked with bombs configured for use against land targets for the second attack contemplated against Midway, a more comprehensive search was not possible. Yet a more adequate search posture using carrier aircraft would have appreciably increased the likelihood of the Japanese carrier force's survival.

Moreover, Nagumo did not order a second-cycle search—a serious and perhaps fatal mistake. Nagumo's search aircraft had a decided advantage in range over those of his American counterparts, except, of course, for the flying boats from Midway, from which he could maintain necessary separation. Exploiting this advantage could have given him as much as one hundred nautical miles' advantage in strike range if the U.S. carriers were located on the outer edge of the search pattern. Failure to take full advantage of the design characteristics of his embarked search and attack aircraft (including those on attached cruisers) was an unconscionable mistake by Nagumo, regardless of the absence of intelligence indicating the presence of U.S. carriers in his vicinity.

Tone's No. 4 search plane did not depart promptly. The launching of seaplanes from the cruiser *Tone* on the number four search line was delayed by thirty minutes. This late launching has often been cited as one of the possible causes of the Japanese failure at Midway. Through an elaborate reconstruction of the events, author Jon Parshall has convincingly established that *Tone*'s late-departing aircraft may well have made contact only because it abbreviated its search pattern, due probably to its late takeoff. Thus luck played an important part in this battle for both the Americans and the Japanese.

Early contact in carrier operations is highly important. Apparently Nagumo did not wish his search planes to be sighted before his attack groups struck a surprise blow at Midway. Though his decision did involve a tradeoff between remaining undetected and locating any U.S. carriers that might have been in the area, and his intelligence supported his actions, the choice for stealth was definitely not worth the huge strike-distance advantage Nagumo would have had if a properly organized dual-cycle search had located the American carriers before they located him.

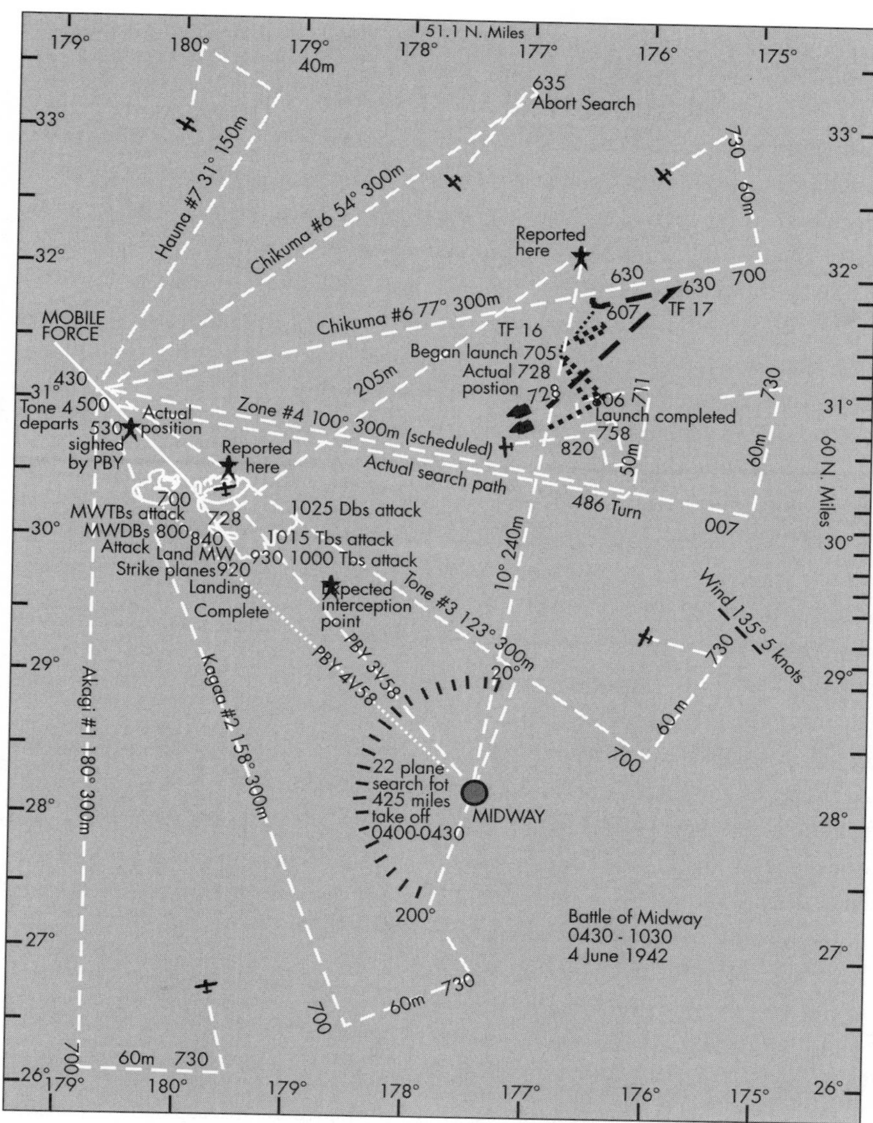

FIGURE 16. Nagumo's search for the American carriers. —*Courtesy of U.S. Naval War College*

At 0552 4V58, a flying boat from Midway, reported "two carriers and main body ships, carriers in front, course 135, speed 25."[118] The American PBY had found the Mobile Force. At 0619 the Japanese air attack approaching Midway from 045 degrees true was intercepted by American Marine fighters.[119] At 0635 the Japanese air raid on Midway started.[120] After shooting down most of the American planes, the Japanese bombed Eastern and Sand Islands, reducing Midway's effectiveness as a base. The Americans on Midway claimed ten Japanese bombers destroyed and four damaged, as well as four fighters shot down and two damaged at a loss of fifteen out of twenty-two Marine planes shot down.[121] The Japanese reported only six total planes lost,[122] and claimed that they had shot down or destroyed on the deck forty-one American fighters, one bomber, and one float reconnaissance plane.[123]

At 0645 the flight commander of the Japanese Midway strike, Lt. Joichi Tomonaga, reported, "We have completed our attack and are homeward bound." At 0700 he reported, "There is necessity for carrying out a second attack wave."[124] At 0710, as the Midway bombers' attack on the Japanese carriers provided all the evidence required of the need for a second attack, the American carriers *Enterprise* and *Hornet* started launching their aircraft for the attack on the Japanese carrier force.[125] Nagumo, of course, was not aware of this.

Tomonaga's call forced Nagumo to make a decision that affected the outcome of the entire battle. He had been advised that another attack was required on Midway. His search planes—now 200 to 250 miles away—had not reported any enemy contact. Half of the planes remaining on his four carriers were standing by armed with torpedoes ready to attack enemy surface units. Aircraft from the first attack on Midway would soon return and require rearming and refueling. Since it seemed there were no American surface forces in the area, Nagumo concluded that it would be necessary to attack Midway again to neutralize its defenses. At 0715 he gave the order, "Planes in second attack wave stand by to carry out attack today. Re-equip yourself with bombs." This decision to change the load of the ninety-three planes Nagumo had ready to attack U.S. carrier forces to bombs configured for a second strike on Midway was most unfortunate for the Japanese.[126] All carriers were unprepared for immediate action.

At 0728, thirteen minutes after the rearming order, Nagumo received a message from the *Tone* seaplane (*Tone* 4) that had been launched a half hour late: "Ten enemy surface ships, in position bearing 010 degrees true, distance 240 miles from Midway, course 150 true, speed over twenty knots."[127] This was the first report of an American surface force. At 0745 Nagumo issued the order, "Prepare to carry out attacks on enemy fleet units. Leave torpedoes on the attack planes which have not as yet been changed to bombs."[128] But Nagumo could not launch an immediate attack because of the rearming order. To the *Tone* search plane he sent the order, "Ascertain types of ships and maintain contact."[129] Here was a situation that challenged his basic plan. If there were carriers with the force, the Japanese situation required immediate action.

At 0755 the Mobile Force was attacked for the second time by sixteen scout bombers from Midway and again at 0810 by fourteen B17s. The Japanese recorded that no hits were made, but Nagumo was forced to make the most fateful decisions of the battle under almost constant attack.

The amplifying report "The enemy is accompanied by what appears to be a carrier" was received from the *Tone* seaplane at 0820, and on getting amplifying information, Nagumo advised Yamamoto that the enemy was present, "composed of one carrier, five cruisers and five destroyers . . . bearing 010 degrees, distance 240 miles from Midway," and the Mobile Force was heading toward them.[130] At 0824 a submarine—the *Nautilus*—was sighted.[131] At 0827 eleven Marine scout bombers made a fourth attack, but once again no hits were made.[132] Nagumo landed the last of his Midway strike aircraft at 0918, changed course to close the enemy, and went to battle speed.[133]

Why this delay of one hour and fifty minutes after the original contact? Nagumo should have contemplated at 0728 why an American force was operating north-northeast of Midway unless it was supporting carrier operations. The answer appears to be that Nagumo realized an all-out first-blow air strike against the U.S. carriers was urgent, but between 0705 and 0830 his Mobile Force was under attack by Midway planes. Between 0738 and 0918 he was recovering planes of the Midway strike. They were low on fuel. They had to be stuck below, in accordance with Japanese doctrine and carrier construction.[134] Planes for the next attack had to be brought up and spotted on deck. This took time—especially when the force was under attack. The frenetic pace and operational realities precluded good judgment from Nagumo.

Much has been made of the timeline for Nagumo's decisions regarding the immediacy of the requirement to strike the reported U.S. carrier. Many historians contend that it was allowing himself to be caught with the airplanes he had ordered configured for a second strike against Midway Island—and his resultant inability to have them change their ordnance loads to be more appropriately suited for the anticarrier mission—that was the critical lapse in Nagumo's decision process, resulting in the loss of all four of his carriers. Others, such as author Dallas Isom, make an excellent case that changing aircraft ordnance loads from torpedoes to bombs took much longer than anyone in the West has recognized, and that consequently Nagumo has been unfairly criticized for lack of good judgment. Isom argues that Nagumo was more the victim of circumstances beyond his control than a flawed commander who lacked resolve.[135] Nagumo's real failure was his lack of attention to retaining enough fighter aircraft both to accompany an attack on the American carriers that might oppose him and still defend his carriers adequately against a possible American attack. Certainly Yamaguchi, his commander of the Second Carrier Division in *Hiryu* and an officer of flair and decision, widely appreciated for his samurai spirit, recommended to Nagumo in the strongest terms that a strike against what was believed to be a single U.S. carrier should be launched immediately and without fighter escort if necessary. Perhaps Frank Snyder evaluated Nagumo's failure best when he said, "I'm convinced that Nagumo just wasn't about to take advice from a 'plebe' admiral!" Such arrogance and intransigence under fire on Nagumo's part makes a lot of sense.

In any case, though it is roundly considered the fatal decision by the Japanese in the battle, in reality getting caught with aircraft rearming did very little to ensure the destruction of the *kido butai*. Regardless of the many books written dissecting the timeline for Nagumo's decisions during the critical rearming phase, the fact remains that the American strike against the carriers had already been launched from *Enterprise* and *Hornet*, commencing at 0701. Regardless of the exact time Nagumo became aware of the presence of a U.S. carrier or of what was taking place on the decks of his carriers, the American air strikes against him had already been set in motion. The best the Japanese could have hoped for was the destruction of all three of the American carriers that would ultimately be revealed (they actually only found one)—a worst-case scenario for the United States in which all aircraft involved in the strike against the Japanese Mobile Force would have to land at Midway or ditch at sea if they ran out of fuel. Though this would have seriously affected the strategic balance of naval power in the Pacific until more U.S. carriers started to join the fleet in the summer of 1943, the outcome of the Battle of Midway—and its overall strategic consequences for the Japanese, including the loss of critical aircraft and irreplaceable pilots—would have remained essentially the same.

FIGURE 17. Aerial view of Midway Islands, with the runway on Eastern Island in the foreground and Sand Island to the rear. —*Courtesy of U.S. Naval Institute Photo Archive*

Prior to the attacks, Captain Simard at Midway had prepared for the expected bombardment. He had cleared his airfield. His battle stations were manned. At 0632 the first bomb fell on Eastern Island. Thirteen more bombs followed. Others hit Sand Island, where the command center of the Naval Air Station's commanding officer was located. The island defense batteries and motor torpedo boats gallantly attempted to repel the attack, but between twenty-one and twenty-seven Japanese bombers and thirty-six fighter planes got through.[136] The power plant on Eastern Island was demolished, cutting electrical supply. Gas lines from the main gasoline storage area were broken. Direct hits were made on one rearming pit, the Marine command post, and the mess hall on Eastern Island. There were numerous casualties to ground personnel. With only three operable fighters to defend Midway and believing he would be bombarded by surface vessels at sunset, Simard decided to evacuate all remaining search planes and all personnel not considered essential to the continued operation of the Naval Air Station.[137]

At 0706 the Japanese carrier group sighted the first two attack groups from Midway:[138] four Marauder B26s and six Avenger torpedo bombers, each armed with a torpedo.[139] The six Navy torpedo planes ran into the vanguard of Japanese fighters attacking Midway, climbed to four thousand feet above the cloud level, and escaped. On reaching the Mobile Force, they dived through the clouds for the carriers. Approaching at a low altitude, they failed to hit any Japanese ships. Five of the six were shot down.[140] The B26 group sighted the Mobile Force about the same time. Two B26s released torpedoes at a carrier without hits. Each ship maneuvered individually. Only two of the four returned to Midway, and they were badly shot up. This was the first time in history that Army planes had attacked warships with torpedoes.[141] Japanese antiaircraft fire had knocked down seven of the ten American planes.[142] Though Nagumo did not yet know it, at that moment Task Force 16 was at a position bearing 065 degrees true and 175 nautical miles from the Mobile Force, and had begun launching a strike from the *Enterprise* and *Hornet*.[143]

The leader of the Marine dive-bomber group, Maj. Lofton R. Henderson,* divided his twenty-eight planes into two groups. When he sighted the Mobile Force he decided on a glide-bombing attack because of the obsolescence of some of his planes and lack of dive-bomb training. No hits were scored. Twelve of the bombers failed to return.[144] The B17s that had been instructed to attack the Occupation Force were ordered to alter their course for the enemy carriers. They attacked from twenty thousand to twenty-three thousand feet. The Japanese recorded no hits on the Japanese ships by the Flying Fortresses, which were undamaged.[145] In these morning air attacks from Midway, there was no fighter support and attacks were uncoordinated, with no air group strike commander assigned. Yet the attacks from Midway were critical to the U.S. cause even though they made no hits on the Japanese Mobile Force.

The five separate and uncoordinated attacks from aircraft from Midway Island put the Japanese Mobile Force constantly in harm's way. However ineffectual their bombing, they represented a threat the Japanese had to contend with. They also caused Nagumo to allocate his scarce remaining aircraft, having already committed 108 planes to the attack on Midway, to defend his four carriers. At this point Nagumo had only three ship-based fighters and eighteen attack planes aboard his flagship *Akagi*, three fighters and twenty-seven attack planes aboard *Kaga*, three fighters and eighteen bombers aboard *Hiryu*, and three fighters and eighteen bombers on *Soryu* ready for action.[146] This further reduced his options for constituting a strike against the American

*Maj. Lofton R. Henderson was shot down and killed in this attack. On 8 August 1942, Maj. Gen. Alexander A. Vandegrift named the field on Guadalcanal taken by his Marines "Henderson Field" in honor of him.

carrier force. With only twelve fighter aircraft remaining on board his carriers, he simply did not have enough to provide either protection for his four carriers or to send a strike group against the American carriers—and certainly not for both. The decisions made about these allocations proved the critical element of the battle.

Midway Carrier Action of 4 June 1942

A side-by-side comparison of the forces at Midway is revealing. The Japanese had the greater number of carriers, four to three; the Japanese had two fast battleships, with sixteen 14-inch guns, the Americans had none; the Americans had more cruisers, eight to three; more destroyers, fourteen to twelve; and more submarines, nineteen to fifteen. The Japanese had a greater number of units with 6-inch guns; both sides had insufficient antiaircraft heavy machine guns. The Americans had a higher task force speed capability, whereas the Japanese had a more balanced fast-carrier task force and a more balanced air striking force.

As for aircraft, the Japanese had 229 carrier-based planes (108 of which had been launched in the 0430 attack on Midway), the Americans 227, though American fighters and torpedo planes were of inferior design. The Americans had a greater number of planes embarked on cruisers, 28 to 14. The Americans also had 110 land-based aircraft for search, reconnaissance, and attack; the Japanese had none except the limited land-based search and reconnaissance from Wake Island.

The American plane models had wildly different speeds and ranges—a decided weakness—while the Japanese had a more homogenous design of planes, permitting several types to be employed tactically as one unit. The American torpedo planes were slow. The American fighter performance was inferior. The Japanese had no self-sealing fuel tanks and less aircraft armor. American torpedo characteristics were poor. The Americans possessed shipboard radar, giving them an important advantage in locating incoming hostile aircraft and vectoring their limited combat air patrol fighters to appropriate locations; the Japanese did not. The Americans could direct fighters using radar and automatic homing equipment on carriers. The Americans had the advantage of being nearer to a major fleet base and logistics support.

The Americans occupied a flanking position, which would enable them to withdraw if necessary and placed the Japanese between American carriers and Midway, essentially giving the enemy a critically placed fourth "carrier"

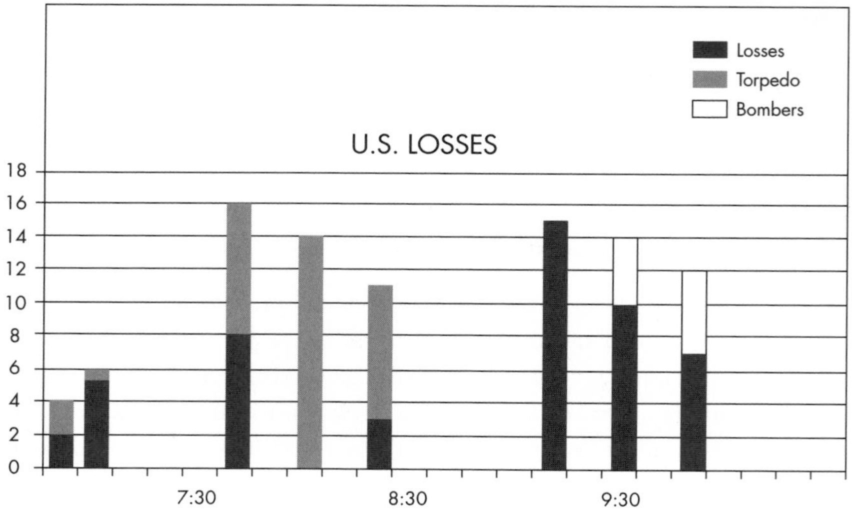

FIGURE 18. Midway air strikes (and U.S. Carrier Torpedo Squadron strikes). —*Courtesy of U.S. Naval War College*

to deal with. This complicated the Japanese decision-making process greatly, as they not only had to defend on two flanks simultaneously, they also had to prioritize their attacks against multiple targets located in opposite directions. The Americans also had superior intelligence and an element of surprise. Yet they were at a disadvantage in their failure to concentrate antiaircraft and fighter defense due to the separation of their two carrier task forces.

The independent American task forces (TF-16 and TF-17) operated under different sets of cruising instructions. These task forces had not operated together prior to this time, unlike the Japanese *kido butai*, which had operated as a unit in every important operation since Pearl Harbor. Moreover, the commander of Task Force 16, Spruance, was a cruiser commander without aviation experience who had just replaced Halsey; Spruance and his air staff had to interact without the security of knowing each other's expectations and preferred operational methods. The *Hornet* air group was new and lacked previous battle experience—a significant and soon–demonstrated shortcoming. The *Yorktown* air group was a composite group from three carriers (*Yorktown*, *Lexington*, and *Saratoga*, which had left most of its air wing in Hawaii while undergoing repairs in Puget Sound) and had never operated as a unit. The Japanese pilots had more combat experience. The results of these asymmetries would be telling. The outcome of the battle hinged on the respective abilities of the commanders to make decisions optimizing their respective strengths and minimizing their vulnerabilities.

Clash of Titans

Fletcher's calculation was that the enemy carrier force would come from the northwest and attack Midway at about dawn on 4 June 1942. His selected position for launching at 0430 would place him on the eastern flank of the enemy's daylight launching position. Fletcher hoped to avoid detection until after the Japanese attack groups had been committed to Midway. He would strike before they could return to refuel and rearm. Fletcher recognized, however, that should the enemy advance on Midway from the north or east, the Japanese would not be between his force and Midway. He would be between the enemy and Midway and open to initial attack.

After he joined Task Force 17 with Task Force 16 on 2 June at 32° 04' N and 172° 45' W, Fletcher directed his Striking Force to proceed to a point two hundred miles north of Midway, with Task Force 16 operating ten miles south of Task Force 17, in anticipation of action.[147] When in position on 4 June, he decided on a dawn search from *Yorktown* in the northern semicircle to a radius of one hundred miles and launched a combat air patrol.[148] This radius, added to his task forces' distance from Midway, would cover the attack radius of the Japanese planes. He also decided to maintain *Enterprise* and *Hornet* in standby condition, pilots in ready rooms and planes spotted on deck for immediate launching.[149]

At 0534 on 4 June *Enterprise* copied the transmission "enemy carriers" from a Midway search aircraft.[150] At 0545 Spruance's command intercepted a report to Midway from a patrol plane stating, "Many planes heading Midway bearing 320, distance 150." At 0552, "Two carriers and battleships bearing 320 degrees, distance 180 nautical miles [from Midway], course 135 degrees, speed twenty-five knots." At 0600 Spruance began to turn to the west in anticipation of attack orders. Seven minutes later Fletcher directed Spruance to "proceed to the southwest and attack enemy carriers when definitely located."[151] The caveat Fletcher attached to this order surely emanated form his experience with flawed reconnaissance aircraft intelligence reports at Coral Sea.

At 0614 Spruance changed course to 240 degrees true and headed for the enemy contact at 25 knots with combat patrol overhead and his air groups ready for takeoff.[152] He was now faced with a vital decision. His informa-

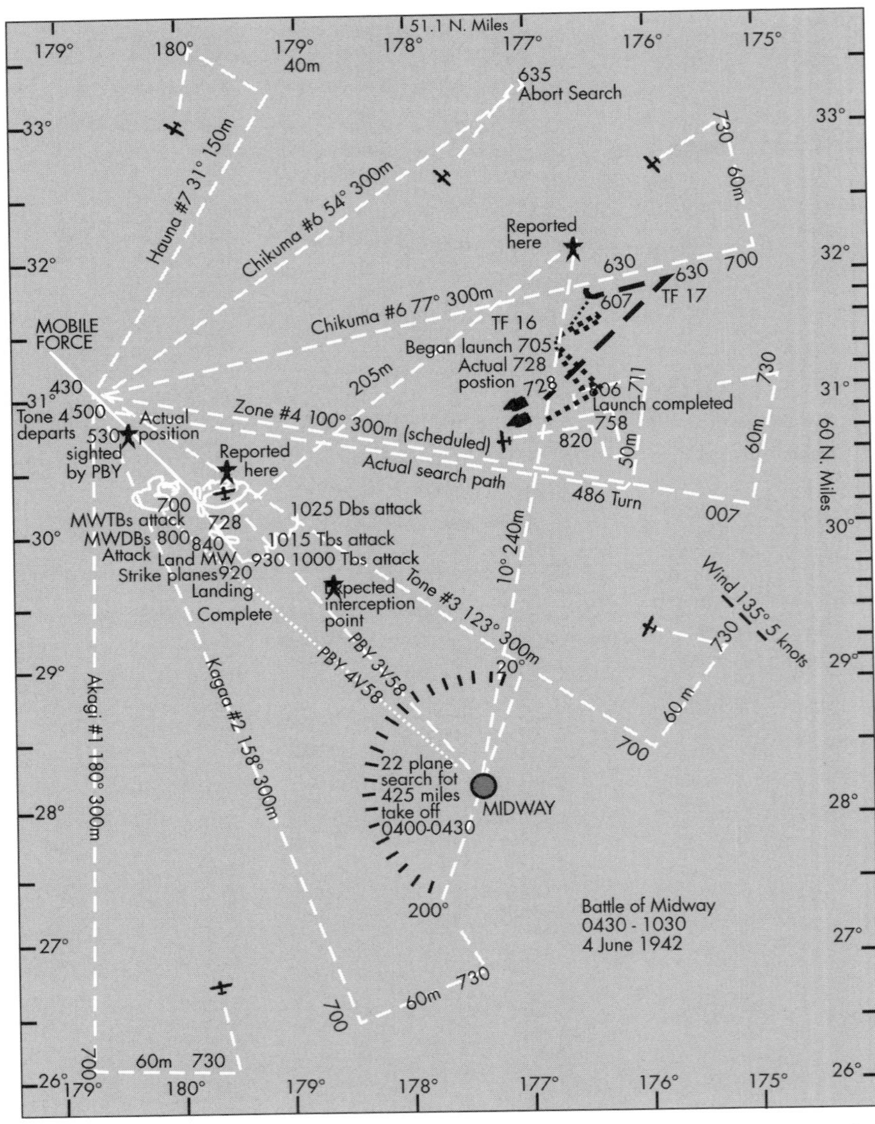

FIGURE 19. Launching points for American carriers in the Battle of Midway —*Courtesy of U.S. Naval War College*

tion indicated that the enemy was located at 247 degrees true, distance 175 miles.[153] His problem was whether his aircraft should launch now at the extreme range of his torpedo planes, or wait until range had been shortened and more reports about enemy strength and position were available. By delaying, it was possible that his formation might lose the advantage of striking first. One consideration weighing heavy on Spruance's mind and reinforced by the events of the Coral Sea was the possibility that the reported position of the enemy carriers was incorrect and that the Japanese attack on Midway might be diverted against him. He was also concerned that his presence was known to the enemy and that his attack groups might break radio silence when launched. Having estimated the situation and weighed his options, Spruance took the calculated risk and delayed launching. It was a courageous decision that paid off handsomely.

At 0700, without further verification of the location of the enemy carriers reported by the Midway search planes, Spruance estimated them at approximately 155 nautical miles distant. In fact the reported position was in error. The Japanese were 40 miles northwest of their reported position.[154] Spruance had separated his task force into two formations so that the carriers could operate individually in case of air attacks. Capt. Mark A. Mitscher* in *Hornet* commanded the second. Mindful of the Coral Sea experience, Spruance separated his task force before any attack rather than having it break apart during one. He started launching from both the *Enterprise* and *Hornet* at 0706 and set their "Point Option" course for recovery as 240 degrees true, speed twenty-five knots.[155]

The *Enterprise* dive-bombers were the first to depart. Since there was a delay with the torpedo planes and their accompanying fighters, Spruance ordered the *Enterprise* dive-bombers to proceed on the mission assigned unescorted by fighter aircraft. The *Enterprise* dive-bombers thus departed at 0752 on a heading of 231 degrees true.[156] This move is open to questioning, as it prevented coordinated bombing and torpedo attacks, which was accepted doctrine at the time. It is possible that Spruance realized that the Japanese Midway Attack Group was soon due back at the Mobile Force and would be refueled, rearmed, and launched again. He wanted to catch as many Japanese

---

*Capt. Mark Mitscher had been selected for rear admiral and his relief as captain of *Hornet* was already onboard when Mitscher was ordered to Midway. In that he was heading for a new assignment, he was probably aware that this could well be his only opportunity to make his mark in combat.

planes on deck as possible. Once again Spruance took a calculated risk to optimize his chance of catching the Japanese Air Wings in the process of rearming on deck. In his After Action Report Fletcher would highlight the importance of hitting the opposing Japanese carriers while their planes were on the deck rather than just hitting the carrier's deck irrespective of the deck load.[157]

The *Enterprise* torpedo squadron (VT-6), noting that the *Enterprise* fighter squadron (VF-6) did not join in formation with them, decided to proceed independently and departed at 0806.[158] The *Enterprise* fighters inadvertently joined with the torpedo planes of the *Hornet* (VT-8) air group, which also departed at 0806.[159] The planes had no markings, identification was difficult, and they were launched at the same time. Thus the *Hornet* air group was escorted by her own fighters and also by those of *Enterprise*. Since bombers must gain altitude and the torpedo planes could not climb over ten thousand feet when armed, the groups unfortunately became separated. If these groups could have proceeded together, the dive-bombers of both carriers might have been combined into one attack group and the torpedo planes into another, with a fighter escort available for each group. This fragmentation and lack of coordination, however, was precisely what made the American attack so successful.

At 0645 *Yorktown* recovered the dawn search planes, which had not located the enemy.[160] Fletcher changed course to 225 degrees true, speed twenty-five knots, to close the enemy. Fletcher now realized that he had to make an important decision. He believed, from available intelligence and based in part on the unreliability of his own pilots' reports from the Coral Sea action, that there were four or five carriers in the Japanese force. Only two had been located. Attack against these two carriers was now imminent by aircraft from Task Force 16, and Fletcher was faced with the problem of deciding whether to reinforce that attack or to wait for information on the possible existence and location of other enemy carriers. Fletcher decided to withhold launching. He may have remembered his experience in the Coral Sea, where the Japanese nearly surprised him. And although he may have believed that it is generally best to throw all available forces at the enemy, as established during war games at the Naval War College, in this case he refrained from doing so.

However, after careful consideration Fletcher realized that to leave the flight decks of two or three enemy carriers undamaged was to invite destruction of his own force. Therefore, at 0838, with no further enemy contacts reported, he decided to reinforce the air groups of Task Force 16 by launching half of his bombers and all of his torpedo planes with fighter support.[161] He directed that the remaining bombers be brought from the hanger deck and readied for attack on additional carriers should they be discovered. Interestingly, this decision to withhold part of his forces was similar to that of Nagumo during his first attack wave on Midway Island. The critical element of this decision, however, had been taken before the battle. Due to Fletcher's recommendation in his After Action Report from the Battle of the Coral Sea, the Midway carriers' fighter complement had been increased from twelve and twenty (thirty-two total on two carriers)[162] to twenty-seven on each carrier,[163] making the allocation decision between defense and strike much easier. This factor alone probably enabled successful defense of Task Force 16 during the battle.

Operations of the *Hornet* Air Group on 4 June

On their way to attack the enemy, the *Hornet* bombing (VB-8) and scouting (VS-8) squadrons flew at twenty thousand feet with their own fighters and those of *Enterprise* in close proximity. The torpedo squadron (VT-8) flew at fifteen hundred feet, beneath the cloud level. Visual contact between them was lost. At 0920 the commander of Torpedo Squadron 8, Lt. Cdr. John C. Waldron, sighted the Japanese carriers to the northwest.[164] He did not report this. Torpedo Squadron 8 headed for the southernmost carrier but was met by the full fury of the Japanese Zeros, drawn down to fifteen hundred feet from their higher-level combat air patrol stations. All fifteen of the slow, cumbersome torpedo planes were shot down.[165] The only survivor, Ens. George H. Gay, launched his torpedo before going down. Ensign Gay survived by shrewdly keeping the seat cushion from his plane over his head, remaining undetected while he watched the Japanese carriers steam by.

Meanwhile, the commander of Fighter Squadron 6 of the *Enterprise*, Lt. James S. Gray Jr., was circling at a high altitude. Clouds prevented him from seeing the fate of Torpedo Squadron 8. He had prearranged with his own Torpedo Squadron 6 that he would respond to a radio call for help. Apparently he had heard no call for help. Still believing he would find enemy fighters at high altitude, he wished to keep an altitude advantage. Presumably, he also believed that by drawing out and engaging the enemy fighters at altitude, he would *de facto* accomplish his primary mission of protecting his torpedo planes and in addition afford protection to the dive-bombers. He reported the composition of the enemy force as two carriers, two battleships, and eight destroyers on a course to the north with no apparent combat air patrol.[166] When he ran short of fuel he returned to *Enterprise* without taking part in the action.

Also at 0920, Torpedo Squadron 8 off *Hornet* sighted the Japanese carriers, but the commander of the *Hornet* air group, Cdr. Stanhope C. Ring, with the dive-bombers and Fighter Squadron 8, failed to see them. Ring was well aware of the fact that he had reached the estimated point of interception. He was faced with the serious problem of finding the enemy. Unfortunately the reasons for his subsequent actions remain unknown and therefore the following analysis is based on the doctrine in force at the time and conjecture.

From Ring's point of view, there were several possibilities. One was that the reported enemy position was in error; a second was that the enemy's estimated course and speed was incorrect; a third was that his own navigation was off because of the effect of drift.[167] Historians John Lundstrom and Frank Snyder are convinced that Ring had been briefed by Mitscher that the Japanese would be operating in two separated groups of carriers, as was the accepted practice in the U.S. Navy at the time, and that the second group would be operating at some distance—probably around twenty nautical miles—behind the first. Thus Ring had been directed to proceed directly to the second expected group of carriers.[168] When they weren't sighted, Ring probably turned toward the expected position of the two carriers that had actually been located. In any of these events, the prescribed procedure was to fly an expanding square. Instead he headed south, assuming that direction was as logical as any. This decision is questionable. Ring did not allow for the enemy slowing to launch and recover planes or to avoid air attacks. He thereby failed to locate the enemy. Some of his planes reached Midway and some were forced down at sea—fifteen ultimately returned to *Hornet*.[169] Ring appropriately earned his place in history as the "goat" of the Midway campaign.

Operations of the *Enterprise* Air Group on 4 June

Lt. Cdr. Eugene E. Lindsey, commander of Torpedo Squadron 6 of the *Enterprise*, sighted the enemy at 0930.[170] Without waiting for the dive-bombers, which by doctrine were supposed to precede him, he attacked. He divided his squadron into two formations for a coordinated approach. The squadron made no hits. Twenty-five Japanese fighters attacked repeatedly. Ten of the fourteen torpedo planes were shot down.[171]

Though the attacks by the *Hornet* and *Enterprise* torpedo planes were unsuccessful, they drew the Japanese fighters from high to low altitudes, permitting the successful bombing attacks that followed. They also caused the Japanese Zero fighters to burn enough fuel to prevent their return to altitude to engage the U.S. bombers. Spread out in chase of the U.S. torpedo planes, the Japanese Zeros soon expended all or most of the sixty rounds they carried for each of their two 20-mm cannons. From the deck it would take the Zeros seven minutes and twenty-seven seconds to climb to the twelve-thousand-foot attack altitude of the incoming U.S. Dauntlesses. At the nominal thirteen-mile maximum visual range experienced that day, an incoming SDB at slightly under its maximum speed of 256 knots would be in its dive in slightly over four minutes. Once in their dives, the Dauntlesses were virtually unstoppable. Thus, even if they were organized to respond to a high-altitude bomber attack—which they were not—the Zeros simply couldn't climb fast enough to engage the incoming dive-bombers. The fate of the *kido butai* was sealed.

When the *Enterprise* Dauntless dive-bombers reached the expected interception point, Lt. Cdr. Clarence Wade McClusky, the air group commander, discovered no enemy fighter aircraft in the vicinity. McClusky reasoned that the assumed enemy carrier speed of advance could not exceed twenty knots, because the carriers would have to maneuver to recover their air groups as well as to avoid the attacking planes from Midway. He therefore concluded that the Japanese must be to the north, and flew an expanding square, as prescribed by existing doctrine. Turning to make the third leg of the square, he sighted a destroyer below him heading northeast at high speed. This was the *Arashi*, which had paused to drop a depth charge on the submarine *Nautilus*.[172] A few minutes later, at 1005, the Mobile Force was sighted and the problem was over.

McClusky's were the most important decisions made by an airborne tactical commander in the Battle of Midway. He approached at nineteen thousand feet, noting four carriers. He decided to lead his sixteen scout bombers against the carrier ahead and to his left, *Kaga*, and directed the fifteen dive-bombers of VB-6, commanded by Lt. R. H. Best, to strike the carrier to their right, *Akagi*. Each squadron divided into three sections of five aircraft each in attack divisions of Vs and columns to protect against fighters until the push-over point. The air group commander, McClusky, turned toward his target, split his flaps, and entered his dive. Successive planes of the first division of dive-bombers repeated the maneuver. There was no fighter opposition, little antiaircraft fire, and the attack was a surprise. The carrier *Akagi* was hit, and burst into flames.[173]

The second squadron, composed of scout bombers armed with the lighter 500-pound bombs, attacked *Kaga*, scoring several hits.[174] They were aided by the second division of dive-bombers and in combination set the *Kaga* afire.[175] The third division of dive-bombers attacked both carriers.[176] The *Enterprise* bombers retired at low levels through gaps in the Japanese screening force. They departed toward Midway to deceive the enemy and then turned toward Point Option, their designated rendezvous point for landing on *Enterprise*. Eighteen bombers failed to return to the *Enterprise*, but four of these landed on the *Yorktown*. Some landed in the water because Task Force 16 could not close Point Option, the predicted position of the carrier on their return. Task Force 16 was about sixty miles northeast of its intended position on account of having to reverse its expected course of 240 degrees true into the diminishing wind to launch aircraft. After doing a circular search, Wade McClusky landed with only two gallons of aviation gasoline left in his tanks. Four to seven planes of his squadron were among those lost due to fuel exhaustion.[177]

Why Spruance failed to inform his returning groups that he was not at Point Option is not clear.[178] In establishing Point Option, he should have taken into consideration all of the factors relating to the critical need to take his returning aircraft aboard. In this case these factors did not change during the air action. Thus Spruance's failure to either be at the prescribed rendezvous point or inform his air crews that the point had been changed is inexcusable. Radio silence to avoid detection was indeed important, but not so important that it justified risking the loss of the majority of one or even two air wings.

Operations of the *Yorktown* Air Group on 4 June

The *Yorktown* air group departed Task Force 17 at 0906 with orders to turn north if it failed to locate the enemy at the presumed interception point.[179] At about 1000 Lt. Cdr. Lance E. Massey, commander of Torpedo Squadron 3 (off *Saratoga* while she underwent repairs at Puget Sound), sighted the Mobile Force. As he approached he was immediately attacked by enemy fighters. *Yorktown*'s Fighter Squadron 3 (also off *Saratoga*, enlarging *Yorktown*'s fighter complement as Fletcher recommended after the Battle of the Coral Sea) tried to defend the torpedo planes but soon became separated. Of the twelve torpedo planes only two returned to their carrier. No hits were scored.[180]

By strange coincidence the *Yorktown* bombing squadron (VB-5), which left one hour and twenty minutes behind the *Enterprise* dive-bombers, sighted the enemy at the same time as Massey.[181] The presence of each was unknown to the other. Fortuitously, the commander of the *Yorktown* squadron, Lt. Cdr. Max F. Leslie, selected one of the carriers, *Soryu*, not attacked by the two *Enterprise* squadrons. Thirteen of his seventeen planes dropped 1000-pound bombs. The first planes made several hits, which soon wrapped the carrier in smoke and flames. Two planes attacked a nearby battleship and two a cruiser. No hits were made.[182] All planes returned to the vicinity of *Yorktown*. At 1159, before they could land, *Yorktown* radar spotted incoming enemy planes bearing 250 degrees true, distance forty-six miles, while fueling fighters of the combat air patrol. The fueling on *Yorktown* was immediately discontinued.

Recapping the Action

At the time the last Midway planes of the *kido butai* were recovered aboard the four Japanese carriers, fifteen American torpedo planes were sighted. This was Torpedo Squadron 8 of the *Hornet*. All ships opened fire and additional fighters were launched. All fifteen American planes were destroyed. A few minutes later Torpedo Squadron 6 off *Enterprise* attacked and lost ten out of fourteen planes. This attack had barely been beaten off when the *Yorktown* torpedo squadron attacked. They lost ten of their twelve planes.

None of these attacks made any hits, but they aided greatly in achieving the final result. All Japanese fighter cover had been drawn to low levels and antiaircraft activity was being directed toward the low-level attacks. This enabled the *Enterprise* and *Yorktown* dive-bombers to approach undetected and unopposed by fighters. At 1024 *Kaga* was attacked by nine dive-bombers of Scouting Squadron 6, which made four hits; at 1025 *Soryu* was attacked by twelve dive-bombers (from *Yorktown*), which made three hits; at 1026 *Akagi* was struck by three dive-bombers from *Enterprise*'s Bombing Squadron 6, which made two hits. In less than two minutes the *kido butai* was reduced to three burning hulks with a single operational carrier—*Hiryu*—still engaged in the action. While Nagumo transferred from the burning *Akagi* to the light cruiser *Nagara*, the commander of Cruiser Division 8, Rear Adm. Hiroaki

FIGURE 20. Diagram of Torpedo Squadrons 8 and 6 attacks —*Courtesy of U.S. Naval War College*

Abe, assumed tactical command. He notified Yamamoto and withdrew to the north. At 1050 he ordered *Hiryu* to attack the enemy carrier or carriers. At 1058 *Hiryu* completed launching eighteen bombers and six fighters to attack the single American carrier reported by the *Tone* seaplane.

The Inevitable Japanese Counterattack

After the sinking of *Lexington* at Coral Sea, fuel lines on *Yorktown* were drained and filled with CO_2. Gas tanks were also surrounded with CO_2. It was believed at the time that this prevented gas fires.[183] The combined combat air patrol of Task Force 16 and Task Force 17 was twenty-eight planes, with twelve of those off *Yorktown* and eight each off *Enterprise* and *Hornet*.[184] The *Yorktown* fighters had been launched so recently that they were still organizing their station assignments at 1152 when their ship first picked up incoming Japanese planes bearing 275 degrees true, distant thirty-two miles.[185] The weather was excellent, and *Hornet*'s captain, Mark Mitscher, could see *Yorktown* on the horizon.[186] The eighteen Japanese dive-bombers and eighteen accompanying fighters from *Hiryu* that attacked

Yorktown at 1207 were broken into small groups by the intercepting fighters and by the circular antiaircraft disposition.[187] Most of the Japanese planes were shot down, but about eight bombers succeeded in attacking *Yorktown*. Three bomb hits were made, causing *Yorktown* to go dead in the water, and the flames from the island structure that resulted made the communication office and Flag Plot untenable.[188] At 1313 Fletcher and his staff, desperately needing the ability to communicate, transferred from the *Yorktown* to the cruiser *Astoria*.

At 1324 the cruisers *Pensacola* and *Vincennes* and destroyers *Benham* and *Balch* from Task Force 16 joined Task Force 17 to assist *Yorktown*. At 1421 *Yorktown* was able to increase speed to fifteen knots. At 1432 she had commenced fueling her fighters when radar picked up another enemy air group. This group was the second strike launched by *Hiryu* at 1331—ten torpedo planes escorted by six fighters.[189] *Yorktown* was caught launching her fighters. All destroyers and cruisers formed in a single circle, probably the first time such a formation was used. Despite maneuvering and fairly effective antiaircraft fire, *Yorktown* was hit on the port side by two torpedoes, the rudder jammed, and the ship became dead in the water and started listing to port, ultimately to twenty-seven degrees.[190]

At 1445 a *Yorktown* scout reported a carrier, two battleships, three cruisers, and four destroyers. This was part of the Mobile Force. The commanding officer of the *Yorktown*, Capt. Elliott Buckmaster, now faced a serious decision. His ship was listing heavily, his power lost, auxiliary power was unusable and an enemy carrier force was only 110 miles away. He decided to abandon ship two and a half hours later.[191] This decision is open to questioning based on a proper analysis of the situation at the time. A carrier was of paramount importance to the United States in mid-1942, and demanded all efforts to save it. It would have been wiser to have removed all but those required in salvage operations and do all that was humanly possible to bring *Yorktown*'s fires under control and tow her back to Hawaii.

A little earlier, at 1200, the commander of the Japanese Second Fleet, Vice Admiral Kondo, had informed Yamamoto that he was heading for the Mobile Force. Kondo did this on his own initiative, and Yamamoto supported the decision. At 1210 Yamamoto received the encouraging news that the *Hiryu* attack group was attacking an enemy carrier. Only one carrier had been reported and now it was being bombed. It was not until *Hiryu*'s second strike an hour and twenty-eight minutes later that the Japanese became aware of the *Enterprise* and *Hornet*.

Yamamoto now conducted his own estimate of the situation and weighed his strengths and weaknesses. He was still, based on available intelligence and contact reports, superior in surface ships. Most of his air strength was destroyed, but apparently so was the enemy's. He decided to seize Midway according to plan. At 1225, aboard *Nagara* and evidently suffering from shock, Nagumo signaled his command that he expected momentary encounter with the enemy and would destroy it by daylight action. At around 1230 *Soryu*'s high-speed experimental reconnaissance plane returned to *Hiryu* when it discovered its own carrier on fire. The pilot, who was having radio problems and was unable to report while airborne, reported that the enemy force had three carriers—*Enterprise*, *Hornet*, and *Yorktown*.[192] Also, a downed American pilot now held as prisoner, an ensign from *Yorktown* taken by Destroyer Division 5, had revealed under torture that the American carriers were *Hornet* and *Enterprise*, escorted by six cruisers and ten destroyers, and *Yorktown* with two cruisers and three destroyers. There were no capital ships left in Pearl Harbor.

This was extremely important information. Yamamoto, learning his enemy was on general westerly courses, felt decisive action was imminent. The entire fleet—Yamamoto's Main Group as well as *Hiryu*, the only carrier remaining of Nagumo's *kido butai*, and the carriers *Ryujo* and *Junyo* and supporting ships of the Second Mobile Task Group of the Aleutian task force—should join the battle. He prepared for night action and made his first modification in his basic plan. He temporarily canceled the Midway and Aleutian operations. He ordered the Second Mobile Task Group of the Aleutians operation (AL) with carriers *Ryujo* and *Junyo* to join Kondo. With *Hosho* of his main force and *Hiryu* of the Mobile Force, this would give him four carriers. Meanwhile, carrying out his orders to prepare for action against the enemy, Yamamoto's Main Group was heading toward the Mobile Force. The Aleutian Support Group had changed course to rejoin the Main Force as well. Cruiser Division 7 was approaching Midway at high speed to bombard the shore installations during the night. Transports and seaplane tenders were retiring northwest. Submarines were tasked to make immediate contact and attack the enemy.[193] At 1331 *Hiryu* launched her second air attack of 16 aircraft against *Yorktown* and two other carriers now known to be operating with her.[194] This strike included ten torpedo planes, including one from *Akagi*, and six fighters, including two from *Kaga*.[195] Since *Yorktown* was making seventeen knots with her fires under control, the Japanese were not sure they hit the same carrier in both attacks. They lost five torpedo planes and three fighters, but made two hits.[196]

Death of the *Kido Butai*

At 1558 a Midway PBY reported three burning ships plus two cruisers bearing 320 at 170 nautical miles from the island.[197] The four operational B17s still on the island were ordered to attack these burning ships. Six B17s arriving from Pearl Harbor turned and attacked at the same time. The Japanese avoided all these high-level strikes by short turns at high speed, even complete circles. Simard on Midway at 1745 received an amplified report: "The three burning ships are Japanese carriers."[198] He ordered Marine Scout Bombing Squadron 241 to make a night attack. This attack group could not locate the targets due to darkness and overcast skies, and returned to Midway without expending weapons.

Soryu sank at 1920. *Kaga* was torpedoed by *Nautilus* at 1359 (the torpedo failed to explode), which resulted in heavy depth charge attacks against *Nautilus*.[199] *Grouper*, which was also in the vicinity, was not as effective as *Nautilus*. Although her commander sighted smoke from two burning ships at a distance of ten to twelve miles, he did not develop these contacts because of enemy depth charges and because he feared an enemy ship might sink him. *Kaga* sank at 1925 as a result of internal explosions.[200] *Akagi*, whose situation was seen as "hopeless" at 1630 on 4 June, was finally scuttled at 0200 on 6 June on Nagumo's orders.[201]

Meanwhile, in Task Force 16, *Enterprise* launched a second attack group of twenty-four dive-bombers, fourteen of them *Yorktown* planes that had flown aboard when their own carrier was torpedoed, and *Hornet* launched sixteen Dauntless dive-bombers.[202] They were unescorted. They attacked independently on enemy dispositions, which were exactly as reported by *Yorktown* planes.[203] Nagumo, taking all precautions for the protection of *Hiryu*, had ordered an unusually broad disposition of screening units. At 1705 planes from *Hornet* and *Enterprise* caught *Hiryu* by surprise, scoring four hits.[204] Surprisingly, only six to twelve Japanese fighters were airborne to meet the U.S. strike—a clear indication of the extent of Japanese plane losses from the day's fighting.[205] At 1730 *Hornet* scout bombers, finding *Hiryu* in flames, dropped fourteen bombs on a nearby battleship and cruiser, claiming three hits on the former and two on the latter.[206] In reality they had expended their ordnance without a single hit.[207]

At 1712 Fletcher in *Astoria* decided to depart company with *Yorktown* and join Task Force 16.[208] His decision is questionable in view of the situation at the time. Fletcher's main strength, Task Force 16, was well to the east. The enemy might attack at any time during the remaining daylight or attempt to destroy *Yorktown* during the night. Fletcher's Task Force 17 forces were weak. Four destroyers were crowded with survivors—about twenty-three hundred in all.[209] He thought the best decision was to retire, transfer the survivors to the cruiser *Portland* during the night and send it on to Pearl Harbor, have *Vincennes* and *Pensacola* rejoin Task Force 16, and return with the remainder of Task Force 17 to *Yorktown* the next morning. This was probably a bad decision. Several weeks after the battle, Nimitz instructed: "In the event a ship receives such severe battle damage that abandonment may be a possibility, a skeletonized crew to affect rescue of the ship shall be ready either to remain aboard or to be placed in an attendant vessel."[210] At 1800 Fletcher, realizing he could not permit *Yorktown* to fall into Japanese hands, directed the destroyer *Hughes* to return and stand by with instructions to sink the carrier to prevent capture or if serious fires developed.

About this time Yamamoto decided to combine his forces and, when joined by *Ryujo* and *Junyo* of Admiral Kakuta's Second Carrier Striking Force from the Aleutian operation with their forty fighters, twenty-one dive-bombers, and twenty-one torpedo planes,[211] strike what remained of the American force in a night action.[212] While sending this dispatch he heard that *Hiryu* was burning fiercely. But at 1915 he directed his command, "The enemy fleet, which has been practically destroyed, is retiring to the east. Combined Fleet units in the vicinity are preparing to pursue the remnants and occupy Midway."[213] This remarkable message shows considerable confusion in Yamamoto as to the authenticity of information available to him and an underestimation of the American commander opposing him. But Yamamoto was evidently determined to seize the advantage during the night, knowing that to abandon the offensive state of mind is to forswear victory.

At 1816 Fletcher received a dispatch from Spruance reporting the attack on the fourth Japanese carrier, *Hiryu*, and asking for instructions for future operations. Fletcher replied "Negative. Will conform to your movements." Fletcher decided at that point to have Spruance assume responsibilities as officer in tactical command (OTC).[214] Fletcher would follow the movements of

Task Force 16 with the remainder of Task Force 17. By 1912 all planes had been recovered and surface forces had rejoined.

Spruance, now in de facto operational command, considered what he should do. He realized that the enemy Mobile Force at 1700 was about 130 miles to the west-northwest with two battleships, three heavy cruisers, and four destroyers, some of which probably had slight damage.[215] They could reach the present location of Task Force 16 by midnight. There was a possibility of another carrier in the area as well, based on initial intelligence of the possibility of four or five carriers.[216] Knowing the Japanese, Spruance reasoned that to save face they would not retire without seeking night action or a landing operation at Midway. He concluded that a move westward during early night hours might run into an ambush. At 1915 he decided to head east, setting a course of 090 degrees true, speed fifteen knots. He would still be in range to support Midway, if necessary.

At about the same time, Kondo, embarked aboard the cruiser *Atago*, received orders that the Second Fleet, the Mobile Force, and the Submarine Force were to contact and attack the enemy immediately.[217] In the light of the Japanese plans for night action Spruance's decision to move east was correct. At midnight Task Force 16 and Task Force 17 were 190 miles from Midway, bearing 050 degrees true.[218]

Japan's Contemplated Night Action

At 2130 Yamamoto received from Nagumo a confusing dispatch, "Total strength of enemy five carriers, six heavy cruisers, fifteen destroyers steaming westward."[219] At 2255 Yamamoto ordered, "Commander Second Fleet will take command of the Mobile Force." He evidently planned to employ the Mobile Force as a striking force. At 2250, however, he had received another dispatch from Nagumo, "The enemy still has four carriers, six cruisers, and fifteen destroyers which are at present steaming westward. All the carriers of our force have become in-operational [*sic*]."[220] Now—with no operational carriers in the Mobile Force—it became a surface force that should possibly be attached to some other commander. The logical choice was Kondo, commander of the Second Fleet. Possibly Yamamoto was also influenced by the fact that Nagumo, judging by his reports, was not in an offensive frame of mind.

Kondo, responding to Yamamoto's order to assume command of the surface force and, after 2200, expecting to encounter the enemy, planned this disposition: "The Mobile Force will turn about and participate in Second Fleet's night engagement; such disposition from right to left will be DesRon 2, CruDiv 5, CruDiv 4 and DesRon 4, with BatDiv 3 ten kilometers behind CruDiv 4, all on course 065 at speed twenty-four knots."[221]

These were the forces that would have been engaged had Task Force 16 and Task Force 17 combined for night action. The U.S. force included two carriers, seven heavy cruisers, one light cruiser, and fourteen destroyers. The Japanese would have opposed them with four battleships, six heavy cruisers, three light cruisers and nineteen destroyers. The Japanese would have had greater firepower and full freedom of action. The Americans would have been forced to remain near their carriers or retire them at high speed on first radar contact. Success here would have given the Japanese command of the sea at Midway. This battle was what the Japanese desired, and it might have happened had the Americans continued westward. Spruance decided otherwise.

Yamamoto, finally convinced of the futility of his position, reversed his earlier decision and decided not to cancel the Aleutian operation.

Operations of 5 June

On the day following the carrier battle, the bulk of the Japanese ships were to the northwest of Midway and moving in a generally westward direction. Spruance, reversing his course of the previous night, gave chase and launched an afternoon strike. The Japanese, unfortunately, were beyond the range of the American planes at that point and the strike returned without success. During the night, two Japanese cruisers—the *Mikuma* and *Mogami*—had collided while trying to avoid the submarine *Tambor*. When Spruance became aware of their situation, and since the augmented Main Body of Yamamoto's force was confirmed to be out of range, Spruance wisely attacked these two ships.

Operations of 6 June

Spruance continued his searches for *Mogami* and *Mikuma*. He launched three strikes against them once they were located. As a result, *Mikuma* was sunk.[222] To avoid being surprised, Spruance then turned away from the area to avoid the Japanese Main Body.

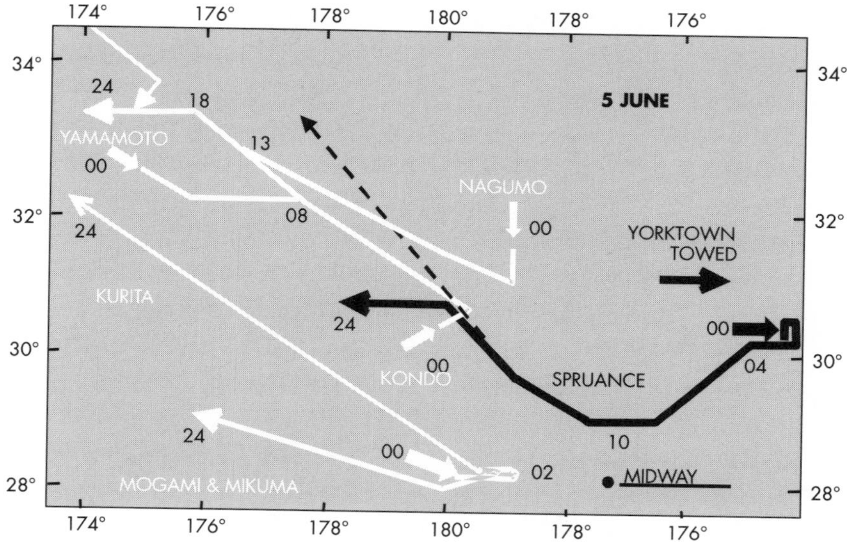

FIGURE 21. Spruance's movements on 5 June 1942. —*Courtesy of U.S. Naval War College*

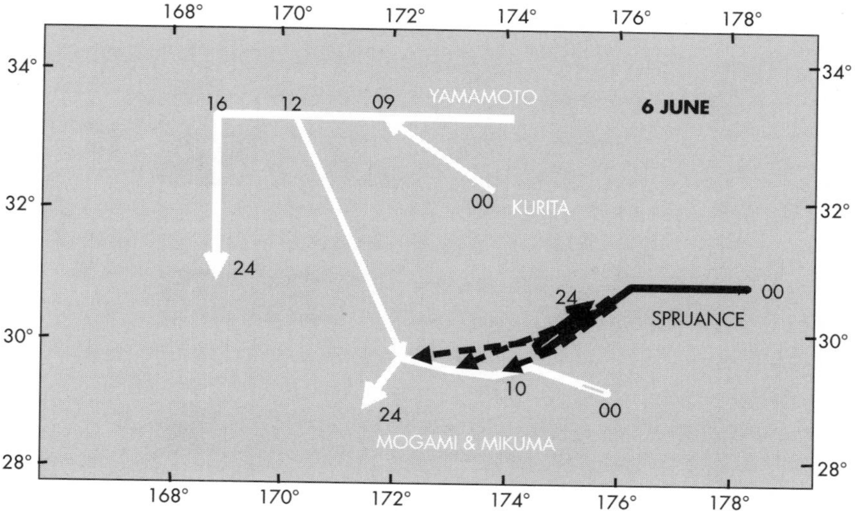

FIGURE 22. Spruance's movements on 6 June 1942. —*Courtesy of U.S. Naval War College*

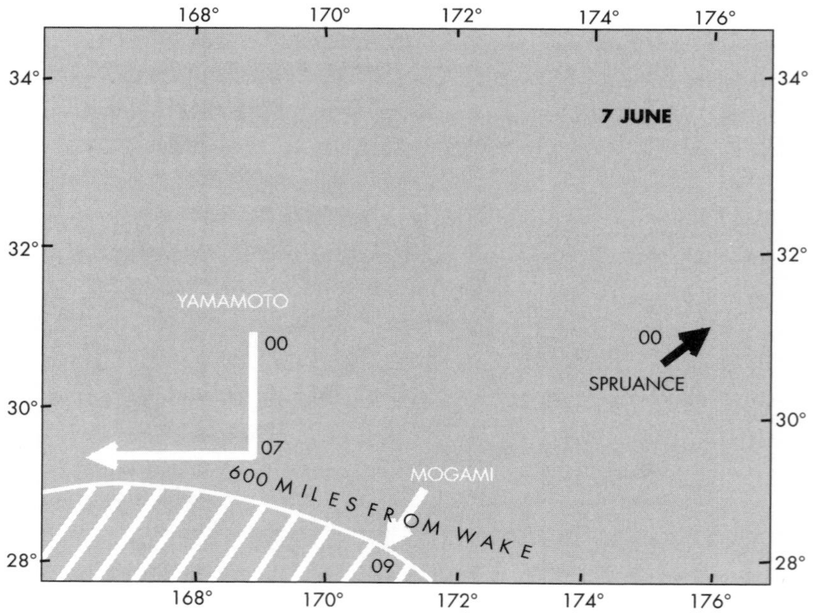

FIGURE 23. Spruance's movements on 7 June 1942. *—Courtesy of U.S. Naval War College*

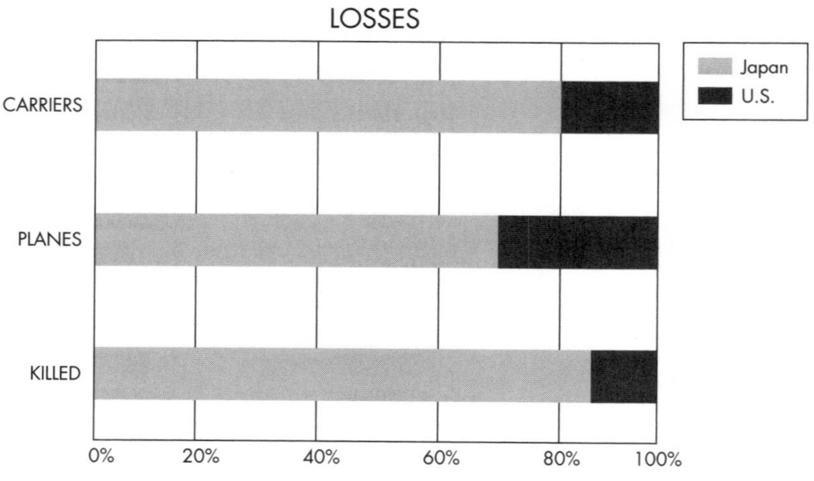

FIGURE 24. Comparison of U.S. and Japanese losses in the Battle of Midway. *—Courtesy of U.S. Naval War College*

"GREATEST GENERATION?"

20s—Pilots/Gunners
~40—ACFT Squadron Commanders
~40—Destroyer COs
50s—Carrier COs/Admirals

FIGURE 25. Three generations of America's "greatest." —*Courtesy of U.S. Naval War College*

Operations of 7 June

Yamamoto, realizing that there was nothing left to gain, departed the Midway area to the west. Spruance departed the area to the northwest. The Battle of Midway had concluded.

The Japanese had lost four carriers, the U.S. one, but almost all of the Japanese planes in the battle were lost when their carriers went down. Most of the U.S. planes that were lost, on the other hand, were either shot down by Zeros or ditched at sea after running out of fuel on their extended attack sorties. In all, just fewer than four thousand men were killed in the Midway action. Many of them went down with their ships.

The television anchorman Tom Brokaw wrote a book about the Americans who fought so gallantly in World War II entitled *The Greatest Generation*. In reality, however, there were three generations of Americans who served so well at Midway. The pilots and gunners, both of the aircraft and in the ships, were in their twenties. The commanding officers of the destroyers and aircraft squadrons were all about forty years of age. The commanding officers of the carriers and cruisers and the flag officers were in their fifties. These three generations of Americans all did their part in achieving a magnificent and strategically critical victory.[223]

Midway in Retrospect: Conclusions

Overcome by fire and explosions, the last ship of the *kido butai* to fight at Midway, the *Hiryu*, was abandoned and scuttled by torpedo from the destroyer *Makigumo*. To the bottom with *Hiryu* went her captain, Tomeo

Kaku, and the commander of the Second Carrier Division—Rear Adm. Tamon Yamaguchi, the ascending star of the Imperial Japanese Navy. As he waived his cap to his men on the destroyers *Kazagumo* and *Makigumo*, he faced his fate in "complete composure."[224] How prophetic that vision must have been. As the cornerstone of the offensive might of the Japanese Navy went to the bottom, utterly destroyed, so did her favorite son. In addition to observing the honorable tradition of joining the fate of his ship, Yamaguchi might also have realized, even this early in the war, that Japan's hopes of victory against a determined United States had vanished. It was 0510 on Friday, 5 June 1942.

Ninety men who fought in the Battle of Midway have ships named after them. Men like Chester W. Nimitz, Frank Jack Fletcher, Raymond Spruance, Mark Mitscher, Wade McClusky, Jimmy Thach, and even Ens. Stephen W. Groves, a fighter pilot on *Hornet*, were honored by their country for their heroism in this historic battle. Henderson Field on Guadalcanal, which was so essential to further success in the war effort, likewise honored a Midway warrior: it was named after Maj. Lofton Henderson, USMC, who was killed while leading the Marine aircraft from Midway against the Japanese carriers.[225] But for what reason were these gallant men so honored?

The strategic consequences of the Japanese navy's operational defeat in the waters north of Midway Island were profound and lasting. Though the Japanese would continue to try to extend their defensive barrier to the southeast from their primary naval base at Rabaul in hopes of severing U.S. communications with Australia, the Americans would now be able to fight them on at least equal terms. Even naval parity could be expected to last only until the industrial might of the United States came into its full potential. But to be seen as a "decisive victory" for the United States, Midway had to place Japan in a situation from which it could not recover. Though the loss of four of six carriers was devastating, the loss of the aircraft aboard those carriers—and the precious pilots who were the best and most experienced in the Japanese navy—was awesome by comparison.

A Japanese eyewitness to the action—Mitsuo Fuchida, a graduate in the 1924 class of the Imperial Japanese Naval Academy, air group commander for Nagumo's flagship *Akagi* during the Battle of Midway, and flight leader of every *kido butai* air strike up to that battle, where he was grounded with an appendicitis attack—attests to the loss of 332 carrier planes by the Japanese navy.[226] Among those he lists 6 aircraft lost in the Midway air strike; 12 fighters lost of the combat air patrol for the carriers; 24 lost in the attacks on

MIDWAY

Nimitz (CVN-68)
Fletcher (DD-992)
Spruance (DD-963)
Mitscher (DDG-57)
McClusky (FFG-41)
Thach (FFG-43)
Stephen W. Groves (FFG-29)

FIGURE 26. U.S. Navy ships honoring those who fought in the Battle of Midway." —*Courtesy of U.S. Naval War College*

the U.S. carriers; 280 planes that went down with the *kido butai*; and 10 seaplanes lost from screening battleships and cruisers.[227] To that at least 5 planes (and one pilot) can be added, acknowledged as lost in the Aleutian Islands operation. That marks an astounding total of 337 aircraft lost in a single unsuccessful operation. While Fuchida notes that those carrier planes in excess of those embarked as part of the operational carrier air wings, 61 in all, are accounted for as fighter aircraft of the Midway Expeditionary Force that was being ferried to Midway in the carriers, the loss of carrier aircraft alone still stands at 261.

Based on the evidence in chapter 2 concerning the numbers of aircraft Japan had at the start of the war, around 561 for the entire First Air Fleet, the Japanese navy had lost 46.5 percent of its carrier-based planes in a single day. Add to this the 56 or so carrier planes lost around Colombo and Trincomalee on Ceylon and in operations in the Southern Resource Area and the 90 aircraft lost in the Battle of the Coral Sea (427 carrier aircraft total), and the Japanese navy had lost at least *76.1 percent* of its initial inventory of carrier aircraft. Aircraft production rate comparisons need not be introduced to demonstrate that First Air Fleet was in rapid decline relative to near-term U.S. fleet aircraft inventories. The Japanese navy simply could not sustain offensive naval operations in the future against their American adversaries. Now it was the Japanese navy, not the U.S., that would be forced to react to its opponent strategically if trends continued.

Any contemplated strategic initiative that required air support would further hazard their effort in the war.

Although aircraft loses could, on the margin, be compensated for, loss of pilots could not. Though pilot losses are much harder to estimate than plane losses since many of the pilots aboard the Japanese carriers were picked up or transferred to other ships in the vicinity, Ikuhiko Hata and Yasuho Izawa list by name thirteen of the seventy-nine fighter pilots they list as killed in all actions including Pearl Harbor and thereafter as killed in action during the Battle of Midway.[228] Using the methodology in chapter 2, of the ninety-seven fighter pilots expected to be aboard the Japanese carriers for the eighty-four operational fighters embarked,[229] thirteen would account for a 13.4 percent loss.

By extension, of the 84 dive-bombers and 93 torpedo planes embarked in an operational status on the Japanese carriers,[230] the expected pilot-to-plane ratio explained in chapter 2 would produce a total of around 204 pilots assigned to fly this complement of planes. Using the same 13.4 percent lost-in-combat ratio as for fighter pilots, another 27 pilots could reasonably be presumed killed. Since the Zero aircraft was acknowledged as superior to anything in the U.S. inventory by American pilots, the Japanese pilots were considerably more experienced, and the Japanese dive-bombers and torpedo planes were shot down at a considerably higher rate—twenty-four compared to twelve—while vulnerable during their attack runs, this number could be as high as 50 additional pilots lost. Taking only the lower numbers, however, at least 40 Japanese pilots were lost at Midway and in the Aleutians.

From the total number of pilots probably assigned to carriers by the Japanese navy at the war's outset—608 or so—operational losses at Midway accounted for at least 7 percent of that number. Considering that 79 fighter pilots alone had been lost since Pearl Harbor,[231] and given the greater number of bomber and torpedo plane pilots assigned to carriers—over twice as many—losses in excess of 237 total carrier pilots could easily have occurred. Thus the Japanese had in all probability already lost 39 percent of their irreplaceable pilots, and probably a lot more. Given that 18 of the fighter pilots and at least 36 of the other pilots were officers, 54 of the 237 pilots—or 17 percent—likely to have been lost were of the leadership cadre. This would also prove telling as the war went on.

The performance in command of Fletcher, Nimitz, and Spruance, who assumed the additional responsibility as acting commander of the Striking

Force as Fletcher directed, will now be considered with respect to the methodology set up on pages 2–3 to evaluate their adherence to the precepts of *Sound Military Decision* imparted during their educational tours of duty at the United States Naval War College. Specifically, each commander's decisions will be evaluated as they relate to the following:

1. The commander's estimate of the situation and grasp of the strategic and operational significance of the decisions he would be required to make. In this area all three commanders deserve a strong A. One could even make a case that Nimitz deserves an A+, especially since he risked all in believing the intelligence information provided for him. Such willingness to accept great risk based primarily on intelligence provided by his staff is an uncommon characteristic in American naval commanders. To his credit, Nimitz not only trusted the intelligence estimate provided for him, but he hedged against any shortcomings it may have had and increased the flexibility of his situation by directing his carrier commanders to base their operations in an area north-northeast of Midway, where they could be arrayed against the Japanese either near Midway or in the Aleutians, as necessary, and where they would be likely to flank the Japanese carriers should they attack Midway initially. This was a masterful stroke by Nimitz executed superbly by Fletcher.

   So also was Nimitz's direction to operate the two American task forces independently. While this decision was in keeping with U.S. doctrine, it violated the experience gained at Coral Sea. It also violated the long-held Navy principle of unity of command, although Fletcher, as the senior commander, maintained ultimate command authority. Owing to *Yorktown*'s need for repairs to the damage she sustained at Coral Sea and to the sudden replacement of Halsey due to his medical condition, prebattle coordination between the two task forces was simply out of the question. Thus Nimitz minimized the potential for working at cross-purposes and in the process increased the lethal potential and likelihood of survival of all three carriers under his strategic direction.

   Likewise, Fletcher astutely grasped the likely employment of the Japanese carriers against the Midway Islands. Nimitz placed him in a position to outflank his opponent and catch him with a significant portion of his aircraft irreversibly employed against a target from which they could not possibly be diverted to threaten Fletcher's carriers. Fletcher demonstrated an excellent understanding of the geostrategic situation.

Perhaps one criticism is in order. As a precursor to the anticipated action and after contact had been gained on the Japanese carriers by Midway scout planes, inadequate attention was paid to providing constantly updated information on the location and movements of the Japanese carriers. This oversight was primarily Nimitz's, but Fletcher and certainly Captain Simard on Midway Island also fell short. This almost caused the failure of the entire Midway operation, as the carrier strike aircraft only managed to locate the Japanese carriers almost by accident and as their fuel was nearly exhausted, assuming the aircraft also wanted to return to their carriers. In all other respects, Simard, the commander of Naval Air Station Midway, correctly and astutely estimated the situation and positioned his command to optimally search, locate, and attack the Japanese as well as defend against attack.

2. The commander's demonstrated ability to formulate a course of action, his ability to convey his decision in mission orders to subordinate commanders concisely and unambiguously, and his flexibility in modifying those orders through strategic and/or operational reappraisal if required. Fletcher once again formulated an aggressive and purposeful course of action, which he conveyed adequately to Spruance. His decision to adhere to Nimitz's order to operate the carrier task forces independently was also sound. Fletcher's decision to launch only aircraft from *Enterprise* and *Hornet* in his initial sortie against the Japanese because of possible misidentification of the presence of carriers among the ships sighted and/or positional errors in the pilot's reporting of the contacts was exceptionally astute. Fletcher maintained his options should errors in the pilots' reports misdirect his initial attack or the additional carriers expected to be in the area be located. He also maximized his ability to defend his carriers.

   Meanwhile, Spruance's most important decision—to turn east and away from a potential night action against a much superior Japanese surface force—was well reasoned and sound. Both of these commanders deserve high marks for their major decisions. Fletcher's failure to ensure constant tracking of the Japanese carriers once they were located by Midway aircraft, a lapse in directing and ensuring surveillance, and his lack of understanding of the importance of making all efforts to save *Yorktown* in view of its strategic importance to the war effort notwithstanding, both commanders deserve a solid A in this important area.

3. The adequacy of command arrangements, the chain of command established, and the communications procedures put into effect to facilitate the exercise of command in battle. Once again, considering the inability to coordinate their actions before the battle, separation and independence of action for Task Force 16 and Task Force 17 was a splendid arrangement for this engagement. However, passing by Fletcher of de facto command to Spruance once he had transferred his Flag to *Astoria* was a questionable decision. Fletcher's choice to pass responsibility for the operation to a junior who was not an aviator—a cruiser commander without previous carrier battle experience, even though Spruance had Halsey's more qualified carrier staff—was an unnecessarily risky decision that worked out well. A B here seems appropriate for Fletcher.

   In contrast, Theobald failed to organize the command for his aviation units in the Alaskan theater either as was the convention at the time or as he was directed by Nimitz. His arrangement contravened unity of command and good judgment. Simard on Midway Island was also left essentially outside the command loop.

4. The commander's adherence to established operational and tactical doctrines where appropriate, his adherence to procedures established prior to the engagement of forces, and his ability to deviate from the same when warranted. Though it went against his experience at Coral Sea, Fletcher adhered to the accepted doctrine of separation of U.S. carriers to increase their independence of action under attack. Normally this would indicate a weakness in his decision process. However, for the reasons he provided to Samuel Eliot Morison enumerated above, this adherence to questionable doctrine was unquestionably the right decision. Moreover, Fletcher optimized his allocation of aircraft for search, strike, and defense, and minimized risk by withholding *Yorktown*'s aircraft from the initial strike long enough to ensure the accuracy of the information he had received on the location and composition of the Japanese force. In doing this he adhered doggedly to

Nimitz's instructions to "be governed by the principle of calculated risk, the avoidance of exposure to attack by superior forces without good prospect of inflicting greater damage to the enemy." He deserves a strong A in this area.

5. The commander's communication of mission requirements to subordinate commanders and the suitability of complementary actions by those subordinates to engage the enemy more effectively. As demonstrated above, all major commanders involved in the Battle of Midway had an excellent appreciation of the mission requirements. This was also true of Theobald, even though he lacked the resources to carry out his assigned mission in Alaska, and it was particularly true of Simard, save for his disregard for providing continuous updates on the location and movement of the Japanese carriers once they were located.

   Perhaps most important, Fletcher in particular and other commanders to a lesser extent placed great trust in the knowledge and instincts of their subordinates. Fletcher refrained from giving Spruance more frequent or numerous directives than were absolutely needed. When he decided that he was no longer in the best position to direct the actions of his Striking Force, he passed authority for completion of the operation to Spruance unhesitatingly—and then refrained from second-guessing Spruance and inserting himself into tactical command once this decision was made. All units of Task Force 16 and Task Force 17 worked smoothly together through the entire battle. Considering the lack of preexecution coordination for such a major naval engagement, as well as the overwhelming eight-to-one disadvantage in ship numbers when compared to the Japanese, such a high degree of mutual understanding and confidence up and down the chain of command is remarkable. Perhaps an A+ is warranted here.

   One must also ask what engendered such a degree of like thinking and mutual confidence. Certainly Fletcher was aware of Spruance's reputation for prudence and confident action. He surely was also aware that Spruance had been both a student and an instructor at the Naval War College. Thus Fletcher had every reason to appreciate Spruance's fundamental grounding in Navy doctrine and expect his adherence to *Sound Military Decision*.

6. The commander's understanding of the engagement's importance within the wider context of achieving U.S. political objectives and his

concomitant appreciation for the appropriate risk and determination of the proper circumstances in which to end the battle. From start to attack to withdrawal, the foregoing discussion should establish this unequivocally in Fletcher's decision process and performance—A+.

7. The commander's audacity and brilliance in conceptualizing, articulating, and executing a plan of action. Here Nimitz deserves most of the credit. He used the available intelligence wisely and positioned his carriers against a vastly superior force in a way that would optimize their chance of success. His instructions on calculated risk conveyed appropriately the relative importance of the immediate strategic situation to the overall and longer-term strategic outcome of the war against Japan. Similarly, Fletcher approached the Japanese in a way that would at once maximize his opportunity for a successful attack leading to destruction of the Japanese carrier force, while simultaneously providing an avenue of escape should an unacceptable risk to his carriers develop. The plan he executed, developed in a compressed time frame, was brilliant. At the risk of losing grading credibility—A+.

8. The commander's ability to learn from the situation and rapidly pass lessons along to the advantage of those commanding in later engagements. As in the Coral Sea engagement, the After Action Reports and lessons learned for the Battle of Midway were complete, well thought out, and timely. This was another strong area attended to in a useful and methodical way. Only a more comprehensive consideration of Japanese mistakes and emerging patterns of operation could have improved the various commanders' performance in this area. An A- is warranted here.

History can hardly deny the success achieved by the U.S. Navy in the Battle of Midway. However, there were flaws in the conduct of that action. Chief among them was the haphazard series of carrier strikes conducted against the Japanese that resulted in sinking of the *Akagi*, *Kaga*, and *Soryu*. The success of those attacks can be attributed more to luck than good planning or proper execution of doctrine. Yet by comparison, the decision processes employed by Yamamoto and Nagumo were flawed in the extreme. Numerical advantage and the superiority of their aircraft design—two major factors that should have worked to the Japanese advantage—were incompetently squandered. Another insurmountable advantage came from Yamamoto's pursuit of the

Port Moresby operation, resulting in the loss of the carriers *Shokaku* and *Zuikaku* for the more important operation at Midway. Considering the other inappropriate decisions discussed above as well, one cannot help but see the advantage the American commanders had in fighting a compliant foe.

The techniques of *Sound Military Decision* employed by officers of the United States Pacific Fleet since Pearl Harbor had evened the naval balance of power in that theater and rolled the Japanese offensive onslaught back on its heels. For the first time since 7 December 1941, things were looking up for the American people and the military effort they had arrayed against Japan.

CHAPTER 4

The Fight for Guadalcanal: The Battle of the Eastern Solomons

FIGURE 27. Adm. Richmond Kelly "Terrible" Turner, commander of Task Group 61.2 for the Marine amphibious landing on Guadalcanal, during one of his lighter moments. —*Courtesy of Naval Historical Center (80-G-309855)*

"**THICK FOG.**" So starts Chief of Staff for Combined Fleet Vice Adm. Matome Ugaki's diary entry for Friday, 5 June 1942.[1] Never in the history of the Imperial Japanese Navy had an officer's diary started a day more appropriately.

Midway fell on Ugaki with the impact of an avalanche. The Japanese were not totally unrealistic, and understood that their plan to seize American territory and lure out the U.S. Fleet posed certain dangers. They could have accepted the loss of a ship or two, but to lose four carriers with all their aircraft plus a heavy cruiser was almost beyond comprehension.

Along with the psychological shock of decisively losing a battle the Japanese had fully expected to win, and the consequent loss of ships and lives, Ugaki experienced deep personal sorrow when an

> academy classmate, one of his closest friends and colleagues, Rear Admiral Tamon Yamaguchi, chose to go down with his flagship, the CV *Hiryu*. Ugaki [was] torn between his grief at this loss and his pride in Yamaguchi's nobility, as he saw it, in thus fulfilling his command responsibility.[2]

The Battle of Midway was a crushing blow for the Japanese. They had no choice but to regroup and rethink their strategy or sue for peace. In a very real sense the "fog of war" had set in, just as Baron Carl von Clausewitz had remonstrated in his treatise *On War*. Analysis and evaluation were in order, followed by an estimate of the situation. Ugaki was responsible for analyzing the fleet engagements so that Yamamoto and his staff might "profit from the experience."[3]

Ugaki's "lessons learned" from the Midway debacle are logical, but also somewhat surprising. Both Ugaki and the Combined Fleet Staff were concerned that the United States was able to gather the intelligence that led to its force's geographically commanding position in relation to Japanese units in the vicinity of Midway—especially when the United States had relatively few carriers and Dutch Harbor and the Aleutian Island chain were so obviously threatened. After exploring several possibilities for the source of this intelligence, they came to the mutual agreement that the most logical source was ship sightings by U.S. submarines. Never in Ugaki's diary is the possibility of compromise of the Japanese navy's JN-25 codes even mentioned until 30 July—well after he had completed his analysis.[4] The Japanese apparently failed to explore an area of huge vulnerability that would continue to hound them throughout the war.

Ugaki also reasoned—and convinced others, including Admiral Yamamoto—that an overconcentration of carriers was a primary cause of the Midway disaster. Suggesting that this was like "offering many eggs in one basket," the Combined Fleet chief of staff argued that the Japanese navy should break with its previous, and for the most part successful, doctrine of concentrating carriers in a single group. Instead two air fleets or task forces were needed so that four to six carriers could be used in two geographically separated but mutually supporting groups.[5]

Ugaki also found that the carriers needed to take measures to reduce vulnerability to an enemy attack while launching against a target in an area separate from where the enemy attack was launched. Ugaki showed some concern that the First Air Fleet Staff had not taken adequate measures to address this vulnerability. They had determined that the lack of adequate air search on flanks was a shortcoming, but no concrete proposal to remedy this problem was offered.[6]

Finally, Ugaki postulated that "the front area of our invasion plan was expanded too widely."[7] This had prevented the concentration of forces for a night engagement after the four carriers of the *kido butai* had been sunk. The 4th Carrier Division of the northern force involved in the Aleutian operations was too far away to join in the action.[8] However, shortening the distance between major groups of ships rather than concentrating them in a single or several closely grouped task forces was accepted as the solution.[9]

By 18 July 1942, only six weeks after the Midway disaster, Ugaki and the Combined Fleet Staff, decided on their future "requirements" and on future near-term Japanese strategy:

1. Increased supply of aircraft.
2. New inventions [unspecified] and supply of weapons.
3. Future policy of directing the war (execution of operations against India).[10]

Thus, rather than conducting a detailed strategic reappraisal, the Combined Fleet merely accepted that mistakes had been made at Midway, vowed to eliminate those mistakes in the future, and decided to continue with a strategy to link up with their German allies in the Indian Ocean. The code name for that objective was Operation Orient. Though Operation Orient was an ongoing effort, Japan had already come to the decision that its feasibility was questionable. The whole concept had suffered a major setback on 19 January 1942, when Combined Fleet Headquarters had received a copy of the new Tripartite Axis military agreement.[11] Though it made a passing reference to Germany's advance eastward in the Caucasus, the agreement said nothing at all with regard to a future mutual offensive effort by Japan and Germany.[12] To further scuttle this operational option, the Japanese army had shown a latent disinclination to support it. By 30 July, Ugaki had become convinced that the army would probably go along with a planned move against India to knock out the crown jewel in the British Empire and deny Persian Gulf oil to the British navy—but not until 1943.[13]

Strategic Reappraisal

Unlike Ugaki and the Combined Fleet Staff, in his strategic reappraisal after Midway Nimitz decided that American options were limited until additional carriers and other needed ships started to arrive in summer of 1943, but that going on the offensive in a limited and calculated way was now a possibility. In reviewing the situation in the Pacific he saw certain Japanese vulnerabilities that had recently started to emerge. Always wary of Japanese capabilities and intentions, Nimitz pressed forward Pacific Fleet planning that aimed to counter the most likely Japanese naval moves, but that also hedged against any potential catastrophe.

Looking to his west, Nimitz saw that Japan's potential for a renewed offensive to take Midway Island was not good. Surely the carriers *Shokaku* and *Zuikaku* still remained available for such an undertaking, along with around 144 aircraft embarked on them. Yet the nominal aircraft load for the four carriers lost by the Japanese at Midway was at least 234, based on prewar estimates and observations, and, even if *Shokaku* and *Zuikaku* were augmented by other light carriers (CVLs)* to bring the count of available aircraft to that number or more, it was unlikely that the Japanese would risk the very viability of their navy on such a risky endeavor. In the North Pacific, a renewed thrust into Alaska remained a possibility, but when Japan pressed its advance at Midway, it had demonstrated limited objectives and a disinclination to try to exploit this region of hostile weather and great distances.

Moreover, Nimitz knew Japan had to have used a considerable amount of its limited petroleum resources to array its vast armada for the Midway and Aleutian Islands offensives. Japan's army, with its distinctively continental focus, needed petroleum to sustain its gains in Southeast Asia and press its advances into China. Japan's domestic situation also called for petroleum resources, both for its economy and for its production of war matériel. The necessary oil lay in adequate amounts and within reasonable distances only in the former Dutch and, to a lesser extent, British holdings

---

*It is worth noting that during World War II fleet carriers (CV) normally carried between ninety and one hundred planes; light carriers (CVL) normally carried from forty-five to fifty planes; and escort carriers (CVE) usually carried from twenty-three to twenty-eight planes. The United States, unlike the Japanese who followed British carrier design parameters and hangared their aircraft belowdecks, used the "deck park" method of carrying planes and used space belowdecks for repairs and other functions. Thus U.S. carriers often carried more aircraft than their displacement would lead one to estimate.

in the maritime regions of Southeast Asia—what the Japanese called the "Southern Resource Area."

Nimitz was acutely aware of the planning the United States had agonized over in the previous decades for a possible war with Japan. War Plan Orange had been formulated and refined repeatedly since 1907 and its implications were clear. Plan Orange was conceived for a two-nation war, and thus no operations south of the equator had been contemplated, but Japan's rapid movement to the south following the attack on Pearl Harbor had expanded the expected area of conflict.[14] The road to Japan, the only place where a final settlement of the war could be reached under the existing circumstances, was through the Gilbert Islands, the Marshall Islands, the Caroline Islands, the Marianas Islands, and the Volcano Islands. This "island hopping," as it became known, had one vital component—access to and through Australia for movement of men and materials. Japan's defense of its gains in the Southern Resource Area and America's road to Tokyo converged at a place in the Solomon Islands known as Guadalcanal. On 7 August 1942 the U.S. 1st Marine Division hit the beaches there.

The operation was not executed without controversy, however. Gen. Douglas MacArthur proposed an offensive of his own on 8 June. Tasked with the primary responsibility of holding the eastern approaches to New Guinea and the sea lines of communication (SLOCs) to Australia, MacArthur advocated a surprise amphibious landing on Rabaul in the Bismarck Archipelago, the primary Japanese naval base in the area.[15] The Joint Chiefs of Staff viewed the plan with favor, as it represented the first opportunity to go on the offensive against Japan since the demoralizing loss of the American foothold in the Philippines. Wary about placing naval forces under the command of an Army General who might well squander scarce assets, Adm. Ernest J. King, Commander in Chief of the United States Fleet (CominCh) recommended the less risky alternative of taking Tulagi in the Solomon Islands chain.[16] Suspecting from intelligence that the Japanese were reinforcing Rabaul and the Southern Resource Area, King pressed for an early offensive.[17] This option supported Admiral Nimitz's concern for maintaining the SLOCs with Australia. Nimitz realized, however, that Tulagi was merely a convenient spot for staging sea plane reconnaissance flights, with little prospect for building an airfield due to its size. Guadalcanal, on the other hand, could serve as a major staging base for Japanese aspirations to the southeast. Nimitz pressed successfully for an American move to take Guadalcanal before the Japanese. But in order to stage naval operations in the Coral Sea in support of a Guadalcanal offensive, it would be necessary to take Tulagi as well, so the Japanese could not use it to enlarge the area they could search.

The Fight for Guadalcanal

Landing simultaneously on Guadalcanal and the nearby island of Tulagi, the Marines drove the Japanese into the jungle. For the Japanese this was an unacceptable turn of events. Vice Adm. Gunichi Mikawa, the newly installed commander of the Japanese Eighth Fleet at Rabaul, six hundred miles north-northwest, responded quickly and with vigor. It would not be until 14 November 1942 that the Japanese were ultimately defeated in their attempt to retake Guadalcanal and the U.S. enclave and important Henderson Field (the base of the CACTUS Air Force) would be secure. The losses the Japanese navy suffered in what historian John Lundstrom has called "the Naval Battle for Guadalcanal"[18]—particularly those of aircraft of the First Air Fleet aboard Japanese carriers—have been cited by Lundstrom and several other authorities as even more decisive with respect to the war in the Pacific than the resounding U.S. victory at Midway. What follows is a consideration of the Naval Battle for Guadalcanal, the two carrier battles that were an integral part of it (the Battle of Santa Cruz will be covered in the next chapter), and the decisions that contributed to the outcomes of those battles.

Choosing a Commander

On 19 June Vice Adm. Robert L. Ghormley assumed duties as commander of the South Pacific Area (COMSOPAC) under Adm. Chester Nimitz. Nimitz informed Ghormley that two two-carrier task forces would rotate patrolling in his area of responsibility, and that there would be four-day overlap periods in their rotational schedule. During this period, Nimitz advised Ghormley that offensive operations against the Japanese might be contemplated.[19] It was yet to be decided who would command these operations if they were ordered.

Five days later the Commander in Chief of the U.S. Fleet, Admiral King, directed that these two-carrier task forces be placed on twelve-hour alert. Nimitz would have four carriers available for the impending fight. USS *Saratoga,* flagship of Vice Adm. "Bull" Halsey's Task Force 11, was en route to Midway Island to deliver aircraft. USS *Enterprise*, flagship of Task Force 16; USS *Hornet*, flagship of Task Force 17; and USS *Wasp* (CV-7), flagship of Task Force 18 and scheduled to be transferred from the Atlantic early in July, were also available.[20] Aboard *Wasp* as commander of Task Force 18 was Rear Adm. Leigh Noyes, the senior commander after Halsey, who was still hospitalized with dermatitis. A graduate of the Naval Academy class of 1906 with Frank Jack Fletcher, Noyes was just three lineal numbers senior to Fletcher.[21] Academics do count! Rear Adm. Raymond Spruance assumed duties as chief of staff for CINCPAC, Admiral Nimitz.

Initially, King ordered Vice Admiral Ghormley to assume personal command of the operation in his theater—Operation Shoestring, as it came to be called because of the deficiencies in ships, aircraft, and equipment to support the struggle for Guadalcanal.[22] Nimitz, however, wanted a combat-tested commander for the operation, and on 21 June recommended to King that Fletcher be promoted to vice admiral and placed in command of the force detailed for the South Pacific.[23] Having commanded Task Forces 16 and 17 in the Battle of the Coral Sea and during the action at Midway, Fletcher not only had more combat experience in command than any other eligible commander in the Pacific, he also had intimate knowledge of the geography and command relationships in the area.

Nimitz pushed for Fletcher's promotion and assignment when he met with King in person on 4 July in San Francisco, and continued his advocacy as late as 14 July when the task forces were all at sea and preparing to rendezvous north of the Fiji Islands for the operation.[24] Nimitz had to overcome a big opponent in King, who was anything but an admirer of Fletcher. King not only perceived Fletcher as a "fixer" for his repeat tours in Washington, but also considered him timid and overly concerned with fueling. (Some thought Fletcher's fueling operations, first during his relief attempt of Wake Island and then in the early stages of the Coral Sea operation, had unnecessarily separated him from Rear Adm. Aubrey Fitch and the *Lexington* task force.) Moreover, Fletcher had done the unthinkable in losing two carriers in action. King gave no sanction to commanders who lost carriers, no matter how strategically important the victories they achieved. Above all, one of the carriers lost was King's beloved *Lexington*, of which he had been the second commanding officer.

Nonetheless, King did succumb to Nimitz's logic, and Fletcher was promoted to vice admiral, retroactive to 26 June when the recommendation had finally been forwarded to President Roosevelt from the Navy Department.[25] Fletcher was designated commander of the Expeditionary Force, and his classmate, Noyes, was designated commander of the Carrier Aircraft of the Expeditionary Force.[26] Fletcher commanded the Expeditionary Force and

Task Force 61, and his Air Support Force commander, Admiral Noyes, as commander of Task Group 61.1, became his immediate subordinate. As task element commanders, under the command of Noyes, were Fletcher as the commander of Task Force 11 in *Saratoga*, as well as Noyes himself as commander of Task Force 18 in *Wasp*, and Rear Adm. Thomas C. Kinkaid, Fletcher's classmate in the Naval War College class of 1930, as commander of Task Force 16 in *Enterprise*.[27] Thus Fletcher was assigned as a task element commander under a subordinate in his own chain of command. The Amphibious Force commander, designated commander of Task Group 61.2, was Rear Adm. Richmond Kelly Turner, and all of these were organized under Vice Admiral Ghormley, COMSOPAC. Arriving to assume command en route to the theater of operations, now Vice Admiral Fletcher gave directions to his subordinates in his Operation Order for "Watchtower," the code name selected for the Solomon Islands operations.

The Battle of Savo Island

When the Marines hit the beach in the Solomon Islands on the early morning of 7 August 1942 the Japanese defenders on Guadalcanal apparently believed it was only a raid and retired into the hills.[28] The terrain prevented similar withdrawal on Tulagi and the smaller surrounding islands, and the Marines, facing strong resistance, could not secure their positions until the evening of 8 August. Two Japanese air attacks on the 7th and another on the 8th delayed the off-loading of the transports and cargo vessels.[29] Having lost twenty of the ninety-nine embarked fighter aircraft in the action, Fletcher requested permission to retire his new flagship carrier, *Saratoga*, and the carriers *Enterprise* and *Wasp*, along with their screening units, from the area.[30] The protraction of the landing placed the 1st Marine Division in a particularly precarious position. If the Japanese could prevent the landing of supplies and equipment, the Marines would be fighting both the Japanese on the islands and those on the beaches behind them. The initiative would pass to the Japanese.

Vice Adm. Gunichi Mikawa, commander of the Japanese Eighth Fleet at Rabaul, responded quickly with the ships that were readily available. At 1800 on 8 August Rear Adm. Richmond K. "Terrible" Turner received notice of a broadcast from Melbourne that a Japanese force of three cruisers, three destroyers, and two gunboats or seaplane tenders only about three hundred miles away off the east coast of Bougainville was headed 120 degrees true at fifteen knots.[31] Since amphibious landings were somewhat new to the U.S. Navy and only a few had ever taken place in the American hemisphere with little or no active resistance, it was felt at the time that the logical commanders for such operations would be those involved in the war planning process. Turner had distinguished himself as a war planner, and thus got the assignment.

Noting the danger to his landing force, Turner decided to withdraw the force on the morning of 9 August. In all there were twenty-four transport ships in Turner's Task Force 14. Nineteen of these were anchored at or nearing Guadalcanal and the other five were at Tulagi.[32] It was the responsibility of Rear Adm. V.A.C. Crutchley, RN, aboard his flagship HMAS *Australia,* to screen the landing operations with two light cruisers, the USS *San Juan* and the Royal Australian Navy's *Hobart*, and two destroyers. Three additional heavy cruisers, *Vincennes*, *Astoria*, and *Quincy*, and two destroyers were stationed to the east of Savo Island, and the area south of the island was patrolled by two more heavy cruisers, USS *Chicago* and HMAS *Canberra*, screened by two destroyers.[33] Two additional destroyers were placed, one on each side of Savo Island, to provide early-warning radar picket duty. The disposition of the U.S. ships in the area and the tracks taken by the attacking Japanese task force on the night of 8–9 August is depicted in figure 28.

Mikawa attacked in the early morning hours of 9 August with seven cruisers, one destroyer, and at least one submarine under conditions of almost total surprise. The attack occurred about an hour and a half after the first in a series of aircraft, assumed to be Japanese, had been detected by radar. Unfortunately, this information was not passed adequately to assure that the appropriate individuals in the U.S. chain of command were alert to a Japanese presence.

The first real signal of trouble for the Allied task force came when enemy ships appeared without warning around the southern tip of Savo Island. In less than half an hour the attack was over and the Japanese force passed east of Savo Island and out to sea. In that short interval they crossed ahead of the U.S. southern cruiser group, putting *Canberra* completely out of action in the first two minutes of the ten-minute engagement. The Japanese force damaged *Chicago*, then crossed astern of the northern cruiser group, battering them so badly that all three sank—*Vincennes* and *Quincy* within an hour of the attack.[34] Inexplicably, Mikawa failed to press home his advantage by destroying the now-helpless transports. This might have been because of a brief and mostly ineffectual air attack on the transports during the surface action. However, a Japanese propensity to overlook "unmanly" nonwarship

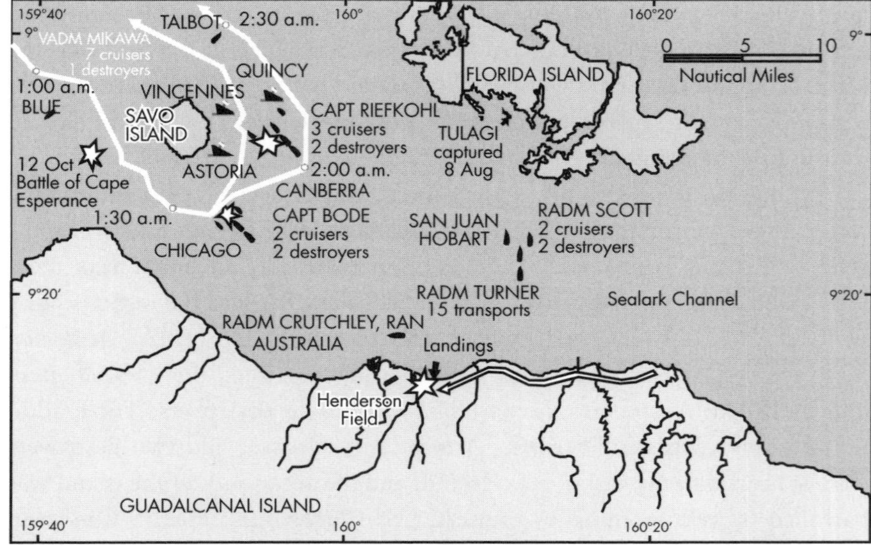

FIGURE 28. Battle of Savo Island, 9 August 1942. —*Courtesy of U.S. Naval War College*

targets, no matter how essential they were to the operation, was also seen at Leyte Gulf in 1944.

In all, the United States and Australia lost four heavy cruisers and a destroyer along with 1,270 officers and men killed and 709 wounded.[35] The Japanese accomplished this—and totally disrupted the Solomon Islands landings—at the cost of only thirty-five men killed and fifty-seven wounded.[36] At the end of 9 August the 6,100 Marines who were to land on Tulagi were left with 39,000 rations, three million rounds of .30-caliber ammunition, and 30,000 rounds of .45-caliber ammunition. The 10,900 Marines on Guadalcanal were left with 567,000 rations and six million rounds of .30-caliber, and six million rounds of .45-caliber ammunition.[37]

This sudden and complete victory for the Japanese would mark the first of a series of attempts to dislodge the U.S. Marine Corps from Guadalcanal. The area in which the five U.S. and Australian ships had been sunk was dubbed "Iron Bottom Sound" as a result of the many warships that had sunk there. Whoever controlled Guadalcanal and its aircraft base Henderson Field would control the SLOCs between Hawaii and Australia. To the Japanese, Guadalcanal was essential to preserving access to vital war-sustaining resources, including oil. To the Americans, control of Guadalcanal was a step toward dictating terms for peace in Tokyo. What follows is a consideration of the carrier battles that were such an important part of the ongoing struggle for Guadalcanal and its valuable and geostrategically important airport.

Where Is Task Force 61? All the World Wonders

Generations of Marines, even those born well after the end of World War II, ask, "Where was Frank Jack Fletcher when we needed him most?"* Most Marines hold him in contempt for "letting them hang out to dry" by failing to relieve them both during their courageous defense of Wake Island at the start of the war and on the beaches and in the jungles of Guadalcanal and the surrounding islands. But was Fletcher really the one to blame for this?

Certainly Vice Adm. George C. Dyer makes a case for Fletcher's culpability in his book, *The Amphibians Came to Conquer*. He lays the blame directly and unequivocally on Fletcher:

> During the main conference [aboard Fletcher's Flagship, USS *Saratoga*, near Koro Island, about a hundred miles south of Suva, Fiji Islands, on 26 July 1942], the most important decision announced by Vice Admiral Fletcher was that the carrier task groups built around the *Enterprise,* flagship of Rear Admiral Thomas C. Kinkaid; the *Wasp*, flagship of Rear Admiral Leigh Noyes; and the *Saratoga*, flagship of Vice Admiral Frank Jack Fletcher, would not be held in a position where they could support the Tulagi-Guadalcanal landings for more than two days; that is, no later than the morning of Sunday, 9 August 1942.
>
> It is easy to say (but not yet proven) that this decision allowed the Japanese Navy to make an unhampered and largely undetected run at our seaborne forces gathered north of Guadalcanal Island the night of 8 August 1942. But there is no question that the carrier task

*The title of this section is a parody on the question asked of Adm. "Bull" Halsey by a radio operator when he left the Leyte Gulf naval battle in an attempt to engage and destroy Admiral Ozawa's carriers. To confuse any Japanese parties who might have decoded the message a radioman added at its beginning "Turkey Trots to Water" and at its end "All the World Wonders." The "All the World Wonders" part of the message added to Admiral Nimitz's query so inflamed Halsey that he reconsidered his aggressive course of action against the carriers.

> force withdrawal provided the Japanese an unpunished retirement after their glorious victory at Savo Island.[38]

Surely a good number of other historians, such as Samuel Eliot Morison, Commo. (later Rear Adm.) Richard Bates (commissioned in 1946 by Adm. Raymond Spruance, president of the Naval War College, to "study and evaluate" the naval battles of World War II), John Keegan, and Richard B. Frank (author of the highly regarded *Guadalcanal*, who "concluded that Fletcher, rightly or wrongly, placed the preservation of his carriers ahead of everything else") have had little good to say about Fletcher's contribution to the war effort.[39] So, too, has Ghormley been roundly criticized. But even Ghormley has been "rehabilitated." In his 1963 book on Guadalcanal, Marine Brig. Gen. Samuel B. Griffith "showed remarkable sympathy for him."[40] Even Morison said in 1949 that "Admiral Ghormley did as well as anyone could have done . . . he was a victim of circumstances."[41] But General Griffith has been less forgiving to Fletcher: "'Haul-Ass' Fletcher, that's what we used to call him. Why, that was his best maneuver. He could break all records getting away from something he didn't like." "There wasn't much left of old 'Haul-Ass' when Sam Morison got through with him."[42]

Other more recent authors, including John Lundstrom and Marvin Butcher, have been more balanced in their treatment of Fletcher. In his defense, there was no real precedent for supporting an amphibious landing with carriers—particularly with air power—in the Pacific war. Also, Fletcher made it clear that he was going to depart the area of Guadalcanal on the morning of 9 August at the pre-execution planning conference. If Admiral Turner or anyone else present had strong objections to that course of action, approved tacitly by Admiral Ghormley, they should have demanded a reversal of the decision before authorizing the plan for the operation. There is no record or indication that they did this, but even so Maj. Gen. Alexander Vandegrift, who commanded the 1st Marine Division at Guadalcanal, decried Fletcher for "running away twelve hours earlier than he had already threatened during our unpleasant meeting."[43] Also, Turner's Operation Plan called for withdrawing the American Amphibious Force incrementally. He expected to release all but five cargo ships and his screening units on the night of 8 August, D+1.[44]

Morison condemned Fletcher as fixated with topping off the fuel of his force. Records indicate that the average fuel on board for all thirteen of Fletcher's destroyers at noon on 8 August was 45.3 percent.[45] Morison also assumed that fleet oilers were waiting close to Guadalcanal to refuel Task

Force 61. In reality, none of the three in the western Pacific area were within a thousand miles of the action.[46] Thus, as six of Fletcher's seven destroyer commanders at Guadalcanal attested in 1976 to Professor Lloyd Graybar, refueling was "necessary and wise."[47]

Moreover, Fletcher's carrier-embarked fighters had taken a real beating on 7 and 8 August. Just before sunset on 8 August, Fletcher had radioed Ghormley (with Admiral Turner as an information addee): "Total fighter strength reduced from 99 to 78. In view of large number of enemy torpedo and bomber planes in area recommend immediate withdrawal of carriers. Request you send tankers immediately to rendezvous decided by you as fuel is running low."[48]

Fletcher's fear for his carriers was not unreasonable. The U.S. landings caught the Japanese by surprise. However, the Japanese quickly developed a menacing submarine presence in the area, as Admiral Fletcher was acutely aware. The *Wasp*, detached to refuel with her screening units,[49] was torpedoed and sunk in the aftermath of the Battle of the Eastern Solomons on 15 September when two torpedoes of a six-torpedo salvo by the Japanese submarine I-19 struck her with devastating effect.[50] Luckily, her planes were able to fly off and reached Espiritu Santo safely. They were, for the most part, embarked aboard *Enterprise* when she returned from repairs at Pearl Harbor during the Battle of Santa Cruz. Fletcher's flagship, USS *Saratoga*, was temporarily taken out of the war when torpedoed on 31 August by I-26 between San Cristobal and the Santa Cruz Islands while conducting morning flight operations.[51] Fletcher cited very real concerns for the security of the only strategic assets in the Pacific, save the soon-to-arrive carrier *Hornet*, and received permission from Admiral Ghormley, COMSOWESPAC, to depart the area—with Turner's full knowledge, and without Turner's objection.

While Marvin Butcher, in his essay "Admiral Frank Jack Fletcher, Pioneer Warrior or Gross Sinner?" comes down forcefully on the side of "pioneer warrior,"[52] John Lundstrom has uncovered perhaps the most powerful and unbiased source to vindicate Fletcher from culpability for the U.S. disaster in the battle of Savo Island.

Lundstrom quotes Col. (later Maj. Gen.) Melvin J. Maas, a reserve officer in the Marine Corps attached to Fletcher's staff for the Guadalcanal action and also a serving congressman—the ranking Republican on the House Naval Affairs Committee while serving under Fletcher—as having written that Fletcher "should be commended for his judgment, courage, and tactical farsightedness" for his decisions during the Marine landings on Guadalcanal.[53] Maas cites ten considerations supporting Fletcher's decision to withdraw. In late August of 1942, while the battles of Savo Island and the Eastern Solomons were still fresh in his mind, he wrote: "Vice Admiral Frank Jack Fletcher. The tops. Finest type Admiral. Experience, brains, exceptional ability. Human, an American in the finest sense. Knows fundamentals of naval tactics and employment. Better than a genius. A man of intelligence. Marked for a 4-star Admiral. 4.0."[54] Though most historians have judged Fletcher harshly for his actions at Guadalcanal on 7–9 August 1942, it would appear that at least one senior Marine in a position to know thought he did the right thing.

The Battle of the Eastern Solomons

A slackening of the action followed the Battle of Savo Island. For the next several weeks the Japanese concentrated on preventing reinforcement and supply of the Marines already ashore. Meanwhile, Japan built up naval units at their main base in the Southern Resource Area at Rabaul on New Britain.

From the Japanese night attack on 9 August through 23 August Japanese cruisers and destroyers bombarded American positions practically every night with relative impunity.[55] "Operating in the close waters between Tulagi and Guadalcanal, these enemy ships would have been good targets for carrier planes and surface ships, in both of which [the U.S.] were superior numerically for a time. However, in order that our carriers' presence might be concealed from the enemy, [Task Force 61] operated . . . well to the south of Guadalcanal, out of range of hostile search planes."[56] The resulting lack of opposition gave the Japanese the opportunity they needed to seriously impede the American logistics flow and enabled them to bring powerful naval units into the area to contest the U.S. presence in the Solomons. By 23 August, the local naval superiority America had enjoyed had vanished. Aerial reconnaissance indicated the Japanese now had three or four aircraft carriers in the vicinity, as many as two battleships, and seven to fifteen cruisers.[57]

The United States still had the carriers *Enterprise*, *Saratoga*, and *Wasp* available to challenge a Japanese move to the south, as well as a battleship, five heavy and one light cruiser, and eighteen destroyers.[58] The primary responsibility of these units was to support the Guadalcanal-Tulagi buildup and maintain the lines of communication between Australia and the Solomons. As a secondary mission, Nimitz tasked Fletcher to destroy enemy forces encountered in the area, but again with the caveat of "calculated risk" limiting action to protect his carriers. An additional task force built around the carrier *Hornet* was dispatched from Pearl Harbor on 17 August when intelligence indicated that battle with the Japanese was imminent.[59] Unfortunately, the *Hornet* group arrived on 29 August, too late to take part in the action.[60]

On Guadalcanal on 9 August, the U.S. Marines had not yet fully developed Henderson Field. This would take another ten days. About twenty fighters and a dozen scout bombers were already stationed there, and more would come as soon as the field could accommodate them. Rear Adm. John S. McCain commanded naval patrol planes in the area as the commander of Air Forces, South Pacific, and had thirty-nine PBYs and thirty B-17s at his disposal. His aircraft searched the area daily in anticipation of the next Japanese attempt to dislodge the Marines from Guadalcanal.[61] In the meantime, Task Force 61 waited in readiness about 100–150 nautical miles southeast of Guadalcanal.

Fletcher wanted to operate with a full range of options, and he was always concerned with keeping his carriers and screening units topped off with fuel. Unaware as yet of any concerted movement by the Japanese against Guadalcanal, he detached Noyes and his *Wasp* task force at about dusk on 23 August to refuel near Espiritu Santo—taking their twenty-six fighters, twenty-six dive-bombers, and eleven torpedo planes with them. That unfortunate choice put the United States at a relative disadvantage as the Japanese began their move south.

The first indication of a Japanese move was the sighting of several transport ships 250 nautical miles north of Tulagi on 23 August.[62] Those ships were out of attack range of Fletcher's carrier aircraft, however, as the U.S. carriers were still operating to the southeast of Guadalcanal. Though two Japanese submarines likely to be screening units for a larger force were sighted heading in a generally southerly direction on that same day, no particular intelligence indication was made of the sightings.

COMAIRSOPAC aircraft reported a contact on the enemy occupation force.[63] Admiral Fletcher launched an attack from his own carrier, *Saratoga*, shortly after 1500, consisting of thirty-one dive-bombers armed with 1,000-pound bombs and six torpedo planes. However, the targeted group of ships had changed course to the northwest about two hours before the attack was launched. This placed the Japanese force beyond the attack range of Task Force 61's aircraft. Due to the distance at which the strike aircraft had been launched not all the planes could make it back to their carrier. With the exception of a single torpedo plane that returned to *Saratoga*, they landed at Henderson Field on Guadalcanal, where they spent the night.[64] A Marine strike group had been launched to attack the same Japanese force just prior to *Saratoga*'s strike, but it was likewise unable to locate its targets.

On the morning of 24 August *Saratoga*'s planes were supposed to rendezvous with her at 0800. The air group commander modified that plan, deciding to delay the return to *Saratoga* until a morning search plan by Marine aircraft from Guadalcanal had been completed. When the search proved negative, the *Saratoga* group of aircraft, minus two dive-bombers that had to return to the island with mechanical problems, returned to their carrier. There they were quickly refueled and rearmed. A Japanese carrier had been located by a carrier search plane at around 0900, and an attack sortie was about to be launched.

Carrier Battle of 24 August 1942

On the morning of 24 August a long-range land-based search plane sighted a Japanese force consisting of one carrier, in all likelihood the *Ryujo,* two cruisers, and one destroyer at 04° 40' S, 161° 15' E on a course of 180 degrees true at 0935, but no speed was given. This contact was copied by personnel aboard *Enterprise* at 1015 and passed immediately to Admiral Fletcher aboard *Saratoga*.[65] The contact placed the Japanese force outside the attack radius of Task Force 61, bearing 343 degrees true at 281 nautical miles.[66] Fletcher launched a morning search in the northern semicircle to a distance of 200 nautical miles. Unfortunately, during the time of the search the *Ryujo* group was 50–100 nautical miles to the north of the planes, which were conducting the search at the limit of their endurance. The planes turned back without contact.[67] The need to turn to the southeast into the wind to launch and recover aircraft frequently made it hard for the U.S. carriers to close enemy targets.[68]

As early as 1100 and thereafter, Task Force 61 was periodically approached by Japanese search planes, and four of these were shot down by carrier combat air patrol fighters.[69] Thus both the Americans and the Japanese knew of the locations of at least a part of their enemy's fleet. The advantage would lie with the force that was able to position their opponent most precisely and launch their aircraft first. Not wanting to be on the defensive at the outset, Admiral Fletcher had *Enterprise* launch twenty-two bombers and seven torpedo planes commencing at 1300 to conduct a search out to 250 nautical miles from his carriers. At 1410 the search gained contact on the Japanese carrier *Ryujo*, one cruiser, and three destroyers bearing 317 degrees true from

Task Force 61 at a distance of 198 nautical miles.[70] Since the same radio circuit was used to direct the combat air patrol fighters, *Enterprise* communications group didn't copy the contact until 1518, and it wasn't passed to Admiral Fletcher on *Saratoga* until 1530. Immediately Fletcher authorized Admiral Kinkaid to launch an attack, if he was satisfied of the accuracy of the locating information.[71]

In the interval, at 1430, the *Enterprise* search plan revealed two additional carriers, four heavy cruisers, six light cruisers, and eight destroyers bearing 340 degrees true at 198 nautical miles from the American force. The two large carriers known to be in the area were *Shokaku* and the *Zuikaku,* commanded by Vice Adm. Nobutake Kondo. Neither U.S. carrier received report of this contact until *Saratoga* copied a transmission stating that two Japanese carriers had been attacked unsuccessfully at 1525.[72]

Though no mention is made of it in the *Enterprise*'s commanding officer's Report of Action and there is only a passing comment on it in Nimitz's similar report to King, the commander of the *Enterprise* air group indicates in his Report of Action that two pilots of Bombing Squadron Six off *Enterprise* attacked one of the two large carriers. That carrier was maneuvering radically and was believed to have sustained no damage by two near misses.[73] *Enterprise* did not acknowledge the pilots' on-scene report of this bombing.

In the meantime, at 1440, four heavy cruisers and three to five destroyers on a bearing of 347 degrees true at 225 nautical miles from Task Force 61 were reported.[74] The Japanese force was spread out on an arc sixty to eighty miles wide, centered at about 162 degrees east longitude, and moving south toward Guadalcanal Island.[75] Two Bombing Squadron Six pilots bombed the largest cruiser in this Japanese formation, but again achieved only two near misses.[76]

At 1330, two hours after returning to *Saratoga* from Henderson Field, the planes of the 23 August search were launched again—this time in a strike against the *Ryujo*—but to her position as passed in the morning at 0935 by land-based search planes, as the *Enterprise* search location was not as yet known. En route to where they believed the *Ryujo* to be, the air group commander leading the strike intercepted a report from an airborne search plane indicating that the *Ryujo* group was seventy-five nautical miles northeast of the position reported by the *Enterprise* search planes. This sighting and a claim by the Army that their B-17s had made bomb hits on a small carrier in the same vicinity four hours after this contact was passed, after the *Saratoga*'s air group had probably already sunk *Ryujo*, gives credence to the possibility that another small carrier was operating in the area as well, bringing the total number of Japanese carriers to four. Not finding a Japanese force at this newly reported position, the *Enterprise* air group commander altered course to the southwest toward the initial contact location and sighted the *Ryujo* group.[77] *Saratoga*'s group of twenty-nine dive-bombers and eight torpedo planes had found their objective anyway, and at 1530 they commenced their attack. It was a well-coordinated attack launched with deadly accuracy. Four of the dive-bombers—all piloted by veterans of the Midway battle—scored hits on the Japanese carrier with their 1,000-pound bombs. As the Dauntlesses departed the Devastator torpedo planes commenced their attack. They scored one "sure" and one probable hit, and one torpedo that missed the *Ryujo* hit and sank an accompanying destroyer.[78] On their return to the *Saratoga*, the Dauntlesses encountered seven Japanese dive-bombers, divided into two groups, and shot down four.[79] As they would soon learn, these Japanese planes were returning from attacking *Enterprise*. Thus the attacks by the Americans and Japanese on the carrier groups opposing them had been, for all intents and purposes, nearly simultaneous.

Figure 29 (see p. 170) provides a chart of the action and the movements of the U.S. and Japanese main forces during the Battle of the Eastern Solomons to show the spatial orientation of the battle.

At about the same time as the U.S. attack on the *Ryujo* the USS *Enterprise* picked up Japanese planes on radar. At 1632 a large number of unidentified aircraft were detected inbound to the force bearing 320 degrees true at eighty-eight nautical miles at an estimated altitude of twelve thousand feet.[80] At the time there were twenty-five *Enterprise* and *Saratoga* fighters airborne in the combat air patrol and another twenty on deck awaiting launch on *Saratoga*.[81] The radar echo immediately faded and wasn't picked up again for seventeen minutes. As a precaution, *Saratoga* launched additional fighters, bringing the total in the air to thirty-eight.

Contact on the inbound Japanese air raid was regained at 1649 on a bearing of 340 degrees true at forty-four nautical miles by *Enterprise*. The first sighting by the combat air patrol was at thirty-three miles on a bearing of 300 degrees true from *Enterprise*. Confusion ensued as the U.S. fighter pilots filled the airwaves with unnecessary chatter, and this greatly diminished the ability of the fighter director officer to vector his planes where needed.[82] While the battle over Task Force 61 was starting, *Saratoga* launched still more fighters, bringing the total airborne to oppose the Japanese attack to fifty-three.[83]

The Japanese dive-bombing attack on the *Enterprise*, which had launched all its ready aircraft and was now making twenty-seven knots and conducting radical maneuvers, did not start until 1711. The Japanese attack group was estimated at between twenty and forty bombers, and they were met immediately by the *Enterprise* and *Saratoga* fighters. Their altitude was close to sixteen thousand feet. Diving at an attack angle of seventy degrees, the Japanese pilots released their bombs at two thousand to fifteen hundred feet. With aircraft coming in at intervals of about seven seconds, the attack lasted for four minutes, interrupted by two respites of twenty to thirty seconds.[84] *Saratoga*, which was distant some ten to fifteen miles on the disengaged side, was not attacked by the Japanese. None of the Japanese torpedo planes reached their objective, as they were intercepted and either shot down or driven off approximately sixty miles from *Enterprise*.[85]

In all, the Japanese were estimated to have launched about seventy-five planes in the attack, including dive-bombers, torpedo planes, and their fighter escorts. Since *Ryujo* was thought to be capable of carrying only about forty aircraft, this was a clear indication that the attack included planes from *Shokaku*, *Zuikaku*, or both, and possibly *Ryujo* as well.[86] The length of time the *Ryujo* strike aircraft would have had to be in the air when they were encountered by U.S. strike aircraft on their return from sinking *Ryujo*—over three hours—indicates that in all probability the *Ryujo* strike was against Guadalcanal, and not the U.S. carriers. Since an attack on Guadalcanal did take place at approximately the same time as that on *Enterprise,* that is almost certainly the case.

At least twenty bombs were released in the vicinity of *Enterprise*.[87] *Enterprise* sustained three direct hits and three near misses. One of the hits inflicted substantial damage and another superficial damage.[88] One bomb hit the starboard corner of the number three elevator, passed through several decks, and exploded, causing extensive damage on several levels of the ship, as well as bulging the deck plates and shattering the wooden flight deck. Another large bomb landed on the starboard side and exploded in the gun galley between the flight deck and the near inboard bulkhead, causing many fatalities and heavy damage and buckling the flight deck forward. A third bomb exploded as it hit, before penetrating the flight deck,[89] again on the starboard side but a bit forward of the second hit, and this damaged the number two elevator. The closest near miss started gasoline fires and damaged arresting wires numbers one and two.

Even with this damage, by 1649 the fires on *Enterprise* were brought under control and she was steaming at twenty-four knots and landing aircraft. The bomb that hit the gun galley inflicted the damage of most immediate

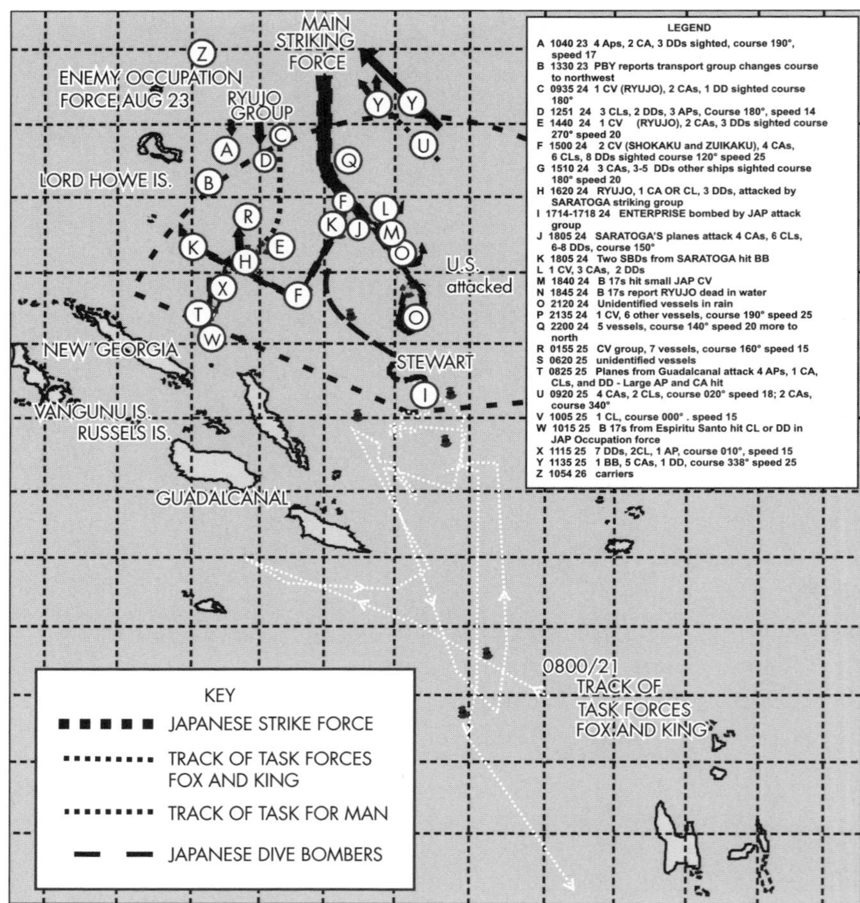

FIGURE 29. U.S. and Japanese force movements in the Battle of the Eastern Solomons (Davis, letter to Commander in Chief, United States Pacific Fleet, dated 5 September 1942, Serial 008, Sept 5, 1942, USS Enterprise Track Chart with contact and Attack Sequence off Solomon Islands, August 23–25, 1942, Enclosure "A," (only page of enclosure). Secret (Downgraded to unclassified). Naval War College Microfilm Collection reel A287, first frame 48173. —*Graphic provided by Jason Peters*

concern, as it caused loss of steering control at 1850, just after sunset, with the rudder jammed at twenty-two degrees when the ship was still making twenty-four knots. Though speed was reduced after a near collision with the destroyer *Balch*, the *Enterprise*'s vulnerability to a submarine attack was greatly increased since only about ten knots could be maintained safely until secondary steering was established about a half hour later. Some *Enterprise* aircraft were able to land aboard their carrier. Others, returning from the unsuccessful strike on *Ryujo*, which they could not locate because of darkness, landed either aboard *Saratoga* or at Henderson Field.[90]

During the action the new battleship *North Carolina*, which had arrived as America's first new-construction major fleet unit at Pearl Harbor in early June, acquitted herself well with antiaircraft gunfire support. This was true for all *Enterprise* screening units. Though as many as sixteen Japanese dive-bombers and eleven level bombers attempted to hit *North Carolina*, her fire was so intense that only three got through to deliver near misses.[91] Firing her twenty 5-inch, four quadruple 1.1-inch mounts, forty 20-mm and twenty-six .50-caliber machine guns, she appeared to be in flames amidships due to the amount of fire she was delivering. In all, she claimed seven Japanese planes splashed.[92] The *Enterprise* Air Group claimed to have splashed twenty-nine Japanese aircraft, and another twenty-four were claimed shot down by the antiaircraft fire of *Enterprise*, *North Carolina*, *Portland*, and *Atlanta*.[93] Some of these, however, might have been claimed by more than one ship, in that they were fired at simultaneously. Another eighteen Japanese aircraft were claimed shot down by *Saratoga*'s fighters, which brought the total to just over seventy.[94]

This large number of Japanese planes lost came at a high price. Two officers and seventy-two enlisted men were killed aboard *Enterprise* and another six officers and eighty-nine men were wounded.[95] Fortunately, only four fighters, four dive-bombers, and two torpedo planes from that ship either went missing, made water landings, or were damaged severely, rendering them beyond repair. Two fighter crews and one bomber crew were missing at sea and presumed lost.[96]

Retirement from the Area and Aftermath

When the fighting had ceased and all air crews in the water in the immediate vicinity had been recovered, Admiral Fletcher had the *Saratoga* and *Enterprise* task groups retire to the south-southeast. Here he intended to refuel them, detach the *Enterprise* group to return for repairs at Pearl Harbor, and rejoin the action with *Wasp,* which was returning from refueling. More action was expected as *Shokaku* and *Zuikaku* with their reduced air contingents were still in the area. But events did not develop as Fletcher had foreseen.

Fletcher's forces rendezvoused with the oilers *Cimarron* and *Platte* at 0800 on 25 August at 13° 4' S and 164° 3' and 30'' E.[97] *Enterprise* was detached, along with the cruiser *Portland* and destroyers *Balch*, *Maury*, *Benham*, and *Ellet* to proceed via Tongatubu to Pearl Harbor for repairs as anticipated. The rest of the ships in company headed north to rejoin the action. On their way, the destroyers *Patterson* and *Monssen* sighted and sank a Japanese submarine with depth charges.[98] Two other Japanese submarines were sighted during the day, and one was sunk by a direct bomb hit from a Scouting Squadron Five aircraft off *Saratoga*.[99]

The Japanese had had enough. Their last gasp was felt when they struck Henderson Field, mostly with land-based heavy bombers, at noon on 25 August. Four men were killed, five wounded, but little other damage was done.[100] This timely retirement was a lucky break, as *Saratoga* was torpedoed and returned to Pearl Harbor for repairs on 31 August, and *Wasp* was torpedoed and sunk by a Japanese submarine on 15 September.

The Battle of the Eastern Solomons in Retrospect

In Admiral Nimitz's own words: "On 23 to 25 August, U.S. Naval Forces in the Southern Pacific, supported by Marine aircraft from the new field at Guadalcanal, and Army aircraft operation from the new field at Espiritu Santo, successfully turned back a large-scale Japanese attempt to recapture Guadalcanal-Tulagi. This major victory, second only to Midway in forces involved, permitted continued consolidation of our position in the Solomons.[101]

"Air losses decided the issue, and the Japanese, all but stripped of carrier aircraft support, broke off the fight although their powerful surface force was still largely intact."[102] Including probables, Fighting Squadron Six aboard *Enterprise* shot down twelve Aichi type-99 dive-bombers, ten Zero fighters, and three Mitsubishi type-97 torpedo planes.[103] Fighting Squadron Five claimed fourteen dive-bombers and three Zeros.[104] At the outset the Japanese outnumbered their American counterparts in aircraft by an estimated 177 to 153.[105] By the end of the action the Japanese had lost almost two carrier groups plus twenty-one land-based or *Ryujo* launched aircraft downed by Marine fighters on Guadalcanal, for a grand total of about ninety aircraft.[106]

The Japanese navy rolled further down the slippery slope toward impotency of the *kido butai.*

Conclusions

Let us turn now to an evaluation of the commanders with respect to the criteria offered on pages 2–3.

1. The commander's estimate of the situation and grasp of the strategic and operational significance of the decisions he would be required to make. This is a very difficult area to assess. Admiral Nimitz demonstrated an excellent grasp of the situation, first in determining that the opportunity existed for the United States to go on the offensive in a limited way after the Battle of Midway, and second in realizing that the most experienced carrier admiral available—Frank Jack Fletcher—should be placed in command of the offensive instrument to do that. Also, in demanding of Admiral King that Fletcher be promoted to vice admiral so that he could be selected to command over the more senior rear admiral, Leigh Noyes, and then being persistent enough to convince a skeptical King that his was the right decision, Nimitz showed real strength of character and excellent insight.

   However, failing to place Fletcher in a position where he could use his air power should the Japanese try to reestablish their control of Guadalcanal once the U.S. Marines had landed there shows an incomplete appreciation of the dynamics of an amphibious landing and buildup on the beach. On balance Nimitz deserves a "B+," but much of the blame for poor operational decisions rests with Fletcher and Richmond Kelly Turner.

   This is not to criticize Nimitz—or Frank Jack Fletcher, for that matter—for their failure to keep the American carriers in the vicinity of the beachhead until all the transports and supply ships had been off-loaded. That, in view of the accurate information now available on the extent of aircraft losses and the fuel situation of the screening units concerned, should be viewed as the proper course of action given a detailed estimate of the situation, notwithstanding the almost universal criticism of historians of the 1940s and 1950s. The real criticism should have been reserved for failing to ensure an adequate search of the area between Rabaul and Guadalcanal by land-based aircraft. Above all, the commander of all land-based Navy search assets, Rear Adm. John S. McCain, should bear the responsibility for adequate coverage of that important area.

As commander of Task Force 63, McCain was commander of aircraft for the Southern Pacific Forces and had responsibility for aircraft temporarily attached as well.[107] In all, around 635 aircraft were available for the Watchtower operation.[108] This included those aircraft of the United States Navy, Marine Corps, Army Air Force, Australian Air Force, and the New Zealand Air Force.[109] Of these 635 aircraft, 238 were Navy aircraft on the carriers *Saratoga*, *Enterprise*, and *Wasp*, and were thus under the control of the commander of Task Group 61.6, Rear Adm. Leigh Noyes.[110] Forty-three more were embarked in the heavy combatant ships of the amphibious force, Task Group 61.2, under the command of Rear Adm. Richmond Kelly Turner.[111]

The remainder, 290 land- and water-based aircraft, were under Admiral McCain's control.[112] While some of these were in rear areas of the South Pacific theater, McCain had 27 B-17s, 10 B-26s, and 38 Army Air Force P-39s in the Guadalcanal-Tulagi area during the amphibious landing phase of the operation; 6 Hudsons from the New Zealand Air Force; 24 Marine SBD scout bombers at Efate, New Hebrides; 22 PBY seaplanes; and 3 scouting planes operating from seaplane tenders—a total of 145 planes with which to provide reconnaissance for the operation.[113] McCain's failure to warn all concerned of the night attack in the Battle of Savo Island, as well as provide continuous tracking information on the Japanese carrier groups once they were located in the Battle of the Eastern Solomons, was a clear failure of his responsibility to the success of the Guadalcanal operation. Thus McCain deserves failing marks, for not ensuring an adequate area search to detect the Japanese cruiser and destroyer group that raided near Savo Island on 9 August 1942, and for not ensuring the continuous tracking of the Japanese carriers heading south on 23–24 August. The latter in all probability accounts for *Shokaku* and *Zuikaku* not being struck while the opportunity existed on the 24th. However, McCain's search plan did uncover the *Ryujo* group, and that mitigates his total failure in his primary area of responsibility. Let us give McCain a D for his efforts.

Admiral Nimitz, on the other hand, did an outstanding job of realizing and ensuring that the most experienced officer of proven decision capacity was given the responsibility for his carrier groups in the South

Pacific. He deserves a high mark for that. Responsibility for adequate search in the Rabaul-Guadalcanal area, however, was ultimately Nimitz's. He, like Admiral McCain, did poorly in this vital area. Also, noting that Admiral Fletcher was probably correct in detaching the *Wasp* task force to refuel, the lack of one or more oilers in the vicinity of the carriers was a serious oversight. This important aspect of the entire operation's success was again the responsibility of Admiral Nimitz. While it should be noted that the number of oilers was inadequate for operations in such distant areas, and Nimitz could do nothing about that, he still failed to provide the flexibility for his operating units that their tasks required. Admiral Nimitz thus had his carriers right where they were needed when they were needed, but failed to support them with land-based air surveillance and readily available fueling capacity—an effort that should lower the B+ awarded earlier to a B.

Rear Admiral Ghormley is culpable for these shortcomings as well. Having just arrived in theater, however, there was little he could do to correct these shortcomings. In fairness, an Incomplete should be assigned.

Now let us consider Frank Jack Fletcher. Fletcher won an important victory in the Battle of the Eastern Solomons that further eroded the Japanese navy's ability to go on the offensive. He was not made aware of a Japanese force movement toward the Guadalcanal landing area, nor was he requested to respond with carrier air once the attack around Savo Island started. In that it was a night attack, there was little that he could have done to prevent it. All that was realistically possible was to respond with an air strike after the damage to the American cruisers and destroyers had already been done. Even that would have been problematic in the dark.

On the other hand, Fletcher's failure to attack the group of two large Japanese carriers that had been reported to him remains a mystery. Circumstances that prevented him from explaining this after the Battle of the Eastern Solomons aside, it can only be surmised that Fletcher understood the futility of launching such a strike under veil of darkness before the carriers could be located. It was his intention to return to the area on 25 August, most likely to seek out and destroy *Shokaku* and *Zuikaku*. The damage to USS *Enterprise* negated that option. Fletcher made an excellent decision in withholding sufficient aircraft for a second strike, either on the *Ryujo* group, if needed, or on the *Shokaku/Zuikaku* group if its position was firmly established. He apportioned his aircraft among search, strike, and defense of his carriers expertly. When the fighting was done, in Admiral Nimitz's own words, the result of the engagement of 24 August was strongly in favor of the United States. And, while USS *Wasp* was most unfortunately sunk by submarine attack on her return from refueling, Fletcher could not reasonably have anticipated that event. Thus he escaped the battle having inflicted considerable damage on Japan's operational objective of retaking Guadalcanal and the air base that commanded the SLOCs between Hawaii and Australia, without the loss of a carrier actually engaged in the action. On balance, Fletcher deserves a weak B+.

Last, but worthy of comment, is Rear Admiral Turner. While, as John Lundstrom emphatically points out,[114] Turner had every opportunity to weigh in against the departure of Fletcher's carriers less than two full days into the amphibious operation, he refrained from doing so. Moreover, he didn't use his own aircraft frequently enough or in any concerted plan in the search phase or ensure that Admiral McCain's air search of the Rabaul-Guadalcanal area was adequate during a period when Japanese naval action to prevent the landing was not only likely but highly probable. Once he failed to request carrier support when the Japanese attacked on 9 August, or in pursuit in the aftermath of the battle, Turner did everything in his power to shift the blame to Fletcher. Turner worked hard for an F and deserves it.

2. The commander's demonstrated ability to formulate a course of action, his ability to convey his decision in mission orders to subordinate commanders concisely and unambiguously, and his flexibility in modifying those orders through strategic and/or operational reappraisal if required. Admiral Nimitz demonstrated great initiative in setting in motion the events that allowed the Navy to take advantage of the great victory at Midway and go on the offensive. Though his organizational arrangement for the operations to wrest Guadalcanal from Japanese control was poor, with Rear Admiral Noyes operating as a subordinate to the carrier task force commander, Vice Admiral Fletcher, but Fletcher in turn reporting to Noyes as commander of the *Saratoga* task force, Nimitz understood that all those involved would work through their situation toward the common goal. All concerned under Nimitz fully understood and appreciated their operational tasks, and chan-

nels remained open to modify those tasks due to such events as the incapacitation of *Enterprise* and the subsequent loss of *Wasp*. Give Nimitz an A in this important area.

Likewise, Fletcher made what was required by his subordinates and what could be expected of him abundantly clear in the preoperation briefings and thereafter. His movements away from Guadalcanal shortly after the amphibious landing were made with the full knowledge and approval of Admiral Ghormley, commander of the Southwest Pacific Area. Here Fletcher deserves at least an A-.

For his inexplicable failure to intercede in the events of the early morning of 9 August, his failure to request support from Fletcher's carrier groups, and his indecision on when to move his transports and supply ships away from their endangered positions near Guadalcanal and Tulagi—even in the aftermath of the Battle of Savo Island—Turner deserves another F. An officer of his experience, with a planning background, should have done much better.

3. The adequacy of command arrangements, the chain of command established, and the communications procedures put into effect to facilitate the exercise of command in battle. For all concerned here, as discussed in this section above, near-failing grades are warranted. To Nimitz, Ghormley, Fletcher, McCain, and Turner, a solid D is assigned.

4. The commander's adherence to established operational and tactical doctrines where appropriate, his adherence to procedures established prior to the engagement of forces, and his ability to deviate from the same when warranted. It should be noted in this area that, after the Battle of Midway, many of the pilots in that engagement and Coral Sea were allowed to take leave.[115] This necessitated putting less experienced pilots and pilots unhardened by combat into the breach at a critical juncture in the Pacific war. They acquitted themselves nicely, indicating that they were well led. Though adherence to doctrine, as amended by experience at Coral Sea and Midway, by the higher levels of command is difficult to evaluate during the battles of Savo Island and the Eastern Solomons, no major deviations can be readily identified from historical records now available. It should also be noted that Fletcher balanced his requirements for search, strike, and defense particularly well; was responsible for the expansion of his carriers' fighter complements

first at Midway and again prior to the August engagements; and that he moved aggressively to strike *Ryujo* before encountering a Japanese strike, while maintaining a second-strike capacity of his own. There seems no reason to assign less than an A to all concerned, and particularly to Fletcher.

5. The commander's communication of mission requirements to subordinate commanders and the suitability of complementary actions by those subordinates to engage the enemy more effectively. As demonstrated above, all major commanders involved in the Battle of the Eastern Solomons had an excellent understanding of the engagement's importance within the wider context of achieving U.S. political objectives, as well as the concomitant appreciation for appropriate risk and determination of appropriate circumstances for battle termination. The same cannot be said for the support phase for the amphibious assault on Guadalcanal and the surrounding islands. For this shortcoming, most historians and Marines assign culpability to Frank Jack "Haul-Ass" Fletcher. An objective review of the facts, however, points the finger at least as convincingly at Richmond Kelly Turner. For Fletcher, a C- for lack of support of the amphibious operation and an A- for the carrier battle with the Japanese navy is reluctantly given. For Turner, a grade of D for his overall conduct of the amphibious operation seems appropriate.

6. The commander's understanding of the engagement's importance within the wider context of achieving U.S. political objectives and his concomitant appreciation for the appropriate risk and determination of the proper circumstances in which to end the battle. Unquestionably, the taking of Guadalcanal, with its geostrategically critical position astride the Allied SLOCs, was the strategic issue in both of these battles. Nimitz certainly understood this—A. Turner seems to have understood this as well, but he failed to take the steps necessary to ensure success in the amphibious assault, landing, and during the build-up phase on Guadalcanal—a weak C-. Fletcher had a responsibility to preserve the only strategic assets the United States had in the Pacific theater, his carriers. He certainly understood this, but after losing a carrier each at Coral Sea and Midway, his caution may have overruled his responsibility for the security of the

Guadalcanal operation—another C-, but one on sounder ground than that assigned to Turner.

7. The commander's audacity and brilliance in conceptualizing, articulating, and executing a plan of action. None of the commanders involved seems to have stood out for his audacity or brilliance. Nimitz and Fletcher did solid jobs. Ghormley's, Turner's, and McCain's efforts were lackluster by comparison. For the former group, B+, and for the latter, D.

8. The commander's ability to learn from the situation and rapidly pass lessons along to the advantage of those commanding in later engagements. One needs only to see the almost thirteen pages of recommendations of Capt. A.C. Davis, the commanding officer of *Enterprise* during this critical period, to appreciate the exhaustive attempt to let other commanders profit quickly from his experiences in the Battle of the Eastern Solomons.[116] Other After Action Reports follow this pattern. Admiral Fletcher chose merely to endorse these recommendations without adding any of his own.[117] The fact that he was able to disseminate lengthy and detailed reports from the commanders of the *Enterprise*, *Saratoga*, *Atlanta*, *Minneapolis*, and commander of Destroyer Division 22—all within two days of the action—attests to the effort to let others profit from Task Force 61's experience in combat as fully and rapidly as possible. Well done! A+.

Epitaph

That this would be Vice Adm. Frank Jack Fletcher's final battle was not immediately certain after the Battle of the Eastern Solomons. What can be reasonably established is that—at Coral Sea, Midway, and the Eastern Solomons—this cruiser admiral with no aviation training acquitted himself and his forces admirably in the war against Japan. In every instance he employed the provisions of *Sound Military Decision* to achieve his assigned strategic objective through a proper, detailed, and often time-constrained Commander's Estimate of the Situation. While his actions could be attributed variously to luck, personal intelligence, and capacity for reasoned decision while under fire, or the incompetence of his adversary, these factors do not adequately support the consistency of his decision process in a naval context. Fletcher approached each situation as had been inculcated in him during his days at the Naval War

College, and expected those serving under him and with whom he interacted to do likewise. His success in the first three carrier battles of World War II and recorded history, to paraphrase a British aphorism of the time relating to their school at Eton, was won "on the playing fields of Newport."

CHAPTER 5

The Battle of Santa Cruz

FIGURE 30. Douglas SBD Dauntless dive-bomber.
—*Courtesy of U.S. Naval Institute Photo Archive*

"We got ourselves another war. A gut-bustin' mother-lovin' Navy war."

—Cdr. Paul Eddington to Capt. Rock Torrey
World War II movie *In Harm's Way*

The Battle for Guadalcanal

AFTER THEIR LOSSES AT MIDWAY and in the Eastern Solomons, one might have expected the Japanese to rethink their commitment to wresting control of Guadalcanal from the United States. Such was not the case. By day the Japanese land forces left on the island fought fiercely with the United States Marines. By night the Japanese bombarded Henderson Field in naval gunnery raids and attempted to reinforce and resupply their troops. This was possible because they had, for the time being, reestablished naval parity in the area: on 15 September, they had sunk USS *Wasp* and inflicted significant damage (a thirty-two-by-fifteen-foot torpedo hole in her hull) to USS *North Carolina*; on 31 August they heavily damaged USS *Saratoga*.[1]

The Japanese wasted little time after the Battle of Santa Cruz in pressing their claim on Guadalcanal. They attacked just before midnight on 11 October

1942, one group intent on shelling Henderson Field while a second group of two seaplane tenders and seven destroyers in advance of the main force off-loaded troops, howitzers, field guns, and an antiaircraft gun on Guadalcanal.[2] The main force of three heavy cruisers and two destroyers, under the command of Rear Adm. Aritomo Goto, rounded Savo Island from the west and headed into what became known after the Battle of Savo Island as "Iron Bottom Sound." Vice Adm. Robert L. Ghormley, commander of the South Pacific Area (COMSOPAC), was ready for them. Waiting in their path was a group of two heavy cruisers, two light cruisers, and five destroyers under the command of Rear Adm. Norman Scott, commander of Task Force 64.[3]

For the American commander, the mission required the development of a cruiser and destroyer doctrine for night surface action. Admiral Scott had a thorough but uncomplicated plan for engaging the Japanese, who had already sunk eight Allied cruisers and three destroyers without losing a single ship in night battles.[4] Instead of assigning several groups to patrol areas or conduct picket duty as Rear Adm. V.A.C. Crutchley, RN, had done in the Battle of Savo Island, Scott stationed his ships in a line abreast, facing the entrance to the sound. He intended to "cap the T," as the British did in the Battle of Jutland in World War I. This would allow his ships to bring maximum firepower—both guns and torpedoes—to bear on the Japanese. The Japanese warships would be illuminated by his destroyers, stationed in the van and at the rear of his cruisers.

Unfortunately for Admiral Scott, he chose as his flagship the heavy cruiser *San Francisco*, which had the worst radar suite of any of his cruisers.[5] Distrusting his radar when *San Francisco* first picked up the advancing Japanese at 2325, Scott executed a 180-degree turn to better triangulate their position. In the process two of his destroyers fell out of formation and wound up between the opposing forces when firing started.

Scott had indeed crossed the T, enabling heavy fire—especially from his two light cruisers with six-inch guns, the *Boise* and *Helena*—and catching the Japanese by surprise. Goto, aboard his flagship *Aoba*, was mortally wounded in the early stages of the battle.[6] The cruiser *Furutaka* rushed between the *Aoba* and the American force, was engulfed in fire by the six-inch guns of the light cruisers, and sank. The destroyer *Fubuki* sank in the same heavy fire. The Japanese hastily retreated to the north to their base at Rabaul. Admiral Scott ordered pursuit of the Japanese to continue the attack and sink the crippled enemy ships at around midnight, but at 0245 he broke off his pursuit of the three remaining. What is now known as the Battle of Cape Esperance was over.

The Japanese lost one heavy cruiser, three destroyers, and at least 565 men, 111 of them taken prisoner off *Fubuki*.[7] However, the Japanese were successful in off-loading the troops and guns brought by the Reinforcement Group, much to the chagrin of the Marines on Guadalcanal.[8]

Though the victory forestalled the Japanese raid on Guadalcanal and Henderson Field, it came at a heavy price. The destroyer *Duncan*, caught between the U.S. and Japanese cruisers when firing started, engaged the Japanese with torpedoes. She was hit repeatedly by both Japanese and U.S. fire and sunk. The light cruiser *Boise* was severely damaged by two eight-inch shells that detonated ammunition in her two forward turrets, and the destroyer *Farenholt* received some damage. Thus three of Scott's eight ships were lost to the war effort at a particularly critical time.

The results of this surface action made it clear to the Japanese that they would have to initiate a more powerful offensive if they were to regain Guadalcanal. The question was whether Admiral Yamamoto was willing to risk his remaining carriers in order to sever the SLOCs between Hawaii and Australia. The answer would come in only two weeks.

Prelude to the Battle of Santa Cruz

Vice Adm. Chuichi Nagumo, commander of the *kido butai* during its attack on Pearl Harbor, its raid on Ceylon, and in every carrier battle of World War II except Coral Sea, seemed the logical choice to settle the issue of control of Guadalcanal and the Solomon Islands chain. His experience notwithstanding, however, Nagumo had fared badly at Midway and the Eastern Solomons, his last two commands.

The picture was less clear on the American side. After commanding in the first three carrier battles of the war, Vice Adm. Frank Jack Fletcher was sent stateside for some well-deserved leave after his flagship, *Saratoga*, was torpedoed on 31 August. Fletcher, in the damaged *Saratoga*, reached Tongatabu on 6 September—only three days after the crippled *Enterprise* had left for Hawaii—and sailed six days later to reach Pearl Harbor on 21 September.[9]

Adm. Ernest J. King, Commander in Chief of the U.S. Fleet (CominCh), had Fletcher come to Washington from his home ("Araby," a 366-acre dairy farm near La Plata, Maryland, where he had spent his time on leave) for a period of debriefings. After that, King assigned Fletcher as commandant of the Thirteenth Naval District in Seattle and commander of the Northwestern Sea Frontier on 18 November 1942.[10] Almost a year later, in October 1943, Fletcher was relieved of his responsibilities as commandant of the Thirteenth Naval District, but continued in his position as commander of the Northwestern Sea Frontier, again under Nimitz, tasked with planning and executing attacks on the Kurile Islands and the occupation of northern Japan.[11] On 15 April of 1944 that position was abolished and Fletcher became commander of the newly established Alaskan Sea Frontier in Adak, Alaska, with additional duty as commander of the North Pacific Force and North Pacific Ocean Area.[12] In this capacity "it was revealed in July 1945, that a task force under his overall command had made the first penetration through the Kurile Islands into the Sea of Okhtosk on March 3 and 4, 1945, and the same task force on February 4, 1944 bombarded Paramushira in the first sea bombardment of the Kuriles."[13] Fletcher was awarded the Distinguished Service Medal for his actions at Coral Sea and Midway, the battle in which "the Japanese suffered the first decisive defeat in three hundred and fifty years, restoring the balance of naval power in the Pacific."[14] Fletcher went on to become chairman of the General Board in Washington before he retired on 1 May 1947. He died on 25 April 1973.[15]

Intelligence indicated an impending Japanese offensive to retake Guadalcanal. With the most experienced carrier commander out of theater, the question of who would command in the looming battle was paramount. The Japanese had intensified their attacks in the Solomons throughout August, especially after the U.S. victory in the Battle of Cape Esperance on the night of 11–12 October.[16] Only two nights later a powerful Japanese force consisting of two battleships, one light cruiser, and eight destroyers bombarded the Marine aircraft on Guadalcanal at Henderson Field for an hour and twenty minutes, destroying or damaging a large number of planes.[17] Numerous Japanese air attacks also caused some damage, but of the total of around six hundred planes making these attacks from 1 to 27 October approximately two hundred were shot down—captured Japanese records admit to only between one-half and two-thirds of that number.[18] In a predawn landing west of Kokumbona on 15 October, the Japanese were able to land much equipment and around ten thousand troops from six transports and cargo vessels supported by a heavy cruiser, two light cruisers, and four destroyers.[19] Additional reinforcements and supplies were landed thereafter, but in lesser quantities. All indications pointed to a full-scale Japanese assault on Henderson Field in the near future.

In the midst of this, Admiral Nimitz in Hawaii was getting the impression that Ghormley had already accepted the likelihood of the Japanese retaking Guadalcanal. On the evening of 15 October Nimitz read a message from Ghormley declaring his forces "totally inadequate" to meet and repel the expected Japanese attack.[20] Nimitz quickly decided to replace Ghormley and obtained King's permission to replace him with Vice Adm. William F. Halsey as COMSOPAC. Learning of his new assignment when he touched down in Noumea harbor three days later, Halsey blurted out, "Jesus Christ and General Jackson! This is the hottest potato they ever handed me!"[21] Halsey was right.

After the damage and losses inflicted by the Japanese in August the only U.S. aircraft carrier in the South Pacific was USS *Hornet* with Rear Adm. George D. Murray embarked as commander of Task Force 17.* In the *Hornet* Task Force were the heavy cruisers *Northampton* and *Pensacola*, along with the antiaircraft light cruisers *Juneau* and *San Diego* and a screen of destroyers.[22] The sole active battleship in the South Pacific was *Washington*.[23] The only other ships available in the theater for Halsey, save for a few destroyers protecting the supply ships being sent to Guadalcanal from Espiritu Santo, were those that survived the Battle of Cape Esperance.[24]

Evidence of a Japanese Offensive

As the Japanese intensified their attacks on the Solomons and increased their efforts to reinforce and resupply their troops on Guadalcanal, air surveillance by U.S. aircraft staging from Espiritu Santo and other nearby locations (operationally assigned to Rear Adm. John S. McCain, Commander, Aircraft, Southwest Pacific Area) revealed a substantial number of ships assembling in the Rabaul-Kavieng and Shortland Island† areas.[25] Japanese submarine activity intensified in an effort to interdict the U.S. supply lines from Espiritu Santo to Guadalcanal, and the U.S. forces noted indications of a concentration of

---

*It should be noted that at this point in the war phonetic task force identifiers based on the first letter of the last name of the task force commander were used in message traffic and radio transmissions to maintain security. The appropriate numerical identifiers will be used here throughout to maintain a proper convention.

†Rabaul was the Japanese advanced area naval base, with about 90,000 men stationed there, at the northeast corner of New Britain Island, just east of the Huon Peninsula on New Guinea. Kavieng is about 120 nautical miles north and west of Rabaul on the northwest corner of New Ireland Island in the upper Solomons, and Shortland Island is in the Solomons just south of the southeast corner of Bouganville Island and about 270 nautical miles southeast of Rabaul.

submarines in the area. All signs pointed toward a major Japanese land offensive on Guadalcanal in the near future—with 23 October established as the most likely date for its start.[26]

The first step for the Japanese would be to capture Henderson Field. This would allow them to bring in supply ships for their troops and aircraft from their carriers to retake and protect the field, and thus achieve air control of the northern part of the Coral Sea and the seaward approaches to it. By cooperating with the carrier and battleship striking force that was assembling in the area around Rabaul, aircraft based at Henderson Field could attack and destroy any American ships or other assets in the area. Only a tremendous defense put up by the 2nd Marines and their reinforcements from the 164th U.S. Army Infantry Regiment of the Americal Division, which landed on 13 October, forced the Japanese to postpone their planned offensive.[27]

The first major attack by the Japanese came on 12 October, the day before the 164th Army Infantry Regiment arrived. The six thousand troops they had stationed on Guadalcanal attacked on the American-held high ground along what would subsequently be known as "Bloody Ridge" in an attempt to move north toward Henderson Field. The Marines were ready for them, holding through the night in what sometimes became hand-to-hand combat, then making good use of 105-mm howitzers and machine guns in the morning. In all the Japanese lost 1,500 men compared to 40 killed and 103 wounded on the U.S. side.

This crushing defeat, resulting in a quarter of their men on Guadalcanal killed, made the Japanese realize that they would need to reinforce quickly or lose the island. By mid-October the Japanese had increased their strength on Guadalcanal to twenty-two thousand men—mostly fresh troops from New Guinea—opposing the twenty-three thousand exhausted and malaria-infected U.S. troops. The Japanese plan was to launch their offensive on 23 October with air support from Vice Adm. Nobutake Kondo's carrier force moving down "the Slot," the well-used direct sea route from Rabaul.

From the observed evidence and intelligence from decoded Japanese JN-25 naval messages, Admiral Nimitz was convinced a major joint naval and land force assault was soon to be launched against American positions on Guadalcanal. He pushed hard for completion of the extensive repairs to *Enterprise* taking place in Pearl Harbor. Once again the construction crews in Hawaii came through. Not enough can be said in praise of these fine workers, whose efforts before the Battle of Midway and the Battle of Santa Cruz were essential to the success of the United States Navy.

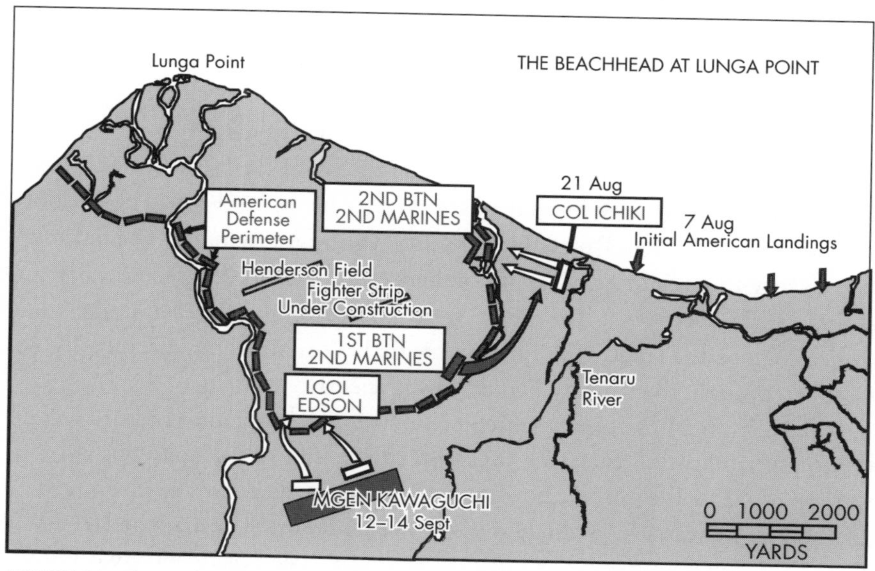

FIGURE 31. The 2nd Marines beachhead on Lunga Point in August and September of 1942. —*Courtesy of U.S. Naval War College*

Enterprise was intended to rendezvous with Admiral Halsey, who was on an aerial reconnaissance mission in the Solomon Islands. Halsey would then resume command of Task Force 16 aboard his old flagship. When Nimitz relieved the defeatist Ghormley, Halsey took over as Commander, South Pacific Forces and Area, responsible for all naval forces, Marine troops, and later Army troops in the South Pacific. Kinkaid, who had been tasked to deliver *Enterprise* to Halsey in the Solomons, remained as commander of Task Force 16 instead.[28] With her repairs complete, *Enterprise* proceeded at high speed from the yard with the battleship *South Dakota* and her screen of destroyers to join with the *Hornet* carrier group and Task Force 17 at 1500 on 24 October at 13° 45' S and 171° 30' E—just in the nick of time to contest the Japanese Joint Force assault on Guadalcanal.[29]

The Battle of Santa Cruz

With the *Enterprise* (CV-6) and *Hornet* (CV-8) Task Forces (TF-16 and TF-17, respectively) now joined, Kinkaid, as the senior officer embarked, took command of the combined Task Force 61. *Hornet* operated close to *Enterprise*, about five miles to the south. Together they set course to sweep the area north of the Santa Cruz Islands to interdict Japanese ships passing down the Slot from Rabaul toward Guadalcanal.[30] "The mission of the force was to support Guadalcanal against an expected large scale attack and occupation, and to destroy any enemy surface forces taking part in this attack."[31]

In addition to the aircraft embarked on the two U.S. carriers, Rear Adm. John S. McCain had sixty-five patrol aircraft and heavy land-based bombers at his disposal. Maj. Gen. Roy S. Geiger's 1st Marine Air Wing on Guadalcanal had twenty-three fighters, sixteen bombers, and one torpedo plane ready for action on 26 October.[32] The latter were unable to fly on 25 October due to heavy rains that made the runway incapable of launching aircraft. By 26 October, though, the runway had dried sufficiently.

At 1250 on 25 October a search plane from Espiritu Santo radioed a contact report indicating that two Japanese carriers and accompanying escorts were at 8° 51' S 164° 30' E, heading 145 degrees true at twenty-five knots.[33] Task Force 61 was 351 nautical miles from the reported contact at 10° 04' S 170° 18' E, on a course of 295 degrees true and speed of twenty-two knots. Kinkaid altered course to close the Japanese carriers and launched a search and attack group from *Enterprise* at 1430 that included twelve scout bombers to search the area in a sector from 280 degrees true to 010 degrees true.[34] The *Hornet* Air Group remained in a ready status to launch when contact with the Japanese force was firmly established.[35]

Fifty minutes later, expecting contact and wanting to strike the Japanese first, Kinkaid launched an attack group of twelve dive-bombers and six torpedo planes escorted by eleven fighters. Neither the search group nor the attack group located the Japanese, since they had reversed course to the north. Due to the overaggressiveness of the attack group commander, who went out to the two-hundred-nautical-mile limit of the search and then continued to search for an additional eighty miles, seven planes and one pilot were lost at sea during the night landings when they returned.[36] Aside from the needless loss of life, this came as a significant blow at a critical time in the engagement. However, the loss of these planes was mitigated by extra aircraft aboard *Enterprise* that had "bingoed"* to her or Henderson Field when *Wasp* sunk in the aftermath of the Battle of the Eastern Solomons.[37]

---

*"Bingoed" is a term used in the military for brevity when an aircraft that is low on fuel, has a mechanical problem, or whose pilot or a member of its crew has a physical problem lands at a base nearer than its home base or intended destination. As used here it denotes those of *Wasp*'s aircraft that were forced to land elsewhere when their carrier was in flames and sinking.

The Japanese were ready to strike. Their major fleet units from Rabaul and some forty ships from the Shortland Islands had gotten underway during the night of 24–25 October.[38] This force included many transport and supply ships to support operations on Guadalcanal, but also at least three carriers to strike any U.S. surface and air forces. As had become their doctrine, the Japanese split their ships into at least three main groups.[39]

Meanwhile, the Japanese intensified their ground operations on Guadalcanal. On 23 October they conducted a heavy artillery bombardment of U.S. positions. A sizeable Japanese attack along the Matanikau River followed, with a force crossing it with tanks and massed infantry. Repeated attacks on the Matanikau River and elsewhere continued unabated through the 24th. This onslaught was supported on 25 October by cruiser and destroyer fire during daylight hours, followed that night by a breakthrough in the American lines and heavy hand-to-hand fighting. The U.S. Marine and Army troops fought well, and the Japanese onslaught was driven back, but with heavy U.S. losses. The situation for the U.S. forces on Guadalcanal was at best tenuous, and heavy rains during the night made Henderson Field unserviceable, preventing the Americans from using land-based air assets against any landing the Japanese were able to make.

During the night of 25–26 October Task Force 61 closed the enemy. At 0110 one of Admiral McCain's land-based search planes radioed that the Japanese had been located at 7° 14' S, 164° 15' E, about three hundred nautical miles from Task Force 61.[40] At dawn *Hornet,* the "duty carrier," had a combat air patrol of fighters overhead and at 0600 *Enterprise* launched a sixteen-plane search group to cover the sector 235-345 degrees true to a distance of two hundred nautical miles.[41] Just after that launch, at 0612, Kinkaid received a report that a patrol plane from Espiritu Santo had located a Japanese force that included the carrier *Zuiho*.[42] Unfortunately, the sighting of *Zuiho* had actually taken place much earlier—at 0410—and her location had been sent as 7° 55' S, 164° 15' E, only two hundred nautical miles from Task Force 61 and on a southerly course at fifteen knots.[43] Somehow transmission of this vital information to Admiral Kinkaid had been delayed for almost two hours. Thus Kinkaid had launched sixteen SBD-3 dive-bombers needlessly, and this diminished his ability to constitute an attack group at the earliest possible time and thus preempt the possibility of being hit first by the Japanese.

Six search aircraft were assigned in pairs to the sector 235–282 degrees true and ten more to the sector 282–345 degrees true.[44] The planes flying in the sub-sector 268–288 degrees true sighted a Japanese force that they

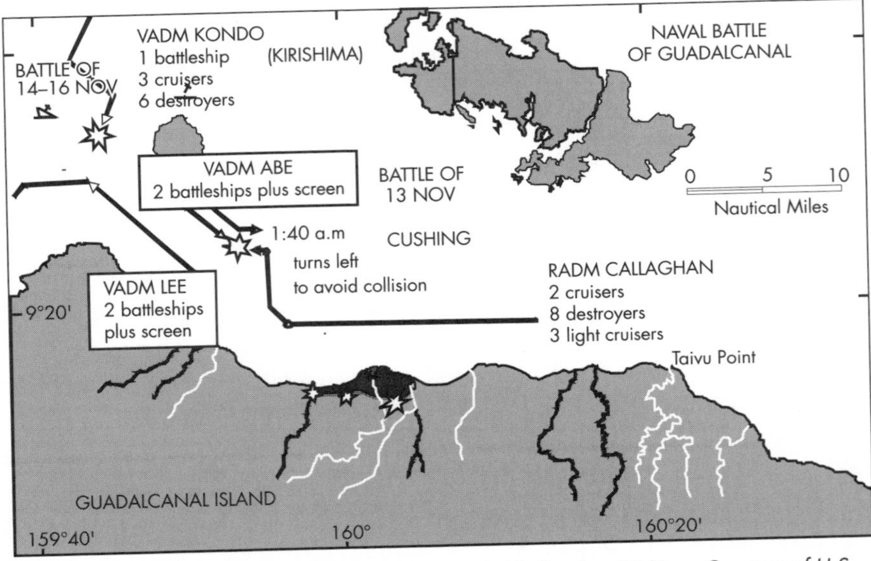

FIGURE 32. The Second Battle of Bloody Ridge, 24–25 October 1942. —*Courtesy of U.S. Naval War College*

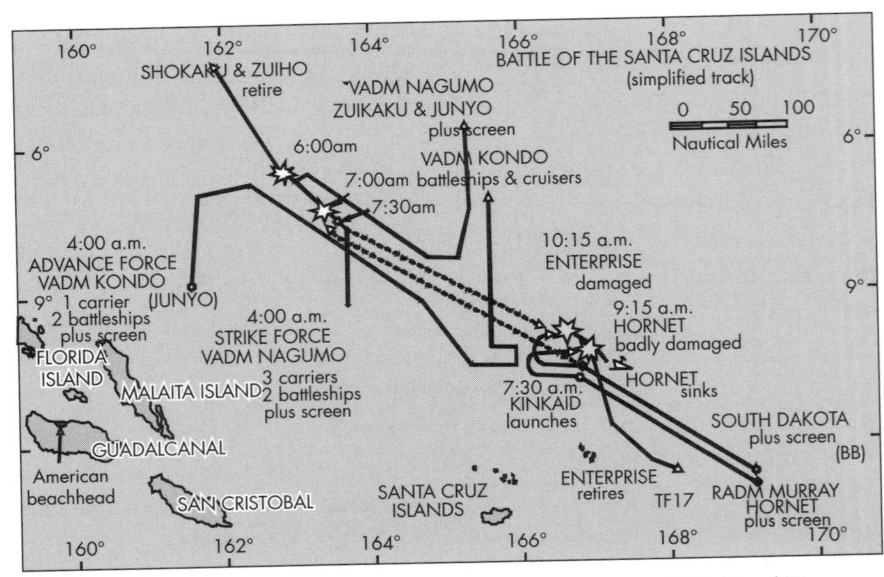

FIGURE 33. The Battle of Santa Cruz, 26 October 1942. —*Courtesy of U.S. Naval War College*

identified as two battleships, one heavy cruiser, and seven destroyers. Not noting any carriers, the crews continued their search to the designated two hundred nautical miles and then returned to *Enterprise* at 1031 after reestablishing the position of the battleship force they had located.[45] The crews had seen a Mitsubishi Type 97 single-engine torpedo bomber flying toward Task Force 61 on their outbound leg and another heading back toward the Japanese force on their return leg but failed to report either sighting.[46]

The crews searching the 298–314 degrees true sector had better luck. They reported at 0750 sighting both *Shokaku* and *Zuikaku* at 7° 05' S, 163° 38' E, with their decks empty. After being attacked by Japanese Zero fighters and shooting two down, the search planes broke off their contact and returned to *Enterprise*.[47]

Another pair of aircraft, assigned to the 330–345 degrees true subsector, copied the 0750 report on the Japanese carriers that had been sighted and departed their track to attack. At 0830, after traversing more than one hundred nautical miles, they attacked *Shokaku,* which was actually in company with *Zuiho* and not the misidentified *Zuikaku*, and delivered two 500-pound bombs to her stern.[48] It seems that *Shokaku*, *Zuikaku*, *Zuiho*, and the converted carrier *Hayataka* had been changing their positions frequently to confuse the U.S. pilots searching for them, and at no time in this battle were any three of these carriers seen in company.[49] *Zuiho* was also attacked and badly hurt, but not crippled.[50]

Enterprise received two transmissions from her search aircraft during this period. The first, received at 0730, was on the contact with the battleship group sighted at 0717. The second, received at 0750, was the one Kinkaid had been waiting for—the Japanese carriers had been located. The *Shokaku* and what was believed to be the *Zuikaku* were two hundred nautical miles from Task Force 61 on a bearing of 300 degrees true, course 330 and speed fifteen knots. Kinkaid also received word that two of the *Enterprise* search planes had hit *Shokaku* with 500-pound bombs.[51] At 0822 a transmission came from an *Enterprise* search plane on the attack frequency that a large Japanese force that did not include any aircraft carriers had been sighted.[52] Kinkaid immediately ordered an attack launched from *Hornet*, and ten minutes later a first-wave strike force of fifteen dive-bombers with 1,000-pound bombs, six torpedo planes, and eight fighters started taking off from her.[53] A second attack wave of nine dive-bombers with 1,000-pound bombs, nine torpedo planes with four 500-pound bombs each,[54] and seven fighters was immediately brought on deck and was in the air by 0910. The *Hornet* air group commander accompanied the second attack wave. Fifteen fighters were maintained continuously for defensive purposes over Task Force 17, the *Hornet* group.[55] Just eight minutes later, concurrent with the end of the launch of a new combat air patrol at 0918, *Hornet* got a radio report from one of her outgoing strikes that two large groups of Japanese carrier planes were headed for Task Force 61.[56]

The situation was beginning to look a lot like the Battle of Midway. As the commander of the South Pacific Area and South Pacific Forces, Halsey, was to observe in his final Report of Action on the Battle of Santa Cruz on 20 November 1942, "narratives and plots of participating units in this action will spotlight the startling similarity in the situation and developments to those existing at Midway on 4 June, 1942. Analysis and conclusions from the action on 26 October should be compared and studied side by side with the Midway engagement."[57] In both these battles the Japanese objective was to wrest control of an island of major strategic importance from the United States. In both cases the Japanese approached the area in multiple separate groups of warships. In both battles the Japanese had to make hard decisions regarding the apportionment of carrier aircraft for search, strike, and defense. Guadalcanal, like Midway, presented the Japanese with essentially an additional carrier with whose aircraft they had to contend (albeit in this case only after Henderson Field dried out sufficiently during the day on 26 October). In both encounters U.S. and Japanese air strikes against their opponents' carriers were in the air simultaneously. And in both carrier battles the opposing commanders would have hard choices to make following their initial successes with a debilitating strike or strikes at a time when the survival of their own force was in jeopardy.

The U.S. Carrier Strike

The first wave of the *Hornet* strike took off with orders to bomb the Japanese carrier task force bearing 300 degrees true at a distance of 190 nautical miles.[58] At 1015 the group flew over and sighted a large cruiser force, but, since it contained no carriers, they continued their search. While passing over what turned out to be an advanced force the *Hornet* strike wave was attacked by nine Zero fighters and lost its own fighter escort in the action, and the Scouting Squadron Seven commander, Lt. Cdr. William J. Widhelm, was shot down. Lt. James E. Vose, commanding officer of Bombing Squadron Eight, assumed command of the strike. They were continually under attack by Japanese fighters from that point on.[59]

At 1030 the *Hornet* strike wave located the Japanese carrier force constructed around one large carrier "with a distinctly pronounced island, which looked fully as large as our *Saratoga* class, also one converted CV."[60] The attack and counterattack profiles are shown in figure 34.

An attack was launched within ten minutes, and eleven of the fifteen planes in the U.S. strike group dropped their bombs. Four direct hits with 1,000-pound bombs were claimed on the large Japanese carrier, which had a single Zero fighter on a "flight deck extending the complete length of the ship, and painted brick red in color."[61] This carrier was later confirmed to be *Shokaku*. Sections of *Shokaku*'s flight deck flew into the air and she was sighted on fire and smoking twenty minutes after the U.S. attack.[62] *Hornet*'s torpedo planes, seeing *Shokaku* in flames, attacked the accompanying heavy cruiser *Chikuma*, scoring two hits.[63] *Hornet*'s second wave strike group torpedo planes scored hits on a *Nachi*-class heavy cruiser and a *Tone*-class cruiser.[64] It appears that *Zuikaku* was not in company with *Shokaku* and *Zuiho* during the U.S. attacks, and thus escaped the engagement without damage.

The Japanese Strikes

A Japanese search plane sighted Task Force 61 at 0750—the precise time when an *Enterprise* search plane radioed that the Japanese carriers had been located—and the Japanese launched an attack group six minutes before the U.S. strike was in the air.[65] Kondo was able to launch immediately due to the longer strike range of his aircraft and the more precise target locating and identifying information his search aircraft passed him. At this time Task Force 61 was at 8° 25' S and 166° 45' E. Fighters from the first Japanese attack group engaged the *Enterprise* attack group that had been launched between 0847 and 0902 and shot down two dive-bombers and two fighters, damaging two other dive-bombers and two fighters sufficiently to cause them to return to *Enterprise*.[66]

Hornet's outgoing strike planes reported two large groups of Japanese planes that included about twenty-four dive-bombers and accompanying Zero fighters while en route to their target.[67] The inbound Japanese strike had been picked up on radar at about the same time, bearing 280 degrees

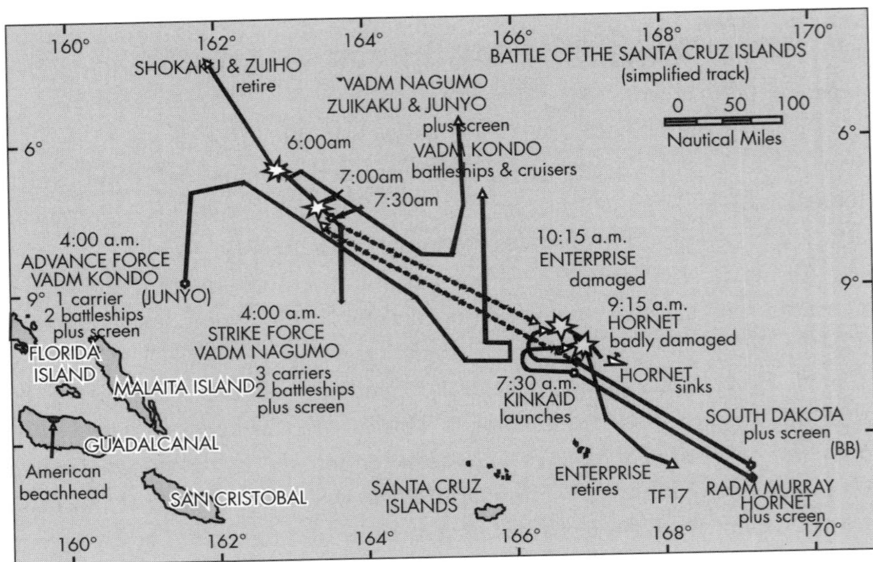

FIGURE 34. The Battle of Santa Cruz, 26 October 1942. —*Courtesy of U.S. Naval War College*

true at sixty miles.[68] Luckily, Task Force 16 was operating eight to ten miles to the northeast of Task Force 17 at that time and was concealed by rain-squalls, making it unlikely that the Japanese would sight it.[69] *Hornet* had fifteen recently launched fighters stationed in her combat air patrol at the time, and they engaged the inbound Japanese strike aircraft, shooting down several before they reached their attack positions.[70]

By 1002 *Hornet* was closing the *Enterprise* group as ordered and her radar held the Japanese strike group at about twenty to thirty miles from the ship, approaching from 230 degrees true.[71] Her fighters were engaging the inbound Japanese strike and she was stationed about midway between that action and *Enterprise*, braced to take the first blow.[72] Task Force 16 was in a circular group with two thousand yards between ships to provide an optimum antiaircraft posture, and maneuvering radically at twenty-eight knots.[73]

At 1010 the Japanese planes dived on *Hornet* and the attack began. It was well coordinated, with both dive-bombers and torpedo planes—about fifteen and twelve respectively—involved. Two minutes into the attack two near misses exploded on the starboard side abreast the bridge. A minute later a Japanese bomber dived vertically into *Hornet*, intent on hitting the bridge or the stack.* He glanced off the stack and hit the flight deck amidships. The plane appeared to be armed with one 500-pound and two 100-pound bombs. One of the 100-pound bombs demolished the signal bridge and part of the stack, killing seven sailors and starting a blazing inferno. The plane itself and the other 100-pound bomb hit the flight deck and exploded, creating a large hole and continuing to the number two ready room below, where another large fire started. Luckily, the 500-pound bomb was a dud, but it still produced a significant hazard until the fires could be put out.[74]

Only two minutes later and only five minutes into the attack, at 1015, *Hornet* was rocked by the force of two torpedoes striking twenty seconds apart near the engineering spaces. Another evaded torpedo had exploded astern on the starboard side. The engine room and two forward fire rooms were flooded and all propulsion and communication power was lost. *Hornet* took on a ten-and-a-half-degree list to starboard, which ultimately righted to seven to eight degrees.

At almost the same time as the two torpedoes struck, *Hornet* was rocked by two more 500-pound bomb hits. The first struck aft, penetrating four decks before exploding. The other exploded while hitting the flight deck just forward of the first bomb and instantly killed thirty men in the hangar and nearby gun batteries. Yet another bomb hit farther forward, piercing *Hornet* and exploding on the third or fourth deck near the messing compartment. Now coasting to a dead stop in the water, *Hornet*'s woes were not over.[75]

Immediately thereafter an unarmed Japanese torpedo plane deliberately dived into *Hornet* from dead ahead.† Miscalculating his approach, the pilot

---

*This was not a kamikaze attack, as the Japanese had not yet initiated that program. Rather, in all likelihood the plane had sustained significant damage from U.S. antiaircraft guns and the pilot realized that he would not be able to return to his ship safely. Akin to the Japanese human-wave suicide tactics that were so often seen in the Pacific island-hopping campaign, it was not uncommon for "doomed" Japanese pilots to ride their aircraft clear to their intended target to ensure maximum damage. In fact, there is at least one report of a pilot attempting to do this as early in the war as the Japanese attack on Pearl Harbor, 7 December 1941.

†Death in battle was thought by many Japanese to assure them of a special and hallowed place in the afterlife. Thus sacrifice of life to assure success in battle was not uncommon for the bravest warriors among them. This attack resembles the bravery demonstrated by the U.S. torpedo squadrons in the Battle of Midway where several of the pilots continued their dangerous runs after the electronic arming attempt on their torpedoes caused the torpedoes to drop well prior to their arrival at their target.

came in in a shallow dive and impacted the port forward gun mount, exploding just outboard of the number one elevator shaft and starting another huge fire. The plane's engine stopped in the junior officer bunk room on the second deck below the flight deck and the plane went into the elevator pit. the Japanese attack was over.[76]

By 1025, only fifteen minutes after the Japanese attack started, there were blazing fires on *Hornet*'s signal bridge, at several places on her flight deck, in her number two ready room, in the chief petty officers' quarters, in the general storeroom, forward messing compartment, the 02 deck on the port side, in the number one elevator pit, in the hangar deck amidships, and on the hangar deck aft in two places. She had lost all fire-main pressure in the attacks. Firefighting went on using only portable "handy-billies" and bucket brigades.[77] The destroyers *Morris* and *Russell*, and later *Mustin* as well, were called alongside to pass over hoses and help fight the fires.[78] The crew prepared to abandon ship and the heavy cruiser *Northampton* was made ready to tow *Hornet* if her fires could be brought under control. Murray, commander of Task Force 17, transferred his flag to USS *Pensacola*.[79]

By 1540 the seriously wounded men, around seventy-five in all, had been transferred to other ships along with about eight hundred nonessential personnel, and faint hopes of saving *Hornet* were reviving. She was under tow by *Northampton* and moving at about three knots. At 1555 the Voice Warning Net, a battery-operated tactical broadcasting system, and flag hoist sent word that another Japanese strike was inbound. At 1620 between four and six Japanese torpedo planes struck. As they approached from a shallow glide from starboard, *Northampton* cast off her tow lines and started evasive maneuvers. Two of the Japanese torpedo planes took her as their target, but missed. The rest of the torpedo planes attacked *Hornet*—a virtual sitting duck. At 1623 a fateful torpedo hit *Hornet* on her starboard side near frame 100. She began taking on water and her list quickly reached fourteen and a half degrees. Capt. C.P. Mason, *Hornet*'s skipper, ordered the ship abandoned. Only the navigator, tactical officer, and gunnery control group remained onboard.[80]

The expected dive-bomber attack came at 1640. Though the five planes in this attack wave made no hits on the defenseless carrier, one near miss shook *Hornet* violently. Her list progressed to twenty degrees, but her guns continued to fire to the very last. Of the twenty planes reported by *Pensacola* to have attacked *Hornet*, over half were shot down prior to releasing their torpedoes.[81]

Six Japanese horizontal bombers dropped their loads on *Hornet* through an obscuring layer of clouds. The navigator and tactical officer, now on the flight deck, saw one bomb strike the starboard corner of the flight deck. The others, probably armor-piercing bombs, landed in a group so small that they appeared to make a single splash. In combination, though they constituted a near miss, their impact was about as damaging as a torpedo hit. Mason was the last to leave the ship, going over the side at 1727. At 1802, with the crew safely away from *Hornet*, she received another hit from one of four dive-bombers making a final attack run. By order of the Task Force Commander, Admiral Murray, the destroyers *Anderson* and *Mustin* fired nine torpedoes and three hundred rounds of 5-inch ammunition into *Hornet* to complete her destruction.[82] By 2136 she was ablaze with a fire that could be seen for over twenty miles.

Anderson and *Mustin* departed the area with *Hornet* still afloat. A Japanese submarine was reported in the area a short time later.[83] During the early action the destroyer *Porter* had also been torpedoed by a submarine while trying to rescue a downed pilot. The immediate threat was serious.[84]

While *Hornet* was being attacked, *Enterprise* had concealed herself in a rainsquall. She recovered her search group between 1031 and 1048 and found that they had shot down seven Japanese Zeros and a torpedo bomber.[85] Unfortunately, one or more of the Japanese planes attacking *Hornet* spotted *Enterprise*. At 1027 a voice transmission passed her presence and location to an inbound strike group.[86]

By 1100 a great number of Japanese planes began to appear on radar. At 1115 Task Force 16 was attacked by an estimated forty-two dive-bombers.[87] The first group of twenty-four dive-bombers attacked *Enterprise*. Seven were shot down while making their attack runs.[88] One bomb hit the forward port corner of the flight deck and a second bomb hit the centerline of the ship just aft of the number one elevator. The fires started by these two bombs were quickly extinguished. Then, at about 1135, about seventeen torpedo planes attacked Task Force 16. An additional twenty-eight dive-bombers followed at 1222. Of these roughly eighty-seven Japanese strike planes, twenty-five were confirmed as shot down and another twenty-three were probably splashed by antiaircraft fire alone.[89] Fifteen of the torpedo planes commenced their attack on *Enterprise*. Maneuvering at twenty-eight knots, *Enterprise* managed to avoid all nine of the torpedoes dropped.[90]

At 1221 another twenty Japanese planes attacked in a shallow dive. Eight Japanese bombers were splashed by *Enterprise*'s antiaircraft fire.[91]

The rest achieved no hits, but a near miss on the starboard side forward, near frame 30, damaged the hull. Soon afterward another ten to fifteen dive-bombers attacked *Enterprise,* but again they achieved no hits.[92] One Japanese bomber slipped through the antiaircraft screen and managed to drop a bomb on *South Dakota*'s number one turret, putting two guns out of commission.[93]

Lt. James Granson Daniels III, a pilot in Fighting Ten aboard *Enterprise* since he received orders to join her in September of 1939, reports that the Japanese Kates that bombed *Enterprise* came right up her stern. Daniels had been with Admiral Halsey when *Enterprise* delivered aircraft to Wake Island, and was bingoed to Pearl Harbor on the evening of 7 December 1941. He received the first Distinguished Flying Cross awarded in World War II for his action in the First Battle of the Marshall Islands on 1 February 1942, where he was credited with shooting down one and a half Kate bombers.

Lieutenant Daniels was credited with another kill at Santa Cruz. By then he was the landing signals officer (LSO) aboard *Enterprise*, responsible for landing all aircraft when they returned from their missions. At the time *Enterprise* had eighty-two aircraft aboard—about ten more than normal—and Daniels had landed the first seventy-two of them. Lt. Robin Scott Lindsey, who would receive the Silver Star for his Santa Cruz service, landed the last ten. When one bomb hit *Enterprise* near her elevator and another by her screws, she was "lifted out of the water." Daniels jumped into the cockpit of one of the two SBDs parked on her stern and opened fire on the incoming Japanese Kates—and actually shot one down. He was given credit for the kill just as he would have been if he had accomplished it in the F4F3A Wildcat fighter aircraft he was assigned to fly at the time.[94]

Daniels also recounts that during the battle several planes from *Enterprise* were forced to bingo to Henderson Field on Guadalcanal. On landing the senior pilot asked to see the commanding officer of the Marines there. He was taken to a Marine major asleep on the wing of an airplane. Once the major was awake, the *Enterprise* pilot saluted and offered that—if the Marines would be so kind as to provide their Navy compatriots with fuel for their airplanes—they would rejoin the battle in whatever capacity the major directed. To this the Marine answered something like, "The only tasking I have for you is to get the hell off my airfield!" So much for cooperation between the Navy and Marine Corps![95]

After the last attack, *Enterprise* resumed landing aircraft. Several made water landings when they ran out of fuel. With the exception of a single attack plane that missed its mark at 1109, *Hornet* was not the subject of any more Japanese attacks during the period they concentrated on *Enterprise*.

Before nightfall, Japanese air reconnaissance sighted Task Force 64, built around the survivors of the Battle of Cape Esperance, which Admiral Halsey had positioned south-southeast of Guadalcanal. Considering that this surface force would attempt to cover *Hornet* from a surface attack, Admiral Yamamoto directed a night cruiser-destroyer attack supported by a strong battleship force before Task Force 64 could get into position to defend *Hornet*. The probability of such an attack played strongly in Admiral Murray's decision to sink *Hornet* by friendly fire while the rest of Task Force 17 retired to the southeast. Unknown to the remaining ships in Task Force 17, two heavy and one light cruiser and eight destroyers were within forty nautical miles and closing on them as they retired. But the Japanese broke off their chase at midnight.[96]

While Task Force 16 and Task Force 17 retired independently to a prearranged fueling area 185 nautical miles southeast of Espiritu Santo, the Japanese continued to search for them. The Japanese Striking Force, minus several carriers hit hard in the battle, returned to their striking position northwest of Guadalcanal to continue their support for the land offensive on the island. That offensive, sometimes fought in hand-to-hand combat, had failed miserably by the morning of 27 October. Late in the day on the 27th, with their operational objective denied, their carriers damaged, and their carrier aircraft depleted, Kondo's force and the two groups of ships supporting it were ordered to retire.[97] The battle for Guadalcanal would continue, but in reality any hope of Japanese victory ended with the Battle of Santa Cruz.

Results of the Battle

In all, about sixty-five aircraft attacked Task Force 17 and *Hornet*. Of these and their additional supporting fighters, only about forty-nine survived engagements with the combat air patrol of Task Force 61. Around eighty planes and their supporting fighters attacked *Enterprise* and Task Force 16. Of these, fifteen were estimated to have been destroyed by U.S. fighters.[98] The new F4F3As that had entered the fleet inventory were proving their worth against their Japanese adversaries, and particularly against the vaunted Zero fighters. Nimitz estimated that as many as two hundred Japanese aircraft had engaged in the series of strikes Kondo sent against his two carriers and their supporting warships—roughly the total air strength expected to be carried aboard four Japanese carriers at this point in the war. Nimitz saw the relatively few aircraft used by the Japanese in their late afternoon attacks on *Hornet* as a likely indication that they had few bombers and torpedo planes left to attack with.[99] The total number of Japanese planes destroyed in the Battle of Santa Cruz is shown in table 7.

Kinkaid sums up the American claims: "It is probable that the air groups of four carriers, (SHOKAKU, ZUIKAKU, ZUIHO and HAYATAKA) about 170 or 180 enemy planes, engaged in this attack. Of these, about 133 actually came within striking range of ENTERPRISE and HORNET. The HORNET was attacked by forty-nine planes, the ENTERPRISE by eighty-four. Some of the planes shot down were hit by our fighters in the enemy surface ship area. Others were downed before and after attacks on our carriers."[100]

The effect on Japanese naval aviation could not have been more devastating. In the words of Nimitz: "This battle cost us the lives of many gallant men, many planes, and two ships that could ill be spared. Despite the loss of about three carrier air groups and damage to a number of ships, the enemy retired with all his ships. We nevertheless turned back the Japanese again in their offensive to regain Guadalcanal, and shattered their carrier air strength on the eve of the critical days of mid-November."[101]

Still, *Saratoga* was in Pearl Harbor undergoing repairs, and *Enterprise* was out of action in Noumea for repairs to the bomb damage she sustained. The main problem in getting *Enterprise* back in action was removing the bulge in the forward sections of her hangar deck and getting her number one elevator operating again. Halsey gave weak assurances to Nimitz in early November that he could have *Enterprise* back on line by 21 November.[102] The Japanese would have the upper hand in the interim. What follows is a recounting of those November days.

Continued Surface Action in the Solomons

On 13 November, just half a month after the Japanese ground offensive on Guadalcanal had been crushed by the U.S. Marines and Army and the naval offensive had been stifled in the Battle of Santa Cruz, the Japanese launched another attack. Increasingly aware that the U.S. had more troops on Guadalcanal than they had initially realized, and that they would not be able to retake the island unless they could neutralize American air power from Henderson Field, the Japanese once again assembled a powerful force built around two battleships—*Kirishima* and *Hiei*. In company with them were a

TABLE 7 Total number of Japanese planes destroyed in the Battle of Santa Cruz

	CERTAIN	PROBABLE	Total
VF-10	16	9	25
VB-10	0	0	0
VS-10	8	0	8
VT-10	2	0	2
Total	26	9	35
VF-72	23	12	35
VB-8	3	2	5
VS-8	15	0	15
VT-6	0	0	0
Total	41	14	55
TF-16 AA	33	15	48
TF-17 AA	23	?	23?
Total	56	15?	71?
Grand Total	123	38?	161?

Source: This table is reproduced exactly from that Kinkaid provided in his report of the battle of Nimitz. Nimitz letter to Commander in Chief, United States' Fleet, dated 6 January, 1943, pp. 11–12.

light cruiser and ten destroyers. All were under the command of Rear Adm. Hiroaki Abe.[103]

The American situation was desperate. Only two heavy cruisers, *San Francisco* and *Portland*; three light cruisers, *Atlanta*, *Juneau*, and *Helena*; and eight destroyers, all under the command of Rear Adm. Daniel J. Callaghan, were available to oppose them.[104] Should the Japanese succeed in their objective of destroying all U.S. aircraft on Guadalcanal, a large group of supply ships was already en route to the island, awaiting the opportunity to resupply and reinforce the Japanese garrison.

Firing started at point-blank range at 0148. Callaghan had attempted to cross the Japanese T, but he misjudged the course and speed of the Japanese ships and wound up on a nearly parallel course. Callaghan had failed to comprehend the strength of the Japanese force. He paid for his errors dearly, and was himself killed in the battle. The USS *Atlanta* was sunk, and all four of

Callaghan's other cruisers were heavily damaged. Four American destroyers were sunk and another heavily damaged. Two Japanese destroyers sunk during the battle, and three more were damaged. At about 0200 Admiral Abe called off his bombardment mission against Henderson Field. [105]

The big loss for the Japanese in the engagement was the battleship *Hiei*, Abe's flagship. *Hiei* was so well armored that she was impervious to broadside gun fire. Her topside compartments and superstructure, however, were considerably more vulnerable. In her duel with *San Francisco*, she took a hit aft from an eight-inch shell that jammed her rudder and flooded her steering machinery compartment.[106] *Hiei* continued to fight, but soon found herself unmaneuverable and reduced to five knots. The next morning Marine SBDs from VMSB-142 and VMSB-131 from Henderson Field and B-17s from the 11th Bombardment Group pounded away at *Hiei,* still very near to Iron Bottom Sound, while she was struggling to return to Rabaul. Shortly after Abe ordered her abandoned, *Hiei* was struck by two more torpedo planes. At least 300 of her crew were killed before she sank.[107]

Though victory could be claimed by the United States in the strategic sense in that the Japanese attempt to neutralize Henderson Field and resupply their forces on Guadalcanal had been denied, the outcome of the First Naval Battle of Guadalcanal was less clear in the broader sense. Since *North Carolina* had been torpedoed along with the *Saratoga* on 31 August, the newly constructed *North Dakota* and *Washington* were the only American battleships in the South Pacific theater. *North Dakota* soon picked up the nickname "Battleship X," since, due to repair in U.S. floating dry docks in the area, she kept reappearing unexpectedly when the Japanese thought they had sunk her. But with four heavy cruisers and one light one sunk and three heavy and three light cruisers damaged in Iron Bottom Sound during the Battle of Savo Island, the Battle of Cape Esperance, and this battle, Halsey was quickly running out of ships to oppose the Japanese in the Solomons.

The Americans did not have long to wait. Only one day after the disastrous losses of Friday the 13th, the *South Dakota* and *Washington* and four accompanying destroyers arrived in Iron Bottom Sound, commanded by Rear Adm. Willis A. Lee. The next day, only two days after their frustrated but damaging foray into the Sound, the Japanese struck again. Figure 35 depicts the action that ensued just before and during the early morning hours of 15 November.

The Japanese had returned to finish the business they had left incomplete on the 13th. Their force consisted of the battleship *Kirishima*, undamaged

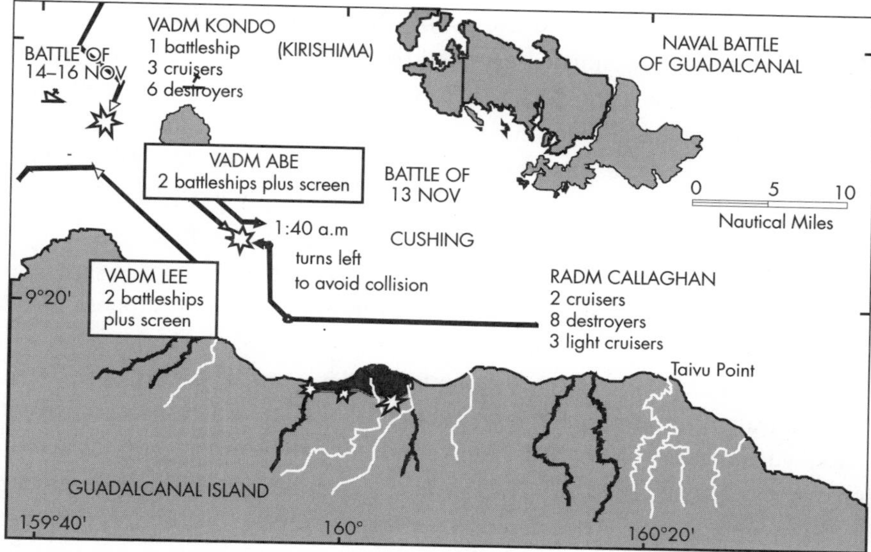

FIGURE 35. First and second naval battles of Guadalcanal, 13 and 14–15 November 1942. —*Courtesy of U.S. Naval War College*

in the pervious battle, two heavy and two light cruisers, and nine destroyers.[108] They were commanded by the very capable Vice Adm. Nobutake Kondo, who inexplicably failed to include the available battleships *Kongo* and *Haruna* in his force.[109]

The Japanese force rounded Savo Island to its west, with several destroyers stationed to its east to ensure the American force was contained. At 2316 on 14 November, Lee, who had spotted Kondo's approaching ships, opened fire.[110] *South Dakota* lost electrical power several times during the fight and took numerous hits on her superstructure from just about every ship in the Japanese force. Her hull was unscathed, as she was equipped to withstand 14-inch shells. Hit twenty-seven times, she was never close to sinking.[111]

Meanwhile, *Washington* closed to within eighty-four hundred yards of *Kirishima* and pounded her with nine 16-inch shells and a barrage of smaller caliber fire.[112] By ten minutes after midnight she was headed for the bottom. *Washington* then turned her fire on the destroyer *Ayanami*, sinking her too before maneuvering rapidly away from the action to avoid Japanese torpedo attacks. The tide had shifted. In just two days the Japanese had lost two battleships, one heavy cruiser, three destroyers, eleven transport ships, and over five thousand troops they had hoped to land on Guadalcanal. In addition to the damage sustained by *South Dakota*, the United States had three destroyers—the *Benham, Preston*, and *Walke*—sunk and another heavily damaged in the Second Naval Battle of Guadalcanal. The Japanese only launched one more major surface battle, on 30 November 1942, before they decided that Guadalcanal was now clearly in the hands of the Americans and abandoned their attempts to retake the island.

The Battle of Tassafaronga was the last attempt to relieve the Japanese garrison on Guadalcanal, a surface action devoid of carrier support. Rear Adm. Raizo Tanaka led a force of eight destroyers to provide supplies for them.[113] Four U.S. heavy cruisers, one light cruiser and four destroyers were lying in wait in Iron Bottom Sound. Though all but two of Tanaka's destroyers had their torpedoes off-loaded to make room for additional stores, those two proved more than enough to contend with when they sighted the American warships and launched their torpedoes. All four U.S. heavy cruisers took hits, and USS *Northampton* was sunk. *Minneapolis*, *New Orleans*, and *Pensacola* were all heavily damaged. Only one Japanese destroyer, the *Takanami*, was sunk by American gunfire, which came much too late. Moreover, the Japanese destroyers succeeded in off-loading their supply barrels before retiring. The supplies the Reinforcement Unit carried were not delivered, however. Admiral Halsey had thus prevented the Japanese from significantly reinforcing their troops on Guadalcanal. He had risked a force in night action and constricted waters—contrary to everything he had learned at the Naval War College—but he achieved his strategic objective. Though vastly superior in torpedo action and superior in night gunnery, the Japanese henceforth lacked the resolve to continue their efforts to wrest Guadalcanal from the Americans. The Naval Battles of the Solomon Islands were over.

Battle of Santa Cruz in Retrospect: Conclusions

Let us turn once again to an evaluation of the commanders.

1. The commander's estimate of the situation and grasp of the strategic and operational significance of the decisions he would be required to make. It would seem that all commanders, including the "defeatist" Ghormley, acutely appreciated the importance of preventing the Japanese from retaking Guadalcanal and severing American sea lines

of communication with Australia. Nimitz demonstrated outstanding judgment even pressed for time and under difficult circumstances. Not only did he correctly evaluate the strategic significance of the intelligence provided him and speed up the extensive repairs to *Enterprise* to ready her for the impending Japanese moves against the Solomon Islands, but he had the good sense and confidence in Halsey to task him to relieve Ghormley just hours before the Japanese onslaught was expected to occur.

Nimitz took this risk knowing full well that his commander, Allied Expeditionary Force Commander of Task Force 61 Rear Adm. Thomas C. Kinkaid, had only been intended to take *Enterprise* to the South Pacific, where Halsey was to have taken command. Moreover, although Murray, now the commander of Task Force 17 aboard *Hornet*, was an aviator (aviator no. 22 in 1915) and had been *Enterprise*'s captain during the early raids on Midway, he had only been promoted to rear admiral shortly before assuming his command on 30 July 1942—just days before the Battle of Santa Cruz.[114] While Halsey was a proven veteran, Kinkaid had considerable carrier experience, and Murray had weathered the Battle of the Eastern Solomons, their lack of time for prebattle planning and coordination and need to operate with unfamiliar subordinates and crews exacerbated any shortcomings in command relationships that might have come to light during the impending battle. Thus the simple command structure Nimitz imposed for the impending Guadalcanal action was particularly useful considering the new faces charged with countering the Japanese. Both Nimitz and Halsey deserve high marks for selecting a proper course of action given their detailed estimates of the situation. Considering their situation, both earn an A+.

The only real criticism that might be levied against any of the commanders in this area is for the failure to ensure continuous tracking once the Japanese carriers had been located in the search of the area between Rabaul and Guadalcanal by land-based aircraft. Commander Aircraft Southern Pacific Forces, Rear Adm. John S. McCain, should have ensured that continuous tracking information on Japanese carrier movements was passed to the other commanders—particularly since his failure to do this in the Battle of the Eastern Solomons proved so costly. McCain deserves better than the failing marks assigned for that battle, particularly considering the success of his search plan on the day before and morning of the Battle of Santa Cruz. But, while he had improved procedures in this important area, as Nimitz later acknowledged, he failed miserably to keep the U.S. carrier task force commanders adequately informed from that point on. Overall, his performance warrants a weak C-.

2. The commander's demonstrated ability to formulate a course of action, his ability to convey his decision in mission orders to subordinate commanders concisely and unambiguously, and his flexibility in modifying those orders through strategic and/or operational reappraisal if required. Nimitz demonstrated great insight and initiative in setting in motion the events that placed two carrier battle groups in position to oppose the Japanese attack on Guadalcanal. Moreover, Nimitz realized at this early stage in the Pacific war the importance of supporting operations ashore by employing Navy units at sea, and in this case, engaging them in battle. "Jointness" in this sense was not something that had been consciously ingrained in Navy leadership. In this instance Halsey mirrored Nimitz's approach. To both, a well-deserved A.

   Kinkaid applied the lessons of the Navy's previous carrier battles well. His decision to continue the search he had launched on the morning of 26 October instead of recalling his much-needed dive-bombers has been questioned by some, but revealing his position could have cost more. His planes were appropriately armed with bombs and could attack any appropriate target—in this case, they were able to attack a Japanese carrier after appropriately resisting opportunities to strike other targets—so this decision gave Kinkaid a weak but possibly important first-strike ability. Operating his carriers somewhat independently, though he advised against it in his After Action Report, probably saved *Enterprise* by allowing her through luck to conceal herself in a rain-squall when the Japanese attacked. This same action, however, may have contributed significantly to the extent of damage to and sinking of *Hornet*. Nonetheless, decisions of this type have to be made. It is unfair to judge a commander after the fact for the consequences of his adherence to existing doctrine. On balance, an A- seems an appropriate grade for Kinkaid.

3. The adequacy of command arrangements, the chain of command established, and the communications procedures put into effect to facilitate the exercise of command in battle. For all concerned here, as discussed

in the first section above, top grades are warranted. To Nimitz, Halsey, and Kinkaid, solid A's are assigned.

4. The commander's adherence to established operational and tactical doctrines where appropriate, his adherence to procedures established prior to the engagement of forces, and his ability to deviate from the same when warranted. In every instance Kinkaid and his subordinates adhered to existing doctrine—for better or for worse. An A is the only appropriate grade. McCain failed not in his adherence to doctrine in directing his land-based aircraft search of the Slot, but rather, in his disinclination to generate doctrine that would have assured continuous tracking information was passed to all appropriate commanders once the Japanese carriers or supporting surface groups were first located. In this area he did a good job initially, but his follow-up was lousy. A C would seem appropriate, as he did aid Kinkaid in locating the Japanese carriers, but he could have done a lot more to ensure that every carrier airplane had a chance to put a bomb or torpedo on target.

5. The commander's communication of mission requirements to subordinate commanders and the suitability of complementary actions by those subordinates to engage the enemy more effectively. As demonstrated above, all major commanders involved in the Battle of Santa Cruz had an excellent understanding of the engagement's importance within the wider context of achieving operational and strategic objectives and concomitant appreciation for appropriate risk and determination of appropriate circumstances for battle termination. This was true despite the fact that all of them were new to their command positions and to the theater. A solid A is warranted for all.

6. The commander's understanding of the engagement's importance within the wider context of achieving U.S. political objectives and his concomitant appreciation for the appropriate risk and determination of the proper circumstances in which to end the battle. Unquestionably, holding Guadalcanal, with its geostrategically critical position astride the Allied SLOCs, was the strategic issue in all of these battles. Nimitz certainly understood this—A. So also did Halsey, Kinkaid, and Murray—A's here too.

7. The commander's audacity and brilliance in conceptualizing, articulating, and executing a plan of action. All of the commanders involved seem to have stood out for their audacity and brilliance, McCain

possibly excepted. Nimitz and Halsey did solid jobs. Kinkaid and Murray did excellent jobs under the circumstances. McCain's efforts were lackluster by comparison. For the former group, A, and for the last, another C.

8. The commander's ability to learn from the situation and rapidly pass lessons along to the advantage of those commanding in later engagements. The Battle of Santa Cruz is without question the best documented of the four carrier battles in World War II in the Pacific theater in 1942. The close proximity of the battles of the Coral Sea and Midway understandably made such extensive analytical documentation difficult. So too did the loss of the Striking Group commander's flagship, *Yorktown*, with much of the battle's documentation in the latter battle. Likewise, the torpedoing of Fletcher's flagship, *Saratoga*, after the Battle of the Eastern Solomons, his departure on leave with expected return to command her, and his subsequent reassignment all conspired to limit after-action analysis of that battle. Those considerations notwithstanding, a commendable job was done for those battles anyway. That done for the Battle of Santa Cruz was superb.

CHAPTER 6

Battle of the Philippine Sea

FIGURE 36. Murderers' Row at Ulithi Atoll Wasp II, Yorktown II, Hornet II, Hancock, and Lexington II. —*Courtesy of U.S. Naval Institute Photo Archive*

Japan's "Absolute National Defense Line"

ADMIRAL YAMAMOTO had promised eighteen months. His promise extended to 7 June 1943. If the United States was not compelled to agree to terminate the war with Japan by that approximate date, he maintained, the industrial might of America would overwhelm the Imperial Japanese Navy, laying open the path to the Japanese home islands. Those in powerful positions in Japan failed to heed Yamamoto's warning. Soon after Yamamoto's deadline, they would see the error in their judgment.

Not much later than eighteen months into the war—early on the morning of 30 September 1943—Emperor Hirohito met with Premier and War Minister Hideki Tojo, President of the Privy Council Yoshimichi Hara; Adm. Osami Nagano, chief of the Navy General Staff; and Vice Adm. Mineichi Koga, commander in chief of the Imperial Japanese Combined Fleet.[1] Their purpose was grim. They had gathered to see what strategic options were open to Japan in the Pacific theater in light of the previous year's reverses. Drawing on the Clausewitzian notion that the defensive is the stronger form of warfare, they reached agreement that Japan's best hope in dealing with the United States—at least for the time being—was to consolidate its defense perimeter and concentrate on islands that could be reached from the Japanese home islands by air either directly or by stops on islands along the way. They hoped such a strategy would give Japan time to build more carriers. In the meantime, lacking the strategic mobility that carriers offered, they would rely on the Eleventh Air Fleet to destroy any major American naval force inside the "Black Line of Defense" that would constitute Japan's "Absolute National Defense Line."[2] They postulated that this plan would ultimately enable Japan to regain the initiative and return to the offensive.

The Black Line of Defense drawn on the chart that day ran from northern Japan north through the Kurile Islands to the southern tip of Sakhalin Island, then from north to south through the Nanpo Shoto—islands south of Honshu—the Bonin, Volcano, and Marianas Islands, thence east beyond Truk in the Carolines, southwest across western New Guinea, and then westerly to the Timor Sea and beyond.[3] From those islands and others lying in between, the Japanese could rely on the part of their naval doctrine that they had failed to follow at Midway. They would force the United States to pass through submarine cordons and islands from which they could stage land-based aircraft in the hopes of destroying roughly 50 percent of all warships attempting to pass. Then the ships of the Imperial Navy would engage the rest. The key would be to ensure that no U.S. carriers passed beyond the Black Line drawn on the chart of the Pacific Ocean with their lethal offensive capability intact. If this strategy proved successful, more planes and carriers could be built and the Japanese could regain the offensive. Should the Americans break through, it would spell disaster not only for Japan's main strategic objectives in Asia, but in all likelihood for Japan itself. Each man, to the last, would be required to fight and, if necessary, die to preserve Japan's Absolute National Defense Line.

SLOCs to Victory Secured

After the Battle of Santa Cruz the United States was left with only a single offensive strategic asset in the Pacific, the badly damaged *Enterprise*. The British "loaned" their carrier HMS *Victorious* to the United States for duty in the Pacific, but she didn't arrive in Norfolk until January 1943 and wasn't ready for active service in the Pacific until May. *Saratoga* was expected back

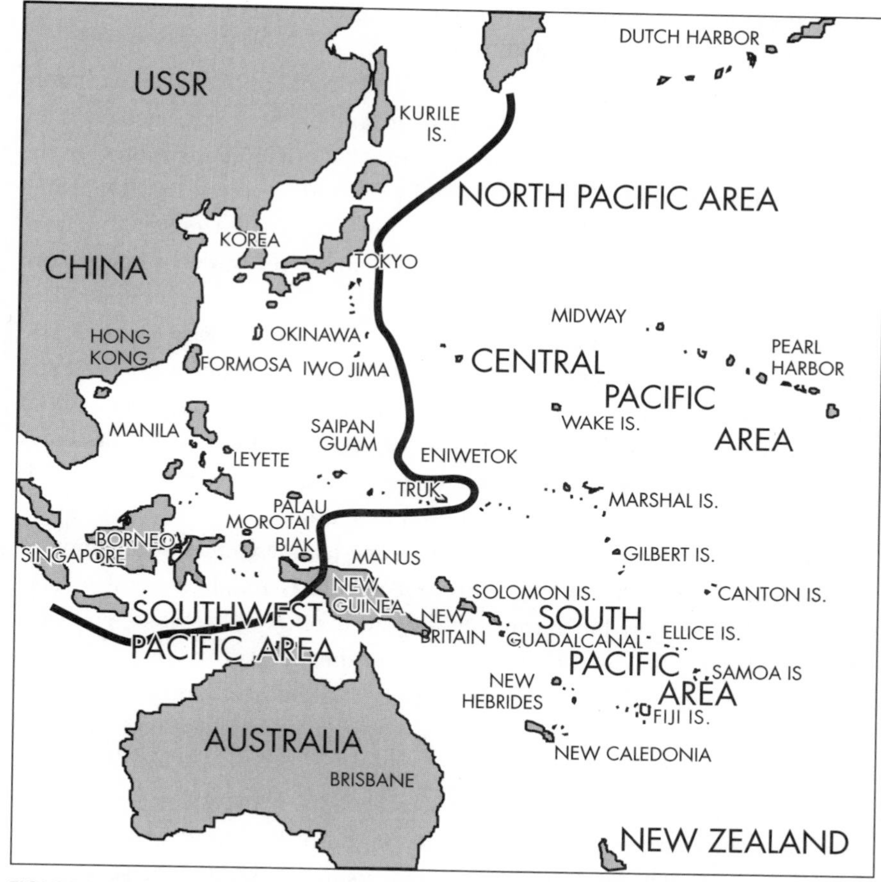

FIGURE 37. Japan's Absolute National Defense Line. —*Graphic provided by Jason Peters*

in the act by about 10 November 1942, and actually did rejoin the action when, along with *Victorious,* she participated in supporting the invasion of New Georgia between 20 and 24 July 1943.[4]

The Japanese still had *Zuikaku* and the fleet carriers *Junyo* and *Hiyo* available to contest Guadalcanal and the Solomons. *Shokaku* was damaged and temporarily out of action. But Santa Cruz had left *Shokaku* and *Zuikaku* without viable air wings. The air combat over and around Guadalcanal had also seriously reduced Japanese air strength. In aerial combat between 7 August and 15 November, VF-5, VF-6, VF-71, VF-72, and VF-10 claimed to have shot down 193 Japanese aircraft, including 54 fighters, 62 dive-bombers, and 15 torpedo planes. Their actual combat score was more like

102 planes total, including 25 fighters, 32 dive-bombers, and 7 torpedo planes, with as many as 20 medium bombers.[5]

At no time from the U.S. invasion of Guadalcanal on 7 August had more than eleven thousand American Marines and soldiers been stationed on it. By 23 October, in anticipation of the major Japanese offensive mentioned in the last chapter, that number rose to around twenty-three thousand. Opposing them were approximately twenty-two thousand Japanese troops brought in for a third major thrust to retake the island.[6] That number grew by about three thousand through early December. The Japanese had begun to realize their position there was untenable, however. On 11 December Rear Adm. Raizo Tanaka, commander of the First Reinforcement Group, made a final attempt to reinforce and resupply Guadalcanal by leading the "Tokyo Express" south through the Slot. His flagship, the new twenty-five-hundred-ton destroyer *Teruzuki,* was torpedoed by American torpedo boats, wounding Tanaka. The Japanese decided to abandon Guadalcanal thereafter.

Meanwhile, Nimitz was still unaware of Japanese intentions, and the United States underwent a major effort to secure the island. In December, General Vandegrift and his 1st Marine Division were relieved by Maj. Gen. Alexander M. Patch, USA, who took command of the Guadalcanal garrison that, including a newly arrived Army division, now stood at a Corps strength of fifty thousand. Patch too was unaware as yet that the Japanese had conceded Guadalcanal.[7]

Patch launched an immediate offensive. His plan was to push west on Guadalcanal from Henderson Field, land fresh troops west of Cape Esperance, and catch the Japanese in a pincers move. While Patch's Marines and Army troops made good progress to their west, the Japanese had other plans than to be caught in his pincers. Admiral Kondo—who still had the carriers *Zuikaku*, *Junyo*, and *Hiyo* available to do battle—once again made use of the Combined Fleet in a move south from the major Imperial Navy base 560 miles away at Rabaul. Admiral Halsey quickly responded by sending two fleet and two escort carriers and a total of five task forces, which included three battleships, from Espiritu Santo, the most forward Allied naval base at 560 nautical miles from Guadalcanal, to greet Kondo's force. But Kondo was not about to risk the few carriers he had left. His move south was a feint to enable swift destroyers to slip in and evacuate the twelve thousand remaining Japanese troops on Guadalcanal. During Kondo's diversion no fleet action occurred, but the cruiser *Chicago* was sunk by torpedo planes staging from the new Japanese airfield on New Georgia.[8]

Patch's pincers made contact on 9 February 1943, but the Japanese troops he had hoped to trap were gone. In three high-speed night runs the Japanese had spirited them away, avoiding their fifth defeat in major land offensives on Guadalcanal. The Japanese chose not to use their carriers in battle again until mid-1944.[9] Thus in the four carrier battles of 1942 and the combined Marine-Army action on Guadalcanal, the United States had rendered the *kido butai* impotent and secured the vital sea lines of communication between Hawaii and Australia. Once the tremendous warship-building programs that Congress had set in motion started sending much-needed capital ships to the Pacific, for the first time since Pearl Harbor, War Plan Orange could be launched against Japan.

MacArthur on a Roll

While the American forces were tightening their grip on Guadalcanal, Gen. Douglas MacArthur was busy. A thousand miles to the west his Australian troops were on the heels of the retreating Japanese over the Owen Stanley Mountains route, while his American troops took a less direct trail across them or were flown in to airfields on the north coast of New Guinea. MacArthur's intent was to have his forces converge on Buna in mid-November in much the same way that General Patch had planned to meet the Japanese troops near Cape Esperance, but MacArthur's troops had to undertake their advance through dense jungle against a well-prepared defensive perimeter.[10]

Unlike the Solomon Islands campaign, the campaign against Buna and Papua on New Guinea never involved major fleet units. Uncharted waters and the proximity to enemy air fields prevented both the Americans and Japanese from hazarding major ships. For both sides, however, resupply by sea was essential.[11]

MacArthur's force ultimately reached almost 30,000, divided equally between Australian and American troops. The Japanese, with only around 12,000 troops who were ravaged by disease and near starvation, collapsed under the pressure of MacArthur's advance in late January of 1943. The costs for the Allies were high—the 3,095 killed was nearly twice the count of those lost on Guadalcanal.[12] But with Guadalcanal in the Solomons and Papua and Buna in northern New Guinea secure, the Joint Chiefs of Staff were due to conduct a strategic reappraisal on the U.S. Pacific campaign. At first the logical next step was generally agreed to be taking Rabaul to deny the Japanese their southern naval staging base. Other viable options soon emerged.

The U.S. Debate on Strategy

While the offensives to retake Guadalcanal and Papua/Buna were in action, the leaders of the Grand Alliance were actively discussing and making strategy. At the Casablanca Conference of January 1943 they had allocated a greater percentage of men and material to the Pacific than to the Atlantic and Europe to take advantage of the successful offensives there, and because the American industrial machine had produced more assets than originally anticipated. At the Washington Conference in May of 1943 the Allies agreed to entrust the conduct of the Pacific War to the American Joint Chiefs of Staff and accepted in principle the Joint Chiefs' strategic plan to defeat Japan. The Joint Chiefs' plan was, in essence, to defeat the Japanese by blockading their home islands, especially by cutting off access to the oil they controlled in the East Indies; bombing Japanese cities; and invading Japan's home islands if necessary.[13]

In order to accomplish this strategy all lines of the Allied advance would converge on Hong Kong to provide a base on the Chinese coast for later operations. The British, with American assistance, would invade Burma and reopen the Burma Road in order to provide supplies to General Chiang Kai-shek's Chinese Army so that they could converge on Hong Kong and the Chinese coast from the west. The British Fleet in the Indian Ocean would fight their way through the Straits of Malacca to join MacArthur's Southwest Pacific forces for a combined force offensive aimed at liberating the Philippines and investing Hong Kong with amphibious units. Most important, Nimitz's Pacific Fleet would unleash the War Plan Orange offensive as planned before the war, advancing through the Marshall and Caroline Island chains to converge with MacArthur's British and American forces on the Chinese coast and take Japanese-held islands so that U.S. Army Air Corps bombers could reach their targets in the Japanese home islands.[14]

The British and Chinese, however, proved not to be up to the task. The British were unable to disengage sufficiently in the Mediterranean to free up enough forces to carry out their agreed part in the plan. The Chinese, likewise, were tied down by a major offensive in China that prevented them from participating—and Chiang Kai-shek's maddening behavior made him a less than reliable ally. The offensive against Japan would be an American show, with as much help as her Australian, New Zealander, and Canadian allies could muster.[15]

The initiatives directed by the American Joint Chiefs of Staff, in order of priority, included the following:

1. A drive through the Central Pacific, advancing westward from Pearl Harbor
2. South Pacific and Southwest Pacific forces cooperating in a drive on Rabaul; Southwest Pacific forces would then press on westward along the north coast of New Guinea
3. North Pacific forces ejecting the Japanese from the Aleutians[16]
4. Intensifying submarine attacks on Japanese naval forces and SLOCs

Executing the Combined Chiefs' Strategy

Due to the American public's concerns over Japan holding American territory, first on the list of objectives was to retake Kiska and Attu Islands in the Alaskan Aleutian chain. Thomas C. Kinkaid, still a rear admiral, had taken over command in that area in January of 1943. He elected to bypass Kiska and take the more distant Attu first. The U.S. 7th Infantry Division initially landed 3,000 troops in a pincers movement on the island, but unexpected Japanese moves and ineffective U.S. naval gunfire ultimately meant that 11,000 troops had to be employed. The landings took place on 7 May, and by the end of May, Attu had been reclaimed at the cost of 600 Americans killed in action and 1,200 more wounded. Of the Japanese garrison of just over 2,600, all were killed or committed suicide in human-wave attacks except 28 who were taken prisoner. A much larger force of 34,500, including 5,300 Canadians, as well as battleships, cruisers, and bombers then assaulted Kiska. When the forces landed on 15 August, however, they met no resistance. The Japanese had spirited away a force twice as large as that on Attu three weeks before. Both Attu and Kiska were back in American hands.[17]

Next on the agenda was a drive through the Central Solomons and along the north coast of New Guinea aimed at capturing the southernmost major Japanese naval base at Rabaul on the northeast corner of New Britain Island. After a large Japanese naval force was defeated by American land-based air attack, Yamamoto decided foolishly to launch an all-out air offensive against American forces in the area.

Yamamoto called up two hundred carrier planes of the Imperial Third Fleet to add to the one hundred planes he already had in the area. While these did destroy several ships and twenty-five Allied aircraft, the Japanese lost forty planes and many of their remaining first-line carrier pilots. This was a disaster their limited pilot training programs could not hope to recover from.[18]

On 16 April 1943 the strategic direction of the Pacific War took a fateful turn for the Japanese. Acting on decoded JN-25 naval code intelligence, Admiral Nimitz was sure that Admiral Yamamoto, his opposite, was making an inspection tour of the Japanese bases around Rabaul and authorized Vice Admiral Halsey to activate Operation Vengeance, which aimed to destroy Yamamoto's plane while it attempted to land on southern Bougainville. Halsey was instructed to conduct his operations without compromising the U.S. intelligence gathering capability with respect to the Japanese naval codes. He sent seventeen P-38 aircraft with drop tanks from Henderson field, and they disposed of the two Japanese bombers—the second carried Vice Admiral Ugaki, Yamamoto's Chief of Staff, who survived the crash of his aircraft at sea—and their accompanying fighters. Yamamoto was succeeded by his handpicked successor, the less capable and much more conservative Adm. Mineichi Koga. Koga lacked Yamamoto's strategic "genius,"* as events were to reveal.[19] In mid-June he sent twenty-four Japanese bombers and seventy accompanying Zero fighters to strike transports in Iron Bottom Sound. Only one of the ninety-four Japanese planes was not shot down, and only six U.S. fighters were lost.[20] Japan's aircraft and pilot losses were mounting quickly.

Central Solomons and New Britain: The Second Phase

The American Joint Chiefs of Staff issued their orders for the second phase of the South Pacific campaign in late March of 1943. MacArthur was to proceed along the north coast of New Guinea and invade New Britain, and Halsey was to push north in the Central Solomons with the ultimate objective of taking and establishing airfields on Bougainville to strike Rabaul.[21]

By the end of June the Allies had enlarged Henderson Field to stage Army Air Corps bombers and had three fighter aircraft runways adjacent to the main air strip. A second and larger bomber base named Carney Field was established five miles away. In the new Air Command Solomons (AIRSOL)

---

*It should be remembered that Yamamoto was the man responsible for Pearl Harbor, Midway, and Guadalcanal. While some have attributed a "genius" for war to Yamamoto, nothing could be further from the truth. Yamamoto was responsible for involving Japan in a war with the United States it could not possibly win. He dispersed his forces at Midway and failed to give Nagumo all available intelligence on the likelihood of U.S. carriers in his vicinity, both contributing to the loss of four of the Imperial Japanese Navy's most powerful carriers. He failed to realize the strategic importance of Guadalcanal to the United States and reinforce it properly as well, thus enabling the U.S. to take the island and use it to thwart Japan's protection of her "Southern Resource Area," and this prevented Japan from cutting U.S. SLOCs between Hawaii and Australia.

contingent, the Allies had 213 fighters, 72 heavy bombers, and 170 light bombers at this complex on Guadalcanal. Likewise, MacArthur's Fifth Air Force had 220 fighters, 80 heavy and 100 medium and light bombers stationed at several airfields on the east coast of New Guinea.[22]

While MacArthur's forces moved forward and prepared to invest New Britain, Halsey's troops moved through the islands of the Central Solomons as depicted in figure 38.

On 30 June Halsey landed troops on Rendova Island south of the important Japanese airfield at Munda, on northwestern New Georgia, and began shelling the field. Five days later he landed another force on the north end of New Georgia and closed in on the heavily entrenched and fortified Japanese contingent. Once Munda was in American hands, Halsey bypassed the large and dug-in Japanese force protecting the Vilna airstrip on Kolombangara Island to the northwest of New Georgia and landed troops on Vella Lavella Island on 15 August.

Unlike a land operation, in which it is almost always inadvisable to bypass an outpost and leave a major force to your rear, Halsey's naval forces were able to isolate the Japanese on Kolombangara and exact a slow death by preventing them from reinforcing or resupplying. Rear Adm. Frederick Moosbrugger and Rear Adm. Arleigh Burke, a destroyer commander, made names for themselves in their actions with the Japanese during this campaign. Unfortunately, Halsey's blockade was not tight enough to completely isolate Kolombangara, and the Japanese extracted around three-quarters of the roughly 12,400 troops there by night.[23]

In the fiasco destroyer battle of Vella Gulf just east of Vella Lavella on 6–7 August 1943, the U.S. lost the destroyer *Chevalier* to a Japanese Long Lance torpedo. Two other U.S. destroyers were heavily damaged and a Japanese destroyer sunk. The only real significance of this battle was that it was the last naval battle the Japanese would win in World War II.[24]

Numbered Fleets

At about this point in the war Adm. Ernest J. King, Commander in Chief of the U.S. Naval Forces, realized that the scope and increasing intensity of combat operations made the makeshift Task Force numbering system then in use obsolete. From the start of the war the Navy had used its old system of assigning numbers to a particular task force commander, and that number would be assigned wherever and whenever that commander was the senior

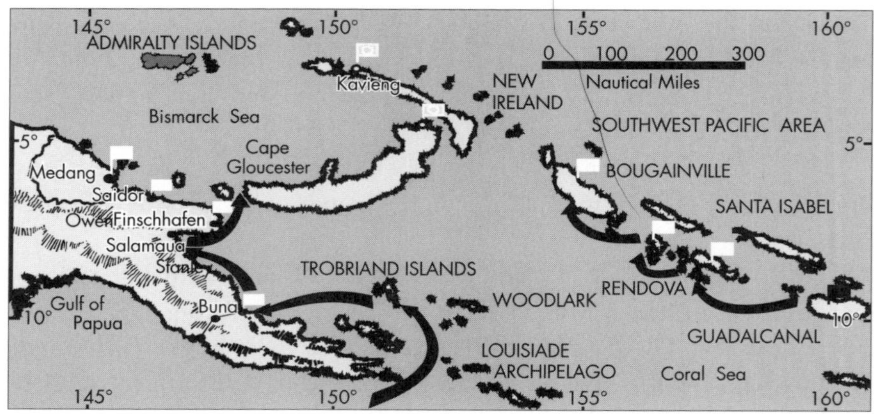

FIGURE 38. Gen. MacArthur's and Vice Adm. Halsey's prongs of the developing two-pronged strategy. —*Courtesy of U.S. Naval War College*

officer assigned to oversee the operation. After the Battle of Midway, in order to preserve the security of command assignments, a system was devised in the Pacific where task forces would be identified by a phonetic letter identifier associated with the first letter of the task force commander's last name. That system quickly showed its limitations.

In March of 1943 Admiral King therefore inaugurated a system using numbers to identify fleets and task forces instead. Under this system all seagoing commands in the Atlantic and Mediterranean were assigned even-numbered identifiers, and all those in the Pacific odd-numbered identifiers. The ships in the Central Pacific became the U.S. Fifth Fleet. Those in the South Pacific under Halsey's command became the U.S. Third Fleet. Navy units not part of Nimitz's Pacific Fleet operating in the Southwest Pacific in support of MacArthur were assigned to the U.S. Seventh Fleet. Their first commander was to be Vice Adm. Arthur S. Carpenter, who was succeeded by Vice Adm. Thomas C. Kinkaid. The U.S. Ninth Fleet operated in the North Atlantic under Vice Adm. Frank Jack Fletcher. Amphibious and other task forces would be designated similarly, with the first digit of their identifying number corresponding to their fleet and a second digit referencing the particular group of ships assigned for an operation. The next level of command subordinate to a task force commander would be a task group command, identified by a number after a decimal point. A task unit would receive another number after a second decimal point, and the same convention would be used for a task element, the last and smallest command designated under King's system.[25]

Operation "Elkton" and the Dual Advance on Rabaul

The next phase planned in the U.S. drive to take Rabaul was a dual advance through the Solomons and New Guinea. In the Solomons, Halsey used AIRSOL aircraft and units of his Third Fleet to springboard his Marines and Army forces toward their objective. Along the north coast of New Guinea General MacArthur did the same by conducting sequential amphibious landings under the cover of land-based aircraft while his combined forces moved in the ships "on loan" from Nimitz to his Seventh Fleet under cover of the gunships and escort carriers at his disposal.

The Japanese countered this dual advance by defending Rabaul from MacArthur's forces with Imperial Army troops and land-based aircraft while the Imperial Navy, with assistance from the Japanese Army, guarded the approaches to Rabaul from the Central Solomons.[26] The campaign was well underway. The next step for the U.S. Navy was the Japanese base at Bougainville. MacArthur's combined force would move against Salamaua and Lae, gateway to New Guinea's Huon Peninsula adjacent to New Britain—but first he would have to take the stronghold of Buna.

Learning from his past experience at Munda and on Vella Lavella, Halsey decided to bypass the Japanese force concentrations on Bougainville and invade halfway up the island at the more weakly defended Cape Torokina in Empress Augusta Bay.[27] By building airstrips there he could threaten Rabaul and force the Japanese to go on the offensive in an attempt to extract his forces from their defensive positions. Lead elements of the force of thirty-four thousand Marines of the 3rd Marine Division and Army troops of the 37th Infantry Division allocated for this operation hit their assigned beachhead at dawn on 1 November.

The Japanese countered Halsey's advance with a hastily organized cruiser and destroyer force sent down from Rabaul to break up the landings by sinking the American troop transports. Task Force 39, already exhausted from the fast pace of recent operations, was all that Halsey had to stop them. This force, commanded by Rear Adm. Stanton Merrill, was the principal U.S. surface force in the entire South Pacific. Halsey chose to risk it in what became the Battle of Empress Augusta Bay in the early morning hours of 2 November 1943. Demonstrating new and daring tactics during this battle, Arleigh Burke brought his force of destroyers alongside the Japanese battle line for a high-speed torpedo run. Admiral Merrill, also maneuvering adroitly, used the superior firing rate of his cruisers' less powerful 6-inch guns to get inside the range of his Japanese opponent and do maximum damage. Though execution on the U.S. side was less than perfect, the Japanese commander, Rear Adm. Sentaro Omori, lost the light cruiser *Sendai* and the bow of his destroyer *Myoko* was ripped off during the fracas. That was enough for Omori; he departed, leaving the American transports untouched. It took the First Marine Amphibious Corps another month to stabilize its expanding defensive perimeter, but Halsey now had a fighter and bomber strip within 220 nautical miles of Rabaul. His preparations were almost complete.[28]

Meanwhile, General MacArthur was moving up the northern coast of New Guinea. On 30 June he had begun putting troops on Kiriwina and Woodlark islands off the Papuan Peninsula and at Nassau Bay, just seventeen miles southeast of the Japanese stronghold at Salamaua. MacArthur made a diversionary attack on Salamaua, then bypassed it. The Japanese there were cut off from reinforcement and resupply unless they drew from Lae. That was just what MacArthur wanted. He landed a force to take Lae, and U.S. destroyers' fire pounded it into submission. MacArthur's next move was to take Finschhafen eighty-two miles up the coast, which he did on 2 October. He then moved to complete his conquest of the Huon Peninsula and continue further up the New Guinea coast. MacArthur's rapid advance, a sharp contrast to his protracted struggle to take Buna, was enabled in part by the amphibious capability provided by the U.S. Navy.[29]

So complete was the cooperation between Halsey and MacArthur that the code name for their operations was "Elkton," referring to the small and then famous town in Maryland renowned for the quick marriages that took place there.[30] Theirs was joint cooperation at its best.

Bypassing Rabaul

In August of 1943 at the Quebec Conference the Combined Chiefs of Staff approved Admiral King's plan to bypass Rabaul and neutralize it with air power and isolation, denying its ninety thousand Japanese inhabitants reinforcement or resupply by sea. MacArthur's next objective was to make a leap of four hundred miles up the coast of New Guinea to Hollandia—code-named

Operation Reckless for the audacity of such a move, but the shortest route to his promised return to the Philippines. As a good Army man, he didn't want Rabaul on his rear, however well neutralized. Thus in mid-December he gained a foothold on New Britain, and the 1st Marine Division stormed ashore on 26 December. The "boxing-in" of Japanese forces at Rabaul was complete by mid-March, and MacArthur was free to advance on Hollandia. Halsey was ordered to Pearl Harbor to assume a command afloat.[31]

The Two-Pronged Strategy

Early in 1943 MacArthur laid before the Joint Chiefs of Staff his plan for an advance on what he called the New Guinea-Mindanao Axis. With new ships expected soon that would allow the extensive prewar planning of War Plan Orange to be executed, Admiral Nimitz advanced the Navy's plan for an island-hopping campaign across the Pacific aimed directly at Tokyo. For months after Admiral King brought this plan up at the Casablanca Conference in January of 1943, the Joint Chiefs considered and debated the merits of the two divergent viewpoints. At the conference, the British had taken the stance that advancing along two separate lines in the Pacific was sure to reduce the scale of any cross-Channel operation in Europe. Yet such an operation would not be possible for some time, and America had produced sufficient resources to make both Pacific options simultaneously possible in the meantime.[32]

The Washington Conference in May had authorized beginning MacArthur and Halsey's initial drives as soon as the Japanese were ejected from the Aleutians. Now in October, a firm decision needed to be made. The Joint Chiefs were divided. At first the Army Air Corps Commander, Gen. Henry H. "Hap" Arnold, sided with Gen. George C. Marshall, the Army Chief of Staff, backing MacArthur's plan. Ultimately, however, when it became clear that the Navy could take the Marianas and provide the Army Air Corps with bases to bomb Japan in their new B-29s, General Arnold swung around to the Navy position. Even though MacArthur assured Arnold that a high priority for his plan would be to take coastal areas of China from which Arnold could stage his B-29s, the prospect of being subordinated to the senior MacArthur was not appealing to the Army Air Corps commander. Thus Arnold threw his weight behind the Navy plan.

Ultimately both MacArthur's and Nimitz's plans were authorized, with the Navy advance to take priority. On 16 November at 0330 the Marines of the 2nd Division launched Operation Galvanic by storming toward beachheads on Makin and Tarawa in the Gilbert Islands. Thus started the amphibious campaign, leading through the Central Pacific to the Marianas. The path of the advance is depicted in figure 39.

Operation Forager and the Battle for the Marianas

The culmination of the campaign through the Central Pacific was as yet seven months away. D-day for the assault on Saipan was set for 15 June 1944. Guam was to be attacked three days later. Vice Adm. Richmond Kelly Turner's Northern Attack Group included the 2nd and 4th Marines and the 27th Infantry Division. Turner was to take Saipan first, and then move on to take Tinian with the same force. Rear Adm. Richard L. Conolly was to move his Southern Attack Group west-northwest from its anchorage at Eniwetok and seize Guam. To do this he had the 3rd Marine Division, the 1st Provisional Marine Brigade, a Corps of artillery, and the 77th Infantry Division, all under the command of Maj. Gen. Roy S. Geiger, USMC. In all, the American assault force numbered 127,571 men. Their task from Nimitz was to "capture, occupy and defend the Marianas." That accomplished, the long-range bombing of the Japanese home islands with B-29s could begin.[33] The thrust of Operation Forager and contemplated follow-on moves is as depicted in figure 40.

Adm. Raymond A. Spruance, commander of the U.S. Fifth Fleet, awaited the action aboard his flagship, USS *Indianapolis*, a proper place for the venerated cruiser man, at anchor at Majuro in the Marshalls. Likewise, Adm. Marc A. Mitscher, commander of Task Force 58, was at anchor at Majuro in his flagship, *Lexington II*. Task Force 58 was powerful indeed. It was built around seven heavy "fast carriers" and eight light carriers.[34] These fifteen carriers carried 954 planes, including 488 fighters, of which 42 were night fighters, 210 dive-bombers, 191 torpedo planes, and 65 floatplanes. Screening this massive juggernaut of air power were seven newly constructed fast battleships, three heavy cruisers, six light cruisers, four antiaircraft cruisers, and fifty-eight destroyers—ninety-three ships in all.[35] To get to the Marines and Army troops investing the Japanese strongholds on Saipan, Tinian, and Guam, the Combined Fleet would have to go through Spruance's and Mitscher's armada.

Spruance and Mitscher left Majuro on 6 June 1944, the same day the Allies sent five divisions across the English Channel to establish a foothold in Europe in Normandy. They intended to launch Operation Forager against

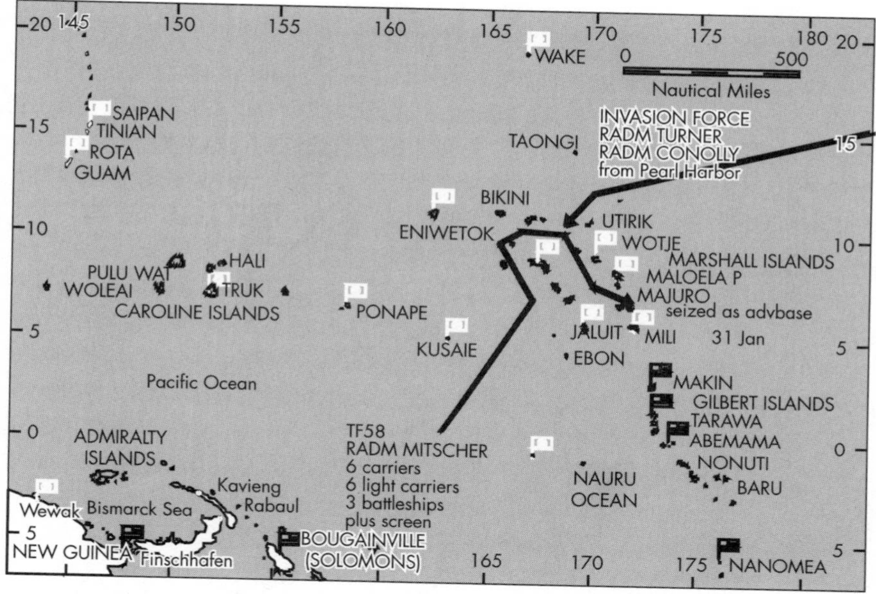

FIGURE 39. First the Gilberts, then the Marshalls: road to the Marianas. —*Courtesy of U.S. Naval War College*

the three Japanese strongholds simultaneously on 12 June, and to support the capture, occupation, and defense of Saipan.[36] Admiral Mitscher convinced Admiral Spruance, without much effort, to launch the first strikes a day early, on the afternoon of 11 June. At 1302, when Task Force 58 was within 200 nautical miles of Guam and 225 nautical miles of Saipan, Mitscher launched his first wave of 225 planes, mostly fighters with a few torpedo planes, against Guam, Saipan, and Tinian simultaneously.

The Japanese air defenses were weak in the Marianas. Pilots and aircraft had been transferred to the New Guinea area, since the Japanese Navy Staff and the Combined Fleet Staff expected the next American naval action to be directed toward Biak in support of General MacArthur's effort to break that stronghold.[37] Of the few planes Admiral Koga had in the Marianas to contest the strikes, eighty-one Zeros that Vice Adm. Kakuji Kakuta sent up were shot down. Twenty-nine other Japanese planes were destroyed on the deck and another twenty-four damaged. Thirteen additional Zeros were probably splashed, but could not be verified. Only eleven Hellcats were lost, and five of their pilots were recovered.[38] Owing to Koga's use of carrier planes in trying to maintain Japan's hold on the northeastern half of New Guinea and

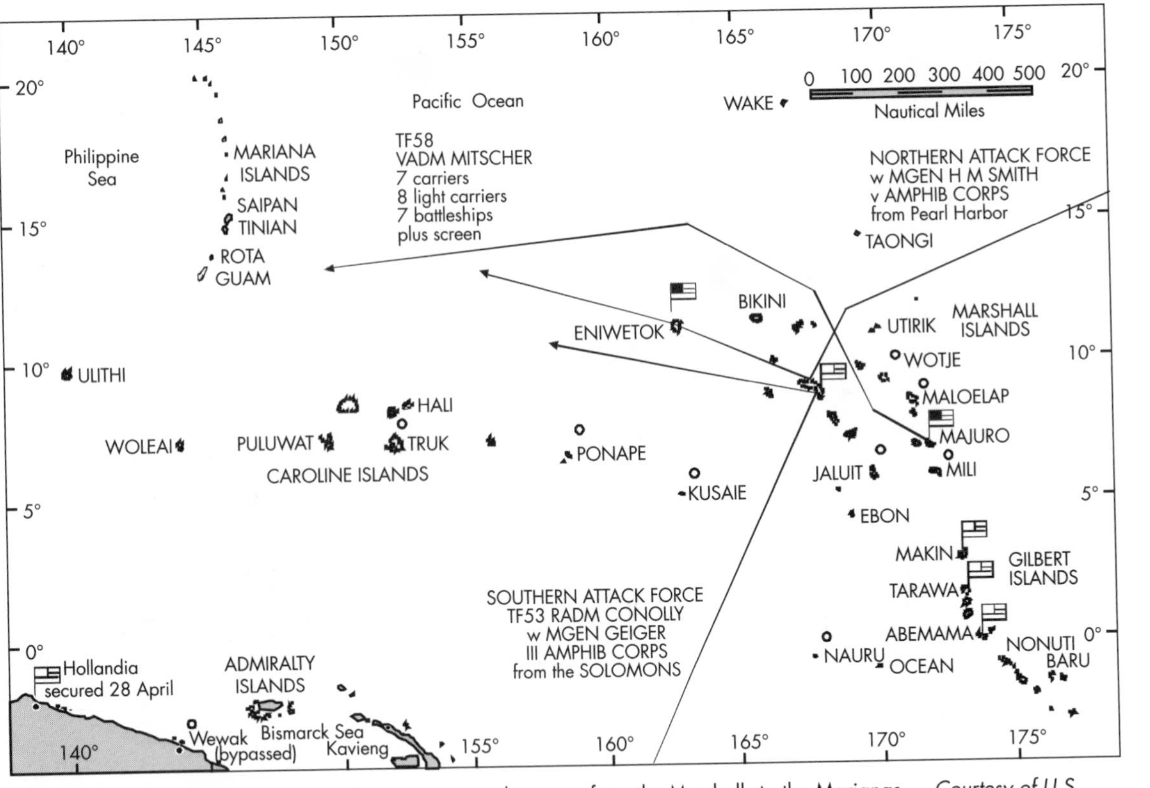

FIGURE 40. Admiral Nimitz's prong of the two-pronged strategy from the Marshalls to the Marianas. —*Courtesy of U.S. Naval War College*

the Central Solomons and the attrition exacted by AIRSOL and the Fifth Air Force there, Japan had neither enough pilots nor enough planes to defend the Marianas adequately. Moreover, in order to meet minimum needs, the Japanese had rushed their new pilots into combat with only about six months of training. They were hardly a match for the more experienced and more numerous Americans they faced.

The Japanese were caught completely by surprise. They expected first that the attack was a diversion for the offensive against Biak they had predicted, and second that the Americans would hit the southern bastion at Guam first in any attack on the Marianas. Mitscher's carriers launched strikes from first light to sunset—171 sorties from his flagship *Lexington II* alone on 12 June—and battered the Japanese for the next four days.[39] Likewise, Vice Adm. William A. "Ching" Lee Jr.'s Battle Line, Task Group 58.7's new fast battleships *Alabama*, *Indiana*, *Iowa*, *New Jersey*, *North Carolina*, *South Dakota*, and *Washington*, and his four heavy cruisers and fourteen destroyers pounded the Japanese on Saipan and Tinian.[40] On 14 June Adm. Jesse Oldendorf's pre–World War II battleships further pulverized the islands from close range. U.S. destroyers fired on the Japanese throughout the night to keep their heads down and U.S. submarines struck at any Japanese destroyer that moved, evaporating the prospect of a Japanese removal to the west.

As D-day for the Marianas operation approached, Admiral Spruance stationed men-of-war on virtually every compass point around Saipan and Tinian. He also had two carrier task groups launch strikes against Iwo Jima, Chichi Jima, and Haha Jima some six to seven hundred miles away to ensure they didn't add to the now almost nonexistent Japanese airpower his landing forces were likely to face.

On 15 June the 2nd and 4th Marines Divisions, well out of sight from shore, prepared to hit the beach between Afetna Point and Agingan Point on the west coast of Saipan. While Admiral Turner's Task Force 51 waited with them over the horizon, USS *Colorado* steamed ahead and troops were lowered into infantry landing craft (LCIs) from cargo nets over the side of transports accompanying her. The LCIs headed toward the beach only to meet heavy fire that broke them repeatedly into seeming confusion. When the third "attempt" to re-form the landing craft failed, the would-be invasion force reembarked their Marines in their transports and, with *Colorado*, steamed back out to sea. The elated Japanese commander of Saipan, Gen. Yoshitsugu Saito, proclaimed immediate victory and sent a highly exaggerated report to Japan that the Americans had been driven off with heavy personnel casualties, one battleship sunk, several carriers damaged, and over 140 planes shot down. The failed landing, however, had been a ruse—a staged event to lure out the Japanese fleet.[41]

In response to this U.S. deception the Japanese launched Operation A-GO. Their plan was to trap the U.S. Fifth Fleet between their remaining carriers and the islands of the Marianas, pounding it by air from two directions. Vice Adm. Jisaburo Ozawa, commanding the mobile carrier force from his base at Singapore, received orders to launch Operation A-GO from Adm. Soemu Toyoda, who had assumed the position of Commander in Chief of the Combined Fleet when Koga's plane was lost in a storm on 8 March. The storm had also forced Koga's chief of staff, Vice Adm. Shigeru Fukudome, to ditch off Cebu, where he was captured by Filipino guerrillas.[42]

The plan was for Ozawa to slip out from his anchorage at Guimaras, slip through the Guimaras Strait and the Visayan Sea, and rendezvous with Ugaki and several groups of supply and replenishment ships in the Philippine Sea on 16 June to surprise the Americans.[43] Less than two hours after Ozawa received the execute order, at 0542, U.S. warships appeared on the horizon and took their firing positions off Saipan's beaches. Soon the Marines were again headed for eleven designated beach landing areas—this time for real. When they reached the reef, the Japanese defenders opened up on them from predetermined flanking positions. Though the fighting was intense, eight thousand Marines of the 2nd and 4th Divisions were on shore by 0900. By the end of the day all twenty thousand Marines detailed to take Saipan were landed. Already they had taken 10 percent casualties.[44]

On 15 June Ozawa's Mobile Fleet, with carriers, battleships, and their screening cruisers and destroyers, emerged from the San Bernardino Strait, about 1,260 nautical miles from Saipan. The Japanese trap was set in motion. But the American submarine SS *Flying Fish*, almost out of fuel and awaiting her relief, was at the right spot to see them. Her skipper, Cdr. R.D. Riser, was unable to count the ships without revealing his position, but as soon as they passed he radioed the news that the huge Japanese force had cleared the Strait heading east-northeast and making twenty knots.[45]

That night another U.S. submarine, SS *Seahorse*, sighted warships two hundred nautical miles east of the Surigao Strait and three hundred nautical miles south of the San Bernardino Strait. The skipper reported this force, Ugaki's ships moving out from Batjan, as on a northeast course at a speed of 16.5 knots.[46] Because of Japanese radio jamming in his area, Spruance didn't get this new intelligence information until 0400 on 16 June. Though Spruance would have enjoyed having the news earlier, its delay didn't really matter. Spruance estimated that Ozawa's carriers could be in position to strike as early as the final hours of 17 June, but that he would be ready to strike the U.S. force no later than some time on 19 June. He would be ready.

The final pieces began to fall into place when SS *Cavalla*, while following several Japanese oilers it came across earlier in the day en route to relieve SS *Flying Fish*, got radar contact on a much larger group of ships. The *Cavalla* submerged and her crew counted propeller sounds, estimating that fifteen warships had passed. When Spruance received *Cavalla*'s report, based on the course and speed passed, he reckoned that Vice Adm. Ozawa's force would be in position to strike in twenty-four hours.[47]

Readying for the Duel

Spruance formed his force into an F shape, oriented from north to south, and inverted so that the horizontal prongs of the F were pointing to the west. At the base of the F was Rear Adm. Alfred E. Montgomery's (USNA '12) Task Group 58.2 with the new fleet carriers *Bunker Hill* and *Wasp II*, two light carriers and a screen of two light cruisers, two light antiaircraft cruisers, and twelve destroyers. Montgomery's task force was formed in a circle with a four-mile radius. Immediately north of Montgomery's force was Rear Adm. John W. Reeves's (USNA '11) Task Group 58.3, which included the Fleet Carriers *Enterprise* and *Lexington II*, two light carriers, the heavy cruiser *Indianapolis*, three light cruisers, one light antiaircraft cruiser, and thirteen destroyers. Embarked aboard *Indianapolis* was the commander of the Fifth Fleet, Adm. Raymond A. Spruance (USNA '07, USNWC '27). Aboard *Lexington II* was Vice Adm. Marc A. Mitscher (USNA '10), the commander of Task Force 58 for Admiral Spruance. Like Montgomery's and the other two carrier Battle Groups, Reeves' Task Group 58.3 was formed on a four-mile radius circle. Immediately above this formidable task group was Task Group 58.1, commanded by Rear Adm. Joseph M.J. "Jocko" Clark (USNA '18). It was composed of the fleet carriers *Hornet II*, *Yorktown II*, two light carriers, a screen of three heavy cruisers, a single antiaircraft cruiser, and fourteen destroyers.[48]

In all likelihood Clark assumed this position at the top of the F and farthest away from the expected Japanese line of advance because he had returned early from the raid Spruance sent him on to destroy the aircraft on or staging from and runways of the Volcano Islands. Clark had arrived

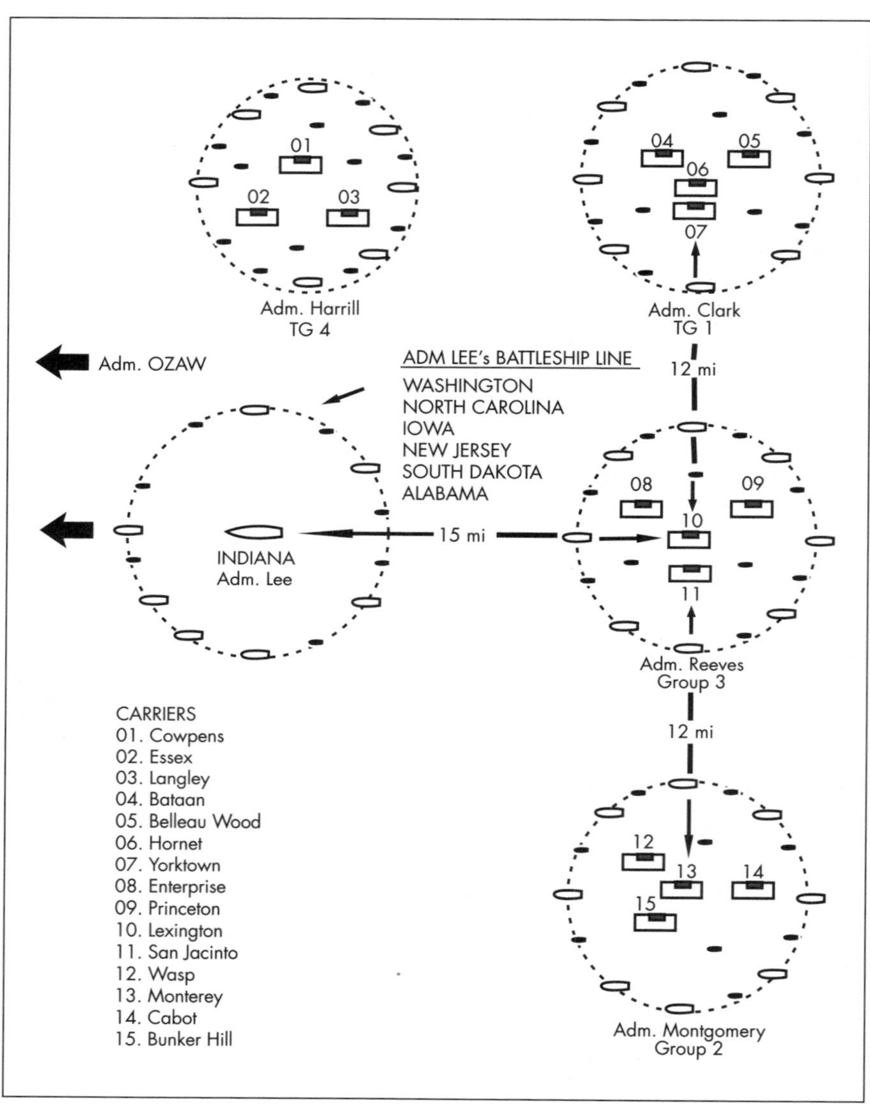

FIGURE 41. Admiral Spruance's battle formation. —*Graphic provided by Jason Peters*

earlier than expected on the evening of 15 June while there was still plenty of light to launch his strikes. He launched strikes from all seven carriers in his task group. Clark's pilots struck again the next day as a nascent typhoon subsided long enough for them to take the Japanese by complete surprise. The first day they splashed ten to twelve Zero fighters and destroyed another twenty-eight planes on the deck. On the 16th they destroyed another sixty planes on the fields they bombed, along with destroying the fuel dumps and cratering runways. The Volcano Islands would not serve as a "shuttle bombing" stop for any aircraft the Japanese could muster to send into the fray from the home islands.[49]

On the northwestern prong of Spruance's F formation was Rear Adm. William K. Harrill's (USNA '14) Task Group 58.4, which had been part of Clark's striking force for the Volcano Islands. Much like the others, it was composed of the fleet carrier *Essex* and light carriers *Langley* and *Cowpens*, three light cruisers, one antiaircraft cruiser, and fourteen destroyers.[50]

Last and of great importance was Vice Adm. "Ching" Lee's group of new fast battleships. Lee was stationed with his flagship *Indiana*, *Alabama*, *Iowa*, *New Jersey*, *North Carolina*, *South Dakota*, and *Washington,* three light cruisers, and fourteen destroyers in a six-mile radius formation.[51] Lee's Task Group 58.7 formed a "gun line" that any Japanese planes seeking to destroy U.S. carriers would likely have to pass through. Spruance had stationed his force to provide defense in depth. Behind it he had another battleship "gun line" in line formation poised between Task Force 58 and Saipan. Should any aircraft get past his armada, the battleships would stop them from hitting the Marines and the reserve force Army 27th Division that had not been landed.

Adding to Spruance's defensive scheme was an "invisible trap" of four submarines placed five hundred nautical miles to the west of Saipan by Rear Adm. Charles A. Lockwood, the commander of submarines in the Pacific (COMSUBPAC). Stationed in a sixty-nautical-mile box along the expected path of the two main Japanese task forces, they awaited their chance to lay waste to anything that passed. Their orders were to "shoot on sight."[52] With the exception of being engaged en route to the battle site by U.S. land-based aircraft from the Marianas, which had not yet been occupied, the Japanese were about to take a taste of their own doctrine—doctrine that they had disastrously failed to follow in the Battle of Midway.

The only question now was what the Japanese would do next. Would the two main task forces of Admirals Ozawa and Ugaki form into a single force and strike directly? Or would the Japanese employ a "cheng" and a "chi"—a normal force and an irregular force so that one could hold the Americans in place while the other approached Spruance's task forces from the flank or rear? If the Japanese attacked at their earliest opportunity, they would be at the limit of their air-striking range and would probably have to organize in a single grouping of warships. Based on the intelligence passed by U.S. submarines, such an attack could come as soon as late in the day on 17 June. If the Japanese failed to strike until later, it was possible that they had assumed the same multiple grouping of ships that they had used at Midway, the Eastern Solomons, and Santa Cruz. It was Spruance's challenge to be ready for anything his Japanese adversaries threw against him.

Opposing the Fifth Fleet were Vice Adm. Takeo Kurita's three battleships, five cruisers, and ten destroyers, supported by three light carriers. Vice Adm. Jisaburo Ozawa's remaining two fleet carrier divisions consisting of six carriers—with 430 warplanes embarked—two battleships, eight cruisers, and fifteen destroyers represented the main Japanese Striking Force.[53] The two Japanese admirals were outnumbered fifteen carriers to nine, and 996 planes to 430. Moreover, excepting the word they got from the commander of the Saipan garrison that four American carriers had been "damaged," they had every reason to know that they were seriously outnumbered in every category of ship and aircraft. The success of the Japanese plan rested with the surprise they hoped to achieve by slipping undetected into the Philippine Sea and the availability of aircraft staged from rear-area bases that would "island hop" to their launching points for repeated sorties against the Americans. Early detection by U.S. submarines took away the first key element of the Japanese plan. With Spruance's raid on the Volcano Islands, "Jocko" Clark had negated any chance of this critical second aspect of the Japanese operational plan coming to pass. Yet the Japanese still had one last advantage—superiority in the distance from which they could launch an air strike—that might even the odds. To exploit this advantage, however, they would have to get through the submarine kill zone, gun line, screening units, and combat air patrol that Spruance had waiting for them.

The Battle of the Philippine Sea

Spruance's plan was simple. He would fly a search out to three hundred nautical miles, and then, if the Japanese were not located, he would sail his force southwest toward the expected Japanese line of advance during the night. The next morning he would reverse his course to get closer to Saipan and to make sure that no Japanese force got in behind him and between him and Saipan. The scheduled amphibious operation to take Guam was postponed.

Admiral Mitscher, anxious to get at the Japanese, contacted Spruance by line-of-sight tactical radio and tried to persuade him to press on to the southwest and engage the Japanese at the earliest opportunity. Spruance, committed to his main objective of ensuring the success of Admiral Turner's amphibious assault on Saipan, resisted Mitscher's advice. He probably considered in his decision that radio operators aboard USS *Indianapolis*, Spruance's flagship, had copied a message from COMSUBPAC in Hawaii to SS *Stingray* asking her to repeat a garbled message she had sent earlier. Since *Stingray* was one of the four submarines Admiral Lockwood had in waiting for the Japanese, the obvious possibility was that she had sighted the Japanese force at about 150 nautical miles from Task Force 58—only half the expected distance based on the earlier sightings by SS *Flying Fish* and SS *Cavalla*. In fact *Stingray* was reporting a fire in her superstructure, but the damage was done. Now believing that the Japanese were considerably closer than originally expected, Spruance informed Mitscher that his desire to steam toward them starting an hour after midnight would open up the possibility of a second Japanese force slipping in behind Task Force 58 during the night and disrupting the main objective of taking Saipan, Tinian, and Guam to stage B-29 bombing runs on Japan.[54]

The Japanese Mobile Force, after refueling at sea on 16 and 17 June, divided into two major components. In the van was Vice Adm. Takeo Kurita with his three light carriers, three battleships, five cruisers, and ten destroyers. Following Kurita about a hundred nautical miles to his southwest was Admiral Ozawa with his six carriers, two battleships, eight cruisers, and fifteen destroyers. During the early morning hours of 19 June, Kurita's air search revealed the basic location of Task Force 58. At 0830 Ozawa, acting on this information, launched his first attack wave of forty-five dive-bombers with 500-pound bombs, eight torpedo planes and 16 Zero fighters.[55] Task Force 58 was still on a southwesterly course and had not located the Japanese within the limits of the three-hundred-nautical-mile search pattern they were flying. Thus the Japanese got off the first blow while still out of the attack range of Fifth Fleet.

This strike range advantage lay with the Japanese not because of better aircraft design, but because they had chosen a trade-off unacceptable to

American strategic culture. Japanese planes lacked armor, bulletproof windscreens, and redundant systems to protect pilots. In the trade-off for greater maneuverability and range, the Japanese had sacrificed pilot safety. Over the long term this was to wreak havoc with Japanese naval aviation, as trained and experienced pilots were even harder to replace than planes. In the war of attrition that World War II in the Pacific theater had become, events from Coral Sea to the Philippine Sea had taken their cumulative toll on Japan's ability to wage war.

Near daybreak on 19 June 1944 a Japanese plane dropped a bomb unsuccessfully near the destroyer *Stockham* in Lee's Task Group 58.7. Another was reported to be over Guam, which, since it had not yet been assaulted, provided a potential "shuttle-bombing" runway for the Japanese. The fight was on. F6F-3 Hellcats were launched and found thirty Zeros and five bombers to contest. This was the first of a good number of dogfights over Guam that day.[56]

While still making twenty-four knots to westward to get the Japanese within the striking range of about 200 nautical miles, Spruance's force got radar contact on approaching bogies. The time was 1000. Though the wind was at his back and the distance to the new contacts was only 150 nautical miles, Mitscher, in tactical command of all aviation assets, decided to continue to close the enemy. After twenty minutes Mitscher turned about into the wind and began to launch. His new Hellcats quickly rose to twenty-five thousand feet altitude, giving them a significant tactical advantage over the Japanese. In the first half hour twenty-seven fighters and torpedo planes were splashed. Then, at 1140, a second and larger wave of forty-seven Zero fighters and sixty-one dive-bombers and torpedo planes arrived from Ozawa's carriers.[57]

When what remained of Ozawa's aircraft returned, those wanting to land on his flagship, *Taiho*,[58] were in for a surprise. Their mother ship was aflame and billowing smoke, requiring them to land on another of Ozawa's carriers. *Taiho*, a thirty-one-thousand-ton carrier, was struck by the last of six torpedoes fired from about fifteen hundred yards at a speed of twenty-seven knots by SS *Albacore*, one of Admiral Lockwood's subs lying in wait. Another torpedo would have hit if a Japanese pilot had not spotted it and become his nation's first kamikaze by diving his plane into it to save *Taiho*. His sacrifice was in vain. While *Albacore* dived to escape, *Taiho* burned out of control.

At about noon a third wave of forty fighters and seven torpedo planes hit Task Force 58. Seven were shot down and the rest were driven off back to their carriers. At 1306 a fourth wave of forty Japanese fighters, thirty-six dive-bombers, and nine torpedo planes struck the American force. This group split in two, with six dive-bombers attacking Task Group 58.3 and achieving little damage. Of the forty Val dive-bombers that tried to land on Guam, nineteen were able to land but were out of commission thereafter with damage. The rest were splashed by Hellcats.[59] The "Marianas Turkey Shoot" was underway.

The surviving planes returning from *Shokaku*'s fourth wave were as surprised as their compatriots from *Taiho* when they returned to find their thirty-thousand-ton carrier in flames. This time the SS *Cavalla*, which had reported the passing of the Japanese Fleet two days earlier but resisted the temptation to launch her fish to preserve the secrecy of the intelligence she provided, was the culprit. Again, one of only four U.S. submarines in the box created by Admiral Lockwood hit her mark. Three of the six torpedoes she launched—the last two while diving to avoid destruction—hit their mark. Of the 105 depth charges *Cavalla*'s crew counted, nearly half were close aboard. *Cavalla* survived. *Shokaku* sank.[60]

It should be noted that the U.S. submarine offensive against the Japanese had just started. The success of this offensive should rightfully give it the status of a "third prong" of the two-pronged strategy employed against the Japanese in the Pacific. To this point, the battle had developed as presented in figure 42.

The Marianas Turkey Shoot

Admiral Ozawa had launched his first attack wave against Task Force 58 at about 0900. He had 222 fighter aircraft, 113 dive-bombers, and 95 torpedo planes—a total of 430 warplanes—on his six carriers to throw against the Americans.[61] By noon Ozawa had lost two of his fleet carriers and his aircraft losses were mounting. For the Americans the fun had just begun.

Stories of individual heroism and masterful airmanship in this battle are numerous. One flier, Ens. Wilbur B. Webb of USS *Hornet II*'s VF-2, was credited with six kills in only a matter of minutes. His F6F-3 Hellcat caught up with a group of six Zero fighters in the pattern attempting to land at Guam Airfield and got in behind them. He approached and fired on every one from the rear until all six flamed to earth.[62] To recount even a few such stories, however, would fail to capture the magnitude of the U.S. triumph in the air that day. Perhaps the recounting of the Marianas Turkey Shoot by the captain of Mitscher's flagship, *Lexington II*, would serve better to do that.

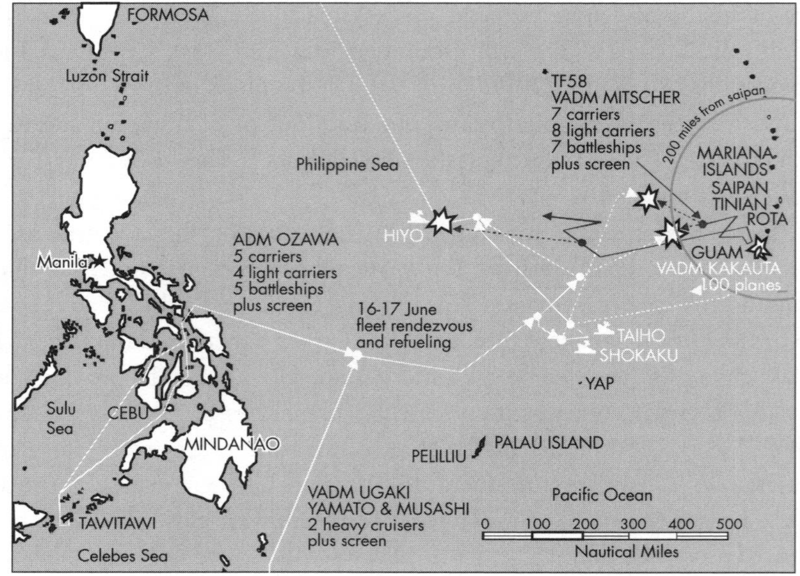

FIGURE 42. Battle of the Philippine Sea. —*Courtesy of U.S. Naval War College*

At 0130 on 19 June 1944 a PBY search plane made radar contact with the Japanese Fleet at 13 degrees 20 minutes North latitude and 137 degrees East longitude. Due to communication difficulties, no report was received of this sighting by Admiral Spruance until eight hours later. Therefore, at 0530 *Lexington II* launched nine torpedo planes and 5 Hellcats to search in five sectors between 205 and 325 degrees true from the ship. At the time no contact was generated as the Japanese Fleet was still 360 nautical miles away. These planes shot down three Japanese torpedo planes, two dive-bombers and a single reconnaissance plane, however, so Admirals Spruance and Mitscher knew that the Japanese were close to attack range.[63]

At 0700 fighters from USS *Belleau Wood* reported enemy planes taking off from Guam. Air combat ensued periodically for the next three hours. At 1001 a "large group of bogies" was sighted and confirmed as 140 nautical miles on a bearing of 245 degrees true from Task Force 58. Task Force aircraft were recalled from Guam and at 1023 *Lexington II* launched thirteen fighters and seventeen dive-bombers as the reported bogies continued to close. At 1032 a

> "tallyho" was received when the Japanese strike was visually sighted, and another "tallyho" came from a *Lexington II* plane ten minutes later. The Japanese got in as close as twenty nautical miles from Task Force 58 before it was fully engaged.[64]
>
> At 1107 a second large group of Japanese planes was sighted, estimated at between fifty and seventy, at 290 degrees true and one hundred and fifteen nautical miles. This second-wave strike was intercepted at forty nautical miles. At 1142 another group of Japanese torpedo planes were closing fast bearing 265 degrees true and again were intercepted at forty nautical miles. At 1146 and 1153 *Lexington II* gunners opened fire on several planes diving on USS *Princeton*. These planes missed their mark, and were of the few Japanese planes that got close to ships of the Task Force that day.[65]
>
> It was apparent that TF 58 was being attacked by succeeding waves of carrier planes. From 1200 until 1500 groups of bogies were detected and intercepted with deadly regularity. No further enemy planes penetrated the screen, and on most occasions interception was effected 40 to 50 miles from the force. At 1500 the USS *Lexington* landed all but six interceptors. Between 1023 and 1500 the 30 VF of VF-16, which were launched as interceptors shot down thirteen Judys [dive-bombers], eight Zekes [fighter aircraft], three Jills [torpedo planes] and two Kates [dive-bombers], and probably shot down two Zekes and one Judy. At 1400 a search group consisting of 8 VT and 5 VF was launched to search sector 225° to 270° true for 325 miles from 14° 04' North 144° 19' East. Again no surface craft were seen, but five Zekes, two Jills and one Judy were shot down, one Zeke probably shot down and several Zekes damaged.[66]

The total score for the *Lexington* Air Group for 19 June was 45 Japanese aircraft shot down, 4 more probably shot down, 1 damaged in the air, 2 destroyed on the ground, 1 probably destroyed on the ground, and 10 damaged on the ground.[67] Air Group Sixteen off *Lexington II* shot down a total of 143 Japanese planes during the Battle of the Philippine Sea and other expeditions, a huge total for a single carrier.[68] Air Groups of the fifteen carriers of Task Force 58 shot down "over 400 enemy planes" on 19 June alone—the largest total in any single day in history.[69] When the smoke had cleared Task Force 58 fighters and other planes had downed 366 enemy aircraft, with 19 more shot down by Battle Force gunners and 17 destroyed on the deck on Guam.[70] Moreover, the resounding victory was won at a comparatively small cost of twenty-seven pilots dead or missing and twenty-nine American planes lost. While the precise reason this battle became known as the Marianas Turkey Shoot is not known, an appropriate myth survived the battle. Many who took part in the destruction of the First Air Fleet relate that one pilot from the deep South remarked to his plane captain when he landed from a mission, "Boy, this sure makes me homesick. It's just like an ol'-fashioned turkey shoot."[71]

During this entire engagement no surface units were struck by U.S. aircraft. The carriers of Task Force 58 had to turn to the east into the wind repeatedly, and as a result were unable to close on the Japanese carriers to their southwest. It was estimated that from the first sighting of the Japanese Striking Force by a PBY and the sighting reported by the submarine *Cavalla* when she torpedoed *Shokaku* the force had traveled eastward about 240 nautical miles. During that same period, Task Force 58 had only averaged about seventeen knots to the west. Searches in the late evening of 19 June failed to locate any Japanese naval units suitable for attacking.[72]

On the Japanese side, even with the loss of two carriers and the three thousand men aboard them, hopes of ultimate victory remained unrealistically high. Admiral Ozawa had every intention of resuming the battle the next day. Ozawa believed that most of his missing planes had landed on Guam or other air strips in the area and would be available for strikes. He also still counted on land-based aircraft shuttled from the Japanese home islands. Perhaps most telling was his reliance on the intelligence provided by his pilots.

Japanese pilots reported on 19 June that they had sunk four Task Force 58 carriers, and that six more were "blazing like bonfires."[73] These reports, of course, were untrue. Yet Ozawa determined that the attack should be resumed after his ships were refueled. His huge aircraft losses did not register until a fleet-wide radio inventory that night revealed that of his 430 original aircraft, he had only 100 that were still capable of going into battle. At 1615 on 20 June Ozawa got word from Admiral Kurita that his force had been spotted by an American search plane.[74] He decided to retire to the west, his own command post (the heavy cruiser *Haguro*, after *Taiho* sank the day before) heading for Okinawa—a Japanese bastion that would not fall until 22 June 1945, with the loss of 107,539 soldiers, sixteen warships and over 800 more planes.[75]

Mopping Up

While Ozawa had had enough, Spruance and Mitscher had not. Throughout the night of 19 June they pursued the Japanese. Though both searches that night and a limited number of searches the next day were conducted, they failed to uncover the Japanese Fleet's location. Then at 1542 on 20 June a garbled message came in from one of the search planes, suggesting that the Japanese carriers had at last been sighted. A little later—at 1605—a more intelligible report placed the Japanese 275 nautical miles to the northwest. This report was corrected ten minutes later to 370 nautical miles, but by then, since Admiral Mitscher had readied a strike based on the 1542 presumed sighting, eighty-five fighters, seventy-seven dive-bombers, and fifty-four torpedo planes were already aloft. The 740-nautical-mile round trip for these planes was too far even with drop tanks. Yet Mitscher, anxious to finish the Japanese off, determined that he could reduce that distance by seventy-five to one hundred miles by steaming "Bendix."* He accepted the risk of losing many aircraft and pilots and boldly let the strike he had launched continue.[76]

When they approached their target they found that the Japanese fleet was divided into three groups. The northern group included one fleet carrier of the *Zuikaku* class, around ten heavy and light cruisers, and from fourteen to sixteen destroyers. The southern group was comprised of three fleet oilers, three CAs, and a destroyer. The western group was five battleships, two fleet carriers of the *Hitaka* class, two escort carriers of the *Ryuho* class, several heavy cruisers, and four destroyers. The air group commander decided to attack the two nearest groups: the southern and western.[77]

By sunset most of the U.S. planes had left the area, but not before doing their damage. The carrier *Hiyo* and the fleet oilers *Genyo Maru* and *Seiyo Maru* were sunk. *Zuikaku* in the northern group was damaged, as were *Junyo* and *Ryuho* of the western group, the heavy cruisers *Chiyoda* and *Maya*, the battleship *Haruna,* and the fleet oiler *Hayasui.*[78] It was also estimated that 22 of the 75 Japanese fighter aircraft launched to counter the attack had been splashed in the encounter. In all, the 100 operational carrier aircraft that the Japanese had available after the Marianas Turkey Shoot were reduced to

*The maker of the instrument that communicates desired ship speed from the bridge to the engine room is made by the Bendix corporation, and their logo is placed near the top possible speed. Hence the term "all ahead Bendix" is synonymous with "full speed ahead."

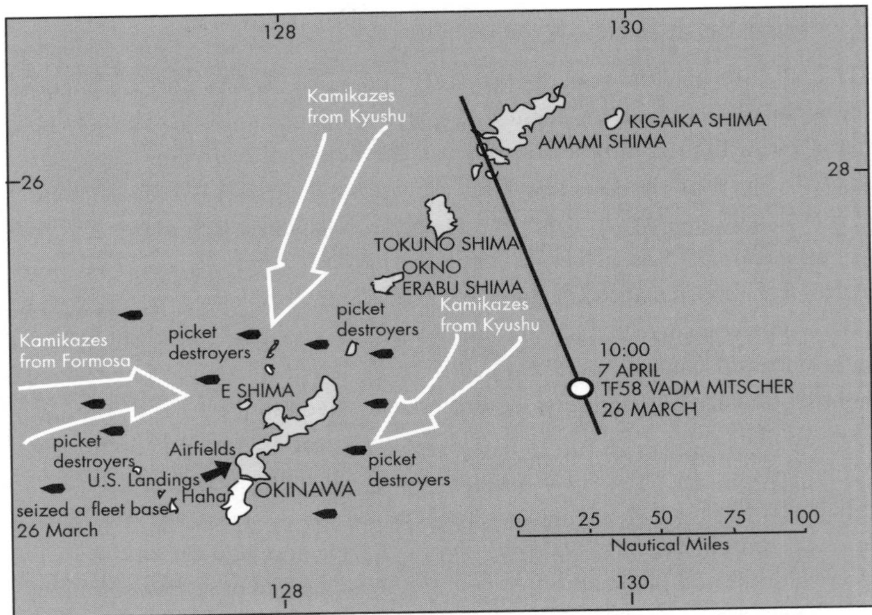

FIGURE 43. The Japanese defense of Okinawa. —*Courtesy of U.S. Naval War College*

less than 50. Of the 9 aircraft carriers the Japanese had when the Battle of the Philippine Sea started, only 2 remained seaworthy. The Imperial Japanese Navy that had once dominated the western Pacific now lacked the air cover and striking power to assume an offensive posture.[79]

But the cost for the U.S. was high. Returning to their carriers after dark and nearing fuel exhaustion, the American pilots were glad to see that Admiral Mitscher had "turned on the lights" for them. Unfortunately, thirty-eight pilots and air crewmen were lost in the strike, and of the 216 planes launched by Task Force 58 carriers only 116 landed safely.[80]

Finishing the Job in the Marianas

By 9 July the Marines and their Army 77th Infantry Division comrades had done their job on Saipan. At a cost of three thousand killed in action and another thirteen thousand wounded they had secured the first base that could bring B-29 bombers within range of Tokyo.[81] Tinian and Guam were next.

Only two weeks after concluding the bloody fighting for Saipan, the Marines of the 2nd and 4th Marine Divisions hit the beaches of Tinian, four miles to the south. In a week they secured control of Tinian, with only four hundred casualties. Marine Gen. Holland M. "Howling Mad" Smith later called this "the perfect amphibious operation of the Pacific War."[82]

Retaking Guam, some 130 nautical miles to the southwest of Tinian, would be another matter. There were no suitable beaches for an amphibious assault on the 30-mile-long island, and its central mountain ridges made perfect defensive positions. The first step was to "soften up" the Japanese garrisons on Guam with two weeks of battleship and smaller unit gunfire—the most for any operation in the Pacific in World War II. When the Marines of the 2nd and 4th Divisions stormed ashore at Agat Beach on 21 July, they were greeted by a "Welcome Marines" notice left by Navy underwater demolition teams. The 77th Infantry Division landed five miles to the north on the other side of Apra Harbor. After five grueling days the two forces linked together and confined most of the Japanese defenders to the narrow Orote Peninsula.[83]

Unable to break out, the Japanese launched wave after wave of suicide attacks. On 10 August, a little over two weeks after the initial U.S. assault, the Japanese made their last stand. Over fifteen hundred Americans and thirty-five hundred Japanese lost their lives in the struggle for Guam. Though organized resistance ended, mopping-up actions were required well into 1945.[84] In fact, the last Japanese soldier didn't come out of hiding to surrender until 1972.*

At long last the Nimitz prong of the two-pronged strategy had paid dividends. The United States, two years after the Japanese had raised their flag on Guam and secured with it their largest base in the Pacific, had regained this valuable stretch of real estate. Once the Seabees had finished improving the runways, U.S. B-29s could start their assault on the Japanese home islands. The beginning of the end was at hand for the Japanese.

Oddly, virtually no one in the Japanese government realized the proximity of downfall until the fall of Saipan. Even then only a few among them fully grasped the gravity of the situation to the east. During 1944 they had launched the *ichi go* offensive on the Asian mainland—in part to counter their inability to transport resources from their "Southern Resource Area" to the Japanese home islands due to the success of the U.S. submarine offensive against their shipping—and had achieved some of their greatest success in the war. With a distinctly continental focus to their overall policy objectives and

*At the time of his surrender, the author happened to be on Guam while flying aerial surveillance missions in the area with the U.S. Navy.

strategy, the Japanese leadership was lulled into a sense of great achievement in their primary area of concern. When Saipan fell, a sense of desperation set in for the first time. Just as Adm. Isoroku Yamamoto had warned, Japan was indeed vulnerable from the east.

When the true extent of the Japanese losses in the Battle of the Philippine Sea or Marianas Turkey Shoot sunk in, Ozawa offered his resignation. It was not accepted. It was not long, however, until his star began to be eclipsed by that of Kurita.

In addition to the strategic advantage it garnered of permitting the U.S, to begin bombing Japan, the demise of Japanese carrier aviation on 19 and 21 June 1944 opened the door to other important operations, including MacArthur's return to the Philippines.

Conclusions

There is no real point in evaluating in detail the decisions of the various commanders for their efforts during the Battle of the Philippine Sea by the criteria used in chapters 2 through 5. By now the U.S. naval leaders were "graduate students" expected to excel in operational art. Moreover, they were graduate students with a large number of the most sophisticated "toys" on the planet. While the Japanese had somehow managed to bring together nine carriers, their air wings mostly composed of fliers who had no more than sixty hours of training and experience, the United States could field fifteen carriers—seven of them of the new and powerful *Essex* class—with experienced pilots, virtually all of whom had a minimum of three hundred hours in the cockpit. Also, though the Japanese Zero fighter was clearly superior to anything the U.S. could put in the air in the early stages of the war, the new F6F-3 Hellcat was more than a match for it. The Zero could, of course, turn faster and maneuver better than the Hellcat, since it lacked the weight of the armor on the U.S. plane. But the Hellcat, aside from having better survivability, had a tremendous power advantage over the Zero. It could also climb higher, allowing it to pounce on any Zero below in an accelerating dive. Further, it could out-accelerate the Zero in level flight, thus making it extremely hard to hit from behind. In combination, the United States had an advantage in both man and machine.

Yet there are several decisions that do stand out in their own right. First, when Admiral Spruance knew from locating information the submarines passed the direction and likely time of approach of the Japanese Fleet, he never strayed from his primary responsibility to ensure the success of the amphibious assaults on Saipan, Tinian, and Guam. Spruance, who had been exposed to *Sound Military Decision* at the Naval War College, overrode Admiral Mitscher, who had not, when he decided to keep Task Force 58 near enough to the Marianas so as not to allow a Japanese force to slip in behind him and his main objectives. While some have criticized Spruance for lacking Mitscher's aggressiveness and losing the opportunity to sink all of the remaining Japanese carriers in the battle, his decision was the correct one. While most of the commanders in the Battle of the Philippine Sea, as "graduate students" who had a huge numerical superiority in ships and airplanes and had undergone a steep learning curve in combat, deserve the expected graduate grade of B+, Spruance clearly merits a strong A for every aspect of his performance and all of his decisions in this battle. Rear Adm. Charles Lockwood, commander of submarines in the Pacific, should likewise receive an A+ for his foresightedness in placing four submarines in the area of most likely operation of the Japanese carriers. His good judgment resulted in a loss in carriers for the Japanese almost as devastatingly complete as the total destruction of their carrier air wings in the Marianas Turkey Shoot.

For the rest of those concerned, the expected minimum grade for this point of the war—B+—is assigned. Only Mitscher, whose recommendation to close the Japanese during the early hours of 19 June would have resulted in a more complete victory, might deserve better, notwithstanding that his plan could have resulted in disaster. His decision to press the attack he had in the air on 21 June was courageous, if costly. His order to "turn on the lights" for returning aircraft was also the right and courageous thing to do.

No victory in naval history was more complete than the Battle of the Philippine Sea and the Marianas Turkey Shoot. So ended the five carrier battles of World War II. (Though Halsey chased and sank several Japanese carriers during the Battle of Leyte Gulf, the inability of those carriers to launch aircraft to contest the outcome disqualifies that episode from consideration as a true carrier battle.) In each of the five carrier battles of World War II, the United States won a strategic—if not operational or tactical—victory. And as with the four previous battles, when evaluated by the tenets of *Sound Military Decision*, the decisions of the commanders in the Battle of the Philippine Sea measured up well.

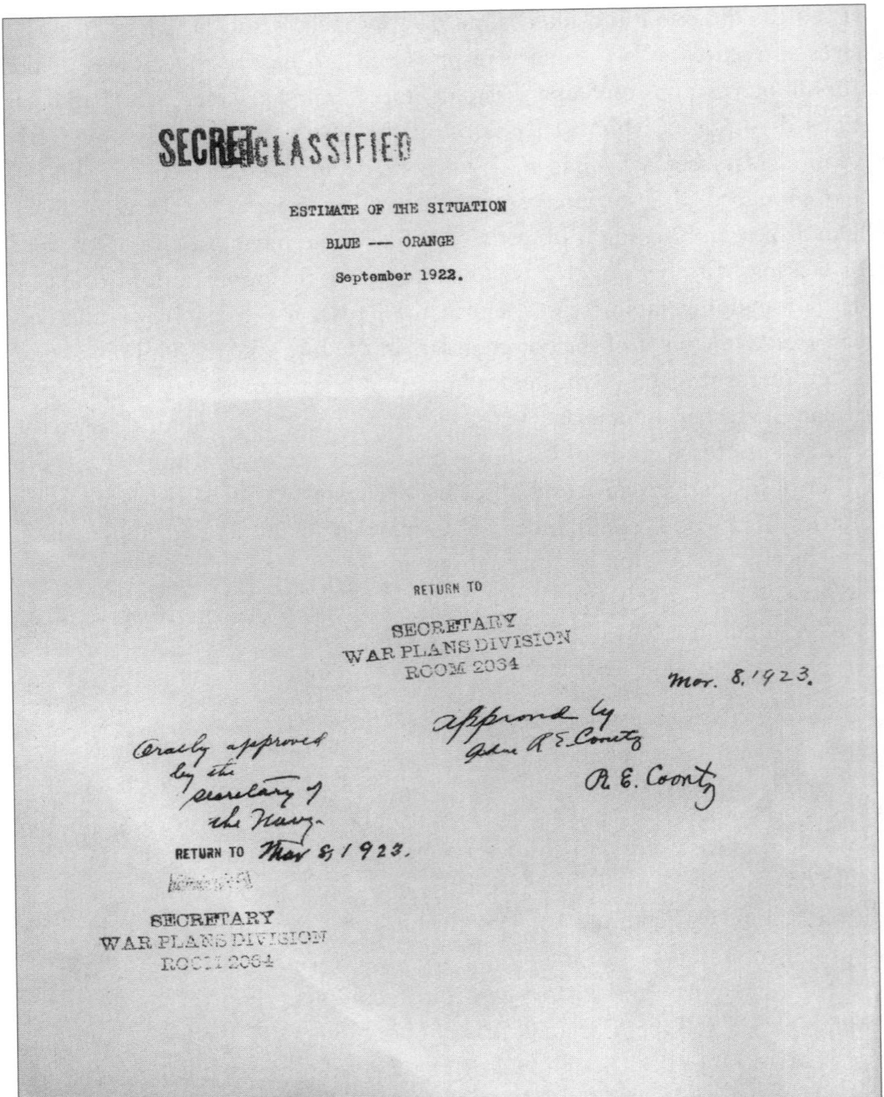

SECRET CLASSIFIED

ESTIMATE OF THE SITUATION

BLUE --- ORANGE

September 1922.

RETURN TO

SECRETARY
WAR PLANS DIVISION
ROOM 2034

Mar. 8, 1923.

approved by
Adm R. E. Coontz

R. E. Coontz

Orally approved
by the
secretary of
the Navy

RETURN TO Mar 8, 1923.

SECRETARY
WAR PLANS DIVISION
ROOM 2034

FIGURE 44. "Estimate of the Situation" Blue [U.S.]—Orange [Japan] 1923. —*Image provided by Edward S. Miller from his lecture "War Pan Orange," U.S. Naval War College*

Conclusions

FIGURE 45. Adm. Chester Nimitz accepts the Japanese surrender as Gen. Douglas MacAuthur, Adm. Bill Halsey, and Adm. Forrest Sherman look on. *—Courtesy of U.S. Naval Institute Photo Archive*

THE UNITED STATES ENTERED WORLD WAR II at a disadvantage in numbers of ships, quality of naval aircraft, and experience in war. Though the Japanese had opposed the Washington Treaty of Naval Limitations of 1922, during the late 1920s and early 1930s it was the most one-sided agreement in their favor that their leadership could have hoped for, and the basis for their rise to world power status and dominance in Asia and the western Pacific. If they had more closely analyzed their situation, the Japanese would have necessarily come to the conclusion that based on the relative state of their economies and their industrial capacities, the United States, unconstrained by its treaty commitments, could have easily built three to five times as many warships as Japan. Moreover, with the United States constrained by its treaty commitments, the Japanese were not faced with the hard decisions inherent in a naval arms race. The Japanese were free to apply their fiscal and intellectual resources to creating the most technologically advanced and operationally experienced navy in the world. Unfortunately for the Japanese, they lacked the foresight to provide for the intellectual refinement of their officer corps and the quantitative training necessary to compete with the United States Navy over the long term.

When the Japanese attacked Pearl Harbor they accelerated the July 1940 Two-Ocean Act, which had already set in motion the industrial machine that would quickly allow the United States to catch up and surpass Japan in all meaningful comparisons of naval might. Yet at the war's outset, Japan held a quantitative and qualitative naval advantage—exacerbated by the U.S. losses at Pearl Harbor—that forced the United States to make up for its disadvantages by superiority in some important area. In the war at sea that decided the outcome of World War II between the Unites States and Japan, the main "equalizer," particularly from December 1941 through about November of 1943, was the quality and consistency of leadership in the United States Navy.

Faced with a need to react to Japanese strategy, and usually outnumbered and qualitatively inferior in ships and aircraft design, the U.S. Navy invariably found a way to go on the offensive successfully. Throughout 1942 the essential element of U.S. success in the Pacific theater was achieving the strategic objective in the four carrier battles that diminished Japan's naval advantage, stopped the expansion of Japanese hegemony, maintained the sea lines of communication with Australia, and opened the door for not one but two axes of offensive action to terminate the war on terms favorable to the United States and its allies. In each of those battles the outcome rested on a few key decisions. Almost invariably, the decisions made in the heat of battle were suitable to the nature of the effect desired, the means available and opposed to achieve that effect, the characteristics of the theater of operations, and the consequences and cost of achieving the effect desired.[1] These were the criteria established as critical in the decision-making process at the Naval War College in *Sound Military Decision* in the period between the first and second world wars.

It would be preposterous to say that education supplanted experience as the main source of a solid decision process that led to success in the Pacific in World War II. It would be even more preposterous to advance the notion that a single part of that educational experience stands out as the absolutely essential element of it—or would it be? The evaluation of the decision process for the commanders in the five carrier battles discussed above reinforces that adherence to the tenets of one major contributor to their education—*Sound Military Decision*—was universally present and indeed important to their reaction to stressful and demanding battle conditions.

It is interesting that the primary prewar planning document for a war between the United States and Japan, approved by the Chief of Naval Operations, Adm. Robert E. Coontz, in 1923, was titled "Estimate of the Situation: Blue–Orange." Equally interesting is the official title given to his diary for the Pacific war, which has become known as the "Gray Book" by Adm. Chester W. Nimitz, Commander in Chief, U.S. Pacific Fleet—"The Running Estimate of the Situation for the Pacific War." The term "estimate of the situation" also appears repeatedly in many of the Battle Reports of the commanders involved in the carrier battles discussed above. That term, "estimate of the situation," is the fundamental underpinning of *Sound Military Decision*, which was used in conjunction with virtually every medium of instruction at the Naval War College in the period between the two world wars. It was thus ingrained in every officer in a key decision-making position through November of 1943, and in most of them thereafter until the end of the war.

Naval Education Between the World Wars

Perhaps the best description of the education received by Navy officers in the period between the two world wars is that given by Adm. William Sowden Sims in his testimony in the Billy Mitchell trial. When asked "Will you tell the court, in a general way, about the Naval War College?" Admiral Sims replied:

> The Naval War College has been established now for approximately 25 or 30 years and, until comparatively recently, it has been there against the opposition of the senior officers of the Service. That has lessened to a considerable extent now. The Navy War College ought not to have been a college at all, because it is not at all in the nature of a college. It is a building with 75 to 100 officers from the fleet, officers of very considerable experience, are ordered, figuratively, to sit around a table and discuss how our fleet would best be handled in case we have war with one of our possible enemies. It is a band of practical officers working out how it should be done. Moreover, having worked out what they believe the tactic ought to be, they are

> tested out on a game board in a room as big as this floor, divided into little squares, and the fleets are represented with small models. They have chart maneuvers that precede this and tactical maneuvers and given a indication of what it means [*sic*]. It is very interesting to see a fine officer come there with 25 years experience, with a good reputation in the Navy, but not a student in any sense—to see him start in with the maneuvers and see the lack of knowledge he has of the proper tactics and strategy, because there is no place in the Navy where it is taught except in the War College, and then to see the man develop through years in the practice. . . .
>
> . . . I wish you had the opportunity of seeing these commanders that I had on one occasion where a demonstration was given for the benefit of a couple of Senators where a decision had to be made, and where one commander made his decision in 20 seconds and the other one in 45 seconds, when modern fleets come together a decision has to be made like that, as was demonstrated in the Jutland battle. A delay of five minutes might be entirely fatal. The object of the War College is to fit officers for high command, and the reason we people who have been interested in the War College all of these years is that although they support the War College and give it lip service, they have never used its products in the selection of the three chief officers of the Navy, the commander-in-chief of the fleet, the chief of naval operations, and the superintendent of the Naval Academy, and that is the matter with the Navy Department today.[2]

When asked further "Should these three key positions be occupied by men who have gone through the War College?" Sims replied: "As Admiral Mahan said, one of the first functions of the War College is not only to train officers, but to find out who ought to be selected as commander-in-chief and chief of operations."[3]

"Has that ever been done?"

"No; never."[4]

"What effect has this action had on the efficiency and morale of the Service?"

"All history shows that it has had a bad effect on the morale of the Service."[5]

Sims, one of the nation's top naval officers and a learned man of great experience who had commanded all U.S. Navy units and operations in World

War I, attested powerfully to the importance of the educational experience at the United States Naval War College received by officers who would go on to command men and warships at sea. Central and critical to that educational experience was the document used to structure officers' critical analytical abilities in formulating optimum courses of action in a variety of challenging and constantly evolving situations—*Sound Military Decision.*

Throughout the discussion of perhaps the most important strategic determinates of World War II in the Pacific theater—the five great carrier battles—this book has applied eight criteria that, in combination, reflect the adherence of the major commanders to the methodologies and tenets of *Sound Military Decision* in their decision processes, especially to the most fundamental aspect, the Commander's Estimate of the Situation. A review of these criteria is in order.

1. The commander's estimate of the situation and grasp of the strategic and operational significance of the decisions he would be required to make. In each of these crucial battles virtually all of the commanders involved deserved and received high marks in this area. Without question this was a strong point for those in the highest echelons of strategic and operational command, from Washington to the far reaches of the Pacific theater. Without a firm grasp of strategic priorities, fleet units would inevitably have been put into high-risk situations and perhaps squandered needlessly. Unlike the Japanese, even when assets were tight, U.S. Navy commanders placed groups of ships in the right place at the right time, and accepted considerable but calculated risk to achieve the necessary strategic outcome.

2. The commander's demonstrated ability to formulate a course of action, his ability to convey his decision in mission orders to subordinate commanders concisely and unambiguously, and his flexibility in modifying those orders through strategic and/or operational reappraisal if required. In this area too all the commanders involved in the decisive carrier battles of the Pacific war did extremely well. Moreover, they did well often under ad hoc situations where preparation times were negligible and assets had to be hastily and incompletely repaired and rushed into battle to provide even a chance of victory. In many of the instances considered, the commanders involved had no prior battle experience together, nor any opportunity to meet in conference to consider their options. What, then, accounts for their high degree

of integration and coordinated action? Unless one attributes their synergistic efforts to luck or divine intervention, it can only be surmised that the coordination of their actions resulted from adherence to a mutually expected method of arriving at their decisions. Once again, the methodology common to their approach to the same basic situation was inherent in their mutual interwar experience with *Sound Military Decision*.

3. The adequacy of command arrangements, the chain of command established, and the communications procedures put into effect to facilitate the exercise of command in battle. With the exception of the hasty command arrangements for the Battle of the Eastern Solomons, when Frank Jack Fletcher was promoted to vice admiral ahead of an officer who was previously three lineal numbers his senior only days before the expected beginning of the battle, this was another strong area. In not one of the five carrier battles did command arrangements significantly impair the proper relationship of subordinates to their commanders, or inhibit the freedom of action of subordinates in achieving their operational and strategic objectives.

4. The commander's adherence to established operational and tactical doctrines where appropriate, his adherence to procedures established prior to the engagement of forces, and his ability to deviate from the same when warranted. Even given the extensive interactions between experienced officers with considerable time in service, and the war games, and other methods used to refine their mutually agreed solutions to naval operational and tactical problems at the War College, in real battle situations the commanders often found the doctrines developed there imperfect. Two things, however, should be considered when evaluating the efficacy of those flawed doctrines. First, they gave a basis for initial action, no matter how flawed, and they served as a benchmark for evaluation essential to the subsequent development of sound doctrines. An ad hoc starting point would have done neither. Second, the assimilation of flawed doctrine helped the Navy decision makers understand, in detail, why that doctrine was flawed, and what needed to be done to make it evolve into sound doctrine. When one commander weighed in with lessons learned from a battle, a mutual awareness of the existing doctrine could lead U.S. naval commanders as a group to appreciate its

deficiencies and then modify it rapidly to reach a consensus on a better way of approaching a given situation.

Examples of both useful doctrine and flaws identified in existing doctrine abound in the carrier battles of World War II. So too does the rapid identification of doctrinal strengths and weaknesses in the After Action Reports of the commanders involved. For once in its history, the U.S. Navy doggedly adhered to doctrine when appropriate and quickly learned to deviate from it when necessary.

5. The commander's communication of mission requirements to subordinate commanders and the suitability of complementary actions by those subordinates to engage the enemy more effectively. Though there were several weak points, this was an area of general strength overall. Two major exceptions bear note. First, the more minor of the two, was the passing of responsibility for conducting air operations from the nonaviator overall commander to an aviator major subordinate. This was an understandable anomaly in normal command relationships that was subsequently rectified when adequate numbers of aviators gained the experience necessary to assume overall command. Second, and a more constant and avoidable problem, was the failure of naval commanders of land-based aircraft to adequately search the areas of expected Japanese naval operations, and their inability to ensure that near-continuous positioning information was generated and passed to the concerned force commanders. Though consistency in searching for, tracking, and reporting Japanese naval locations and movements did improve over the course of the war, this was a serious problem that introduced much unnecessary risk during strategically critical battles.

6. The commander's understanding of the engagement's importance within the wider context of achieving U.S. political objectives and his concomitant appreciation for the appropriate risk and determination of the proper circumstances in which to end the battle. Here Adm. Chester Nimitz excelled beyond any reasonable expectation. All but the last of the five carrier battles of World War II were near-run events. In all of the first four the United States was at a numerical disadvantage. All five were critical and essential to the U.S. strategy to defeat Japan. Admiral Nimitz, best of all the Navy commanders in World War II, showed an appreciation of the existing strategic situation and accepted the risks—often

great risks—that had to be taken to achieve the nation's immediate and long-term political objectives. Nimitz initiated or accepted naval engagements only when and where they were needed. When simultaneously faced with challenged strategic objectives in several areas of the Pacific, he invariably estimated the situation correctly and came up with a proper response. No officer comes to mind who adhered to this element of *Sound Military Decision* more consistently than Nimitz.

So too did Nimitz know when to terminate an engagement and preserve his scarce assets once the strategic objective had been secured. He showed great restraint by resisting the temptation to pursue the enemy and administer a more complete drubbing at Midway, Santa Cruz, and the Philippine Sea. In every case his evaluation of the situation revealed that the costs could well exceed the benefits of continued action, and he acted accordingly.

Of course it was Nimitz's job to understand the engagement's importance within the wider context of achieving U.S. political objectives, appreciate the appropriate level of risk, and determine the right circumstances for terminating the battle in the Pacific theater. In doing this he uniformly conveyed to his subordinates an urgency and appreciation for the consequences of their engagements. Nimitz appreciated the relationship between what was going on at sea and on land, as during the naval campaign for Guadalcanal, and did not hesitate to change an important commander close to an expected battle, as he did with Halsey, the commander of the South Pacific Area, just before the Battle of Santa Cruz. This aspect of *Sound Military Decision* was a definite strong point for the naval leadership in the Pacific, and Admiral Nimitz in particular.

7. The commander's audacity and brilliance in conceptualizing, articulating, and executing a plan of action. The action plan for the Battle of Midway stands out as an exclamation point for audacity and brilliance in conceptualizing, articulating, and executing a plan. Throwing a three-carrier force with the primary subordinate commander (Spruance) thrust quickly and unexpectedly into his command position and a carrier needing months of repair but getting only seventy-two hours of it against an armada of over two hundred Japanese ships certainly shows audacity. So too does the acceptance of the accuracy of

available intelligence implied in taking such a risk. Flanking the *kido butai* by sandwiching it between the available U.S. carriers and the Midway Islands so that the Japanese would have to make quick and vital choices on the employment of their air assets—and make them correctly—shows brilliance.

Understanding the importance of maintaining the U.S. sea lines of communication early in the war and sending two carrier groups to the Coral Sea also demonstrates brilliance. So too does Spruance's impenetrable formation at the Battle of the Philippine Sea and his appreciation that taking Saipan, Tinian, and Guam took primacy over the destruction of the opposing Japanese Fleet.

While the Battles of the Eastern Solomons and Santa Cruz were more reactive to Japanese strategic initiatives, and thus less likely to be conducted in accordance with an audacious or brilliant prior plan, it would be correct to say that those engagements were also conducted with a degree of audacity and brilliance. Thus, to a measured extent, the naval leaders involved did quite well in this area too.

8. The commander's ability to learn from the situation and rapidly pass lessons along to the advantage of those commanding in later engagements. The Battle of the Coral Sea ended on 11 May and the Battle of Midway started on 3 June. In this short period of time, and as a result of lessons provided in the After Action Report of Rear Adm. Frank Jack Fletcher after Coral Sea, the air wings of the carriers at Midway were increased from eighteen to twenty-seven fighter aircraft. This factor made victory at Midway possible. Without the extra planes, there is no doubt that the outcome would have been different. This incident attests strongly to the rapidity of feedback on and action taken as a result of the lessons learned in a previous battle.

One cannot help but be impressed with the quality and completeness of the lessons learned and provided in the After Action Reports of the commanders at all levels of every carrier battle of the Pacific war. Likewise, one can easily see that the actions taken to resolve deficiencies in doctrine, materials of war, and ship design paid huge dividends in warship lethality and durability and in lives spared in subsequent actions. From top to bottom, this was a uniformly strong point in the Navy's leadership in the Pacific.

***Sound Military Decision*, Good Decisions, and the Defeat of Japan**

The proof of any position is, as they say, in the pudding. In establishing the relationships first between the education officers received in the interwar period and the quality of their decisions in battle during World War II in the Pacific theater, and second between those decisions and the strategic outcomes they achieved, the totality of the results achieved is the surest measure available. Perhaps the best statement on which to measure those linkages comes from a speech given by Vice Admiral Frank Jack Fletcher during Navy Day celebrations at Des Moines, Iowa, on 27 October 1946:

> What, then, prompted [Japan's] surrender? Was it the atomic bombs or was it Russian entry into war? **Neither!** Japan who had so easily started the war in December 1941 was desperately striving for a way to quit before the Berlin conference, before either of the events mentioned. Never in any period had a nation so powerfully armed so abjectly surrendered. I will tell you why. Her navy was sunk! Her raw materials were exhausted. Her fuel oil and fuel products were gone. Her soldiers and her people were hungry. Her war industries were shattered. Her supply lines were completely cut. Atom bomb or no atom bomb, her surrender was inevitable. Russian entry into the war did not shorten it one day. Control of the sea was ours! In all of recorded history, whenever or wherever great nations bounded by the seas have fought, control of those seas has become the dominant factor in deciding the issue. How was the extraordinary accomplishment achieved? In early December 1941 Senior American Naval Officers in the Pacific were gravely concerned because the balance of naval strength in the Pacific lay with the Japanese. After that fateful event of 7 December the preponderance favoring the enemy was tremendous.
>
> Now statistics are usually dull as dish water, but let me give you a few as to what happened to the Japanese Navy that are dynamic. It was not a force or a fleet that was defeated, or damaged, or even sunk. It was the whole Navy that was sunk, a Navy that at the outset was third strongest in the world and more powerful than all the forces we could then muster in the Pacific. Give your attention to these figures: Of 12 battleships, 11 were sunk, 1 was heavily damaged

and inoperative. Of 26 aircraft carriers, 21 were sunk, 5 were damaged in varying degrees, none were operable. Of 43 cruisers, 38 were sunk, 2 were heavily damaged and out of action in Singapore, the remaining 3 were out of action in Japan. All, I repeat all of the foregoing damage was inflicted by the aircraft, submarines and surface ships of the American Navy, except 2 cruisers sunk by British ships and 1 by our own army aircraft. But that is not all. Japan had 179 destroyers. 135 were sunk—121 of them by your Navy, 14 by army aircraft. Only two of the 44 that remained afloat were fully operable. She had 193 submarines, 129 were sunk. As to the remaining 64, damage, lack of spare parts, destruction of repair facilities, lack of fuel, made only a handful operable. Of her merchant marine, our submarines alone had sent 1042 ships of 4,779,000 tons to the bottom. Navy and Army aircraft and surface vessels—ships and planes of our Allies—and mines disposed of another 2,800,000 tons.*

Very very few ships over 1,000 tons remained to move troops or munitions or to bring to Japan vitally essential food, fuel and raw materials. Remember it was our seapower that brought Japan to her knees. When she surrendered she still had a large army intact and a substantial air force, both more than double the forces she had on December 7, 1941. Our enemy had seen his fleet destroyed, his sea lanes cut off, many of his islands captured or neutralized and his vital supply forces eliminated—all by our control of the sea—on it, under it and over it.[6]

Fletcher's speech accurately reflects the totality of the victory the U.S. Navy achieved against the Imperial Japanese Navy in World War II. Fletcher also mentions how important education and training were to achieving victory—but in the enlisted ranks. So too was education important in the officer ranks.

*The numbers of ships sunk by the U.S. Navy and other Services and by Allies in World War II is confirmed by Ernest J. King, Fleet Admiral, U.S. Navy, *U.S. Navy at War 1941–1945*, Washington: Unites States Navy Department, 1946, Appendix A, pp. 233–251, with one exception. The fleet carrier *Kasagi* was under camouflage at Sasebo, fitting out, and had not yet been commissioned when the war ended.

Contemporary Relevance

In Admiral Sims's testimony cited above, he talks about the rapidity with which information has to be evaluated and a decision reached in battle. Sims testified in 1925. Today, with long-range sensors and highly accurate missiles, and with supersonic aircraft and enormously lethal ship- and land-launched projectiles, quick and correct decisions are perhaps even more critical to battle at sea than in Sims's era. In fact, the relatively new discipline of Information Warfare attests to the currency of Sims' position. Though rote in their presentation, the tenets of *Sound Military Decision* still apply exactly to the high-paced warfare likely to be encountered by the U.S. Navy.

But what about the importance of education for the officers of the Navy and Marine Corps? True, most have recent experience in battle—but none have had the occasion for experience in naval battle since 1945. And the degree of their success in battle from the sea is likely to decrease the likelihood of more combat in the foreseeable future. Thus, just as between the two world wars, education in lieu of firsthand experience is sure to be a necessary component of future success in war. Moreover, to a greater degree than ever, war in the future will be conducted in a Joint environment. Thus education that focuses on interaction and the contemplation of warfare problems that could be encountered by members of *all* the Armed Services is critical to success in future wars. One can only hope that the quality of that education will be on the level of that provided to the leaders of the United States Navy prior to World War II.

Yet one cannot help but be skeptical. Admiral Sims stated in his testimony that "until comparatively recently [the Naval War College had] been there against the opposition of the senior officers of the Service . . ." There are many, particularly in Newport, who would echo that sentiment even today. Why? Admiral Sims also stated that the three top leaders in the Navy—the Chief of Naval Operations, the Commander in Chief of the Fleet (now combatant commanders) and the superintendent of the Naval Academy—should all be graduates of the Naval War College, which had never happened. As of June 2005 neither the Chief of Naval Operations nor any of the Navy's combatant commanders are graduates of any war college. This has been the case, with a few noted exceptions, over the past decade and longer. At present, only the superintendent of the Naval Academy is a product of the Naval War College, and then as its president and not as a student. Is it any wonder that the importance of refining analytical abilities, decision processes, and operational and tactical concepts receives little attention when almost none of those leading the Navy are products of this educational experience—an experience that, as Sims testified, "There is no place in the Navy where it is taught except the War College"?

Moreover, the Naval War College has evolved its curriculum to be much more *de*scriptive and less *pro*scriptive than in the interwar period. While the "Commander's Estimate of the Situation" is still held as central to Operational Art at sea, operations and tactics are now more often described than developed by the students and faculty at Newport. Success in "sinking the Japanese Navy" in World War II was a product of both adherence to the decision processes put forward in *Sound Military Decision* and working through difficult problems at sea before they occurred, developing strategic, operational, tactical, and doctrinal concepts in the classrooms and on the game floor at the War College in Newport. Focusing on such basics can and will serve the U.S. Navy well in the future.

Sound Military Decision

Decisions count. It is difficult to refine the decision process without immersion in situations like those in which the actual decision will be made. This is possible, and it was achieved with important results in World War II in the Pacific theater. While no two people will agree with the grades assigned to the naval commanders under discussion, the fact remains that those commanders achieved an unprecedented degree of success. They did not enjoy superior capacity for waging war over the Japanese until 1944. Thus much of this success resulted from something other than a mismatch in hardware and technology. Hopefully this book has established the value of a professional education—and in particular the relevance of *Sound Military Decision* to that education—as the reason at least in part for that success. And hopefully, future generations of Navy, Marine, Army, Air Force, and Coast Guard officers will profit from access to a similar educational experience to lead them to similar success in their profession of arms.

APPENDIX

Plans for the New Order in East Asia and the South Seas

This appendix represents the "Land Disposal Plan in the Greater East Asia Co-Prosperity Sphere," reproduced in total in appendix II of Richard Storry's seminal work, *The Double Patriots: A Study of Japanese Nationalism*, pp. 317–319. According to Storry,

> The scope of the proposed New Order—or 'Co-Prosperity Sphere' as it came to be called—has already been suggested . . . but it is not perhaps generally realised [*sic*] how ambitious were the plans for future expansion of Japanese power.
>
> Certain countries in Asia—such as Burma and the Malay States—were to be organized as independent monarchies. Australia, New Zealand and Ceylon were to be incorporated in the Japanese Empire under Governors-General. There were, also, to be Governors-General of Alaska (including the Yukon district of Canada, Alberta, British Columbia and the State of Washington), and of Central America (not including Mexico, but embracing the other Latin American republics in that area as well as the British, French and Dutch West Indies). It was appreciated that such spoils could hardly be gathered in one war. Therefore it was anticipated that having gained the British, French and Dutch Asiatic colonies by taking part in the European War—and these colonies, together with the Philippines, constituted the "smaller" Co-Prosperity Sphere, or "the South Seas of the first sense"—Japan must prepare for a further great war some twenty years later. These plans were prepared by the Research Section of the Ministry of War, in collaboration with the Army and Navy General

Staffs and the Overseas Ministry. They were completed in December, 1941. (p. 276)

In that this document, placed into evidence in the war crime trials conducted by the International Military Tribunal established for that purpose in the Far East, establishes the grandiose nature of Japanese political objectives at the war's outset, this document has been reproduced in its entirety here.

1. Regions to be under the jurisdiction of the Government-General of Formosa:
   - Hong Kong
   - Macao (to be purchased)
   - The Philippine Islands
   - Paracel Islands
   - Hainan Island (to be purchased from China)
2. To be administered by the South Seas Government Office:
   - Guam
   - Nauru
   - Ocean Island
   - Gilbert Islands
   - Wake
3. The Melanesia Region Government-General or South Pacific Government-General (provisional titles):
   - New Guinea (the British and Australian mandated territories east of Long. 141°E.)
   - The Admiralty Archipelago
   - New Britain, New Ireland and the islands in the vicinity
   - The Solomons
   - Santa Cruz Archipelago
   - Ellice Islands
   - Fiji Islands
   - New Hebrides
   - New Caledonia
   - Loyalty Island
   - Chesterfield Island
4. Eastern Pacific Government-General:
   - Hawaii

Howland, Baker and Phoenix Islands
Rain Islands
Marquesas and Tuamotu Islands
Society Islands
Cook and Austral Islands
Somoa
Tonga

5. The Australian Government-General:
The whole of Australia, and Tasmania

6. The New Zealand Government-General (provisional title):
The North and South Islands of New Zealand
Macquarie Island
The sea, south of the Tropic of Capricorn and east of Long. 160° E., as far as the S. Pole region

7. The Ceylon Government-General:
Ceylon; and India lying south of the following boundary: from the west coast on the Northern frontier of Portuguese Goa, thence to the north of Dharwar and Bellary and to the River Penner, and along the north bank of the Penner to the east coast at Nellore
Laccadive Islands
Maldive Islands
Chagos Islands
Seychelles
Mauritius

8. Alaska Government-General:
Alaska
The Yukon Province, and the land between that Province and the Mackenzie River
Alberta
British Columbia
The State of Washington

9. The Government-General of Central America:
Guatemala
San Salvador
Honduras
British Honduras

Nicaragua
Costa Rica
Panama
Columbia, and the Maracaibo district of Venezuela
Ecuador
Cuba
Haiti
Dominica
Jamaica
Bahamas
The future of Trinidad, British and Dutch Guiana and British and French possessions
The Leeward Islands to be decided by agreement between Japan and Germany after the war

10. In the event of her declaring war on Japan, Mexico to cede territory east of Long. 95° 30'.
    Should Peru join in the war against Japan it must cede territory north of Lat. 10°; and if Chile enters the war it shall cede the nitre zone north of Lat. 24°

Independent States

1. The East Indies Kingdom:
    All Dutch possessions in the E. Indies
    British Borneo, Labuan, Sarawak, Brunei
    Cocos
    Christmas Island
    Andamans
    Nicobars
    Portuguese Timor (to be purchased)
2. The Kingdom of Burma:
    British Burma and Assam, together with part of Bengal between the Ganges and Brahmaputra
3. The Malay Kingdom
4. The Kingdom of Thailand

5. The Kingdom of Cambodia:
   Cambodia and French Cochin China
6. The Kingdom of Annam:
   Annam, Laos and Tongking

Notes

Chapter 1

1. Nimitz, Chester W., Fleet Admiral, USN. Letter to Vice Adm. Charles Melson, President of the United States Naval War College, dated 19 September 1965 on display in McCarty—Little Hall at the U.S. Naval War College, Newport, R.I.
2. Ibid., pp. 1–2.
3. Ibid., p. 3.
4. Battle of Sable Island Manuscript, Serial No. 71, dated October–November 1923. United States Naval War College Archives (hereafter referred to as "USNWCA") Record Group (RG) 14/15, 128 pages plus accompanying diagrams.
5. Stein, Steven. *Washington Irving Chambers: Innovation, Professionalism, and the New Navy, 1872–1913*. Unpublished dissertation manuscript, Ohio State University.
6. Merrill, James M. *A Sailor's Admiral: A Biography of William F. Halsey.* New York: Thomas Y. Crowell Company, 1976, p. 11.
7. Ibid., p. 13.
8. *United States v. War Department: Trial by General Courts Martial in the case of Colonel William Mitchell, Air Service*, "Opinion of the Board of Review, Taylor, Abbott and Korn, Judge Advocates," dated 20 January 1926, p. 1. Record Group (hereafter "RG") 153, Records of the Office of the Judge Advocate General (Army), Box No. 9214-2, Folder 1, p. 1. National Archives of the United States of America, NA-2, College Park, Md.
9. Ibid., pp. 3–8.
10. Ibid., p. 4.
11. Ibid., pp. 4–6.
12. Ibid., p. 2.
13. Ibid., p. 2.
14. Ibid., p. 3.
15. Ibid., p. 4.

16. Ibid.
17. It is indeed ironic that Grand Joint Exercise No. 4 of February 1932 would evaluate a land-based attack on Rear Adm. Harry E. Yarnell's carrier force northeast of Hawaii as having done that with aircraft claimed by Admiral Yarnell as destroyed on the deck in a previous raid from his carriers during that exercise. Grand Joint Exercise No. 4 will be discussed at greater length later in this chapter.
18. *United States v. War Department*, Mitchell court-martial, p. 5.
19. Hone, Thomas C., Norman Friedman, and Mark D. Mandeles. *American and British Aircraft Carrier Development 1919–1941*. Annapolis, Md.: Naval Institute Press, 1999, pp. 28–29. This book is an indispensable asset to anyone looking for a comprehensive examination of the history of development of naval aviation and/or of the maturation of concepts for the employment of and designs of aircraft carriers in the U.S. Navy. It covers in great depth the controversy over the role of aviation assets in the Navy and should be viewed as a companion to this chapter.
20. Ibid., p. 28.
21. Ibid., p. 29.
22. Ibid.
23. Ibid.
24. *United States v. War Department*, Mitchell court-martial, pp. 9–10.
25. Hone, *American and British Aircraft Carrier Development*, pp. 20 and 31.
26. Miller, Edward S. Conversations with Douglas V. Smith regarding Navy policy on aircraft carriers, aircraft, and their roles in naval combat in the 1920s and 1930s held in Luce Hall, Room 123, at the Naval War College on Thursday, 4 December 2003.
27. General Courts Martial, William Mitchell Case Records, 1925 (Case No. 168771). RG 153, Records of the Office of the Judge Advocate General (Army). Col. William Mitchell, Air Service, Trial by General Court-Martial, Washington, D.C., 18 November 1925, Volume 12, 168771, Alexander H. Galt Official Reporter, 715 Woodward Building, Washington, D.C. College Park, Md.: National Archives No. II, Box No. 9214-2, section 1018-1147, part 1097.
28. Ibid., part 1097–98.
29. Ibid., part 1098.
30. Ibid.
31. Ibid.
32. Ibid.
33. Sims declined the Distinguished Service Medal from the United States government for his wartime service, but did accept the Grand Cross of the Order of St. Michael and St. George from Great Britain in 1918, and was made a Grand Officer of the Legion of Honor in France in 1919; a Grand Cordon, First Class,

in the Order of the Rising Sun of Japan in 1920; a Grand Cordon of the Order of Leopold by Belgium, also in 1920; and a Grand Officer of the Crown of Italy in 1921. His honors from colleges and universities included Yale (1919), Harvard (1920), Columbia (1920), Pennsylvania (1920), University of California (1923), Wesleyan (1923), Tufts (1919), Williams (1920), Juanita (1919), Stevens Institute (1921), Union College (1922), Cambridge, England (1921), McGill's (1922) and Queens (1922) of Canada. Ibid., part 1098–99.

34. Ibid., part 1103.
35. Ibid., part 1102.
36. Ibid.
37. Ibid., part 1100–1102.
38. Ibid., part 1101.
39. Ibid., part 1106.
40. Ibid., part 1110.
41. General Courts Martial, William Mitchell Case Records, 1925 (Case No. 168771). RG-153, Records of the Office of the Judge Advocate General (Army). Col. William Mitchell, Air Service, Trial by General Court-Martial, Washington, D.C., 18 November 1925, Volume 12, 168771, Alexander H. Galt Official Reporter, 715 Woodward Building, Washington, D.C. College Park, Md.: National Archives No. II, Box No. 9214-4, section 2570–85, part 2570.
42. Ibid., part 2570–71.
43. Ibid., part 2571.
44. Ibid.
45. Ibid.
46. Ibid.
47. Ibid., part 2573.
48. Ibid., part 2584.
49. Ibid.
50. Ibid., part 2585.
51. Hattendorf, John B., B. Mitchell Simpson, III, and John R. Wasdleigh. *Sailors and Scholars: The Centennial History of the U.S. Naval War College*. Newport, RI: Naval War College Press, p. 327.
52. Hone, *American and British Aircraft Carrier Development*, p. 11.
53. Ibid., p. 30.
54. Ibid.
55. McMurtrie, Francis E., A.I.N.A., ed. *Jane's Fighting Ships 1941* (issued 1942). New York: The Macmillan Company, 1942, p. 462.
56. Ibid., p. 295. *Kaga* was rebuilt after being sunk at Midway in June 1942 and had a capacity of ninety aircraft.
57. Ibid.
58. Ibid., pp. 294 and 296.

59. Hone, *American and British Aircraft Carrier Development*, pp. 44–46.
60. Ibid., p. 48.
61. Parkes, Oscar, O.B.E., M.B., Ch.B., ed. *Jane's Fighting Ships 1933*. London: Sampson Low, Marston & Co., Ltd., 1933, p. 479.
62. Hone, *American and British Aircraft Carrier Development*, p. 53.
63. Rhodes, James B., archivist of the United States. *Records Relating to United States Navy Fleet Problems I to XXII 1923–1941*. National Archives No. 1 (NA-1), Records of the Office of the Chief of Naval Operations Record Group 38; General Records of the Department of the Navy Record Group 80; and Records of Naval Operating Forces Record Group 313.
64. Yarnell, H.E., Rear Admiral, USN, Commander Aircraft, Battle Force. *Operations of the Blue Air Force in Grand Joint Exercise No. 4, 1–12 February 1932*, from Commander Aircraft, Battle Force, dated 27 February 1932, p. 2. USNWCA: RG-8, Box 61, Folder 3.
65. Ibid., pp. 1–2.
66. Ibid., pp. 3 and 7.
67. Ibid., pp. 6–7.
68. Ibid., p. 5.
69. Ibid.
70. Linn, Brian M. *Guardians of Empire: The U.S. Army and the Pacific, 1902–1940*. Chapel Hill, N.C.: University of North Carolina Press, p. 208.
71. Linn, Brian M. Conversations with Douglas V. Smith regarding Grand Joint Exercise No. 4 held in Luce Hall, Room 123, at the Naval War College on Thursday, 17 June 2004.
72. Reynolds, Clark G. *Admiral John H. Towers: The Struggle for Naval Air Supremacy*. Annapolis, Md.: Naval Institute Press, pp. 237–238.
73. Yarnell, H.E. First Endorsement on Umpire Reports, Grand Joint Exercise No. 4 dated Feb. 16, 1932, p. 1. USNWCA:RG-8, Box 61, Folder 3.
74. Fleming, Thomas. "Early Warning: February 7, 1932, A Date That Would Live In . . . Amnesia." In *American Heritage*, July/August 2001, p. 54.
75. Ibid.
76. Churchill, Winston S. *The Second World War, Volume II: Their Finest Hour*. London: Cassell & Co., Ltd., 1949, p. 481.
77. Insight provided by Mr. Daniel Martinez, historian of the USS *Arizona* Memorial, while lecturing to elective course of Douglas V. Smith entitled "World War II in the Pacific Theater," in Chairman's Classroom, Connolly Hall, U.S. Naval War College, Thursday, 11 March 2004.
78. The archives searched include: National Archives No. 1, Washington, D.C.; National Archives No. 2, College Park, Md.; U. S. Naval War College Archives; U.S. Naval Academy Archives; U.S. Army War College Archives; U.S. Marine Corps Archives, Gray Library, Marine Corps University, Quantico, Va; U.S.

Naval Historical Center Archives, Washington, D.C.; American Historical Center, University of Wyoming, Laramie, Wyo.; Hoover Institute Library and Archives, Stanford University, Palo Alto, Calif.; and a national electronic search of libraries and archives conducted by the Research Librarians of the Naval War College.

79. Nofi, Albert A., Ph.D., senior analyst, Center for Naval Analyses. Conversations with Douglas V. Smith regarding Grand Joint Exercise No. 4 of 1–12 February, 1932, and United States Navy Fleet Problems I through XXII conducted between 1923 and 1941 in Sims Hall, at the Naval War College on Thursday, 1 September 2004.
80. Miller, Edward S. *War Plan Orange: The U.S. Strategy to Defeat Japan, 1897–1945*. Annapolis, Md.: Naval Institute Press, 1991. This award-winning documentary of the Navy's planning effort for a drive across the Pacific to defeat Japan is an indispensable companion to this study.
81. Ibid., p. 164.
82. Ibid., p. 142.
83. Ibid., p. 175.
84. McMurtrie, *Jane's Fighting Ships 1941*, p. 460.
85. Hanson, Victor Davis. *The Western Way of War: Infantry Battle in Classical Greece*. Alfred A. Knopf: New York, 1989, p. 31. Here the author points out that in the fifth and fourth centuries, battle occurred in the Greek world nearly two out of every three years.
86. This insight was provided by Prof. Emeritus Frank Snyder, captain, USN (Ret.), based on research he has conducted on World War I activities of subsequent Naval War College graduates.
87. United States Naval Academy Memorandum from Capt. W.W. Smith, USN, Mathematics Department, to the superintendent, "Subject: Survey of the Curriculum of the United States Naval Academy," dated 1 April 1939, p. 1. Document provided by Mr. Gary LeValley, archivist, U.S. Naval Academy library.
88. Ibid., p. 2.
89. Ibid., p. 3.
90. Ibid., p. 5.
91. Ibid., p. 10.
92. Ibid., p. 12.
93 Ibid.
94. For a detailed development of this theme, see Vlahos, Michael. *The Blue Sword: The Naval War College and the American Mission, 1919–1941*. U.S. Naval War College Historical Monograph Series, No. 4. Newport, R.I.: Naval War College Press, 1980, chapters I–V.

95. Warren, Mame, and Marion E. Warren. Excerpt from special dispatch to the Baltimore Sun dated 12 April 1905. *Everybody Works But John Paul Jones: A Portrait of the U.S. Naval Academy, 1845–1915*. Annapolis, Md.: Naval Institute Press, 1981, p. 48.
96. Hagan, Kenneth J. *This People's Navy: The Making of American Sea Power.* New York: The Free Press (a Division of Macmillan), 1991, p. 239.
97. Ibid.
98. Ibid.
99. Ibid.
100. Kennedy, John Gerald. *United States Naval War College, 1919–1941: An Institutional Response to Naval Preparedness*. USNWCA, 1975. Unpublished manuscript. This manuscript provides an excellent narrative of the development of and changes in the curriculum at the Naval War College during the interwar period, as well as of the imprint made by each president of the War College during that period.
101. Sims, William S., Rear Admiral, USN. Graduation Address, 22 May 1919. USNWCA: RG-14/15, p. 2.
102. Sims, William S. Rear Admiral, USN. Commencement Address, 2 June 1919. USNWCA: RG-14/15, p. 4.
103. Ibid., p. 3.
104. Hattendorf, *Sailors and Scholars*, p. 155.
105. Plunkett, C.P., Rear Admiral, USN. USNWCA:RG-14/15. Remarks to the Opening Course for Class of July, 1921, p. 1.
106. Ibid., p. 2.
107. Ibid.
108. Ibid., p. 4.
109. Pratt, W.V., Rear Admiral, USN. Graduation Address, 27 May 1927. USNWCA: RG-14/15, p. 12.
110. Ibid., pp. 1–7.
111. Laning, Harris, Rear Admiral, USN. Opening Address to the Classes of 1931, delivered 2 July 1930, p. 2.
112. Ibid., p. 1.
113. Rowan, S.C., Captain, USN. Opening Address to the Classes of 1934, delivered 1 July 1933, p. 4.
114. Kalbfus, Edward Clifford, Admiral, USN. Graduation Address to the Class of 1941. USNWCA: RG-14/15, p. 1.
115. Ibid., p. 6.
116. *Sound Military Decision*. U.S. Naval War College, Newport, R.I., 1942, copy 3394, p. 36. Declassified Ref: ALNav 59–53 of 12/15/53.
117. Ibid.
118. Ibid., pp. 38–39.

119. *Register of the Alumni, Graduates and Former Naval Cadets and Midshipmen, United States Naval Academy Alumni Association, Inc., 1845–1985,* 1985 edition. Published by the United States Naval Academy Alumni Association. Also *The Register*, manuscript listing of U.S. Naval War College Faculty and graduates, provided by Dr. Evelyn Cherpak, archivist, U.S. Naval War College. Please note that all listings of graduation dates from the Naval Academy and Naval War College are drawn from these two publications.
120. *Annual Report of the Secretary of the Navy—Fiscal Year 1946*, pp. 23 and 27.
121. Nimitz, C.W, Fleet Admiral, USN. Address of the Chief of the Bureau of Navigation to the graduating class, 2 December 1941, USNWCA: RG-14/15, p. 3.

Chapter 2

1. JN-25, unlike the Magic diplomatic code that needed the "Purple" sixteen-selector (electronic pathway) or later "Jade" twenty-selector transmission units akin to the German Enigma machine for encryption and decryption, required use of two books: a code book (with less than 33,333 entries) to convert words or letters to five-number groups, and a related cipher book (of 100,000 five-number groups arranged in a random sequence). For encryption, each code group was then added to the next cipher group in sequence. No machine was used. (Insights here provided by Prof. Emeritus Frank Snyder of the United States Naval War College in a letter responding to the author, Herman Wouk, concerning his presentation on the Battle of Midway given on its Fiftieth Anniversary in Newport, Rhode Island).
2. Prados, John. *Combined Fleet Decoded: The Secret History of American Intelligence and the Japanese Navy in World War II*. New York: Random House, 1995, p. 305.
3. Lundstrom, John B. *The First Team: Pacific Naval Air Combat from Pearl Harbor to Midway*. Annapolis, Md.: Naval Institute Press, 1984, p. 4.
4. Ibid., p. 9.
5. Interview of Capt. James Granson Daniels, USN (Ret.), participant as fighter pilot in all carrier battles of World War II except the Battle of Midway, 18 February 2002, Honolulu, Hawaii.
6. Daniels interview 18 February 2002.
7. Miller, Edward S., note to Douglas V. Smith of 8 December 2005.
8. Bates, Richard W., Rear Admiral, USN (Ret.). *The Battle of Midway Including the Aleutian Phase, June 3 to June 14, 1942: Strategical and Tactical Analysis*. Defense Documentation Center, Defense Logistics Agency: Cameron Station, Alexandria, Va., 1947, pp 5–6. (Previously classified document.)
9. Fuchida, Mitsuo, and Masatake Okumiya. *Midway: The Battle that Doomed Japan, The Japanese Navy's Story*. Edited by Clark H. Kawakami and

Roger Pineau. Annapolis, Md.: Naval Institute Press, 1955, reprinted 1992, pp. 33–89.

10. Agawa, Hiroyuki. *The Reluctant Admiral: Yamamoto and the Imperial Navy*. Tokyo: Kodansha International Ltd., 1979, pp. 295–297.
11. Ugaki, Matome, Admiral, Imperial Japanese Navy. *Fading Victory: The Diary of Admiral Matome Ugaki 1941–1945*. Translated by Masataka Chihaya. Pittsburgh, Pa.: University of Pittsburgh Press, 1991, pp. 109–110.
12. Prang, Gordon. *Miracle at Midway*. New York: McGraw-Hill Book Company, 1982, pp. 22–23.
13. Miller, Edward. S. *War Plan Orange: The U.S. Strategy to Defeat Japan, 1897–1945*. Annapolis, Md.: Naval Institute Press, 1991. Miller chronicles the vicissitudes in planning between the "thrusters," who wanted to defend the Philippines at the outset of any war with Japan, and the "cautionaries," who favored a more gradual island-hopping approach to victory in the Pacific in World War II.
14. Willmott, H.P. *Empires in the Balance: Japanese and Allied Naval Strategies to April 1942*. Annapolis, Md.: Naval Institute Press, 1982, Appendix A: Nominal Orders of Battle of the Imperial Japanese and U.S. Navies Between 7 December 1941 and 2 September 1945, pp. 525–530.
15. Ibid., pp. 171–172. Please note that all figures for both Japanese and U.S. fleets here are taken from this source.
16. Bates, Richard W., Rear Admiral, USN (Ret.). *The Battle of the Coral Sea, May 1 to May 11 Inclusive, 1942, Strategical and Tactical Analysis*. Appendix 2, p. v. Unpublished manuscript prepared for the Bureau of Naval Personnel, 1947, now held by the Defense Documentation Center, Defense Logistics Agency, Cameron Station, Alexandria, Va., and at other authorized military installations.
17. H.P. "Ned" Willmott. *Empires in the Balance: Japanese and Allied Naval Strategies to April 1942*. Annapolis, Md.: Naval Institute Press, 1982, Appendix A: Nominal Orders of Battle of the Imperial Japanese and U.S. Navies Between 7 December 1941 and 2 September 1945, pp. 525–530.
18. Mahan, Alfred Thayer. *The Influence of Sea Power Upon History 1660–1783*. New York: Dover Publications, Inc., 1987. Original publication Boston: Little, Brown and Company, 1890, 557 pages.
19. Vice Adm. Yoji Koda provides these insights on Japanese naval doctrine in World War II. Koda was assigned as a student in the Naval Command College of the United States Naval War College in 1992 where he was my student in a seminar on World War II in the Pacific theater. A naval scholar who had several previous tours in the United States, Koda was every bit as much my teacher as student. He provided insightful commentary and analysis after every seminar session, and many of his insights will be included later in this and other chapters.

20. Bates, *The Battle of the Coral Sea*. Relative positions of all elements of the Japanese force are taken from pages 12–13.
21. The *kido butai*, or "mobile force," was the striking group of large carriers in Vice Adm. Chuichi Nagumo's Third Fleet, normally employed in the Central Pacific.
22. Lunsdtrom, John B. Lecture entitled "The Role of the Aircraft Carrier in Pacific Fleet Strategy from Pearl Harbor to Guadalcanal" delivered at the Naval War College for elective WE-576, "World War II in the Pacific Theater," Prof. Douglas V. Smith, Chairman's Classroom, Thursday, 13 January 2005.
23. Bates, *The Battle of the Coral Sea*, p. 32.
24. Ibid., p. 17.
25. Bates, *The Battle of the Coral Sea*, pp. 29 and 34.
26. Fletcher, Frank Jack, Rear Admiral, USN. Commander Task Force 17 letter to Commander in Chief, U.S. Fleet, dated 27 May 1942, "Subject: The Battle of the Coral Sea, May 4–8, 1942." Naval War College Microfilm Collection reel A39, starting frame 41078, p. 2. (Previously classified document.)
27. Bates, *The Battle of the Coral Sea*, p. 33.
28. Fletcher, letter to Commander in Chief, United States Fleet dated 27 May 1942, p. 3.
29. Bates, *The Battle of the Coral Sea*, p. 34.
30. Ibid.
31. Ibid., p. 35.
32. Lundstrom, John B. Lecture entitled "Frank Jack Fletcher—Black Shoe Carrier Admiral" for elective WE-576 of Douglas V. Smith, given Thursday, 13 January 2005, in Chairman's Classroom, room C-138, U.S. Naval War College.
33. Bates, *The Battle of the Coral Sea*, pp. 36 and 38.
34. Ibid.
35. Ibid.
36. Fletcher, letter to Commander in Chief, United States Fleet dated 27 May 1942, p. 3.
37. Bates, *The Battle of the Coral Sea*, pp. 35–38.
38. Ibid., p. 38.
39. Ibid., p. 39.
40. Ibid., p. 34.
41. Ibid.
42. Ibid., p. 33.
43. Lundstrom provided insights on the relative ranges achievable for U.S. and Japanese carrier air strikes in "Black Shoe Carrier Admiral" (lecture).
44. Bates, *The Battle of The Coral Sea*, pp. 39 and 42.
45. Bates, *The Battle of The Coral Sea*, pp. 42–43.

46. Ibid., p. 45.
47. Ibid., p. 43.
48. Ibid., p. 43.
49. Ibid., pp. 44–45.
50. Ibid., p. 45.
51. Fitch, Aubrey W., Rear Admiral, USN. *War Diary, Commander Task Force Eleven (Commander Carrier Division One)* dated 31 May 1942. Commander Task Group 17.5 Action Report, letter to Commander Task Force Seventeen dated 18 May 1942, p. 1. Naval War College Microfilm Collection reel A39, first frame 41078. (Previously classified document.)
52. Ibid., p. 2.
53. Fletcher, letter to Commander in Chief, United States Fleet dated 27 May 1942, p. 3. Also Bates, *Battle of the Coral Sea*, p. 53–54.
54. Bates, Ibid., p. 54.
55. Ibid., p. 56.
56. Ibid., p. 55.
57. Sherman, Frederick C. *War Diary, Commander Task Force Eleven (Commander Carrier Division One)* dated 31 May 1942. Commanding Officer, USS *Lexington* Report of Action, letter to Commander in Chief, United States Pacific Fleet dated 15 May 1942, p. 1–2. Naval War College Microfilm Collection reel A39, first frame 41078. (Previously classified document.)
58. Bates, *The Battle of The Coral Sea*, p. 55.
59. Fitch, Aubrey W. Commander Task Group 17.5 (Commander Carrier Division One) letter to Commander Task Force 17 dated 18 May 1942: Action Report—Coral Sea—May 7–8, 1942, p. 2. Naval War College Microfilm Collection reel A39, first frame 41078. (Previously classified document.)
60. Fletcher, letter to Commander in Chief, United States Fleet dated 27 May 1942, p. 5.
61. Bates, *The Battle of the Coral Sea*, p. 56.
62. Fitch, *CTF-11 War Diary*, CTG-17.5 letter to CTF 17, p. 2.
63. Sherman, *CTF-11 War Diary*, letter to Commander in Chief, United States Pacific Fleet dated 15 May 1942, p. 2.
64. Bates, *The Battle of the Coral Sea*, pp. 58–59.
65. Fletcher, letter to Commander in Chief, United States Fleet dated 27 May 1942, p. 10.
66. Lundstrom, John B. *The First Team: Pacific Naval Air Combat from Pearl Harbor to Midway*. Annapolis, Md.: Naval Institute Press, 1984, Table of Japanese Carrier Plane Strength, p. 188.
67. Lundstrom, *The First Team*, p. 205, and Hata, Ikuhiko and Yasuho Izawa. *Japanese Naval Aces and Fighter Units in World War II*. Annapolis, Md.: Naval Institute Press, 1989, p. 377. Numbers given are a compromise between figures provided in these two sources.

68. Koda provided insight here. See note 21.
69. Ibid.
70. Okumiya, Masatake and Jiro Horikoshi. *Zero!* New York: E.P. Dutton & Co., Inc., p. 57.
71. Starting with the opening attacks on U.S. military bases, the parallels between the American Civil War and the Pacific war are striking. Between 1941 and 1945 Japan was to the United States what the Confederacy had been exactly eighty years before. Both wars saw the United States opposed by enemies that relied on allegedly superior material qualities to overcome demographic, industrial, and positional inferiority, and in both wars the United States' superior material resources and ability to mount debilitating blockades proved decisive to the outcome. In both wars the United States was able to use the advantages of a secure base and exterior lines of communications to bring overwhelming strength against its enemies. These enemies were plagued by divided counsels and committed to a defensive strategy of holding widely separated positions along an extended perimeter, which were not mutually supporting and which could not be properly supplied for want of adequate transportation infrastructure. In both wars the enemies of the United States, intent on forcing it to recognize their existence or conquests, sought to wage wars of attrition and exhaustion against a far superior enemy, and in the process were divided and conquered.

    The Union drive down the Mississippi that resulted in the capture of Vicksburg in July 1863 has its parallel in the drive to the Philippines that separated Japan from the southern resources area; both Tennessee and the march to the sea have as their counterpart the Central Pacific offensive that, in the form of blockade and the strategic bombing offensive, took the war to the enemy homeland. Both efforts for the United States were characterized by mass firepower and shock action, though on this point a certain caution needs to be exercised because the parallels are not exact. Stretching the point, one could assert that the battles in the Southwest Pacific in 1942 and 1943 were equivalent to the battles in Maryland and Virginia in 1862, in that the outcome of these battles ensured that the Confederacy and Japan had to win quickly or not at all. Moreover, in both conflicts Europe loomed large. In the American Civil War the Confederacy looked to European intervention to ensure its victory and in World War II Japan tied itself to the German cause in the hope that Germany's victory would ensure the neutralization of the United States. Neither European hope was realized.

    Much like the Confederacy in the U.S. Civil War, which, after the fall of the rail hub of Chattanooga in November of 1863, could not use interior lines to transport troops to meet superior Union numbers where needed, the Japanese reached a point after which they no longer possessed the offensive capability to withstand the production of fast carriers, well-trained pilots, and capable aircraft fielded by the United States starting in the summer of 1943. The Japanese had placed themselves in a position where their geostrategic advantage of interior lines with fast-moving carriers to compensate for greater American numbers of ships would erode rapidly, should their offensive capacity fall below some critical level.

72. Fitch, *CTF-11 War Diary*, CTG-17.5 letter to CTF 17, p. 2.
73. Bates, *The Battle of the Coral Sea*, p. 66.
74. Bates, *The Battle of the Coral Sea*, pp. 64–65.
75. Ibid., pp. 65–66.
76. This graphic has been derived from information in *Jane's Fighting Ships of World War II*, foreword by Antony Preston. New York/Avenel, New Jersey: Crescent Book, 1946/1947; published in the U.S. in 1989 and reprinted in 1992; and Bates, *The Battle of the Coral Sea*, p. 81.
77. Bates, *The Battle of the Coral Sea*, p. 78.
78. Fitch, *CTF-11 War Diary,* CTG-17.5 letter to CTF 17, p. 2.
79. Bates, *The Battle of the Coral Sea,* p. 81.
80. Sherman, *CTF-11 War Diary*, letter to Commander in Chief, United States Pacific Fleet dated 15 May 1942, p. 4.
81. Fitch, Aubrey, Vice Admiral, USN. Oral History of the Battle of the Coral Sea. Statement given to Commo. R.W. Bates, USN, Head Analyst, Naval War College, 30 November 1946.
82. Commander Task Force 17 Operation Order No. 2-42, dated 1 May 1942, paragraph 3(e)(2), p. 4.
83. Bates, *The Battle of the Coral Sea*, p. 85.
84. Fletcher, letter to Commander in Chief, United States Fleet dated 27 May 1942, p. 8.
85. Bates, *The Battle of the Coral Sea*, p. 86.
86. *United States Strategic Bombing Survey*, Naval Analysis Division: Interrogation of Captain Watanabe, Imperial Japanese Navy, Commander in Chief Combined Fleet Log—Coral Sea Action, 8 May 1942, p. 539.
87. *United States Strategic Bombing Survey*. Interrogation of Captain Yamaoka, Imperial Japanese Navy Operations Officer, Staff, 5th Air Flotilla, Naval Analysis Interrogation of Japanese Officials: Volume I—Interrogation, Naval No. 10, p. 53.
88. Sherman, *CTF-11 War Diary*, letter to Commander in Chief, United States Pacific Fleet dated 15 May 1942, p. 5.
89. Bates, *The Battle of the Coral Sea*, p. 93.
90. Fitch, *CTF-11 War Diary,* CTG-17.5 letter to CTF 17, p.3
91. Bates, *The Battle of the Coral Sea*, p. 96.
92. Fitch, *CTF-11 War Diary,* CTG-17.5 letter to CTF 17, p.3
93. Bates, *The Battle of the Coral Sea*, p. 98.
94. Ibid., p. 99.

95. Ibid.
96. Thach, John S. "Jimmy," Rear Admiral, USN (Ret.). Annapolis, Md.: Oral Histories of the United States Naval Institute, Oral History No. 58, Thach No. 3, pp. 272–273.
97. Sherman, *CTF-11 War Diary*, letter to Commander in Chief, United States Pacific Fleet dated 15 May 1942, , pp. 7 and 11.
98. Bates, *The Battle of the Coral Sea*, p. 102.
99. Fitch, *CTF-11 War Diary*, CTG-17.5 letter to CTF 17, p. 5.
100. Sherman, letter to Commander in Chief, United States Pacific Fleet dated 15 May 1942, p. 9.
101. Ibid., p. 13.
102. Bates, *The Battle of the Coral Sea*, p. 101.
103. Ibid., p. 100.
104. Ibid.
105. Ibid., p. 101.
106. Ibid., p. 103.
107. Ibid., pp. 105, 107–108.
108. Bates, Richard W., Rear Admiral, USN (Ret.). *The Battle of Midway Including the Aleutian Phase, June 3 to June 14, 1942: Strategical and Tactical Analysis.* Defense Documentation Center, Defense Logistics Agency: Cameron Station, Alexandria, Va., p. 2. (Formerly classified document.)
109. Please see explanatory note for option three on page 46.
110. Uhlig, Frank Jr. Letter to historian Edward S. Miller dated 10 December 2004, p. 1.
111. Ibid., p. 2.
112. Ibid., p. 3.
113. Clasuewitz, Karl von. *On War*. Princeton, N.J.: Princeton University Press, 1776, p. 87.
114. Bates, *The Battle of the Coral Sea*, appendix II, p. vii.
115. Okumiya, *Zero!*, pp. 50–54.
116. Ibid., pp. 48 and 51. Please note that numbers for the *Hosho*, *Zuiho*, and *Shoho* (which joined the fleet in January of 1942) are derived from other sources.
117. Okumiya, *Zero!*, p. 54.
118. Bates, *The Battle of the Coral Sea*, appendix II, p. vii.
119. Wildenberg, Thomas. "Midway: Sheer Luck or Better Doctrine?" in *Naval War College Review*. Newport, R.I.: Naval War College Press, Volume 58, Number 1 (Winter 2005), pp. 121–136.
120. Ibid.
121. *Yorktown* numbers are from Buckmaster, E., Captain, USN. *War Diary, Commander Task Force Eleven (Commander Carrier Division One)* dated

31 May 1942. Commanding Officer, USS Yorktown letter to Commander in Chief, United States Pacific Fleet dated 25 May 1942, p. 48. Naval War College Microfilm Collection reel A39, first frame 41078. (Previously classified document.) *Lexington* numbers are from Bates, *Battle of the Coral Sea*, p. 81.

122. Lundstrom, "Black Shoe Carrier Admiral" (lecture) in note 36.
123. Fletcher, letter to Commander in Chief, United States Fleet dated 27 May 1942, pp. 6 (para. 19) and 9 (para. 26).
124. Ibid., p. 6, para. 19.
125. Ibid., p. 9, para. 26.
126. Ibid.

Chapter 3

1. Insights for Japanese naval doctrine in World War II were provided by Vice Adm. (then Capt.) Yoji Koda of the Japanese Maritime Self-Defense Force. Vice Admiral Koda was assigned as a student in the Naval Command College at the United States Naval War College in 1992, where he was my student in a seminar on World War II in the Pacific theater. A naval scholar who had several previous tours in the United States, Koda was every bit as much a teacher as a student. He provided insightful commentary and analysis after every seminar session, and many of his insights will be included later in this and other chapters.
2. H.P. "Ned" Willmott. *Empires in the Balance: Japanese and Allied Naval Strategies to April 1942*. Annapolis, Md.: Naval Institute Press, 1982, Appendix A: Nominal Orders of Battle of the Imperial Japanese and U.S. Navies Between 7 December 1941 and 2 September 1945, pp. 525–530.
3. McMurtrie, Francis E., A.I.N.A., ed. *Jane's Fighting Ships 1943–4* (issued 1944). New York: The Macmillan Company, 1944, p. 296.
4. Ibid., pp. 171–172. Please note that all figures for both Japanese and U.S. fleets here are taken from this reference.
5. Lundstrom, John B., author of *The First Team* and *The First Team and the Guadalcanal Campaign*. Conversations with Douglas V. Smith regarding the research on National Archives No. 2, CINCPAC Secret and Confidential Message File, Record Group 313, he has completed for his forthcoming book on Adm. Frank Jack Fletcher and his decisions at the battles of Coral Sea, Midway, and the Eastern Solomons, via phone on Friday, 19 November 2004.
6. Ibid.
7. Bates, Richard W., Rear Admiral, USN (Ret.). *The Battle of Midway Including the Aleutian Phase, June 3 to June 14, 1942: Strategical and Tactical Analysis*. Unpublished manuscript prepared for the Bureau of Naval Personnel, now held by the Defense Documentation Center, Defense Logistics Agency, Cameron Station, Alexandria, Va., and at other military installations, 1948, p. 81.

8. Willmott, *Empires in the Balance*, p. 172.
9. Potter, E.B. and Chester W. Nimitz, eds. *Sea Power: A Naval History*. Englewood Cliffs, N.J.: Prentice-Hall, Inc., 1960, p. 672.
10. *The Lucky Bag 1906*. Annapolis, Md.: U.S. Naval Academy. Vol. XIII, p. 82. Excerpt from the United States Naval Academy yearbook for 1906, Admiral Frank Jack Fletcher Collection, Box 1, Folder 2, Bibliographical File, American Heritage Center, University of Wyoming, Laramie, Wyo.
11. Admiral Frank Jack Fletcher Collection, Biographical Sketch, Box 1, Folder 2, Bibliographical File.
12. Bureau of Navigation letter No. 6132-1 of 13 February 1908. Admiral Frank Jack Fletcher Collection, Box 1, Folder 2, Bibliographical File.
13. Bureau of Navigation, Navy Department letter No. 6132-17 of 31 July 1911. Admiral Frank Jack Fletcher Collection, Box 1, Folder 2, Bibliographical File.
14. Bureau of Navigation, Navy Department letter No. 6132-23 of 6 March 1912. Admiral Frank Jack Fletcher Collection, Correspondence File, Box 1, Folder 6.
15. *The Washington Post*: Sunday, January 13, 1929. "Inside Story of American Fiasco at Vera Cruz in 1914 Absolves Admiral [Frank Friday] Fletcher of All Blame, Says Witness." (Lead story, p. 1.)
16. Daniels, Josephus [Secretary of the Navy]. Navy Department letter of Commendation dated 12 June 1914 to Lt. F.J. Fletcher via Commander in Chief, Atlantic Fleet. Admiral Frank Jack Fletcher Collection, Correspondence File 1914, Box 1, Folder 7.
17. Eberle, E.W. [Secretary of the Navy]. Navy Department letter of 19 January 1916 to Lt. Frank J. Fletcher; "Subject: Medal of Honor." Admiral Frank Jack Fletcher Collection, Correspondence File 1915–1916, Box 1, Folder 8.
18. Admiral Frank Jack Fletcher letter from USS *Kearsage* to Admiral Winslow dated 18 April 1917. Admiral Frank Jack Fletcher Collection, Correspondence File 1915–1916, Box 1, Folder 8.
19. Sims, William Sowden, Admiral, USN. U.S. Naval Forces Operating in European Waters letter, Reference No. S 1 17102, dated 11 May 1918. Admiral Frank Jack Fletcher Collection, Correspondence File 1918–1920, Box 1, Folder 9.
20. Daniels, Josephus [Secretary of the Navy]. Navy Department letter to Cdr. Frank J. Fletcher serial N-32/FJS-LL dated October 29, 1918. Admiral Frank Jack Fletcher Collection, Correspondence File 1918–1920, Box 1, Folder 9.
21. Chandler, W.D., Jr. Navy Department, Bureau of Navigation letter serial N221-DBB, dated 23 October 1920. Admiral Frank Jack Fletcher Collection, Correspondence File 1918–1920, Box 1, Folder 9.
22. Daniels, Josephus [Secretary of the Navy]. Secretary of the Navy citation on behalf of the president awarding the Navy Cross to Cdr. Frank J. Fletcher, USN, for service in the World War dated 11 November 1920. Admiral Frank Jack Fletcher Collection, Correspondence File 1918–1920, Box 1, Folder 9.

23. Williams, C.S., President, U.S. Naval War College. Naval War College, Newport, RI, letter serial 444 Cl-ma dated 18 July 1924. Admiral Frank Jack Fletcher Collection, Correspondence File 1924–1926, Box 1, Folder 12.
24. Chief of the Bureau of Medicine and Surgery letter to Cdr. Frank Jack Fletcher dated 13 March 1928. Admiral Frank Jack Fletcher Collection, Correspondence File 1927–1928, Box 1, Folder 13.
25. Cdr. Frank Jack Fletcher, U.S. Navy letter from San Diego, Calif., dated 11 October 1928. Admiral Frank Jack Fletcher Collection, Correspondence File 1927–1928, Box 1, Folder 13.
26. Leigh, R.H. Navy Department, Bureau of Navigation letter serial Nav-31-R of 2 January 1929. Admiral Frank Jack Fletcher Collection, Correspondence File 1930–1932, Box 1, Folder 15.
27. *The Register*, manuscript listing of U.S. Naval War College Faculty and Graduates, p. 39. Provided by Dr. Evelyn Cherpak, archivist, U.S. Naval War College.
28. Leigh, R.H. Navy Department, Bureau of Navigation letter serial Nav-3-P dated 21 February 1930. Admiral Frank Jack Fletcher Collection, Correspondence File 1930–1932, Box 1, Folder 15.
29. Admiral Frank Jack Fletcher Collection, Biographical Sketch, Box 1, Folder 2, Bibliographical File.
30. Admiral Frank Jack Fletcher Collection, Correspondence File 1935–1936, Box 1, Folder 17.
31. Auphaill, F. Navy Department, Bureau of Navigation letter serial Nav-313-UB dated 18 August 1930. Admiral Frank Jack Fletcher Collection, Correspondence File 1930–1932, Box 1, Folder 15.
32. Ibid., p. 3.
33. Butcher, Marvin E., Lieutenant Commander, USN "Admiral Frank Jack Fletcher, Pioneer Warrior or Gross Sinner?" In *Naval War College Review*, Winter 1987, p. 70.
34. Fuchida, Mitsuo, and Masatake Okumiya. *Midway: The Battle That Doomed Japan, The Japanese Navy's Story*. Edited by Clarke H. Kawakami and Roger Pineau. Annapolis, Md.: Naval Institute Press, 1955 and 1992, p. 105. This book, which first appeared in its Japanese version in 1951, was the first to chronicle the magnitude of the defeat suffered at Midway by the Imperial Japanese Navy. Mitsuo Fuchida, flight leader of the attack on Pearl Harbor and every other carrier operation conducted by the *kido butai* prior to Midway, was the senior Air Wing commander aboard the carrier *Akagi* (under Vice Adm. Cuichi Nagumo, commander of the First Striking Force's flagship) during the battle. His manuscript, which was edited to produce *Midway*, was prepared primarily from the Top Secret debrief and reconstruction of the actual events which Fuchida was commissioned to prepare after the Midway operation and which "appeared in his foot locker after the War."

35. Ibid., p. 107.
36. Ibid.
37. Ibid., p. 114.
38. Ibid., p. 124.
39. Prados, John. *Combined Fleet Decoded: The Secret History of American Intelligence and the Japanese Navy in World War II*. New York: Random House, 1995, p. 305.
40. Ibid., p. 300.
41. Ibid., p. 316.
42. Ibid., p. 320.
43. Bates, *The Battle of Midway*, p. 2.
44. Bates, Ibid.
45. Bates, Ibid.
46. Lundstrom, John B. *The First South Pacific Campaign: Pacific Fleet Strategy December 1941–June 1942*. Annapolis, Md.: Naval Institute Press, 1976, pp. 137–149.
47. Ibid., pp. 120–128.
48. Ibid., p. 124.
49. Ibid.
50. Willmott, H.P. *The Barrier and the Javelin: Japanese and Allied Pacific Strategies February to June 1942*, Annapolis, Md.: U.S. Naval Institute Press, 1983, p. 107.
51. Fuchida, *Midway: The Battle That Doomed Japan*, p. 108.
52. Ibid., pp. 107–108.
53. Ibid., p. 109.
54. Ibid.
55. Ibid.
56. Willmott, *Empires in the Balance*, p. 105.
57. Fuchida, *Midway: The Battle That Doomed Japan*, p. 109.
58. Ibid.
59. Bates, *The Battle of Midway*, p. 21.
60. Ibid.
61. Ibid., p. 22.
62. Ibid.
63. Ibid.
64. Ibid., p. 23.
65. Ibid., pp. 24–25.
66. Prados, *Combined Fleet Decoded*, pp. 318–319.
67. Simard, Cyril T, Captain, USN. Letter to Commander in Chief, United States Pacific Fleet, Report of Engagement with the Enemy, Battle of Midway, 30 May to 7 June 1942, dated 18 June 1942, *Diary*, p. 2. Naval War College Microfilm Collection reel A55, first frame 41571. (Previously classified document.)

68. Ibid., p. 3.
69. Bates, *The Battle of Midway*, p. 39.
70. Ibid.
71. Ibid., p. 40.
72. Ibid.
73. Ibid., pp. 62 and 65.
74. Ibid., p. 40.
75. Morison, Samuel Eliot. "Coral Sea, Midway and Submarine Actions May 1942–August 1942," in *History of United States Naval Operations in World War II*, Vol. IV. New York: Little, Brown and Company, 1949, p. 81.
76. Ibid., p. 66.
77. Bates, *The Battle of Midway*, p. 67.
78. Ibid., p. 81
79. Karig, Walter, Captain, USNR, and Eric Purdon, Commander, USNR. *Battle Report: Pacific War: Middle Phase (Prepared from Official Sources)*. New York: Rinehart and Company, Inc., 1947, p. 32.
80. Lundstrom, John B. Lecture entitled "The Role of the Aircraft Carrier in Pacific Fleet Strategy from Pearl Harbor to Guadalcanal" delivered at the Naval War College for elective WE-576, "World War II in the Pacific Theater," Prof. Douglas V. Smith, Thursday, 13 January 2005.
81. Morison, Samuel Eliot. Letter to Vice Adm. Frank Jack Fletcher, USN (Ret.) dated 22 November 1947, p. 1. Admiral Frank Jack Fletcher Collection, Correspondence File 1930–1932, Box 1, Folder 26.
82. Fletcher, Frank Jack. Commander North Pacific Force, United States Pacific Fleet, letter to Captain [Samuel Eliot] Morison (undated), p. 1. Admiral Frank Jack Fletcher Collection, Correspondence File 1930–1932, Box 1, Folder 26.
83. Thach, John S., "Jimmy," Rear Admiral, USN (Ret.). Oral History No. 58, Thach #3. Annapolis, Md.: Oral Histories of the United States Naval Institute, pp. 272–273.
84. Fuchida, *Midway: The Battle That Doomed Japan*, pp. 171–173.
85. Morison, Samuel E. *History of United States Naval Operations in World War II, Volume IV, Coral Sea, Midway and Submarine Actions May 1942–August 1942*. New York: Little, Brown and Company, 1949, p. 176.
86. Bates, *The Battle of Midway*, p. 4.
87. *Register of the Alumni, Graduates and Former Naval Cadets and Midshipmen, United States Naval Academy Alumni Association, Inc., 1845–1985*, 1985 edition. Published by United States Naval Academy Alumni Association. Also *The Register*, manuscript listing of U.S. Naval War College faculty and graduates, provided by Dr. Evelyn Cherpak, archivist, U.S. Naval War College. All listings

of graduation dates from the Naval Academy and Naval War College are drawn from these two publications.

88. Morison, *History of United States Naval Operations*, p. 166 (footnote).
89. Bates, *The Battle of Midway*, p. 73; and Morison, *History of United States Naval Operations*, p. 166.
90. Willmott, *Empires in the Balance*, p. 326 and Bates, *The Battle of Midway*, p. 73.
91. Bates, *The Battle of Midway*, p. 73.
92. Morison, *History of United States Naval Operations*, p. 161.
93. Bates, *The Battle of Midway*, p. 74.
94. Morison, *History of United States Naval Operations*, p. 179.
95. Ibid., p. 181.
96. Ibid.
97. Ibid., p. 180.
98. Ibid., p. 184.
99. Simard, *Diary*, p. 1.
100. Ibid.
101. Bates, *The Battle of Midway*, p. 78.
102. Simard, *Diary*, p. 2. This group of ships is referred to by Captain Simard as "Main Body" in his *Diary*.
103. Ibid.
104. Ibid.
105. Ibid., and Bates, *The Battle of Midway*, p. 79.
106. Simard, *Diary*, p. 2.
107. Bates, *The Battle of Midway*, p. 79.
108. Simard, *Diary*, 2.
109. Bates, *The Battle of Midway*, p. 109.
110. Ibid., p. 110.
111. Nimitz, Chester W., Admiral, USN. Commander in Chief, United States Pacific Fleet, letter to Commander in Chief, United States Fleet [Admiral King], "Subject: Battle of Midway," dated June 28, 1942, p. 7. Naval War College Microfilm Collection reel A55, first frame 41571. (Previously classified document.)
112. Simard, *Diary*, p. 3.
113. Ibid.
114. Bates, *The Battle of Midway*, pp. 110–111.
115. Ibid., p. 111.
116. Ibid.

117. Nagumo, *The Japanese Story of the Battle of Midway*, p. 10. The time of 0130 given in the text is Tokyo time and has been corrected above to local time. All times hereafter from this source will likewise be changed to reflect local time.
118. Simard, *Diary*, p. 3.
119. Bates, *The Battle of Midway*, p. 88.
120. Simard, *Diary*, p.3.
121. Ibid., p. 4.
122. Nagumo, *The Japanese Story of the Battle of Midway*, p. 67.
123. Ibid.
124. Ibid., p. 11.
125. Fletcher, Frank Jack, Rear Admiral, USN. Commander, Cruisers, Pacific Fleet letter to Commander in Chief, United States Pacific Fleet, "Subject: Battle of Midway," dated 14 June 1942, p. 1. (Previously classified document.) All times have been corrected to local time in the vicinity of the action. Naval War College Microfilm Collection reel A55, first frame 41571.
126. Nagumo, *The Japanese Story of the Battle of Midway*, pp. 11–12, and Morison, *History of United States Naval Operations*, p. 107.
127. Ibid., p. 24.
128. Morison, *History of United States Naval Operations*, p. 107.
129. Ibid.
130. Ibid., pp. 11–12.
131. Bates, *The Battle of Midway*, p. 91.
132. Ibid.
133. Ibid., p. 92.
134. Peatie, Mark R. *Sunburst: The Rise of Japanese Naval Air Power 1909–1941*. Annapolis, Md.: Naval Institute Press, 2001, pp. 63–76.
135. Isom, Dallas W. "The Battle of Midway: Why the Japanese Lost." In *Naval War College Review*, Summer 2000, pp. 60–100.
136. Bates, *The Battle of Midway*, p. 111.
137. Ibid., p. 117.
138. Nagumo, *The Japanese Story of the Battle of Midway*, p. 13.
139. Bates, *The Battle of Midway*, p. 89.
140. Ibid.
141. Ibid., p. 112.
142. Ibid.
143. Ibid., p. 88.
144. Ibid., pp. 112–114.
145. Ibid., p. 114.
146. Nagumo, *The Japanese Story of the Battle of Midway*, p. 12.

147. Fletcher, Commander Cruisers, Pacific Fleet, to Commander in Chief, United States Pacific Fleet letter dated 14 June 1942, p. 1. Naval War College Microfilm Collection reel A55, first frame 41571. (Previously classified document.)
148. Ibid.
149. Ibid.
150. Murray, G.D. Commanding Officer, USS *Enterprise* (CV 6) letter to Commander in Chief, U.S. Pacific Fleet, "Subject: Battle of Midway, June 4–6, 1942, Report of," dated June 8 1942, p. 2. Naval War College Microfilm Collection reel A55, first frame 41571. (Previously classified document.)
151. Ibid.
152. Morison, *History of United States Naval Operations*, p. 113.
153. Distances based on plotting carriers' positions.
154. Morison, *History of United States Naval Operations*, p. 103.
155. Ibid., p. 2. Also Fletcher, Commander Cruisers, Pacific Fleet, to Commander in Chief, United States Pacific Fleet letter dated 14 June 1942, p. 1, and Spruance, R. A., Commander Task Force 16, 16 June 1942 letter to Commander in Chief, U.S. Pacific Fleet, p. 1.
156. Lundstrom, *The First Team*, p. 335.
157. Fletcher, Frank Jack, Rear Admiral, USN. Commander Task Force 17 letter to Commander in Chief, United States Pacific Fleet, "Subject: Battle of Midway—Forwarding of Reports," dated June 26, 1942, p. 1. Naval War College Microfilm Collection reel A55, first frame 41571. (Previously classified document.)
158. Lundstrom, *The First Team*, pp. 335–336.
159. Ibid.
160. Fletcher, Frank Jack, Commander Cruisers, Pacific Fleet, to Commander in Chief, United States Pacific Fleet letter dated 14 June 1942, p. 1. Fletcher switched from using his Commander Task Force 17 designation to Commander, Cruisers, U.S. Pacific Fleet on moving his flag to USS *Astoria* when *Yorktown* was abandoned.
161. Ibid., pp. 1–2.
162. Bates, *The Battle of the Coral Sea*, p. 81.
163. Sherman, Frederick C. Commanding Officer, USS *Lexington* letter to Commander in Chief, United States Pacific Fleet dated 15 May 1942, p. 12, Recommendations, paragraph 31-3. Naval War College Microfilm Collection reel A55, first frame 41571. (Previously classified document.) Fletcher subsequently endorsed this recommendation most strongly.
164. Bates, *The Battle of Midway*, p. 127.
165. Ibid., p. 128.
166. Ibid.
167. Ibid., p. 129.

168. Conversations of Douglas V. Smith with John B. Lundstrom and Professor Emeritus Frank Snyder conducted at the Reading Room in Newport, Rhode Island, on Thursday, 13 January 2005.
169. Bates, *The Battle of Midway*, p. 130.
170. Ibid.
171. Ibid., p. 131.
172. Ibid., p. 132.
173. Nimitz, Commander in Chief, United States Pacific Fleet letter to Commander in Chief, United States Fleet [Admiral King] dated 28 June 1942, p. 12. Spruance, Commander Task Force 16 letter of 16 June 1942, p. 2.
174. Nimitz, letter to Commander in Chief, United States Fleet dated 28 June 1942 p. 12. Spruance, Spruance, Commander Task Force 16 letter of 16 June 1942, p. 2.
175. Nimitz, letter to Commander in Chief, United States Fleet dated 28 June 1942, p. 12. Spruance, Commander Task Force 16 letter of 16 June 1942, p. 2.
176. Nimitz, letter to Commander in Chief, United States Fleet dated 28 June 1942 p. 12. Spruance, Spruance, Commander Task Force 16 letter of 16 June 1942, p. 2.
177. Morison, Samuel E. *History of United States Naval Operations*, p. 130.
178. Bates, *The Battle of Midway*, 136–137.
179. Ibid., p. 133.
180. Ibid., pp. 133–134.
181. Ibid., p. 135.
182. Ibid.
183. Nimitz, letter to Commander in Chief, United States Fleet dated 28 June 1942, p. 13.
184. Nimitz, letter to Commander in Chief, United States Fleet dated 28 June 1942, p. 14. Murray, Commanding Officer, USS *Enterprise* (CV 6) letter dated June 8 1942, p. 3. Mitscher, M.A., Captain, USN. Commanding Officer, USS *Hornet* letter to Commander in Chief, United States Pacific Fleet, dated 13 June 1942, "Subject: Report of Action"—4–6 June 1942, p. 3. (Previously classified document.)
185. Fletcher, Commander Cruisers, Pacific Fleet letter to Commander in Chief, United States Pacific Fleet dated 14 June 1942, "Subject: Battle of Midway," p. 2.
186. Mitscher, letter to Commander in Chief, United States Pacific Fleet dated 13 June 1942, p. 3.
187. Fletcher, letter to Commander in Chief, United States Pacific Fleet dated 14 June 1942, p. 2. Nimitz, letter to Commander in Chief, United States Fleet dated 28 June 1942, p. 13.

188. Fletcher, letter to Commander in Chief, United States Pacific Fleet dated 14 June 1942, p. 2.
189. Nagumo, *The Japanese Story of the Battle of Midway*, p. 12. Nagumo lists the correct composition of the strike as four fighters and nine torpedo planes from the *Hiryu* supplemented by two fighters from the *Kaga* and one torpedo plane from the *Akagi*.
190. Fletcher, Commander Cruisers, Pacific Fleet letter dated 14 June 1942, p.3. Buckmaster, E[lliott]., Captain, USN. Commanding Officer, USS *Yorktown* letter to Commander in Chief, U.S. Pacific Fleet, "Subject: Report of Action for June 4, 1942, and June 6, 1942," dated 18 June 1942, p. 5. Naval War College Microfilm Collection reel A55, first frame 41571. (Previously classified document.)
191. Fletcher, letter to Commander in Chief, United States Pacific Fleet dated 14 June 1942, p. 3. Buckmaster, letter to Commander in Chief, United States Pacific Fleet dated 18 June 1942, pp. 5–6.
192. Fuchida, *Midway: The Battle That Doomed Japan*, p. 228.
193. Ibid., p. 248.
194. Bates, *The Battle of Midway*, p. 98.
195. Fuchida, *Midway: The Battle That Doomed Japan*, p. 228.
196. Bates, *The Battle of Midway*, p. 98.
197. Simard, *Diary*, p. 6.
198. Ibid., p. 6.
199. Bates, *The Battle of Midway*, p. 145. Nagumo, *The Japanese Story of the Battle of Midway*, p. 15.
200. Ibid., p. 14.
201. Nagumo, *The Japanese Story of the Battle of Midway*, p. 14.
202. Nimitz, letter to Commander in Chief, United States Fleet dated 28 June 1942, p. 15.
203. Ibid.
204. Murray, Commanding Officer, USS *Enterprise* letter dated June 8 1942, p. 3.
205. Ibid.
206. Mitscher, letter to Commander in Chief, United States Pacific Fleet dated 13 June 1942, p. 3.
207. Bates, *The Battle of Midway*, p. 142.
208. Ibid., p. 141.
209. Fletcher, Commander Cruisers, United States Pacific Fleet letter dated 14 June 1942, p. 3.
210. Ibid., p. 142.
211. Fuchida, *Midway: The Battle That Doomed Japan*, p. 110.
212. Ibid., pp. 243–249.

213. Fuchida, *Midway: The Battle That Doomed Japan*, p. 248.
214. Ibid., pp. 142–143.
215. Ibid., p. 143.
216. Ibid.
217. Morison, *History of United States Naval Operations*, p. 139.
218. Bates, *The Battle of Midway*, p. 144.
219. Nagumo, *The Japanese Story of the Battle of Midway*, p. 17. Fuchida, *Midway: The Battle That Doomed Japan*, p. 149.
220. Nagumo, *The Japanese Story of the Battle of Midway*, p. 17.
221. Nagumo, *The Japanese Story of the Battle of Midway*, p. 60.
222. Bates, *The Battle of Midway*, p. 169.
223. Insights for this section were provided by Prof. Emeritus Frank Snyder in his presentation on the Battle of Midway, and used with his permission.
224. Nagumo, *The Japanese Story of the Battle of Midway*, p. 15.
225. Morison, *History of United States Naval Operations*, pp. 110, 261, and 286.
226. Fuchida, *Midway: The Battle That Doomed Japan*, p. 289. Biographical information was taken from the cover jacket of this volume.
227. Ibid.
228. Hata, Ikuhiko, and Yasuho Izawa. *Japanese Naval Aces and Fighter Units in World War II*. Annapolis, Md.: Naval Institute Press, 1989, appendix B, pp. 375–378.
229. Fuchida, *Midway: The Battle That Doomed Japan*, p. 108.
230. Ibid.
231. Hata, *Japanese Naval Aces*, appendix B, pp. 375–378.

Chapter 4

1. Ugaki, Matome, Admiral, Imperial Japanese Navy. *Fading Victory: The Diary of Admiral Matome Ugaki 1941–1945*. Translated by Masataka Chihaya. Pittsburgh, Pa.: University of Pittsburgh Press, 1991, p. 138.
2. Ibid., p. 133.
3. Ibid.
4. Ibid., pp. 139–142 and 174.
5. Ibid., pp. 144–145.
6. Ibid., pp. 140–141.
7. Ibid., p. 144.
8. Ibid.
9. Ibid., pp. 144–145.
10. Ibid., p. 172.
11. Fuchida, Mitsuo, and Masatake Okumiya. *Midway: The Battle That Doomed Japan, The Japanese Navy's Story*. Edited by Clarke H. Kawakami and Roger Pineau. Annapolis, Md.: Naval Institute Press, 1955, p. 77.

12. Ibid.
13. Ugaki, *Fading Victory*, p. 174.
14. Insight provided by Edward S. Miller, author of *War Plan Orange*, in marginal notes to the manuscript for this work, which he graciously critiqued prior to submission for publication.
15. Lundstrom, John B. *The First Team and the Guadalcanal Campaign*. Annapolis, Md.: Naval Institute Press, 1994, p. 5.
16. Ibid.
17. Ibid.
18. Lundstrom, *The First Team and the Guadalcanal Campaign*, Part V (title of section), pp. 461–524.
19. Ibid., p. 5.
20. Ibid., pp. 5–6.
21. Dyer, George Carroll, Vice Admiral, USN (Ret.). *The Amphibians Came to Conquer: The Story of Admiral Richmond Kelly Turner*, Volume I. Washington, D.C.: U.S. Government Printing Office, 1972, p. 293.
22. Butcher, Marvin E., Lieutenant Commander, USN. "Admiral Frank Jack Fletcher, Pioneer Warrior or Gross Sinner?" In *Naval War College Review*, Winter 1987, p. 75.
23. Ibid.
24. Dyer, *The Amphibians Came to Conquer*, p. 293.
25. Ibid., p. 294.
26. Ibid.
27. Ibid., pp. 292–294.
28. Lewis, Winston B., Ensign, USNR, and Henry A. Mustin, Lieutenant Junior grade, USNR. *The Battle of Savo Island 9 August 1942 and the Eastern Solomons 23–25 August 1942*. Washington, D.C.: Naval Historical Center, Department of the Navy, 1943 (Republished in 1994), Combat Narratives Series, Solomon Islands campaign, 2–3, p. 1.
29. Ibid.
30. Ibid.
31. Ibid., pp. 1–2. It should be noted that observers dispute Admiral Turner's recollection of when he first became aware of the Japanese force of ships, indicating that this actually took place earlier in the day.
32. Ibid., p. 2.
33. Ibid., pp. 2–3.
34. Lewis, *The Battle of Savo Island*, pp. 5 and 12.
35. Ugaki, *Fading Victory*, p. 180.
36. Ibid.
37. Lewis, *The Battle of Savo Island*, p. 44, footnote 82.
38. Dyer, *The Amphibians Came to Conquer*, p. 300.

39. Lundstrom, John B. Lecture entitled "Frank Jack Fletcher—Black Shoe Carrier Admiral," delivered at the Naval War College for elective WE-576, "World War II in the Pacific Theater," Prof. Douglas V. Smith, Thursday, 13 January 2005. Quotation is taken from lecture notes given by Lundstrom and used with his permission, p. 26.
40. Ibid., p. 16.
41. Ibid.
42. Ibid., pp. 16 and 17.
43. Ibid., p. 25.
44. Ibid., p. 27.
45. Ibid., p. 30.
46. Ibid., p. 31.
47. Ibid., p. 23.
48. Ibid., p. 25.
49. Lundstrom, *The First Team and the Guadalcanal Campaign*, p. 105.
50. Ibid., pp. 220–229.
51. Ibid., p. 171.
52. Butcher, "Pioneer Warrior or Gross Sinner?," pp. 69–79.
53. Lundstrom, lecture notes for "Frank Jack Fletcher—Black Shoe Carrier Admiral," p. 33.
54. Ibid., p. 35.
55. Mustin, *The Battle of the Eastern Solomons*, p. 49.
56. Ibid.
57. Ibid., pp. 49–50.
58. Ibid., p. 50.
59. Ibid.
60. Ibid.
61. Ibid.
62. Davis, A.C. Commanding Officer, USS *Enterprise* letter to Commander in Chief, United States Pacific Fleet letter of 5 September 1942, "Subject: Action of August 24, 1942, Including Air Attack on USS *Enterprise*; Report of," p. 2. Naval War College Microfilm Collection reel A99, first frame 42790. (Previously classified document.)
63. Ibid., p, 52.
64. Ibid.
65. Nimitz, C.W., Admiral, U.S. Navy. Commander in Chief, United States Pacific Fleet letter to Commander in Chief, U.S. Fleet dated 27 September 1942, "Subject: Solomon Islands Campaign—Action of 23–25 August," p. 6. Naval War College Microfilm Collection reel A99, first frame 42790. (Previously classified document.)
66. Mustin, *The Battle of the Eastern Solomons*, p. 54.

67. Nimitz letter to Commander in Chief, United States Fleet dated 27 September 1942, p. 6.
68. Ibid.
69. Ibid.
70. Ibid.
71. Ibid., p. 7.
72. Ibid.
73. Nimitz letter to Commander in Chief, United States Fleet dated 27 September 1942, p. 7. Davis letter to Commander in Chief, United States Pacific Fleet dated 5 September 1942, p. 3. Leslie, M.F. Commander, Enterprise Air Group letter of 2 September 1942, to Commander in Chief, United States Pacific Fleet, "Subject: Report of Action in the Solomon Islands Area August 22–25, 1942," p. 3. Naval War College Microfilm Collection reel A99, first frame 42790. (Previously classified document.)
74. Nimitz letter dated 27 September 1942, p. 7.
75. Mustin, *The Battle of the Eastern Solomons*, p. 55.
76. Ibid.
77. Ibid., p. 56.
78. Nimitz letter to Commander in Chief, U.S. Fleet dated 27 September 1942, p. 7.
79. Ibid.
80. Davis, letter to Commander in Chief, United States Pacific Fleet, dated 5 September 1942, Serial 008 Sept 5, 1942, USS *Enterprise* Track Chart with contact and Attack Sequence off Solomon Islands, August 23–25, 1942, p. 3. Secret (downgraded to unclassified). Naval War College Microfilm Collection reel A287, first frame 48173.
81. Ibid.
82. Ibid., p. 4.
83. Ibid.
84. Ibid., pp. 4–5.
85. Ibid., p. 5.
86. McMurtrie, Francis E., ed. *Jane's Fighting Ships 1941*. New York: The Macmillan Company, 1942, pp. 293–296 lists *Ryujo* as capable of embarking around twenty-four aircraft. Her actual complement, according to this informed Japanese source, was fourteen aircraft more than western observers expected. This was typical of *Jane's* underestimates for all Japanese carrier classes.
87. Ibid., p. 7.
88. Ibid., pp. 6–7.
89. Ibid., pp. 7–10.
90. Ibid., p. 6.
91. Mustin, *The Battle of the Eastern Solomons*, p. 67.

92. Ibid., pp. 67–68.
93. Ibid., p. 12.
94. Ibid.
95. Ibid., p. 11.
96. Ibid., pp. 11–12.
97. Mustin, *The Battle of the Eastern Solomons*, p. 70.
98. Ibid.
99. Ibid.
100. Ibid, p. 71.
101. Nimitz letter to Commander in Chief, United States Fleet dated 27 September 1942, p. 1.
102. Mustin, *The Battle of the Eastern Solomons*, p. 53.
103. Ibid., p. 63.
104. Ibid.
105. Lundstrom, *The First Team and the Guadalcanal Campaign*, p. 106.
106. Mustin, *The Battle of the Eastern Solomons*, p. 72.
107. Dyer, *The Amphibians Came to Conquer*, p. 292.
108. Ibid., p. 297.
109. Ibid.
110. Ibid., pp. 297–298.
111. Ibid., p. 298.
112. Ibid.
113. Ibid.
114. Lundstrom, John B. Lecture entitled "The Role of the Aircraft Carrier in Pacific Fleet Strategy from Pearl Harbor to Guadalcanal" delivered at the Naval War College for elective WE-576, "World War II in the Pacific Theater," Prof. Douglas V. Smith, Thursday, 13 January 2005.
115. Lundstrom, *The First Team and the Guadalcanal Campaign*, pp. 1–2.
116. Davis letter to Commander in Chief, United States Pacific Fleet dated 5 September 1942, pp. 13–25.
117. Fletcher, Frank Jack. Commander Task Force 61 letter to Commander in Chief, United States Pacific Fleet dated 26 September 1942, "Subj: Report of Action on August 24, 1942," p. 1 (only page of report).

Chapter 5

1. Lundstrom, John B. *The First Team and the Guadalcanal Campaign*. Annapolis, Md.: Naval Institute Press, 1994, p. 227.
2. Frank, Richard B. *Guadalcanal*. New York: Random House, 1990, pp. 295–297.
3. Ibid., pp. 293–295.

4. Ibid., p. 293.
5. Ibid., p. 294.
6. Ibid., pp. 302–303.
7. Ibid., p. 309.
8. Ibid., p. 312.
9. Lundstrom, *The First Team and the Guadalcanal Campaign*, p. 173.
10. Admiral Frank Jack Fletcher Collection, Biographical Sketch, p. 3., Box 1, Folder 2, Bibliographical File, American Heritage Center, University of Wyoming, Laramie, Wyo.
11. Ibid.
12. Ibid.
13. Ibid.
14. Ibid.
15. Ibid., p. 4.
16. Nimitz, Chester W., Admiral, USN. Commander in Chief, United States Pacific Fleet, letter to Commander in Chief, United States Fleet [Admiral King], "Subject: Solomon Islands Campaign, Battle of Santa Cruz—26 October 1941," dated 6 January 1943, Naval War College Microfilm Collection reel A193, starting frame 45530, p. 4. (Previously classified document.) Please note that in this and all other official correspondence relating to this period of the war Guadalcanal was referred to by its assigned code word, "Cactus," and Espiritu Santo by its assigned code word, "Button."
17. Ibid.
18. Ibid.
19. Ibid.
20. Lundstrom, *The First Team and the Guadalcanal Campaign*, p. 328.
21. Ibid.
22. Poor, Henry V., Ensign, USNR, Henry V. Mustin, Lieutenant Junior Grade, USNR, and Colin G. Jamison, Lieutenant Junior Grade, USNR. *The Battles of Cape Esperance 11 October 1942 and Santa Cruz Islands 26 October 1942.* Washington, D.C.: Naval Historical Center, Department of the Navy, 1943 Combat Narratives Series, Solomon Islands campaign, 4–5, p. 31. Republished in 1994.
23. Ibid.
24. Ibid. It should be remembered that *Salt Lake City*, *Boise*, and *Farenholt* had received heavy damage and the destroyer *Duncan* had been sunk during the Battle of Cape Esperance.
25. Nimitz, letter to Commander in Chief, United States Fleet dated 6 January 1943, p. 4.
26. Ibid.
27. Ibid., pp. 4–5.

28. Lundstrom, *The First Team and the Guadalcanal Campaign*, p. 328.
29. Nimitz, letter to Commander in Chief, United States Fleet dated 6 January 1943, p. 5.
30. Mason, C.P., Captain, USN. Commanding Officer, USS *Hornet*, letter to the Secretary of the Navy and Commander in Chief, United States Pacific Fleet, dated 30 October 1942, "Subject: Report of Action, October 26, 1942, and subsequent loss of USS *Hornet*," Naval War College Microfilm Collection reel A193, starting frame 43846, p. 2. (Previously classified document.)
31. Ibid.
32. Nimitz letter to Commander in Chief, United States Fleet dated 6 January 1943, p. 5.
33. Ibid.
34. Ibid. Also, Mason letter to the Secretary of the Navy and Commander in Chief, United States Pacific Fleet dated 30 October 1942, p. 2.
35. Mason, letter to the Secretary of the Navy and Commander in Chief, United States Pacific Fleet dated 30 October 1942, p. 2.
36. Nimitz letter to Commander in Chief, United States Fleet dated 6 January 1943, p. 5. Kinkaid, Thomas C., Rear Admiral, USN. Commander Task Force 61 letter to Commander in Chief, United States Pacific Fleet, "Subject: USS *Hornet* Report of Action, October 26, 1942—Comments on," dated 6 November 1942, p. 1. (Previously classified document.) In this report Admiral Kinkaid opines in paragraph 2, "Late return of the attack group was not due to the difficulty of keeping Point Option [as stated in CO USS *Hornet* Ltr. CV8/A16-3 (5) Secret Serial 00100 of October 30, 1942] but to the zeal of the striking group commander in pressing on beyond the scouting line in an endeavor to find the enemy."
37. Interview of Capt. James Granson Daniels, USN (Ret.), participant as fighter pilot in all carrier battles of World War II except the Battle of Midway, 18 February 2002, Honolulu, Hawaii.
38. Nimitz letter to Commander in Chief, United States Fleet dated 6 January 1943, p. 5.
39. Ibid.
40. Nimitz letter to Commander in Chief, United States Fleet dated 6 January 1943, p. 6.
41. Poor, *The Battles of Cape Esperance*, p. 36.
42. Ibid., p. 35.
43. Ibid., p. 36.
44. Ibid., p. 41.
45. Ibid.
46. Ibid.
47. Ibid., p. 42.

48. Ibid.
49. Ibid., footnote 7, p. 36.
50. Ibid., p. 43.
51. Nimitz letter to Commander in Chief, United States Fleet dated 6 January 1943, p. 7.
52. Mason letter to the Secretary of the Navy and Commander in Chief, United States Pacific Fleet, dated 30 October 1942, p. 2.
53. Ibid., p. 3.
54. While it seems odd that "VT" (torpedo planes) would be loaded with bombs, this is a verbatim entry in the After Action Report of the Commanding Officer, USS *Enterprise*, Mason, to the Secretary of the Navy and Commander in Chief, United States Pacific Fleet, dated 30 October 1942, p. 3, para. 7.
55. Ibid.
56. Ibid.
57. Halsey, William F., Vice Admiral, USN. Commander South Pacific Area and South Pacific Forces letter to Commander in Chief, United States Pacific Fleet, "Subject: Report of Action, October 26, 1942, and subsequent loss of USS *Hornet*," dated 20 November 1942, Naval War College Microfilm Collection reel A193, starting frame 45530, p. 1. (Previously classified document.)
58. Vose, J.E., Lieutenant, USN. Commander Bombing Squadron 8 letter to Commanding Officer, USS *Hornet*, "Subject: Action on 26 October 1942," dated 29 October 1942, Naval War College Microfilm Collection reel A193, starting frame 45530, p. 1. (Previously classified document.)
59. Ibid.
60. Ibid., p. 2.
61. Ibid.
62. Ibid.
63. Ibid. Also Nimitz letter to Commander in Chief, United States Fleet, dated 6 January 1943, p. 8.
64. Nimitz, letter to Commander in Chief, United States Fleet, dated 6 January 1943, p. 8.
65. Ibid.
66. Ibid.
67. Ibid.
68. Ibid.
69. Ibid.
70. Ibid.
71. Mason letter to the Secretary of the Navy and Commander in Chief, United States Pacific Fleet, dated 30 October 1942, p. 3.
72. Ibid., pp. 3–4.
73. Ibid., p. 4.

74. Ibid.
75. Ibid, pp. 4–5.
76. Ibid., p. 5.
77. Ibid., p. 4.
78. Ibid., p. 5.
79. Ibid., p. 6.
80. Ibid., p. 7.
81. Nimitz letter to Commander in Chief, United States Fleet dated 6 January 1943, p. 8.
82. Mason letter to the Secretary of the Navy and Commander in Chief, United States Pacific Fleet dated 30 October 1942, pp. 7–8.
83. CTF 17 (Rear Admiral Murray) message of 260507Z42 to CTG 17.4 directing "As soon as all personnel are picked up torpedo Hornet," with CTG 17.4's response to CTF 16 and CTF 17 reporting on completion of tasking, Naval War College Microfilm Collection reel A193, starting frame 43846, p. 1. (Previously classified document.)
84. Kinkaid, T. C., Rear Admiral, USN. Commander Task Force 61 letter to Commander in Chief, United States Pacific Fleet Serial 0077 (no date given), "Subject: Report of Carrier Action North of the Santa Cruz Islands, 26 October 1942," Naval War College Microfilm Collection reel A193, starting frame 44248, p. 5. (Previously classified document.)
85. Nimitz letter to Commander in Chief, United States Fleet dated 6 January 1943, p. 9.
86. Ibid.
87. Tisdale, Mahlon S., Captain, USN. Commander Cruisers, Task Force 16 letter to Commander in Chief, United States Pacific Fleet dated 29 October 1942, "Subject: Report of Action—October 26, 1942," Naval War College Microfilm Collection reel A193, starting frame 44692, p. 2. (Previously classified document.)
88. Hardison, O.B., Captain, USN. Commanding Officer, USS *Enterprise* letter to Commander in Chief, Unites States Pacific Fleet dated 10 November 1942, "Subject: The Battle of Santa Cruz, October 26, 1942, Report of," Naval War College Microfilm Collection reel A193, starting frame 44181, p. 4. (Previously classified document.)
89. Tisdale letter to Commander in Chief, United States Pacific Fleet dated 29 October 1942, p. 2.
90. Nimitz letter to Commander in Chief, United States Fleet dated 6 January 1943, p. 9.
91. Hardison letter to Commander in Chief, Unites States Pacific Fleet dated 10 November 1942, p. 6.
92. Kinkaid letter to Commander in Chief, United States Pacific Fleet Serial 0077 (no date given), pp. 4–5.

93. Nimitz letter to Commander in Chief, United States Fleet dated 6 January 1943, pp. 9–10.
94. Interview of Capt. James Granson Daniels, USN (Ret.), participant as fighter pilot in all carrier battles of World War II except the Battle of Midway, 18 February 2002, Honolulu, Hawaii. Captain Daniels, who was the last surviving pilot from both the battle of the Eastern Solomons and Santa Cruz, died in 2003. He related in this interview that the normal Air Group of *Enterprise* was eighteen fighters, eighteen dive-bombers, eighteen scout bombers, and eighteen torpedo planes—a total of seventy-two aircraft. The ten extra planes aboard *Enterprise* were the result of the sinking of USS *Wasp* just after the Battle of the Eastern Solomons.
95. Ibid. In this story Captain Daniels offered that the Marine major was the legendary "Pappy" Boyington. No attempt has been made here to authenticate Major Boyington's presence on Guadalcanal at this point in the war.
96. Nimitz letter to Commander in Chief, United States Fleet dated 6 January 1943, pp. 11–12.
97. Ibid., p. 12.
98. Ibid.
99. Ibid.
100. Kinkaid letter to Commander in Chief, United States Pacific Fleet Serial 0077 (no date given), p. 1.
101. Nimitz letter to Commander in Chief, United States Fleet dated 6 January 1943, p. 18.
102. Lundstrom, *The First Team and the Guadalcanal Campaign*, p. 463.
103. Frank, *Guadalcanal,* p. 434.
104. Ibid., pp. 434–435.
105. Ibid., p. 451.
106. Ibid.
107. Ibid., pp. 454–455.
108. Ibid., pp. 470–471.
109. Ibid., pp. 462–463.
110. Ibid., p. 475.
111. Ibid., p. 480.
112. Ibid., p. 481.
113. Ibid., p. 505.
114. Lundstrom, *The First Team and the Guadalcanal Campaign*, p. 168.

Chapter 6

1. Lockwood, Charles A., Vice Admiral, USN (Ret.), and Hans Christian Adamson, Colonel, USAF (Ret.). *The Battle of the Philippine Sea.* New York: Thomas Y. Crowell Company, 1967, p. 1.

2. Ibid., pp. 1–3.
3. Ibid., pp. 1–2.
4. Lundstrom, John B. *The First Team and the Guadalcanal Campaign*. Annapolis, Md.: Naval Institute Press, 1994, pp. 283, 465, and 527.
5. Ibid., p. 528.
6. For a comprehensive treatment of the battles of the Tenaru River and Bloody Ridge see Potter, E.B., editor, Chester W. Nimitz, Fleet Admiral, USN, associate editor. *Sea Power: A Naval History*. Englewood Cliffs, N.J.: Prentice-Hall, Inc., 1960, chapter 37, "Guadalcanal."
7. Potter, *Sea Power*, pp. 707–709.
8. Ibid.
9. Ibid.
10. Ibid., p. 708.
11. Ibid.
12. Ibid.
13. Ibid.
14. Ibid., p. 711.
15. Ibid.
16. Ibid.
17. Ibid., pp. 714–715.
18. Ibid., p. 717.
19. Costello, John. *The Pacific War 1941–1945*. New York: Quill, 1982, pp. 401–403.
20. Potter, *Sea Power*, p. 717.
21. Ibid.
22. Ibid.
23. Potter, *Sea Power*, pp. 718–722.
24. Ibid., p. 722.
25. Ibid., p. 712.
26. Ibid., p. 715.
27. Ibid., p. 722.
28. Ibid., pp. 722–728.
29. Ibid., p. 729.
30. Ibid., p. 731.
31. Ibid., pp. 729–731.
32. Ibid., p. 736.
33. Lockwood, *The Battle of the Philippine Sea*, p. 59.
34. Litch, E.W. Captain, USN. Commanding Officer, USS *Lexington*, letter to Commander in Chief, United States Fleet dated 30 June 1944, "Subj: Attack on the Marianas Islands from June 11 through June 19, 1944 (East Longitude dates) in support of the occupation of Saipan and the engagement of the Japanese Fleet

on 19 and 20 June, 1944 (East Longitude dates)—Action Report of," Naval War College Microfilm Collection reel A9, starting frame 79537, pp. 1–2. (Previously classified document.)

35. Lockwood, *The Battle of the Philippine Sea*, p. 28.
36. Litch letter to Commander in Chief, United States Fleet dated 30 June 1944, p. 1.
37. Lockwood, *The Battle of the Philippine Sea*, p. 65.
38. Ibid., pp. 64–65.
39. Litch letter to Commander in Chief, United States Fleet dated 30 June 1944, p. 4.
40. Lockwood, *The Battle of the Philippine Sea*, pp. 64 and 69.
41. Ibid., pp. 78–79.
42. Costello, *The Pacific War 1941–1945*, p. 473.
43. Lockwood, *The Battle of the Philippine Sea*, p. 79.
44. Ibid., pp. 80–81.
45. Ibid., p. 82.
46. Ibid., p. 82.
47. Ibid., p. 87.
48. Lockwood, *The Battle of the Philippine Sea*, pp. 85 and 62–64.
49. Ibid., p. 83.
50. Ibid., pp. 85 and 64.
51. Ibid.
52. Ibid., p. 87.
53. Ibid., p. 91.
54. Ibid., p. 88.
55. Ibid., p. 91.
56. Ibid., p. 92.
57. Ibid., p. 93.
58. King, Ernest J., Fleet Admiral, USN. *U.S. Navy at War 1941–1945*. Washington: United States Navy Department, 1946, p. 234.
59. Lockwood, *The Battle of the Philippine Sea*, p. 94.
60. Ibid, pp. 94–95.
61. Ibid., p. 95.
62. Ibid., p. 106.
63. Litch letter to Commander in Chief, United States Fleet dated 30 June 1944, p. 8.
64. Ibid., p. 9.
65. Ibid.
66. Ibid., p. 10.
67. Ibid.
68. Ibid.
69. Ibid.
70. Lockwood, *The Battle of the Philippine Sea*, p. 108.

71. Ibid., p. 106.
72. Ibid.
73. Ibid., p. 109.
74. Ibid.
75. Costello, *The Pacific War 1941–1945,* p. 578. For a most complete consideration of the amphibious operations of the United States Marine Corps and Army in the Pacific war, as well as the Japanese defenses against their assaults, please see Gatchel, Theodore L., Colonel, USMC (Ret.). *At the Water's Edge.* Annapolis, Md.: Naval Institute Press, 1996.
76. Lockwood, *The Battle of the Philippine Sea*, p. 110.
77. Ibid., p. 112. Also Litch, letter to Commander in Chief, United States Fleet dated 30 June 1944, p. 11.
78. Lockwood, *The Battle of the Philippine Sea*, p. 124.
79. Ibid.
80. Ibid., p. 123.
81. Costello, *The Pacific War 1941–1945,* p. 484.
82. Ibid., p. 485.
83. Ibid.
84. Ibid., p. 486.

Conclusions

1. *Sound Military Decision.* U.S. Naval War College, Newport, R.I., 1942, copy 3394, p. 36. Declassified Ref: ALNav 59–53 of 12/15/53.
2. General Courts Martial, William Mitchell Case Records, 1925 (Case No. 168771). RG 153, Records of the Office of the Judge Advocate General (Army). Col. William Mitchell, Air Service, Trial by General Court-Martial, Washington, D.C., 18 November 1925, Volume 12, 168771, Alexander H. Galt official reporter, 715 Woodward Building, Washington, D.C. College Park, Md.: National Archives No. II, Box No. 9214-2, section 1018–1147, parts 1112–13.
3. Ibid., part 1114.
4. Ibid.
5. Ibid.
6. Fletcher, Frank Jack, Vice Admiral, USN. Speech on 27 October 1946 at Des Moines, Iowa, pp. 2–3. Admiral Frank Jack Fletcher Collection, Box 2, Folder 73, Speeches File, American Heritage Center, University of Wyoming, Laramie, Wyo.

Bibliography

Battle Reports and Combat Narratives

Bates, Richard W., Rear Admiral, USN (Ret.). *The Battle of the Coral Sea, May 1 to May 11 Inclusive, 1942, Strategical and Tactical Analysis.* Unpublished manuscript prepared for the Bureau of Naval Personnel, 1947, now held by the Defense Documentation Center, Defense Logistics Agency, Cameron Station, Alexandria, Virginia, and at other authorized military installations. (Previously classified document.)

———. *The Battle of Midway Including the Aleutian Phase, June 3 to June 14, 1942: Strategical and Tactical Analysis.* Unpublished manuscript prepared for the Bureau of Naval Personnel, 1948, now held by the Defense Documentation Center, Defense Logistics Agency, Cameron Station, Alexandria, Virginia, and at other military installations. (Previously classified document.) This study, commissioned after World War II by the U.S. Navy, makes use of formerly classified and unclassified sources from both the United States and Japan, as well as interviews with the participants wherever possible, and is the most definitive and exhaustive study on the Battle of Midway available. It is drawn from substantially as an original source document by such eminent and seminal works as the fifteen-volume set entitled *History of United States Naval Operations in World War II* by the noted historian Samuel Eliot Morison, which remains so popular that it is now in reprint forty-six years after its initial publication.

———. *The Battle of Savo Island, August 9th, 1942: Strategical and Tactical Analysis.* Unpublished manuscript prepared for the Bureau of Naval Personnel, 1950, now held by the Defense Documentation Center, Defense Logistics Agency, Cameron Station, Alexandria, Virginia, and at other military installations, 377 pages. (Previously classified document.)

———. *Diagrams for The Battle of Savo Island, August 9, 1942: Strategical and Tactical Analysis.* Unpublished manuscript prepared for the Bureau of Naval

Personnel, 1950, now held by the Defense Documentation Center, Defense Logistics Agency, Cameron Station, Alexandria, Virginia, and at other military installations, 29 pages. (Previously classified document.)

Edwards, R.S., Chief of Staff. *Battle Experience from Pearl Harbor to Midway, December 1941 to June 1942, Including Makin Island Raid 17–18 August.* Secret—Declassified DOD Dir 5200.9. Washington, D.C.: Headquarters of the Commander in Chief, Navy Department, Washington, D.C., 15 February 1943, 132 pages.

Karig, Walter, Captain, USNR and Eric Purdon, Commander, USNR. *Battle Report Pacific War: Middle Phases (Prepared from Official Sources).* New York: Rinehart and Company, Inc., 1947, 434 pages.

King, Ernest J., Fleet Admiral, USN. *U.S. Navy at War 1941–1945.* Washington, D.C.: United States Navy Department, 1946, 305 pages.

Office of the Secretary of Defense Weapons Systems Evaluation Group (WSEV) Study No. 4. *Operational Experience of Fast Carrier Task Forces in World War II.* Confidential—Declassified by authority of OJCS Declassification Branch on 17 May 1979. Washington, D.C.: Office of the Secretary of Defense Ser. 385, 15 August 1951, 234 pages. USNWCA: RG-23.

Unidentified Authors. *Combat Narratives: Solomon Islands Campaign—IV Battle of Cape Esperance, 11 October 1942 [and] V Battle of Santa Cruz Islands, 26 October 1942.* Confidential—Declassified DOD Dir 5200.9, for official use only. Washington, D.C.: Publications Branch, Office of Naval Intelligence, United States Navy, 1943, 66 pages.

Unidentified Authors. *Naval Chronology, World War II.* Washington, D.C.: United States Government Printing Office, 1955, 214 pages. Prepared in the Naval History Division, Office of the Chief of Naval Operations, Navy Department.

Books

Agawa, Hiroyuki, translated by John Bester. *The Reluctant Admiral: Yamamoto and the Imperial Navy.* New York: Kodansha International Ltd., 1979, 397 pages.

Annual Report of the Secretary of the Navy for Fiscal Year 1946. Washington, D.C.: United States Government Printing Office, 1947, 77 pages.

Baer, George W. *One Hundred Years of Sea Power: The U.S. Navy, 1890–1990.* Stanford, Calif.: Stanford University Press, 1994, 553 pages.

Bell, Christopher M. *The Royal Navy, Seapower and Strategy Between the Wars.* Stanford, Calif.: Stanford University Press, 2000, 232 pages.

Bell, P.M.H. *The Origins of the Second World War in Europe.* New York: Longman, 1986, 326 pages.

Boyle, John Hunter. *China and Japan at War 1937–1945.* Stanford, Calif.: Stanford University Press, 1972, 430 pages.

Buell, Thomas B. *Master of Sea Power: A Biography of Fleet Admiral Ernest J. King*. Boston, Little, Brown and Company, 1980, 609 pages.

Burns, Eugene. *Then There Was One: The U.S.S.* Enterprise *and the First Year of War.* New York: Harcourt, Brace and Company, 1944, 179 pages.

Bywater, Hector C. *The Great Pacific War: A History of the American Japanese Campaign of 1931–33*. Boston: Houghton Mifflin Company, 1925, 317 pages.

Caidin, Martin. *Zero Fighter.* New York: Ballantine Books, Inc., 1969, 160 pages.

Chihaya, Masatake, translator. *Fading Victory: The Diary of Admiral Matome Ugake, 1941–1945*. Pittsburgh, Pa.: University of Pittsburgh Press, 1991, 731 pages.

Churchill, Winston S. *The Second World War, Volume II: Their Finest Hour*. London: Cassell & Co., Ltd., 1949, 271 pages.

Clausewitz, Karl von. *On War*. Princeton, N.J.: Princeton University Press, 1976.

CMH Pub 104-21. *The German Campaign in Russia: Planning and Operations (1940–1942)*. Washington, D.C.: Center of Military History, United States Army, 1988, 187 pages.

Costello, John. *The Pacific War 1941–1945*. New York: Quill, 1982, 742 pages.

Cutler, Thomas J. *The Battle of Leyte Gulf 23–26 October 1944*. New York: Harper Collins Publishers, 1994, 343 pages.

Dull, Paul S. *A Battle History of The Imperial Japanese Navy (1941–1945)*. Annapolis, Md.: Naval Institute Press, 1978, 402 pages.

Dyer, George Carroll, Vice Admiral, USN (Ret.). *The Amphibians Came to Conquer: The Story of Admiral Richmond Kelly Turner*, Volume I. Washington, D.C.: U.S. Government Printing Office, 1971, 596 pages.

Evans, David C. and Mark R. Peattie. *Kaigun: Strategy, Tactics, and Technology in the Imperial Japanese Navy 1887–1941*. Annapolis, Md.: Naval Institute Press, 1997, 661 pages.

Forrestel, E.P., Vice Admiral, USN (Ret.). *Admiral Raymond A. Spruance, USN: A Study in Command*. Washington, D.C.: U.S. Government Printing Office, 1966, 275 pages.

———. *Annual Report Fiscal Year 1945: The Secretary of the Navy to the President of the United States*. Washington, D.C.: Navy Department of the United States of America, 1945, 143 pages.

Frank, Richard B. *Guadalcanal*. New York: Random House, 1990, 800 pages.

Fuchida, Mitsuo, and Masatake Okumiya. *Midway: The Battle That Doomed Japan, The Japanese Navy's Story*. Edited by Clarke H. Kawakami and Roger Pineau. Annapolis, Md.: Naval Institute Press, 1992, 310 pages.

Gatchel, Theodore L., Colonel, USMC (Ret.). *At the Water's Edge*. Annapolis, Md.: Naval Institute Press, 1996, 266 pages.

Glassford, William A., Captain, USN. *Jutland Decisions,* Ser. No. 32. Newport, RI: Naval War College, December 1930, 92 pages.

Goldstein, Eric and John Maurer. *The Washington Conference, 1921–1922: Naval Rivalry, East Asian Stability and the Road to Pearl Harbor*. Ilford, Essex, U.K.: Frank Cass, 1994, 319 pages.

Gooch, John, ed. *Decisive Campaigns of the Second World War.* London: Frank Cass, 1990, 198 pages.

Greenfield, Kent Roberts. *American Strategy in World War II: A Reconsideration.* Malabar, Fla.: Robert E. Krieger Publishing Company, 1963, 145 pages.

———, ed. *Command Decisions*. CMH Pub 70-7. Washington, D.C.: Center of Military History, United States Army, 1960, 565 pages.

Gunston, Bill, forward by. *Jane's Fighting Aircraft of World War II*. London: Butler & Tanner, Ltd., 1989, 318 pages.

Hagan, Kenneth J. *This People's Navy: The Making of American Sea Power.* New York: The Free Press, 1991, 434 pages.

Halsey, William F., Fleet Admiral, USN. *Admiral Halsey's Story.* New York: McGraw-Hill Book Company, Inc., 1947, 310 pages.

Hammel, Eric. *Carrier Strike: The Battle of the Santa Cruz Islands, October 1942.* Pacifica, Calif.: Pacifica Press, 1999, 409 pages.

Hanson, Victor Davis. *The Western Way of War: Infantry Battle in Classical Greece.* Alfred A. Knopf: New York, 1989.

Harries, Merion, and Susie Harries. *Soldiers of the Sun: The Rise and Fall of the Imperial Japanese Army*. New York: Random House, 1991, 569 pages.

Hata, Ikuhiko and Yasuho Izawa, translated by Don Cyril Gorham. *Japanese Naval Aces and Fighter Units in World War II*. Annapolis, Md.: Naval Institute Press, 1989, 442 pages.

Hattendorf, John B., B. Mitchell Simpson III, and John R. Wadleigh. *Sailors and Scholars: The Centennial History of the U.S. Naval War College*. Newport, R.I.: Naval War College Press, 1984, 354 pages.

Heinrichs, Walso. *Threshold of War: Franklin D. Roosevelt & American Entry into World War II*. New York: Oxford University Press, 1988, 279 pages.

Hone, Thomas C., Norman Friedman, and Mark D. Mandeles. *American and British Aircraft Carrier Development 1919–1941*. Annapolis, Md.: Naval Institute Press, 1999, 248 pages.

Humble, Richard. *United States Fleet Carriers of World War II 'In Action.'* Poole, Dorset UK: Blandford Press, 1984, 160 pages.

Joint Army-Navy Assessment Committee. *Japanese Naval and Merchant Shipping Losses During World War II By All Causes*. Washington, D.C.: U.S. Government Printing Office, 1947, 57 pages.

Karig, Walter, Captain, USNR, and Eric Purdon, Commander, USNR. *Battle Report: Pacific War, Middle Phase*. New York: Rinehart and Company, Inc., 1947, 434 pages.

King, Ernest J., Fleet Admiral, USN. *U.S. Navy at War 1941–1945*. Washington: United States Navy Department, 1946, 305 pages.

Kitchen, Martin. *Europe Between the Wars: A Political History*. New York: Longman, 1988. 350 pages.

Larrabee, Eric. *Commander in Chief*. New York: Harper & Row, Publishers, 1987, 723 pages.

Lewis, Winston B., Ensign, USNR, and Henry A. Mustin, Lieutenant Junior Grade, USNR. *The Battle of Savo Island 9 August 1942 and the Eastern Solomons 23–25 August 1942*. Washington, D.C.: Naval Historical Center, Department of the Navy, 1943 (Republished in 1994), Combat Narratives Series, Solomon Islands campaign, 81 pages.

Liddell Hart, B.H. *History of the Second World War*. New York: Perigee Books, 1982, 768 pages.

Linn, Brian M. *Guardians of Empire: The U.S. Army and the Pacific, 1902–1940*. Chapel Hill, N.C.: University of North Carolina Press, 343 pages.

Lockwood, Charles A., Vice Admiral, USN (Ret.), and Hans Christian Adamson, Colonel, USAF (Ret.). *Battle of the Philippine Sea*. New York: Thomas Y. Crowell Company, 1967, 229 pages.

Loxton, Bruce, with Chris Coulthard-Clark. *The Shame of Savo: Anatomy of a Naval Disaster*. Annapolis, Md.: Naval Institute Press, 1994, 319 pages.

Lundstrom, John B. *The First Team: Pacific Naval Air Combat from Pearl Harbor to Midway*. Annapolis, Md.: Naval Institute Press, 1984, 547 pages.

———. *The First Team and the Guadalcanal Campaign: Naval Fighter Combat from August to November 1942*. Annapolis, Md.: Naval Institute Press, 1994, 626 pages.

———. *The First South Pacific Campaign: Pacific Fleet Strategy December 1941–June 1942*. Annapolis, Md.: Naval Institute Press, 1976, 240 pages.

Mahan, Alfred Thayer. *The Influence of Sea Power Upon History 1660–1783*. New York: Dover Publications, Inc., 1987, 557 pages. Original publication by Little, Brown and Company of Boston in 1890.

McDonald, J. Kenneth, Ernest J. King, chair of Maritime History, U.S. Naval War College. *The Second World War in the Pacific: Plans and Reality*. National Maritime Museum, Grenwich, London SE10 9NF, *Maritime Monographs and Reports No. 9-1974*. Newport, R.I.: Naval War College, 1974, 19 pages. USNWCA: RG-37.

McMurtrie, Francis E., A.I.N.A., editor. *Jane's Fighting Ships 1938* (Issued December 1938). London: Sampson Low, Marston & Co., Ltd., 1938, 541 pages.

———. *Jane's Fighting Ships 1939* (Issued November 1939). London: Sampson Low, Marston & Co., Ltd., 1939, 543 pages.

———. *Jane's Fighting Ships 1940* (Issued January 1941). London: Sampson Low, Marston & Co., Ltd., 1940, 527 pages.

———. *Jane's Fighting Ships 1941* (Issued 1942). New York: The Macmillan Company, 1942, 530 pages.

Merrill, James M. *A Sailor's Admiral: A Biography of William F. Halsey.* New York: Thomas Y. Crowell Company, 1976.

Messenger, Charles. *The Chronological Atlas of World War Two.* New York: Macmillan Publishing Company, 1989, 255 pages.

Miller, Edward S. *War Plan Orange.* Annapolis, Md.: Naval Institute Press, 1991, 509 pages.

Millot, Bernard A. *The Battle of the Coral Sea.* Annapolis, Md.: Naval Institute Press, 1974, 166 pages.

Morison, Samuel Eliot. *History of United States Naval Operations in World War II.* Fifteen volumes. Edison, NJ: Castle Books, 2001.

Morison, Samuel Eliot. *Coral Sea, Midway and Submarine Actions May 1942–August 1942*, in *History of United States Naval Operations in World War II*, Vol. IV. New York: Little, Brown and Company, 1949, 296 pages.

———. *The Struggle for Guadalcanal and the Marianas August 1944–February 1943*, *History of United States Naval Operations in World War II*, Vol. VI. New York: Little, Brown and Company, 1949, 389 pages.

———. *Breaking the Bismarcks Barrier 22 July 1942–1 May 1944*, in *History of United States Naval Operations in World War II*, Vol. VI. New York: Little, Brown and Company, 1950, 463 pages.

———. *New Guinea and the Marianas March 1944–August 1944*, in *History of United States Naval Operations in World War II*, Vol. VII. New York: Little, Brown and Company, 1949, 435 pages.

———. *The Two-Ocean War.* New York: Galahad Books, 1963, 611 pages.

Murray, Williamson. *The Change in the European Balance of Power, 1938–1939.* Princeton, N.J.: Princeton University Press, 1984, 494 pages.

Murray, Williamson and Allan R. Millett. *A War to be Won: Fighting the Second World War 1937–1945.* Uncorrected page proof, Harvard University Press, 2000, 640 pages.

———. *Strategy for Defeat: The Luftwaffe 1933–1945.* Maxwell Air Force Base, Ala.: Air University Press, 1983, 365 pages.

——— and Allan R. Millett. *Calculations: Net Assessment and the Coming of World War II.* New York: The Free Press, 1992, 353 pages.

Nagumo, Chuichi, Admiral, Imperial Japanese Navy, Commander in Chief, First Air Fleet. *The Japanese Story of the Battle of Midway* (A Translation). OPNAV P32-1002, Office of Naval Intelligence, United States Navy, June 1947, p. 6. Department of the Navy – Naval Historical Center, 805 Kidder Breese SE – Washington Navy Yard, Washington D.C. 20374-5060. This document can be accessed over the Internet at: http://www.history.navy.mil/library/special/midway/midway.htm.

National Maritime Museum (author not listed). *The Second World War in the Pacific: Plans and Reality*, Maritime Monographs and Reports No. 9-1974. Greenwich, London: National Maritime Museum, 1974, 49 pages.

Naval Chronology, World War II. Washington, D.C.: United States Government Printing Office, 1955, 214 pages.

The Navy Department: Duties and Functions of Its Bureaus. Annapolis, Md.: United States Naval Academy, 1913, 163 pages.

Newcomb, Richard F. *Savo: The Incredible Naval Debacle off Guadalcanal.* New York: Holt, Rinehart and Winston, 1961, 278 pages.

Offner, Arnold A. *The Origins of the Second World War: American Foreign Policy and World Politics, 1917–1941.* Malabar, FL: Robert E. Krieger Publishing Company, 1986, 268 pages.

Okumiya, Masatake, and Jiro Horikoshi. *Zero!* New York: E.P. Dutton & Co., Inc., 1956, 424 pages.

Parkes, Oscar, O.B.E., M.B., Ch.B., and Francis E. McMurtrie, A.I.N.A., joint editors. *Jane's Fighting Ships 1924.* London: Sampson Low, Marston & Co., Ltd., 1924, 424 pages.

———. *Jane's Fighting Ships 1926.* London: Sampson Low, Marston & Co., Ltd., 1926, 448 pages.

———. *Jane's Fighting Ships 1930.* London: Sampson Low, Marston & Co., Ltd., 1930, 450 pages.

Parkes, Oscar, O.B.E., M.B., Ch.B. *Jane's Fighting Ships 1933.* London: Sampson Low, Marston & Co., Ltd., 1933, 528 pages.

———. *Jane's Fighting Ships 1934* (Issued December, 1934). London: Sampson Low, Marston & Co., Ltd., 1933, 531 pages.

———. *Jane's Fighting Ships 1943–4* (Issued 1944). New York: The Macmillan Company, 1944.

Peattie, Mark R. *Sunburst: The Rise of Japanese Naval Air Power 1909–1941.* Annapolis, Md.: Naval Institute Press, 2001, 312 pages.

Polmar, Norman, in collaboration with General Minoru Genda, Japanese Air Self-Defense Force, Captain Eric M. Brown, O.B.E., Royal Navy, and Professor Robert M. Langdon, U.S. Naval Academy. *Aircraft Carriers: A Graphic History of Carrier Aviation and Its Influence on World Events.* Garden City, New York: Doubleday & Company, Inc., 1969, 785 pages.

Poor, Henry V., Ensign, USNR, Henry V. Mustin, Lieutenant Junior Grade, USNR, and Colin G. Jamison, Lieutenant Junior Grade, USNR. *The Battles of Cape Esperance 11 October 19422 and Santa Cruz Islands 26 October 1942.* Washington, D.C.: Naval Historical Center, Department of the Navy, Washington, D.C.: Naval Historical Center, Department of the Navy, 1943 (Republished in 1994), Combat Narratives Series, Solomon Islands campaign, 4-5, 80 pages.

Potter, E.B. *Nimitz.* Annapolis, Md.: Naval Institute Press, 1976, 507 pages.

———. *Bull Halsey*. Annapolis, Md.: Naval Institute Press, 1988, 421 pages.

Potter, E.B., and Chester W. Nimitz, editors. *Sea Power: A Naval History.* Englewood Cliffs, New Jersey: Prentice-Hall, Inc., 1960, 932 pages.

Potter, John Deane. *Yamamoto: The Man Who Menaced America.* New York: Viking Press, 1965, 332 pages.

Prados, John. *Combined Fleet Decoded: The Secret History of American Intelligence and the Japanese Navy in World War II.* New York: Random House, 1995.

Prange, Gordon W., Donald M. Goldstein and Katherine V. Dillon. *Miracle at Midway.* New York: McGraw-Hill Book Company, 1982, 469 pages.

Puleston, W.D., Captain, USN. *The Armed Forces of the Pacific: A Comparison of the Military and Naval Power of the Unites States and Japan.* New Haven, Conn.: Yale University Press, 1941, 273 pages.

Register of the Alumni, Graduates and Former Naval Cadets and Midshipmen, United States Naval Academy Alumni Association, Inc., 1845–1985. Annapolis, Md.: United States Naval Academy Alumni Association, publishers, 1985 edition.

Reynolds, Clark G. *The Carrier War.* Alexandria, Va: Time-Life Books, 1982, 176 pages.

———. *Admiral John H. Towers: The Struggle for Naval Air Supremacy.* Annapolis, Md.: Naval Institute Press, 1989, 676 pages.

———. *War in the Pacific.* New York: Military Press, Archive Publishing, Ltd., 1990, 160 pages.

Roberts, J. M. *Europe 1880–1945.* Second Edition. New York: Longman, 1967, 1989, 631 pages.

Sakai, Saburo, with Martin Caidin and Fred Saito. *Samurai!* New York: ibooks, Distributed by Simon and Schuster, Inc., 2001, 382 pages.

Slim, Field Marshal the Viscount. *Defeat into Victory.* New York: David McKay Company, Inc., 1963, 468 pages.

Spector, Ronals H. *Eagle Against the Sun.* New York: The Free Press, 1985, 589 pages.

Stalin, Joseph (Ministry of Foreign Affairs of the U.S.S.R.). *Stalin's Correspondence with Churchill and Attlee 1941–1945* New York: Capricorn Books, 1965, 401 pages.

Storry, Richard. *The Double Patriots: A Study of Japanese Nationalism.* Westport, Connecticut: Greenwood Press, Publishers, 1973, 335 pages.

Thorn, Christopher. *Allies of a Kind: The United States, Britain, and the War Against Japan, 1941–1945.* New York: Oxford University Press, 1978, 772 pages.

United States Strategic Bombing Survey, Naval Analysis Division. Interrogation of Captain Watanabe, Imperial Japanese Navy, Commander in Chief Combined Fleet Log—Coral Sea Action, 8 May 1942.

United States Strategic Bombing Survey. Interrogation of Captain Yamaoka, Imperial Japanese Navy Operations Officer, Staff, 5th Air Flotilla, Naval Analysis Interrogation of Japanese Officials: Volume I–Interrogation, Naval No. 10.

Vlahos, Michael. *The Blue Sword: The Naval War College and the American Mission, 1919–1941*. Newport, R.I.: Naval War College Press, 1980, 214 pages.

Ware, Leonard, Lieutenant, USNR. *The Landing in the Solomons 7–8 August 1942*. Washington, D.C.: Naval Historical Center, Department of the Navy, 1943 (Republished in 1994), Combat Narratives Series, Solomon Islands campaign, 1, 101 pages.

Warner, Denis, and Peggy Warner, with Sadao Seno. *Disaster in the Pacific: New Light on the Battle of Savo Island*. Annapolis, Md.: Naval Institute Press, 1992, 298 pages.

Warren, Mame and Marion E. Warren. *Everybody Works But John Paul Jones: A Portrait of the U.S. Naval Academy, 1845–1915*. Annapolis, Md.: Naval Institute Press, 1981, 121 pages.

Watt, Donald Cameron. *How War Came: The Immediate Origins of the Second World War 1938–1939*. New York: Pantheon Books, 1989, 736 pages.

Weinberg, Gerhard L. *A World at Arms*. Cambridge, UK: Cambridge University Press, 1994, 1178 pages.

Willmott, H.P. *The Great Crusade*. New York: The Free Press, 1989, 500 pages.

———. *Empires in the Balance: Japanese and Allied Pacific Strategies to April 1942*. Annapolis, Md.: Naval Institute Press, 1982, 487 pages.

———. *The Barrier and the Javelin: Japanese and Allied Pacific Strategies February to June 1942*. Annapolis, Md.: Naval Institute Press, 1983, 595 pages.

———, edited by John Keegan. *The Second World War in the Far East*. London: Cassell & Co., 1999, 224 pages.

Archival Documents

Auphaill, F. Navy Department, Bureau of Navigation letter serial Nav-313-UB dated 18 August 1930. Admiral Frank Jack Fletcher Collection, Correspondence File 1930–1932, Box 1, Folder 15, American Heritage Center, University of Wyoming, Laramie, Wyo.

Bureau of Navigation letter No. 6132-1 of 13 February 1908. Admiral Frank Jack Fletcher Collection, Box 1, Folder 2, Bibliographical File, American Heritage Center, University of Wyoming, Laramie, Wyo.

Bureau of Navigation, Navy Department letter No. 6132-17 of 31 July 1911. Admiral Frank Jack Fletcher Collection, Box 1, Folder 2, Bibliographical File, American Heritage Center, University of Wyoming, Laramie, Wyo.

Bureau of Navigation, Navy Department letter No. 6132-23 of 6 March 1912. Admiral Frank Jack Fletcher Collection, Correspondence File, Box 1, Folder 6, American Heritage Center, University of Wyoming, Laramie, Wyo.

Chandler, W.D., Jr. Navy Department, Bureau of Navigation letter serial N221-DBB, dated 23 October 1920. Admiral Frank Jack Fletcher Collection, Correspondence File 1918–1920, Box 1, Folder 9, American Heritage Center, University of Wyoming, Laramie, Wyo.

Chief of the Bureau of Medicine and Surgery letter to Cdr. Frank Jack Fletcher dated 13 March 1928. Admiral Frank Jack Fletcher Collection, Correspondence File 1927–1928, Box 1, Folder 13, American Heritage Center, University of Wyoming, Laramie, Wyo.

Daniels, Josephus [Secretary of the Navy]. Navy Department letter of commendation dated 12 June 1914 to Lt. F.J. Fletcher via Commander in Chief, Atlantic Fleet. Admiral Frank Jack Fletcher Collection, Correspondence File 1914, Box 1, Folder 7, American Heritage Center, University of Wyoming, Laramie, Wyo.

Daniels, Josephus [Secretary of the Navy]. Navy Department letter to Cdr. Frank J. Fletcher serial N-32/FJS-LL dated October 29, 1918. Admiral Frank Jack Fletcher Collection, Correspondence File 1918–1920, Box 1, Folder 9, American Heritage Center, University of Wyoming, Laramie, Wyo.

Daniels, Josephus [Secretary of the Navy]. Secretary of the Navy citation on behalf of the president awarding the Navy Cross to Cdr. Frank J. Fletcher, USN. for service in the world war dated 11 November 1920. Admiral Frank Jack Fletcher Collection, Correspondence File 1918–1920, Box 1, Folder 9, American Heritage Center, University of Wyoming, Laramie, Wyo.

Eberle, E.W. [Secretary of the Navy]. Navy Department letter of 19 January 1916 to Lt. Frank J. Fletcher; "Subj: Medal of Honor." Admiral Frank Jack Fletcher Collection, Correspondence File 1915–1916, Box 1, Folder 8, American Heritage Center, University of Wyoming, Laramie, Wyo.

Admiral Frank Jack Fletcher Collection, Biographical Sketch, Box 1, Folder 2, Bibliographical File, American Heritage Center, University of Wyoming, Laramie, Wyo.

Fletcher, Frank Jack, letter from USS *Kearsage* to Admiral Winslow dated April 18, 1917. Admiral Frank Jack Fletcher Collection, Correspondence File 1915–1916, Box 1, Folder 8, American Heritage Center, University of Wyoming, Laramie, Wyo.

———. U.S. Navy letter from San Diego, Calif., dated 11 October 1928. Admiral Frank Jack Fletcher Collection, Correspondence File 1927–1928, Box 1, Folder 13, American Heritage Center, University of Wyoming, Laramie, Wyo.

Admiral Frank Jack Fletcher Collection, Correspondence File 1935–1936, Box 1, Folder 17, American Heritage Center, University of Wyoming, Laramie, Wyo.

Fletcher, Frank Jack. Commander North Pacific Force, United States Pacific Fleet, letter to Captain [Samuel Eliot] Morison (undated). Admiral Frank Jack Fletcher Collection, Correspondence File 1930–1932, Box 1, Folder 26, American Heritage Center, University of Wyoming, Laramie, Wyo.

Leigh, R.H. Navy Department, Bureau of Navigation letter serial Nav-31-R of 2 January 1929. Admiral Frank Jack Fletcher Collection, Correspondence File 1930–1932, Box 1, Folder 15, American Heritage Center, University of Wyoming, Laramie, Wyo.

Leigh, R.H. Navy Department, Bureau of Navigation letter serial Nav-3-P dated 21 February 1930. Admiral Frank Jack Fletcher Collection, Correspondence File 1930–1932, Box 1, Folder 15, American Heritage Center, University of Wyoming, Laramie, Wyo.

The Lucky Bag 1906. Annapolis, Md.: U.S. Naval Academy. Vol. XIII, p. 82. Vol. XIII, p. 82. Excerpt from the United States Naval Academy yearbook for 1906, Admiral Frank Jack Fletcher Collection, Box 1, Folder 2, Bibliographical File, American Heritage Center, University of Wyoming, Laramie, Wyo.

Morison, Samuel Eliot. Letter to Vice Adm. Frank Jack Fletcher, USN (Ret.), dated 22 November 1947. Admiral Frank Jack Fletcher Collection, Correspondence File 1930–1932, Box 1, Folder 26, American Heritage Center, University of Wyoming, Laramie, Wyo.

Sims, William Sowden, Admiral, USN. U.S. Naval Forces Operating in European Waters letter, Reference No. S 1 17102, dated 11 May 1918. Admiral Frank Jack Fletcher Collection, Correspondence File 1918–1920, Box 1, Folder 9, American Heritage Center, University of Wyoming, Laramie, Wyo.

Williams, C.S., President, U.S. Naval War College. Naval War College, Newport, R.I., letter serial 444 Cl-ma dated 18 July 1924. Admiral Frank Jack Fletcher Collection, Correspondence File 1924–1926, Box 1, Folder 12, American Heritage Center, University of Wyoming, Laramie, Wyo.

Government Records/Documents

Annual Report of the Secretary of the Navy—Fiscal Year 1946.

Army-Navy Game football program dated 29 November 1941, p. 181. Records of the U.S. Naval Academy Archives.

Campaign Plan for Operations of the Pacific Ocean Areas, 1944 GRANITE. Headquarters of the Commander in Chief, United States Pacific Fleet and Pacific Ocean Areas, 13 January 1944.

Col. William Mitchell, Air Service, Trial by General Court-Martial, Washington, D.C., 18 November 1925, Volume 12, 168771, Alexander H. Galt Official Reporter, 715 Woodward Building, Washington, D.C., sections 1018-1147. College Park, Md.: National Archives No. II, Box 9214-2.

Col. William Mitchell, Air Service, Trial by General Court-Martial, Washington, D.C., 18 November 1925, Volume 12, 168771, Alexander H. Galt Official Reporter, 715 Woodward Building, Washington, D.C., sections 2062-2096 and 2570-2585. College Park, Md.: National Archives No. II, Box 9214-3.

General Courts Martial, William Mitchell Case Records, 1925 (Case No. 168771). RG 153, Records of the Office of the Judge Advocate General (Army). Col. William Mitchell, Air Service, Trial by General Court-Martial, Washington, D.C., 18 November 1925, Volume 12, 168771, Alexander H. Galt Official Reporter, 715 Woodward Building, Washington, D.C. College Park, Md.: National Archives No. II, Box No. 9214-2, section 1018–1147.

General Courts Martial, William Mitchell Case Records, 1925 (Case No. 168771). RG 153, Records of the Office of the Judge Advocate General (Army). Col. William Mitchell, Air Service, Trial by General Court-Martial, Washington, D.C., 18 November 1925, Volume 12, 168771, Alexander H. Galt Official Reporter, 715 Woodward Building, Washington, D.C. College Park, Md.: National Archives No. II, Box No. 9214-4, section 2570–2585.

Kalbfus, E.C., Rear Admiral, USN (Ret.). *Sound Military Decision.* Restricted—Unclassified—REF: ALNAV 59-53 12/15/53. Newport, R.I.: U.S. Naval War College, September 21, 1942, 243 pages. USNWCA: RG –

Kimmel, Husband E., Rear Admiral, USN (Ret.). Statement before the Joint Committee on the Investigation of the Pearl Harbor Attack, Senate Congressional Resolution 27. Confidential—Released for publication on appearance of Rear Admiral Kimmel before the Committee. Laramie, Wyoming: American Heritage Foundation Archives, File Group 76, Box 2, 108 pages.

Knox, Frank, Secretary of the Navy. Board to Study the Methods of Educating Naval Officers, designation of Rear Admiral. William S. Pye as President, 3 Mar 1944. USNWCA: RG – 28.

Oexle, A.W. Air Intelligence Group Message "The Air War Against Japan 1–15 February 1945, Serial 579 dtd 28 February 1945. Secret: Unclassified by Authority NND0968133/KW Nara Date 12/19. College Park, Md.: National Archives No. II.

Records Relating to United States Navy Fleet Problems I to XXII, 1923–1941. National Archives Microfilm Publication. Washington: National Archives and Records Service, General Services Administration, 1975.

Register of Officers 1884–1977, The United States Naval War College. Forward dated 11 July 1977. USNWCA: RG-27.

Rhodes, James B., archivist of the United States. *Records Relating to United States Navy Fleet Problems I to XXII 1923–1941.* National Archives No. 1 (NA-1), Records of the Office of the Chief of Naval Operations Record Group 38; General Records of the Department of the Navy Record Group 80; and Records of Naval Operating Forces Record Group 313.

Sound Military Decision. U.S. Naval War College, Newport, R.I., 1942, copy 3394. Declassified Ref: ALNav 59-53 of 12/15/53.

Smith, W. W., Captain, USN. Survey of the Curriculum of the United States Naval Academy. Annapolis: United States Naval Academy Department of Mathematics, 1 April 1939, 13 pages. U.S. Naval Academy Archives (hereafter USNAA).

Stearns, Robert L., Chairman; Dwight D. Eisenhower, General of the Army, Vice Chairman; James P. Baxter, Frederick A. Middlebush, George D. Stoddard, Edward L. Moreland, Bryant El Moore, Major General, USA, James L. Holloway, Rear Admiral, and David M. Schlatter, Major General, USAD, members. *A Report And Recommendation To The Secretary of Defense by the Service Academy Board.* Department of Defense, January 1950. USNAA.

United States v. War Department: Trial by General Courts Martial in the case of Colonel William Mitchell, Air Service, "Opinion of the Board of Review, Taylor, Abbott and Korn, Judge Advocates," dated 20 January 1926, p. 1. Record Group (hereafter "RG") 153, Records of the Office of the Judge Advocate General (Army), Box No. 9214-2, Folder 1. National Archives of the United States of America, NA-2, College Park, Md.

United States vs. Colonel William Mitchell, Air Service. "Opinion of the Board of Review, Taylor, Abbott and Korn, Judge Advocates." War Department, in the office of the Judge Advocate General, Washington, D.C., 20 January 1926, 82 pages. College Park, Md.: National Archives No. II, Box 9214-1.

Watters, James E., Commander, USNR, Walt Johnson, Commander, USNR, and Mel Chaloupka, Captain, USNR (Lt. Cdr. Christopher Haskell, USNR, ed.). *U.S. Naval Reserve: The First 75 Years.* Newport, R.I.: United States Naval War College Center for Naval Warfare Studies, Advanced Concepts Department, 30 September 1992.

Yarnell, H.E., Rear Admiral, USN, Commander Aircraft, Battle Force. *Operations of the Blue Air Force in Grand Joint Exercise No. 4, 1–12 February 1932,* from Commander Aircraft, Battle Force, dated 27 February 1932. USNWCA: RG-8, Box 61, Folder 3.

Yarnell, H.E. First Endorsement on Umpire Reports, Grand Joint Exercise No. 4, dated 16 February 1932. USNWCA: RG-8, Box 61, Folder 3.

Interviews

Daniels, James Granson, Captain, USN (Ret.), participant as fighter pilot in all carrier battles of World War II except the Battle of Midway, 18 February 2002, Honolulu, Hawaii.

Linn, Brian M. Conversations with Douglas V. Smith regarding Grand Joint Exercise No. 4 held in Luce Hall, Room 123, at the Naval War College on Thursday, 17 June 2004.

Lundstrom, John B., author of *The First Team* and *The First Team and the Guadalcanal Campaign*. Conversations with Douglas V. Smith regarding the research on National Archives No. 2, CINCPAC Secret and Confidential Message File, Record Group 313, he has completed for his forthcoming book on Adm. Frank Jack Fletcher and his decisions at the battles of Coral Sea, Midway, and the Eastern Solomons, via phone on Friday, 19 November 2004.

———, and Prof. Emeritus Frank Snyder. Conversations with Douglas V. Smith conducted at the Reading Room in Newport, Rhode Island, on Thursday, 13 January 2005.

Miller, Edward S. Conversations with Douglas V. Smith regarding Navy policy on aircraft carriers, aircraft, and their roles in naval combat in the 1920s and 1930s held in Luce Hall, Room 123, at the Naval War College on Thursday, 4 December 2003.

Nofi, Albert A., Ph.D., senior analyst, Center for Naval Analyses. Conversations with Douglas V. Smith regarding Grand Joint Exercise No. 4 of 1–12 February, 1932, and United States Navy Fleet Problems I through XXII conducted between 1923 and 1941 in Sims Hall, at the Naval War College on Thursday, 1 September 2004.

Journal Articles

Blee, Ben W., Captain, USN (Ret.). "Whodunnit?" Annapolis, Md.: United States Naval Institute Proceedings, July 1982, 5 pages.

Buell, Thomas B., Commander, USN. "Admiral Edward C. Kalbfus and the Navy Planner's 'Holy Scripture': *Sound Military Decision.*" Newport, R.I.: Naval War College Press. In *Naval War College Review*, Volume XXV, Number 5/Sequence Number 243, May–June 1973, pp. 31–40.

Butcher, Marvin E., Lieutenant Commander, USN. "Admiral Frank Jack Fletcher, Pioneer Warrior or Gross Sinner?" In *Naval War College Review*, Winter 1987.

Cullen, Charles W., USN. "From the Kriegsacademie to the Naval War College: The Military Planning Process," a lecture delivered at the Naval War College. Newport, R.I.: *Naval War College Review*, March 1971, pp. 52–63.

Fleming, Thomas. "Early Warning: February 7, 1932, A Date That Would Live In . . . Amnesia." *American Heritage*, July/August 2001.

Hone, Trent. "The Evolution of Fleet Tactical Doctrine in the U.S. Navy, 1922–1941." *The Journal of Military History*, 67 (October 2003), pp. 1107–48.

Knox, Dudley W., Lieutenant Commander, USN. "The Role of Doctrine in Naval Warfare," Prize Essay, 1915. Annapolis, Md.: United States Naval Institute Proceedings, Vol. 41, No. 2, March–April, 1915, 40 pages.

Polmar, Norman and Thomas B. Allen. "Invasion Most Costly." Naval Institute *Proceedings*, August 1994, pp. 51–56.

Wildenberg, Thomas. "Midway: Sheer Luck or Better Doctrine?" in *Naval War College Review*. Newport, R.I.: Naval War College Press, Volume 58, Number 1 (Winter 2005).

Lectures

Best, Richard "Dick" Halsey, Lieutenant Commander, USN (Ret.). Videotaped lecture entitled "Battle of Midway Strikes" presented as part of a series of lectures commemorating The Battle of Midway, Tape 4, 17 May 2001. Monterey, Calif.: Dudley Knox Library of the Naval Postgraduate School, 17 May 2001.

Frost, H.H., Lieutenant Commander, USN. "The North Sea Operations of April 1916: A Study of Naval Strategy." Newport, R.I.: Naval War College, 5 August 1926, 35 pages. Confidential–Declassified IAW DOD Memo 3 May 1972, "Subj: Declassification of WW II Records." USNWCA: RG-15.

Lundstrom, John B. Lecture entitled "The Role of the Aircraft Carrier in Pacific Fleet Strategy from Pearl Harbor to Guadalcanal" delivered at the Naval War College for elective WE-576, "World War II in the Pacific Theater," Prof. Douglas V. Smith, Chairman's Classroom, Thursday, 13 January 2005.

Lundstrom, John B. Lecture entitled "Frank Jack Fletcher: Black Shoe Carrier Admiral" given Thursday, 13 January 2005, for elective course WE-576, "World War II in the Pacific Theater," Prof. Douglas V. Smith in Chairman's Classroom, room C-138, U.S. Naval War College.

Martinez, Daniel, historian of the USS *Arizona* Memorial. "Forgotten Images of Pearl Harbor." Lecture given in Chairman's Classroom, Connolly Hall, U.S. Naval War College, Thursday 11 March 2004 to elective course of Prof. Douglas V. Smith entitled "World War II in the Pacific Theater."

Pye, William S., Captain, USN. "War Plans." Lecture delivered at the Naval War College, 7 January 1926. Secret–Declassified IAW memo of 3 May 1972, "Subj: Declassification of WW II Records." Newport, R.I.: Naval War College, 12 January 1926, 29 pages. USNWCA: RG-15.

Spruance, Raymond A., Admiral (then captain), USN. "The Nature of Naval Warfare" (presentation). Restricted—Declassified IAW DOD memo of 3 May 1972: "Subj: Declassification of WW II Records." Newport, R.I.: Naval War College, 7 July 1937, 23 pages. USNWCA: RG-14.

Spruance, Raymond A., Admiral, USN. Untitled address on the war in the Pacific delivered before the Royal United Service Institution, 30 October 1946. Newport, R.I.: Naval War College, 31 pages. USNWCA: RG-28.

Letters

Fletcher, Frank Jack, Vice Admiral, USN, Commander North Pacific Force, United States Pacific Fleet. Letter (1947, undated) responding to Capt. Samuel Eliot Morison's letter dated 22 November 1947, indicating that Admiral Fletcher had "automatically assumed command of all the task forces" when the USS *Yorktown* arrived on the eve of the battle of Midway. Admiral Frank Jack Fletcher Collection, Box 1, Folder 26, American Heritage Center, University of Wyoming, Laramie, Wyo.

Morison, Samuel Eliot, Captain, USN. Letter to Adm. Frank Jack Fletcher, USN (Ret.) at "Araby," La Plata, Md., dated 22 November 1947 requesting clarification from Admiral Fletcher on whether he or Admiral Spruance was in command (O.T.C.: Officer in Tactical Command) at the Battle of Midway on 4 June 1942, to clarify for publication of *The History of United States Naval Operations in World War II*. Admiral Frank Jack Fletcher Collection, Box 1, Folder 26, American Heritage Center, University of Wyoming, Laramie, Wyo.

Nimitz, Chester W., Fleet Admiral, USN. Letter to Vice Adm. Charles Melson, president of the United States Naval War College, dated 19 September 1965 on display in McCarty-Little Hall at the U.S. Naval War College, Newport, R.I.

Sims, William S., Rear Admiral, USN. Letter from the president of the United States Naval War College to Mr. Frederic W. Wile concerning the relative merits of battleships and aircraft carriers in battle. 77 Rhode Island Avenue, Newport, R. I., October 16, 1924. USNWCA: MS-Item 240.

Uhlig, Frank Jr. Letter to historian Edward S. Miller dated 10 December 2004.

Microfilm

The Battle of the Coral Sea

Buckmaster, E., Captain, USN. Commanding Officer, USS *Yorktown* letter to Commander in Chief, United States Pacific Fleet dated May 11, 1942, "Subj: Attack made by Yorktown Air Group on Enemy Forces in Tulagi and Gavutu Harbors." Naval War College Microfilm Collection reel A39, first frame 41078. (Previously classified document.)

———. Commanding Officer, USS *Yorktown* letter to Commander in Chief, United States Pacific Fleet dated 16 May 1942, "Subj: Air Operations of Yorktown Air Group against Japanese Forces in the vicinity of the Louisade Archipelago on May 7, 1942." Naval War College Microfilm Collection reel A39, first frame 41078. (Previously classified document.)

———. Commanding Officer, USS *Yorktown* letter to Commander in Chief, United States Pacific Fleet dated 25 May 1942, "Subj: Report of action of Yorktown and

Yorktown Air Group on May 8, 1942." Naval War College Microfilm Collection reel A39, first frame 41078. (Previously classified document.)

———. *War Diary, Commander Task Force Eleven (Commander Carrier Division One)* dated 31 May 1942. Commanding Officer, USS *Yorktown* letter to Commander in Chief, United States Pacific Fleet dated 25 May 1942. Naval War College Microfilm Collection reel A39, first frame 41078. (Previously classified document.)

Fitch, Aubrey W., Rear Admiral, USN. *War Diary, Commander Task Force Eleven (Commander Carrier Division One)* dated 31 May 1942. Commander Task Group 17.5 Action Report, letter to Commander Task Force 17 dated 18 May 1942. Naval War College Microfilm Collection reel A39, first frame 41078. (Previously classified document.)

———. Commander Task Group 17.5 (Commander Carrier Division One) letter to Commander Task Force 17 dated 18 May 1942: Action Report—Coral Sea—May 7–8, 1942. Naval War College Microfilm Collection reel A39, first frame 41078. (Previously classified document.)

———. Commander Task Force 17 Operation Order No. 2-42, dated 1 May 1942. Naval War College Microfilm Collection reel A39, first frame 41078. (Previously classified document.)

Fletcher, Frank Jack, Rear Admiral, USN. Commander Task Force 17 letter to Commander in Chief, United States Fleet, dated 27 May 1942, "Subj: The Battle of the Coral Sea, May 4–8, 1942." Naval War College Microfilm Collection reel A39, starting frame 41078. (Previously classified document.)

Seligman, M.T., Commander, USN. Executive Officer, USS *Lexington* letter to Commanding Officer, USS *Lexington* dated 14 May 1942, "Subj: Action in the Coral Sea, May 8, 1942—report of." Naval War College Microfilm Collection reel A39, first frame 41078. (Previously classified document.)

Sherman, Frederick C. *War Diary, Commander Task Force Eleven (Commander Carrier Division One)* dated 31 May 1942. Commanding Officer, USS *Lexington* Report of Action, letter to Commander in Chief, United States Pacific Fleet dated 15 May 1942. Naval War College Microfilm Collection reel A39, first frame 41078. (Previously classified document.)

———. Commanding Officer, USS *Lexington* letter to the Secretary of the Navy dated 18 May 1942, "Subj: Action in the Coral Sea, May 8, 1942, report of." Naval War College Microfilm Collection reel A39, first frame 41078. (Previously classified document.)

The Battle of Midway

Buckmaster, E[lliott]., Captain, USN. Commanding Officer, USS *Yorktown* letter to Commander in Chief, United States Pacific Fleet, "Subj: Report of Action for June

4, 1942, and June 6, 1942, dated 18 June 1042." Naval War College Microfilm Collection reel A55, first frame 41571. (Previously classified document.)

Dubose, L.T., Captain, USN. Commanding Officer, USS *Portland* letter to Commander in Chief, United States Pacific Fleet, "Subj: Action Report dated June 11, 1942." Naval War College Microfilm Collection reel A55, first frame 41571. (Previously classified document.)

Fletcher, Frank Jack, Rear Admiral, USN. Commander Cruisers, Pacific Fleet letter to Commander in Chief, United States Pacific Fleet, "Subj: Report of Action, June 4, 1942, dated 11 June 1942." Naval War College Microfilm Collection reel A55, first frame 41571. (Previously classified document.)

———. Commander Cruisers, Pacific Fleet letter to Commander in Chief, United States Pacific Fleet, "Subj: Battle of Midway, dated 14 June 1942." Naval War College Microfilm Collection reel A55, first frame 41571. (Previously classified document.)

———. Commander Task Force 17 letter to Commander in Chief, United States Pacific Fleet, "Subj: Battle of Midway—Forwarding of Reports," dated 26 June 1942. Naval War College Microfilm Collection reel A55, first frame 41571. (Previously classified document.)

Hoover, Gilbert C., Commander, USN. Commander Task Group 17.4 (Commander Destroyer squadron 2) letter to Commander in Chief, United States Fleet, "Subj: Report of Action, June 4, 1942, dated 4 June 1942." Naval War College Microfilm Collection reel A55, first frame 41571. (Previously classified document.)

Jarrett, H.B., Lieutenant Commander, USN. Commanding Officer, USS *Morris* letter to Commander in Chief, United States Fleet, "Subj: Midway Island Action of June 4, 1942—Report of, dated June 13, 1942." Naval War College Microfilm Collection reel A55, first frame 41571. (Previously classified document.)

Loomis, D.W., Captain, USN. Commanding Officer, USS *Pensacola* letter to Commander in Chief, United States Pacific Fleet, "Subj: Report of Engagement with Enemy Aircraft on June 4, 1942." Naval War College Microfilm Collection reel A55, first frame 41571. (Previously classified document.)

Mitscher, M.A., Captain, USN. Commanding Officer, USS *Hornet* letter of 13 June 1942, to Commander in Chief, United States Pacific Fleet, "Subj: Report of Action—4–6 June 1942." Naval War College Microfilm Collection reel A55, first frame 41571. (Previously classified document.)

Murray, G.D. Commanding Officer, USS *Enterprise* (CV 6) letter to Commander in Chief, United States Pacific Fleet, "Subj: Battle of Midway, June 4–6 1942, Report of, dated June 8, 1942." Naval War College Microfilm Collection reel A55, first frame 41571. (Previously classified document.)

Nimitz, Chester W., Admiral, USN. Commander in Chief, United States Pacific Fleet, letter to Commander in Chief, United States Fleet [Admiral King], "Subj: Battle of Midway, dated June 28, 1942." Naval War College Microfilm Collection reel A55, first frame 41571. (Previously classified document.)

Sauer, E.P., Commander, USN. Commander Task Group 17.4 (Commander Destroyer Squadron 6) letter to Commander Task Force 17, "Subj: Japanese Torpedo Plane Attack on U.S.S. Yorktown During Battle of Midway, June 4, 1942—Report of June 12, 1942." Naval War College Microfilm Collection reel A55, first frame 41571. (Previously classified document.)

Sherman, Frederick C., Commanding Officer, USS *Lexington* letter to Commander in Chief, United States Pacific Fleet dated 15 May 1942. Naval War College Microfilm Collection reel A55, first frame 41571. (Previously classified document.)

Simard, Cyril T., Captain, USN. Commanding Officer, Naval Air Station Midway Island letter to Commander in Chief, United States Pacific Fleet, Report of Engagement with the Enemy, Battle of Midway, 30 May to 7 June 1942, dated 18 June 1942, *Diary*. Naval War College Microfilm Collection reel A55, first frame 41571. (Previously classified document.)

Spruance, Raymond A., Rear Admiral, USN. Commander Task Force 16, 16 June 1942 letter to Commander in Chief, United States Pacific Fleet, "Subj: Battle of Midway; forwarding of reports." Naval War College Microfilm Collection reel A55, first frame 41571. (Previously classified document.)

Tobin, R.G., Captain, USN. Commander Destroyer Division 4 letter to Commander in Chief, United States Pacific Fleet, "Subj: Battle, Report of, dated 7 June 1944." Naval War College Microfilm Collection reel A55, first frame 41571. (Previously classified document.)

The Battle of the Eastern Solomons

Davis, A.C., Commanding Officer, USS *Enterprise* letter to Commander in Chief, United States Pacific Fleet letter dated 5 September 1942, "Subj: Action of August 24, 1942, Including Air Attack on USS *Enterprise*; Report of." Naval War College Microfilm Collection reel A99, first frame 42790. (Previously classified document.)

———. Commanding Officer, USS *Enterprise* letter to Commander in Chief, United States Pacific fleet dated 5 September 1942, "Subj: Action of August 24, 1942, Including Air Attack on USS *Enterprise*, Report of, Enclosure 'A' to *Enterprise* Secret (Downgraded to Unclassified) Serial 008 Sept 5, 1942, USS Enterprise Track Chart with contact and Attack Sequence off Solomon Islands August 23–25, 1942" (only page of enclosure). Naval War College Microfilm Collection reel A99, first frame 42790. (Previously classified document.)

Fletcher, Frank Jack, Vice Admiral, USN. Commander Task Force 61 letter to Commander in Chief, United States Pacific Fleet dated 26 September 1942, "Subj:

Report of Action on August 24, 1942." Naval War College Microfilm Collection reel A99, first frame 42790.

Leslie, M.F., Commander, *Enterprise* Air Group letter dated 2 September 1942, to Commander in Chief, United States Pacific Fleet, "Subj: Report of Action in the Solomon Islands Area August 22–25, 1942." Naval War College Microfilm Collection reel A99, first frame 42790. (Previously classified document.)

Nimitz, C.W., Admiral, USN. Commander in Chief, United States Pacific Fleet letter to Commander in Chief, United States Fleet dated 27 September 1942, "Subj: Solomon Islands Campaign—Action of 23–25 August," p. 6. Naval War College Microfilm Collection reel A99, first frame 42790. (Previously classified document.)

The Battle of Santa Cruz

Halsey, William F., Vice Admiral, USN. Commander South Pacific Area and South Pacific Force letter to Commander in Chief, United States Pacific Fleet, "Subj: Report of Action, October 26, 1942, and subsequent loss of USS *Hornet*." dated 20 November 1942. Naval War College Microfilm Collection reel A193, starting frame 45530. (Previously classified document.)

Hardison, O.B., Captain, USN. Commanding Officer, USS *Enterprise* letter to Commander in Chief, United States Pacific Fleet dated 10 November 1942, "Subj: The Battle of Santa Cruz, October 26, 1942, Report of." Naval War College Microfilm Collection reel A193, starting frame 44181. (Previously classified document.)

Kinkaid, Thomas C., Rear Admiral, USN. Commander Task Force 61 letter to Commander in Chief, United States Pacific Fleet dated 3 November 1942, "Subj: Preliminary Report of Action, October 26, 1942" (First Endorsement on CTF-17 Secret letter A16-3 (11t) Serial 0050 dated 30 October 1942. Naval War College Microfilm Collection reel A193, starting frame 44181. (Previously classified document.)

———. Commander Task Force 61 letter to Commander in Chief, United States Pacific Fleet, "Subj: USS *Hornet* Report of Action, October 26, 1942, Comments on," dated 6 November 1942. Naval War College Microfilm Collection reel A193, starting frame 43846. (Previously classified document.)

———. Commander Task Force 61 letter to Commander in Chief, United States Pacific Fleet dated 8 November 1942, "Subj: Preliminary Report of Action, October 26, 1942" (Second Endorsement on CTF-17 Secret letter A16-3 (11t) Serial 0050 dated 30 October 1942. Naval War College Microfilm Collection reel A193, starting frame 44181. (Previously classified document.)

———. Commander Task Force 61 letter to Commander in Chief, United States Pacific Fleet Serial 0077 (no date given), "Subj: Report of Carrier Action North of the

Santa Cruz Islands," 26 October 1942. Naval War College Microfilm Collection reel A193, starting frame 44248. (Previously classified document.)

Mason, C.P., Captain, USN. Commanding Officer, USS *Hornet*, letter to the Secretary of the Navy and Commander in Chief, United States Pacific Fleet, dated 30 October 1942, "Subj: Report of Action, October 26, 1942, and subsequent loss of USS *Hornet*." Naval War College Microfilm Collection reel A193, starting frame 43846. (Previously classified document.)

Murray, G.D., Rear Admiral, USN. Commander Task Force 17 letter to Commander in Chief, United States Pacific Fleet dated 30 October 1942, "Subj: Preliminary Report of Action October 26, 1942." Naval War College Microfilm Collection reel A193, starting frame 43846. (Previously classified document.)

———. Commander Task Force 17 letter to the Secretary of the Navy dated 12 November 1942, "Subj: Final Report of Action Santa Cruz Islands, October 26, 1942." Naval War College Microfilm Collection reel A9, starting frame 79537. (Previously classified document.)

———. Commander Task Force 17 message of 260507Z42 to Commander Task Group 17.4 directing "As soon as all personnel are picked up torpedo *Hornet*," with CTG 17.4's response to CTF 16 and CTF 17 reporting on completion of tasking. Naval War College Microfilm Collection reel A193, starting frame 43846. (Previously classified document.)

Nimitz, Chester W., Admiral, USN. Commander in Chief, United States Pacific Fleet, letter to Commander in Chief, United States Fleet [Admiral King], "Subj: Solomon Islands Campaign, Battle of Santa Cruz—26 October 1941," dated 6 January 1943. Naval War College Microfilm Collection reel A193, starting frame 45530. (Previously classified document.)

———. Commander in Chief, United States Pacific Fleet, letter to Commander in Chief, United States Fleet [Admiral King], "Subj: Solomon Islands Campaign, Battle of Santa Cruz—26 October 1941," dated 6 January 1943, Naval War College Microfilm Collection reel A193, starting frame 45530. (Previously classified document.)

Sanchez, H.G., Lieutenant Commander, USN. Commander Fighting Squadron 72 to Commander Task Force 17 dated 2 November 1941, "Subj: Action Report of October 26, 1942." Naval War College Microfilm Collection reel A193, starting frame 44181. (Previously classified document.)

Souchek, A., Captain, USN. Commanding Officer, USS *Hornet* letter to the Secretary of the Navy dated 30 October 1942, "Subj: Report of Action, October 26, 1942, and subsequent loss of USS *Hornet*." Naval War College Microfilm Collection reel A193, starting frame 44692. (Previously classified document.)

Tisdale, Mahlon S., Captain, USN. Commander Cruisers, Task Force 16 letter to Commander in Chief, United States Pacific Fleet dated 29 October 1942, "Subj:

Report of Action—October 26, 1942." Naval War College Microfilm Collection reel A193, starting frame 44692. (Previously classified document.)

Widhelm, W.J., Lieutenant Commander, USN, and J.E. Vose, Lieutenant, USN. Commander Scouting Squadron 8 and Bombing Squadron 8 letter to Commanding Officer, USS *Hornet*, "Subj: Action on 26 October 1942," dated 29 October 1942. Naval War College Microfilm Collection reel A193, starting frame 45530. (Previously classified document.)

The Battle of the Philippine Sea

Gardner, M.B., Captain, USN. Commanding Officer, USS *Enterprise*, letter to Commander in Chief, United States Fleet dated 9 July 1944, "Subj: USS *Enterprise* War Diary for June 1944—Forwarding of." Naval War College Microfilm Collection reel A9, starting frame 79537. (Previously classified document.)

Litch, E.W., Captain, USN. Commanding Officer, USS *Lexington*, letter to Commander in Chief, United States Fleet dated 30 June 1944, "Subj: Attack on the Marianas Islands from June 11 through June 19, 1944 (East Longitude dates) in support of the occupation of Saipan and the engagement of the Japanese Fleet on 19 and 20 June, 1944 (East Longitude dates)—Action Report of." Naval War College Microfilm Collection reel A9, starting frame 79537. (Previously classified document.)

Newspaper Articles

"Adm. Fletcher Receives DSM: 9 Other Area Men Decorated." Source and date unknown. Admiral Frank Jack Fletcher Collection, Box 3, Folder 96, American Heritage Center, University of Wyoming, Laramie, Wyo.

"Adm. Fletcher Wins D.S.M. for Midway, Coral Sea Battles." Source and date unknown. Admiral Frank Jack Fletcher Collection, Box 3, Folder 96, American Heritage Center, University of Wyoming, Laramie, Wyo.

"Admiral Tough on Jap Nerves: Admiral's Transfer to Sea Frontier Is Significant," *Seattle Post-Intelligencer*, 24 Oct. 1943. Admiral Frank Jack Fletcher Collection, Box 3, Folder 98, American Heritage Center, University of Wyoming, Laramie, Wyo.

"Air Forces General Cites Adm. Fletcher For Pacific Operations." Source and date unknown. Admiral Frank Jack Fletcher Collection, Box 3, Folder 96, American Heritage Center, University of Wyoming, Laramie, Wyo.

Book review, "Unified Command Plan Is Supported in 'The Case Against the Admirals.'" Review of *The Case Against the Admirals*, by William Bradford Huie (216 pages): E.P. Dutton & Co., Inc., New York. Admiral Frank Jack Fletcher Collection, Box 3, Folder 96 (Newspaper Clippings), American Heritage Center, University of Wyoming, Laramie, Wyo.

"Capt. Fletcher Swanson's Aide." Source and date unknown. Admiral Frank Jack Fletcher Collection, Box 1, Folder 2, American Heritage Center, University of Wyoming, Laramie, Wyo.

Capt. Miller Freeman, USNR (Ret.). "Background for War in the Pacific," reprinted from October 1915 issue of *Pacific Motor Boat*. Admiral Frank Jack Fletcher Collection, Box 2, Folder 98 (Newspaper Clippings: Miscellaneous), American Heritage Center, University of Wyoming, Laramie, Wyo.

"Combat Teams of Sea, Air, Land Units Making Naval Hisatory in the Pacific," *St. Louis Post-Dispatch*, Sunday Morning, 2 April 1944. Admiral Frank Jack Fletcher Collection, Box 3, News Scrapbook Folder, American Heritage Center, University of Wyoming, Laramie, Wyo.

Elizabeth Oldfield. "Did You Happen to See—Vice Admiral Frank J. Fletcher." Source and date unknown. Admiral Frank Jack Fletcher Collection, Box 2, Folder 96, American Heritage Center, University of Wyoming, Laramie, Wyo.

"Fletcher, Coral Sea Commander, Named to Be Vice Admiral." Source and date unknown. Admiral Frank Jack Fletcher Collection, Box 3, News Scrapbook Folder, American Heritage Center, University of Wyoming, Laramie, Wyo.

"Frank Jack Fletcher '06." Obituary, source and date unknown. Admiral Frank Jack Fletcher Collection, Box 1, Folder 2, American Heritage Center, University of Wyoming, Laramie, Wyo.

"Inside Story of American Fiasco at Vera Cruz in 1914 Absolves Admiral [Frank Friday] Fletcher of All Blame, Says Witness," *The Washington Post*, Sunday 13 January 1929, p. 1. Admiral Frank Jack Fletcher Collection, Box 1, Folder 7 (Correspondence File 1914), American Heritage Center, University of Wyoming, Laramie, Wyo.

"Kurile Raids May Start Drive From Aleutians," *Seattle Post-Intelligencer*, 20 Jan. 1944. Admiral Frank Jack Fletcher Collection, Box 3, Folder 98, American Heritage Center, University of Wyoming, Laramie, Wyo.

Warren, Mame, and Marion E. Warren. Excerpt from special dispatch to the *Baltimore Sun* dated 12 April 1905. *Everybody Works But John Paul Jones; A Portrait of the U.S. Naval Academy, 1845–1915*. Annapolis, Md.: Naval Institute Press, 1981, p. 48.

Oral Histories

Thach, John "Jimmy" S., Admiral, USN, 1905–1981. *Oral History of Admiral John S. "Jimmy"* Thach. COC. U.S. Naval Forces, Europe, 1965–1967, Vol. I, O.H. 58. Education, USNA, 1927; USS *Mississippi,* USS *California*, 1927–1929; Naval Aviation School, Pensacola, Fla., 1929–1930; Squadron VF-1, USS *Saratoga*; Patrol Squadron 9, USS *Wright*, 1934–1936; Scouting Squadron 6-B, USS *Cincinnati*, 1936–1937; Patrol Squadron 5-F, Panama Canal Zone; VF-3 Squadron, USS *Saratoga*; Developed Thach Weave Technique for dealing with the enemy in aerial combat, 1941; Navy Operational Training Command, Pilot Training, Jacksonville, Fla.; USS *Yorktown* and Battle of Midway, 1942; USS *Lexington* and Operation Forager, 1944–1945; Witness to Japanese surrender on USS *Missouri*, 1945. Annapolis, Md.: U.S. Naval Institute. Oral Histories of the United States Naval Institute, Oral History No. 58, Thach #3.

Fitch, Aubrey, Vice Admiral, USN. Oral History of the Battle of the Coral Sea: Statement given to Commo. R.W. Bates, U.S. Navy, Head Analyst, Naval War College, 30 November 1946.

Speeches

Best, The Honorable Sir Matthew Robert, Vice Admiral, K.C.B., D.S.O., RN, Commander in Chief American and West Indies Station, Flag Captain H.P. Boxer, RN, Commander of HMS *York*, and Commander A.B. Fanshawe, RN, Executive Officer of HMS *York*. "Jutland." Restricted: Not to pass out of the custody of Officers of the U.S. Naval or Military Service. Newport, R.I.: Naval War College, February, 1936, 41 pages. USNWCA: RG-15.

Kalbfus, E.C., Rear Admiral, USN. Notes used by Rear Adm. E.C. Kalbfus, USN, in introducing Rear Adm. H.E. Yarnall, USN, at Graduation Day Exercises, 18 May 1940, 3 pages. USNWCA: RG-16.

———. Address by the president of the U.S. Naval War College to the graduating classes of 1941. Newport, R.I.: U.S. Naval War College, 1941. USNWCA: RG-16.

———. Extract from remarks made by Rear Adm. E.C. Kalbfus, USN, at Graduation Exercises, 2 December 1941. Newport, R.I.: United States Naval War College, 2 Dec 1941. USNWCA: RG-16.

Laning, Harris, Rear Admiral, USN. "Opening Address Before the Staff and Classes of 1931." Newport, R.I.: United States Naval War College, delivered 2 July 1930, USNWCA: RG-16.

Nimitz, C.W., Rear Admiral, USN. (Chief of Bureau of Navigation). Graduation Address, United States Naval War College. Newport, R.I.: Naval War College, 2 December 1941. USNWCA: RG-16.

Nimitz, C.W, Fleet Admiral, USN. Address of the Chief of the Bureau of Navigation to the graduating class, 2 December 1941. USNWCA: RG-16.

Plunkett, C.P., Rear Admiral, USN. Address of the president of the Naval War College opening the course for the class of July, 1921, Naval War College, 1 July 1921. Newport, R.I.: Naval War College, 1 July 1921, 6 pages. USNWCA: RG-16.

Pratt, W.V., Radm. Extracts from the address of the president of the Naval War College to the graduating class entitled "The Three Phases of a Naval Career: Some reflections of an Older Officer." Newport, R.I.: Naval War College, 27 May 1927, 13 pages. USNWCA: RG–16.

Pye, William S., Rear Admiral, USN. "Address of the President of the Naval War College to Student Officers of Phase I of the Army-Navy Staff College Course at the Naval War College." Newport, R.I.: United States Naval War College, 1 August 1942. USNWCA: RG-16.

———. "Remarks of President, Naval War College at Opening of College on January 1, 1943." Newport, R.I.: United States Naval War College, 1 January 1943. USNWCA: RG-16.

Rowan, S.C., Captain, USN, acting chief of staff. "The Course of Study at the Naval War College." Newport, R.I.: United States Naval War College, 1 July 1933, 21 pages. USNWCA: RG-16.

Rowan, S.C., Captain, USN. "Opening Address to the Classes of 1934, delivered 1 July 1933." USNWCA: RG-16.

Sims, W.S., Rear Admiral, USN. "Graduation Address delivered by the President, Naval War College." 22 May 1919, 25 pages. USNWCA: RG-16.

———. "Address delivered by the President, Naval War College, Opening the Course for the Class commencing the course in June of 1919." Newport, R.I.: United States Naval War College, 2 June 1919. USNWCA: RG-16.

———. "Address delivered by the President, Naval War College, Opening the Course for the Class of December, 1919." Newport, R.I.: Naval War College, 2 December 1919, 38 pages. USNWCA: RG-16.

———. Graduation address, 22 May 1919. USNWCA: RG-16.

———. Commencement address, 2 June 1919. USNWCA: RG-16.

Spruance, Raymond A., Admiral, USN. Notes for Admiral Spruance's address for the entering class of 1946 (Adm. Spruance spoke extemporaneously—no copy of his remarks was made). Newport, R.I.: United States Naval War College, 13 July 1946, 10 pages. USNWCA: RG-16.

Unpublished Manuscripts

Battle of Sable Island Manuscript, Serial No. 71, dated October–November 1923. United States Naval War College Archives (hereafter referred to as "USNWCA") Record Group (RG) 14/15, 128 pages plus accompanying diagrams.

Buell, Thomas B., Commander, USN. Unpublished draft of article entitled "Admiral Edward G. Kalbfus and the Naval Planner's 'Holy Scripture,' *Sound Military Decision*." Newport, R.I.: U.S. Naval War College, 7 March 1973, 10 pages.

Campbell, Mark Allen. *The Influence of Air Power Upon the Evolution of Battle Doctrine in the U.S. Navy, 1922–1941*. M.A. Thesis: University of Massachusetts, December 1992.

Cooke, Charles M. Jr., Commander, USN. Senior Class of 1934 thesis on *The Relationship in War of Naval Strategy, Tactics, and Command with Special*

Reference to Aircraft and Submarines. Newport, R.I.: Naval War College, 7 May 1934, 22 pages. Hoover Institute: Charles M. Cooke Collection, Box 13.

Kennedy, John Gerald. *United States Naval War College, 1919–1941: An Institutional Response to Naval Preparedness*. USNWCA, 1975. Unpublished dissertation manuscript for University of Minnesota. Newport, R.I.: U.S. Naval War College Department of Advanced Research, June 1975, 376 pages. This manuscript provides an excellent narrative of the development of and changes in the curriculum at the Naval War College during the interwar period, as well as of the imprint made by each president of the War College during that period.

Koda, Yoji, Captain, Japanese Maritime Self-Defense Force (JMSDF). "A Commander's Dilemma: Gap Between Pre-planned Military Strategy, Tactics, Force Strength Built on these Concepts, Pre-hostility Training and Actual Execution. Case: Imperial Japanese Navy." Newport, R.I.: Paper produced for elective Course SE-575, "World War II in the Pacific Theater," dated 29 May 1992, 13 pages.

Nimitz, C.W., Commander, USN. Class of 1923 thesis on policy. Newport, R.I.: Naval War College, 1 September 1922, 25 pages. USNWCA: RG-13.

———. Class of 1923 thesis on tactics. Newport, R.I.: Naval War College, 28 April 1923, 52 pages. USNWCA: RG-13.

Spruance, Raymond A., Commander, USN. Class of 1927 thesis on command. Newport, R.I.: Naval War College, 11 September 1926, 11 pages. USNWCA: RG-13.

———. Class of 1927 thesis on policy. Newport, R.I.: Naval War College, 4 December 1926, 31 pages. USNWCA: RG-13.

Snyder, Frank. "Sound Military Decision." Newport, R.I.: U.S. Naval War College, 25 March 2002, 17 pages.

———. "The Knox-King-Pye Board." Newport, R.I.: Naval War College, date unknown, 8 pages.

Stein, Steven. *Washington Irving Chambers: Innovation, Professionalism, and the New Navy, 1872–1913*. Unpublished dissertation manuscript, Ohio State University.

Turner, Richmond K., Captain, USN. *The Foreign Relations of the United States*. Unpublished Theses, Senior Class of 1936. Newport, R.I.: Naval War College, 30 March 1936, 136 pages. USNWCA: RG-13.

War Game Reports

Craig, Martin, Major General, Commanding General Blue Army Expeditionary Force. *Report of Army Participation in Grand Joint Exercise No. 4*, Hawaii, February, 1932. Secret: Downgraded at three-year intervals: Declassified after twelve years. DOD Dir 5200.10. Regraded Unclassified by authority of DOD Dir. 5200.1R, 29 Mar 1995. U.S. Army Historical Institute, 26 May 1932. On loan from Army War College, Carlisle Barracks, Pa.

Lanning, Harris, Captain, USN. *The Battle of Sable Island as Maneuvered at the U.S. Naval War College by the Class of 1924, History and Tactical Critique* Serial No. 71). Newport, R.I.: Naval War College, October–November, 1923, 174 pages. Confidential—Declassified IAW DOD Memo of 3 May 1972, "Subj: Declassification of WW II Records." USNWC: RG-4.

Index

Illustration page locators are in italics.

About the Author

DOUGLAS V. SMITH is professor of strategy and policy and head of the Strategy and Policy Division of the College of Distance Education at the U.S. Naval War College. He is a graduate of the U.S. Naval Academy, class of 1970, the Naval Postgraduate School, and the Naval War College, and holds a Ph.D. in military history from Florida State University. A career naval officer, he was Head of War Planning for Commander in Chief, United States Naval Forces, Europe and U.S. Commander Eastern Atlantic, where he directed strategic and long-range planning for the Navy and Marine Corps in Europe. He was also the executive officer of the Naval Facility, Midway Islands, during his 28 years of naval service.

THE NAVAL INSTITUTE PRESS is the book-publishing arm of the U.S. Naval Institute, a private, nonprofit, membership society for sea service professionals and others who share an interest in naval and maritime affairs. Established in 1873 at the U.S. Naval Academy in Annapolis, Maryland, where its offices remain today, the Naval Institute has members worldwide.

Members of the Naval Institute support the education programs of the society and receive the influential monthly magazine *Proceedings* and discounts on fine nautical prints and on ship and aircraft photos. They also have access to the transcripts of the Institute's Oral History Program and get discounted admission to any of the Institute-sponsored seminars offered around the country.

The Naval Institute also publishes *Naval History* magazine. This colorful bimonthly is filled with entertaining and thought-provoking articles, first-person reminiscences, and dramatic art and photography. Members receive a discount on *Naval History* subscriptions.

The Naval Institute's book-publishing program, begun in 1898 with basic guides to naval practices, has broadened its scope to include books of more general interest. Now the Naval Institute Press publishes about seventy titles each year, ranging from how-to-books on boating and navigation to battle histories, biographies, ship and aircraft guides, and novels. Institute members receive significant discounts on the Press's more than eight hundred books in print.

Full-time students are eligible for special half-price membership rates. Life memberships are also available.

For a free catalog describing Naval Institute Press books currently available, and for further information about subscribing to *Naval History* magazine or about joining the U.S. Naval Institute, please write to:

Member Services
U.S. NAVAL INSTITUTE
291 Wood Road
Annapolis, MD 21402-5034
Telephone: (800) 233-8764
Fax: (410) 571-1705
Web address: *www.navalinstitute.org*